THE OLD TESTAMENT WORLD

THE OLD TESTAMENT WORLD
Second Edition

Philip R. Davies
and
John Rogerson

WESTMINSTER
JOHN KNOX PRESS
LOUISVILLE • KENTUCKY

© 2005 John Rogerson and Philip Davies

First published in Great Britain as *The Old Testament World:
Completely Revised and Expanded Edition* by T&T Clark International,
A Continuum Imprint
The Tower Building
11 York Road
London SE1 7NX

and in the United States of America by
Westminster John Knox Press
100 Witherspoon Street
Louisville, Kentucky 40202-1396

Photographs taken and supplied by John Rogerson

This book is printed on acid-free paper that meets the
American National Standards Institute Z39.48 standard.   ∞

PRINTED IN GREAT BRITAIN BY
ANTONY ROWE LTD., CHIPPENHAM, WILTSHIRE

05 06 07 08 09 10 11 12 13 14 -- 10 9 8 7 6 5 4 3 2 1

Library of Congress Cataloging-in-Publication Data is on file at
the Library of Congress, Washington, D.C.

ISBN 0-664-23025-3

CONTENTS

Part III
LITERATURE AND LIFE

Part IV
THE FORMATION OF THE OLD TESTAMENT

Chapter 16
ORAL TRADITION AND COLLECTIONS PRIOR TO THE DEPORTATIONS

Chapter 17

PREFACE

Since the appearance of the first edition of *The Old Testament World* in 1989 our knowledge of that world has changed considerably. What was intended then as a 'progressive' account of the subject now looks rather conservative. We hope that this second edition will once again render the book 'progressive' in the sense that it will represent the direction in which our understanding is going rather than where it has come from.

Some of the major developments of the last fifteen years affect the book generally in the following ways. The term 'Old Testament' is now largely absent from most scholarly textbooks because it refers to the first part of the Christian Bible. Instead, it is more common to speak of the 'Hebrew Bible' which, though presenting the contents in a different order, contains the same writings as the Protestant Old Testament. But although 'Hebrew Bible' better reflects the primary role of these writings as Jewish or proto-Jewish (in a way that they are not proto-Christian), it is an ungainly term. 'Bible' is a Christian category and implies a type of canonical status that it does not enjoy in Judaism. Further, while the writings were originally almost entirely in Hebrew, they were not exclusively so. In any case it is impossible to write about the world of the 'Old Testament' without reference to texts that are not in the 'Hebrew Bible' but are found in a separate section designated 'The Apocrypha' in Protestant Bibles or as an integral part of the 'Old Testament' in Catholic Bibles. In the end, we have retained the title of the original in order to show that this is a new edition of *The Old Testament World*. Had we written it anew, we might have chosen a different title.

'Ancient Israel' has become another problematic term. The Old Testament (or Hebrew Bible) uses the name Israel in a number of ways: to denote a 'united kingdom' under David and Solomon, a part of a 'divided kingdom' after Solomon's death, and in a theological sense to denote the people chosen by Yhwh. Historically and archaeologically the matter is complicated by the fact that of two kingdoms, Israel and Judah, only the latter, Judah, survived and then increasingly adopted the role and name of Israel, for reasons that we shall try to explain in this book. For the sake of clarity, we shall mostly try to use 'Israel' to designate the 'northern' kingdom that probably existed from the tenth to the eighth centuries BCE, and Judah for the 'southern' kingdom that probably existed from the ninth century onwards. 'Palestine', used today in archaeological scholarship to denote roughly the area occupied by the modern state of Israel, Gaza and the occupied territories of the West Bank, is an ancient name. It is found first in Assyrian sources of the eighth century BCE, was used by classical writers such as Herodotus, and became the name of a Roman province. From early Christian times it was used to designate the 'Holy Land', and it is used in modern reference works such as the *Anchor Bible Dictionary* and *The Oxford Encyclopedia of Archaeology in the Near East*. We have continued to follow that tradition.

The proper name of the God of the Old Testament is usually not given in English Bibles but is represented as 'the Lord', following ancient Jewish practice. We know its consonants, YHWH, but do not know how they were pronounced. In some biblical names it is vocalised as 'yah, 'yo' or 'yahu'. In non-biblical texts it appears also as 'Yao' or 'Yaw'. We have reproduced it simply as 'Yhwh'.

Finally, as we tried to make clear in the first edition, the phrase 'Old Testament World' can have two meanings. There is the ancient world from which it sprang, which informed its writers and readers/hearers and within which it made sense. Without a knowledge of this world it will not make sense to us. But it also *creates* a world of its own, one that reverberates in Jewish and Christian culture over two millennia and more. The two worlds sometimes coincide, sometimes conflict and sometimes lie apart. Where they diverge, the issue is, of course, not whether the Bible is 'reliable' or 'true'. This is an issue that belongs to religious belief (although paradoxically it seems to obsess many archaeologists a great deal!). Rather, such divergence points us away from seeing the Old Testament as a mere witness to history and towards an appreciation of a cultural and philosophical achievement that has deep roots in the scribal culture of the ancient Near East, Persia and Greece. And after the historical world has long passed away, that other world remains, and deserves to be studied and, as far as we are able, understood and appreciated.

In preparing this second edition we have been greatly helped by Keith Mears and Duncan Burns, to whom we offer our grateful thanks. We should also like to thank our students in the Biblical Studies Department in Sheffield, for whom this was a course book in the 1990s, on the basis of which we enjoyed many stimulating discussions and contacts. Quotations from the Bible, where not our own translations, are taken from the New Revised Standard Version.

Suggested Reading and References

Throughout the volume we have referred to J.B. Pritchard (ed.), *Ancient Near Eastern Texts Relating to the Old Testament* (Princeton, NJ: Princeton University Press, 3rd edn, 1969) (abbreviated as *ANET*). Although this is now dated, it is still readily available in libraries. For a more recent edition of comparative material see W.W. Hallo and K.L. Younger (eds.), *The Context of Scripture: Canonical Compositions, Monumental Inscriptions and Archival Documents from the Biblical World* (Leiden: E.J. Brill, 1997–2002).

For Dictionaries, see D.N. Freedman (ed.), *The Anchor Bible Dictionary* (New York: Doubleday, 1992) and D.N. Freedman (ed.), *Eerdmans Dictionary of the Bible* (Grand Rapids: Eerdmans, 2000).

For archaeology, see E.M. Myers, *The Oxford Encyclopedia of Archaeology in the Near East* (New York: Oxford University Press, 1997).

For one-volume commentaries on the Bible see J. Barton and J Muddiman (eds.), *The Oxford Bible Commentary* (Oxford: Oxford University Press, 2001); J.D.G. Dunn and J.W. Rogerson (eds.), *Eerdmans Commentary on the Bible* (Grand Rapids; Eerdmans, 2003).

Part I

THE SETTING

Wadi En Jamil in the Hill Country of Judah

Chapter 1

GEOGRAPHY AND ECOLOGY
OF ANCIENT PALESTINE

'A certain man went down from Jerusalem to Jericho' (Luke 10:30). Although these words are from the New Testament rather than the Old, they well illustrate how much the study of the Bible can be enriched by a knowledge of its geography and social setting.

The road from Jerusalem to Jericho descends over 3000 feet (900 m) in the space of 15 miles (24 km). It passes through wilderness—that is, land which supports sheep, goats, and camels for the five or six months of the rainy winter season (October to March), but which is bare in the summer. This landscape is weird and unfriendly, the result of erosion of the hills by rain and wind over thousands of years. The road winds along valleys overlooked by hills which have many caves—caves that served as refuges for robbers until quite recent times. This bleak and dangerous landscape is referred to in the simple words, 'went down from Jerusalem to Jericho'. With this sort of picture in our minds, we use our imagination as we read the story. We are not surprised that a man should be robbed on such a road, nor are we surprised that two travellers did not want to linger, even though they saw a man in need. The action of the man who stopped to help becomes even more praiseworthy; he was running quite a risk by stopping.

But it is not only a knowledge of geography that we need to grasp the full meaning of the story. If we know something about Old Testament purity laws—for example, the regulations concerning priests in Leviticus 22:4-7—we may interpret the action of the priest and levite as follows: they may have been on their way up to the temple to officiate there. If the man by the roadside were dead, and they touched him, they would become unclean and would not be able to officiate that day. The full power of the story is, however, conveyed by the fact that the traveller who helped the wounded man was a Samaritan, and that relations between Jews and Samaritans were far from cordial. The story therefore challenges its readers to act in a way that puts the needs of a human being above the enmities that separate races; but this point would be lost if we had no idea who Samaritans were, and that they were disliked, if not hated, by many Jews. In the first two chapters of this book, we shall try to write about the land and social organisation of the Old Testament in a way designed to illuminate the text, and to stimulate the imagination of readers.

The Land

By far the best way of visualising ancient Palestine was suggested by George Adam Smith (1931: 48). We are to think of six strips placed side by side, and going from the top to the bottom of a page (north to south), as in Map 1, below.

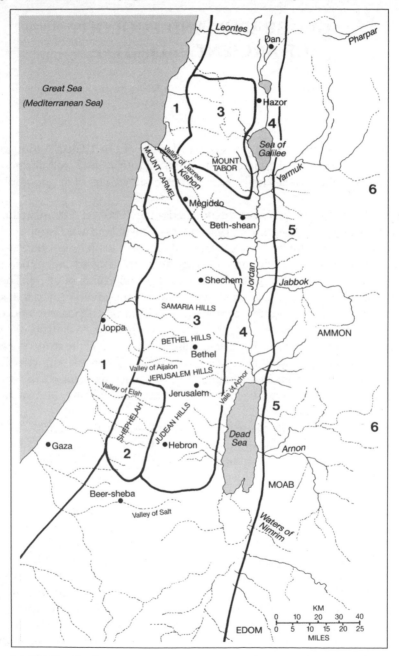

Map 1. *The 'Six Strips' of Palestine (according to George Adam Smith [1931])*

The Coastal Plain

The first strip, on the extreme left (the west), is the coastal plain. It begins about 15 miles (24 km) south of Tyre and is a narrow strip with the sea on one side and mountains on the other. As it comes south it merges into the broad valley of Jezreel on its eastern side, while to the west it becomes the beautiful bay that sweeps in a semicircle from Akko to Haifa. At this point it ends, because the hills that make up Mt Carmel block its progress any further south. To continue along the coastal plain you must either go round the edge of Mt Carmel where it almost reaches the sea, or you must cross the Carmel ridge by one of three passes.

Of all the parts of Israel, the area around Haifa has probably undergone the greatest changes in the centuries between Old Testament times and the present. Then, the coastline was about half a mile (less than 1 km) farther to the east; along the southern edge of the bay, the delta of the river Kishon made it impossible to travel farther south. The modern town of Haifa, which lies at the foot of Mt Carmel and extends up its side, did not exist. This part of the coastal plain is hardly mentioned in the Old Testament.

The Coastal Plain (Strip 1). Looking South towards Mt Carmel

South of the place where Mt Carmel meets the sea, the coastal plain continues, at first as a very narrow strip between sea and mountains, then broadening out and running on until it merges into the Negev region. In Old Testament times parts of this section of the coastal plain were covered with pine forests, the last of which were felled by the Turks during the First World War. Other parts of the plain were swampy. This was because the river channels that carried the waters from the central hills to the Mediterranean Sea could not cope with the volume of water, particularly in the winter. Their passage was partially blocked by two barriers of hard limestone which were formed in geological time when the sea twice receded and returned, each time to a lower level.

Like the northern part of the coastal plain, the section to the south of Mt Carmel is rarely mentioned in the Old Testament. It had only one natural harbour, at Joppa

(Hebrew *Yafo*), from which Jonah set sail in his attempt to avoid going on a mission to Nineveh (Jonah 1:3). To the south of Joppa, the coastal plain was occupied by the Philistines. Their cities of Gaza, Ashdod, and Ekron are the scene of the exploits of Samson (Judges 16) and of the disastrous effects of their capturing the Israelites' Ark of the Covenant (1 Samuel 5). Otherwise, the lack of mention of this area is probably due to the fact that it contained part of the major international route from Egypt to Damascus and beyond, known as the Way of the Sea (Isaiah 8:23). This was generally controlled by Egypt or by one of the northern powers, such as Assyria. Only rarely did the Israelites exert any effective authority in this region, and few Israelites lived there.

The Shephelah

The second strip is really only half a strip, and is to be found separating the part of the coastal plain where the Philistines were settled, from the hill country of Judah. It is almost parallel with the Dead Sea, two strips to its right. Called the Shephelah, which in Hebrew means lowlands, it is a transitional area between the coastal plain and the central hills, and rises to 1500 feet (4·60 m) at its highest points.

The Shephelah (Strip 2). The Valley of Elah

Today, this area is one of the most beautiful parts of the land, especially where it has been planted with forests, even if the trees are different species from those in Old Testament times. Then, the region was well known for its sycamore trees (1 Kings 10:27) and for sheep farming (2 Chronicles 26:10). It is mentioned in the Old Testament first of all as the scene of encounters between Samson and the Philistines and between Judah and the Philistines (Judges 14–15; 1 Samuel 17). It was quite natural that the Philistines, as they tried to expand their territory, should concentrate on the lowlands immediately to their east. In the period of the monarchy, the route running along the western edge of the Shephelah, from Beth-shemesh to Lachish was fortified, so as to prevent potential enemies from attacking Judah by way of the Shephelah. Its capital, Lachish, was the second most important city in Judah after Jerusalem, and when the Assyrian king Sennacherib captured the town in 701 BCE, he regarded this as a feat worthy to be depicted in the massive stone reliefs that can be seen in the British Museum in London.

The Highlands

The third strip is the central hill country. It is the most important and the most varied of the six strips, and can be divided into three main areas: Galilee, the Samaria and Bethel hills, and the Hebron hills. Galilee itself is usually divided into Upper and Lower Galilee, a division based on the fact that the hills of Upper Galilee are on average 1000 feet (300 m) higher than those of Lower Galilee. This is not the only difference. Upper Galilee is made up of high peaks and narrow gorges. No routes cross it in any direction, and it was hardly suitable for settlement in Old Testament times. Thus, it does not really figure in the Old Testament. Lower Galilee is quite different; its mountains are more isolated from each other, and there are broad valleys and basins which offer natural routes. One of its mountains, Mt Tabor, has become completely isolated from the surrounding hill country, and stands in a plain like a giant upturned bowl. Conditions for settlement were much more favourable compared with Upper Galilee, although there was no really important city in the region. Yet even Lower Galilee is rarely mentioned in the Old Testament, whereas in the New Testament it figures prominently as the place where Jesus spent most of his life and where he concentrated his ministry. The reason for this is that Galilee was always under threat from the northern kingdom of Israel's neighbours, Syria and Assyria. In about 900 BCE, the king of Damascus invaded Galilee and destroyed some of the towns on the edges of its hill country (1 Kings 15:20). Although the region was later recovered, it was lost again around 740 BCE to the Assyrians. Galilee's prominence in the New Testament was the result of its conquest in 103 BCE by King Aristobulus I, and its incorporation into the Jewish kingdom.

The progress of the central hill country southwards is interrupted by the valley of Jezreel. The word 'valley' is misleading, because the area is in fact a triangular plain nearly 50 miles (80 km) wide from the coast to the Jordan valley and 20 miles (32 km) across from north to south. It is a large catchment area for the rains that come from the surrounding hills, and these waters are conducted to the sea by the river Kishon. In Old Testament times the Kishon could not cope with heavy rain, and the plain was liable to flooding. This made it marshy and partly unsuitable for travel or settlement. It did, however, contain important routes, such as that from the coastal plain to the west to the Jordan valley in the east via the Harod valley, and it was an area where horses and chariots could be deployed in battle. Judges 4–5 records a victory won by the Israelites when the plain became flooded and the Canaanite chariots were bogged down (Judges 5:21). It is also the setting for the story in which Saul tried in vain to defeat the Philistine chariots, and lost his life on the nearby mountain range of Gilboa (1 Samuel 31:1-6; 2 Samuel 1:6).

The journey from Lower Galilee into the valley of Jezreel involves even today a steep descent down a twisting and turning road. On the other side of the valley, however, the ascent into the Samaria hills is quite gentle, and the hills enclose other broad basins or valleys. Finally, the road enters a long narrow plain running roughly north to south, and where this is crossed almost at right angles by a valley which runs from the coastal plain to the Jordan valley, the heartland of the Samaria hills is reached. Where the valleys intersect stood the city of Shechem, flanked on either side by Mt Ebal and Mt Gerizim.

As the road continues to the south, the broad valleys enclosed by the hills become rarer, until the road enters the Bethel hills and begins to twist and turn along valleys at the foot of them. Here the hills seem to be packed tightly together, and there are no obvious routes in any direction. In Old Testament times the settlements were not far from what served as the main north–south route.

The Hebron hills are separated from the Bethel hills by the Jerusalem Saddle. This country is lower than the Bethel or Hebron hills, and has broad valleys and a plain on which an airstrip was built in the last century. It also provides a number of routes from the coastal plain to the central hills, being flanked on the coastal side by the Lod triangle, a wedge of land running into the hills from the coastal plain. Towards the southern end of the Jerusalem Saddle is Jerusalem itself, at 2400 feet (730 m) a strategically located city at the crossing of routes from north to south and west to east. It is to be noticed that Jerusalem is more or less level with the northern end of the Dead Sea, and therefore commands the most southerly route across the Jordan valley and into Transjordan.

The Hebron hills begin just south of Bethlehem. They rise to over 3000 feet (900 m) and then fall away into the Negev region. They are much less wide than the Bethel hills, because they are flanked on the west by the Shephelah, or lowlands. Access was always far more difficult from the coastal plain on to the Bethel hills, compared with access to the Jerusalem Saddle, and to the Hebron hills via the Shephelah.

Bethel hills (Strip 3). View from Khan el-Laban

The Jordan Valley

The fourth strip is the Jordan valley, part of a geological fault that extends into East Africa, and which is the lowest natural surface in the world. At its most northern end was the city of Dan, at one of the several sources of the River Jordan. To the south of Dan was the Lake Huleh region, an area of swamps and pools, which today has been drained. To the south of Lake Huleh and on the edge of Upper Galilee was the city of Hazor, which controlled north south and east–west routes. Almost exactly opposite the Bay of Haifa on the coast, the Jordan valley broadens out to become the Sea of Galilee. This is about 12 miles (19 km) long and 5 miles (8 km) wide, the surface of the lake being 600 feet (180 m) below sea level. Again, it is remarkable that this lake, so prominent in the New Testament in the ministry of Jesus, is hardly mentioned in the Old Testament. The hills around the Sea of Galilee were volcanic in geological time, with the result that much black basalt stone is found on its western and northern sides.

Jordan Valley (Strip 4). Waterfall Near Sources of the River Jordan

South of the Sea of Galilee the River Jordan resumes the journey down the valley, following a very tortuous path until it flows into the Dead Sea, about 65 miles (105 km) away. In biblical times, the Dead Sea did not extend as far to the south as it does today. It is 1200 feet (370 m) below sea level and has a very high salt content, in spite of being fed constantly by the fresh waters of the Jordan. It figures hardly at all in the Old Testament, a notable exception being the vision in Ezekiel 47, where the prophet sees a stream issuing from the Jerusalem Temple and running down into the Dead Sea, making its waters fresh and life-supporting. South of the Dead Sea, the rift valley continues, and it eventually rises to 650 feet (198 m) above sea level before sloping down to meet the Red Sea at the Gulf of Aqabah.

The Transjordanian High Lands

The fifth strip, to the east of the Jordan Valley, consists of the hills of Transjordan (Hebrew *'Ever Hayarden*, 'the land beyond the Jordan') which rise like a steep wall out of the Jordan Valley to heights of 4000 feet (1220 m). Opposite Galilee was the region of Bashan, with a plateau which enjoyed good agricultural conditions. In the Old Testament, bulls or cows of Bashan are regarded as fierce (Psalm 22:13) or well-fed (Amos 4:1). South of the River Yarmuk, which enters the Jordan Valley at the south end of the Sea of Galilee, is the area of Gilead. Here, in hilly, forested country, some Israelites related to the tribe of Ephraim settled. It was the country of Jephthah (Judges 11), and it was also the setting for the battle of David's forces against those led by his rebellious son Absalom (2 Samuel 18:6-18). To the south of Gilead and towards the east was the territory of the Ammonites, on the site of whose capital, Ammon, now stands Amman, the capital of Jordan. To the south of the Ammonites, level with the upper half of the Dead Sea, was the kingdom of Moab, dominated by a broad plateau which was good for agriculture and for sheep farming. The story of Ruth reflects the agricultural advantages of Moab over the Judean hills, when it depicts the family of Naomi leaving Bethlehem for Moab in order to find food (Ruth 1:1). Finally, in strip five was the territory of Edom, to the south of the Arnon gorge.

Transjordan (Strip 5). Evergreen Oak Forest Near Ajlun

The Desert

About strip six there is little to say. It is the desert extending eastwards into what is now Saudi Arabia.

It will be clear from this description that the geographical features of ancient Palestine make it very unusual, if not unique. Where else in the world is there a large inland sea whose surface is 1200 feet (370 m) below sea level? Where else can you go, in the space of 15 miles (24 km), from the cool climate of Jerusalem in winter to the summer-like warmth of the Jordan valley? In fact, the geography of the land left its mark on the language to a surprising degree. Although there is a general Hebrew verb meaning 'to go', there are also verbs specifically meaning 'to go up' and 'to go down', and these were used advisedly in a land where there was a lot of going up and down.

Climate and Vegetation

Visitors who go to modern Israel in the summer (June to September) are sometimes surprised to discover a landscape bare of grass and flowers, except where there has been artificial watering. In fact, the growing cycle there is very different from that of Europe or North America, where the winter months are 'dead' months because of the cold. It is cold in the winter months in modern Israel, too, although the average temperature in Jerusalem in January is around 10C (50F), compared with an average for Sheffield in northern England of 3C (36F). What is decisive in modern Israel is the fact that rains fall only from October to April, and that the ground temperature in these months is high enough to encourage growth. From May to September there is no rain, and the soil dries out completely under the hot sun, producing the brown and bare effect that sometimes disappoints visitors in those months.

The distribution of rain varies in the different regions. In the Dead Sea area annual rainfall is 4 inches (100 mm), whereas in Jerusalem it is 22 inches (550 mm). The southern end of the Hebron hills receives about 16 inches (400 mm), while Upper Galilee has an annual rainfall of 28 inches (700 mm). Thus there is a tendency for rain to increase as one goes northwards. However, there is evidence to suggest that the rains were more unreliable in areas of lower rainfall than in areas of higher rainfall (Hopkins 1985: 90).

Reliability of rainfall was also an important factor in Old Testament times. Ideally, for agriculture, the early rains (Hebrew *yoreh*) came in October, softening the hard-baked earth sufficiently for ploughing and planting. The main rains, 70 per cent of the total, then fell in December to February, and the season ended with the latter rains (Hebrew *malqosh*), which gave a final boost to the maturing of the crops. Unfortunately, this ideal occurs only a third of the time (Hopkins 1985: 87). For about another third of the time the winter consists of the alternation of wet and dry spells; other patterns include a wet early season followed by dry weather and an early dry season followed by a late wet season. The latter is particularly unhelpful to agriculture, as it is almost impossible, or was in Old Testament times, to plough the hard-baked soil until the first rains had softened it. In view of the variability of rainfall from year to year, it is not surprising that 'rain at the proper times' was considered to be a blessing from God (Leviticus 26:4), and that the word 'famine' occurs frequently (Genesis 12:10; Ruth 1:1).

Given that 70 per cent of the rainfall is ideally concentrated into three months, it is clear that the rains, when they do fall, are heavy. For example, Sheffield, located in one of the rainier areas of England, has an average annual rainfall of just over 31.5 inches (800 mm), but this is distributed over twelve months. If 70 per cent of Jerusalem's 21.5 inches (550 mm) falls in three months, this gives about 5 inches (130 mm) for each of those months, compared with 3½ inches (86 mm) for Sheffield's wettest month. Furthermore, even that amount in Jerusalem is concentrated into no more than 50 days. Thus, when it rains in the wettest months, the rain is very heavy indeed; this has implications for the soil and for the retention of moisture in a land characterised mainly by hills and valleys.

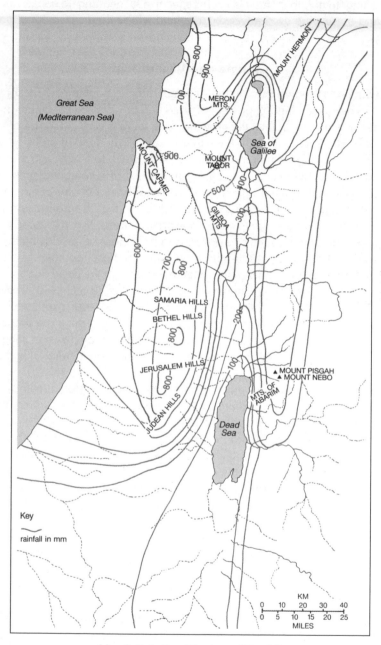

Map 2. *Palestine: The Annual Rainfall*

The modern visitor to Israel and the West Bank sees a land whose hills are often bare, except where forests have been planted in recent times, or where terracing is in use. In Old Testament times the landscape looked very different. In the hills of Galilee and in the Samaria, Bethel, and Hebron hills there were forests of the evergreen oak *Quercus calliprinos*, the deciduous oak *Quercus ithaburensis*, and the pine *Pinus halepensis*, along with their associated undergrowth. Of these trees, the evergreen oak predominated especially in mountainous areas. Thus, the initial force of the heavy rains was broken by the leaves of the evergreen oaks, and the moisture was retained by the root systems of the undergrowth. With the clearing of the forests, however, there was nothing to prevent the heavy rains from washing the soil from the side of the hills into the valleys, thus producing the sort of bare landscape familiar to modern visitors to some parts of the country.

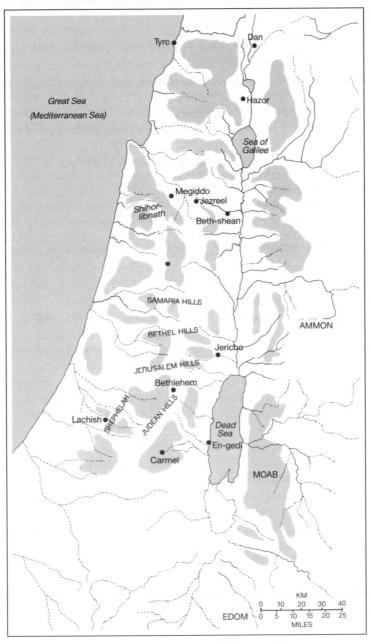

Map 3. *Forested Areas of Ancient Palestine, c. 1200 BCE*

We do not know exactly how extensive the forests still were at the beginning of the Old Testament period (c. 1200 BCE). The text itself certainly has many references to forests and woods, and to the wild animals such as lions and bears that lived in them. Although we can only guess about the extent of the forests in 1200 BCE, it is likely that the central core of Upper Galilee was completely forested (remains of the ancient forest can still be found here). In Lower Galilee the basins and valleys had been cleared, as had the areas around the main routes. In the Samaria hills, the basins and valleys and main routes were cleared, but away from settlements the forests remained, The Bethel hills were probably still largely forested, especially on their western side. The Jerusalem Saddle, on the other hand, was probably much more open country, while the Hebron hills were not so densely covered as those of Bethel. Parts of the Shephelah had probably been cleared of trees. Whether or not this guesswork is correct, it is important to realise that modern visitors to Israel and the West Bank see a very different landscape from that of Old Testament times.

Population and Agriculture in 1200 BCE

The scholarly reconstruction of the history of ancient Israel and therefore of the history of its land use is undergoing radical change in contemporary biblical scholarship, and is an area of great disagreement. In what follows, and for the sake of simplicity, a fairly traditional critical reconstruction of the history and land use will be given. Readers are referred to Chapter 4 for fuller discussion and for a reconstruction that will differ in some respects from what here serves as an historical outline to illustrate the subject of land use. Hopkins (1985: 137-70) gives a cautious review of the geographical and ethno-archaeological questions involved.

The beginning of the biblical period in Israel in the Early Iron Age is marked by the establishment of new, small settlements, and by the reoccupation of sites that had been abandoned during the Late Bronze Age. The overall impression is of the dispersion of settlements, not of their concentration in particular areas. Some of the new settlements were located in remote parts of the countryside, where conditions for agriculture were not always ideal. Perhaps remoteness, and therefore the unlikelihood of being attacked by enemies, was more important to these communities than good agricultural conditions.

The villages or small towns in which the inhabitants lived had populations ranging from about 150 to 1000. The people lived in houses that were often variations on the so-called four-roomed house, of which the central 'room' was probably a courtyard. There may have been an upper storey on the rear part of the house. Each house would contain a nuclear family of about five people, although this might vary from three to seven or even eight persons. In the case of large and strategically located settlements, there would be defensive walls, public buildings, and a square where public transactions could take place.

The life of a village revolved around the agricultural cycle, for each settlement produced all its own food needs. We possess, in the shape of the so-called Gezer Calendar (found in the remains of that ancient city), a list of agricultural duties that needed to be attended to year-by-year, and although it is at least 300 years later than the period under examination, it can be briefly considered here (Borowski, 1987: 32-44). The first activity listed is olive harvesting. This would be done in September and October, and presumably the gathering-in would include the pressing of the olives, which were grown mainly for their oil.

The second and third activities were sowing cereals and then sowing pulses, such as lentils and chickpeas, with two months allotted to each. Precisely when this was done depended on the arrival of the first rains, without which the hard soil could not be ploughed prior to sowing. Also, given the unpredictability of the pattern of the rainfall, as described above, the farmers probably prolonged the planting season in order to see how the weather developed before planting the whole of the crop. The next activity is hoeing weeds (one month). This was probably done between February and March and involved collecting grasses and other weeds to be used as hay. The next task, also requiring a month, is harvesting barley. This grain was widely grown, because it was more tolerant of harsh conditions than wheat, and it matured earlier. This harvest occurred during April, and was followed six weeks or so later by the harvest of wheat (although this crop may not have been grown in the hill country). The final activities were the harvesting of grapes, probably in July and August, and the harvesting of figs and dates in September.

These activities demanded some co-ordination of effort, and they raise questions about social organisation. Most obviously, the harvest periods required as many men, women, and children as possible to complete the task. For the harvests that took place in the dry months the main hazard was not, as in northern Europe, for example, rain or storms, but heat. Again, the ploughing demanded some co-operation, especially if the oxen used were owned by the village as a whole, rather than by individual families.

With the life of settlements largely devoted to agriculture, and given the importance of the various harvests, it is to be expected that the completion of harvests was marked by communal celebrations. We have some glimpses of these celebrations from later periods in the Old Testament. The book of Ruth, for example, suggests that the barley harvest was a communal activity, which was followed by drinking, wooing, and lovemaking (Ruth 3). From the point of view of the later developed religion of the Old Testament, agricultural celebrations were linked to key events in the people's faith. The barley harvest was the Festival of Unleavened Bread, the wheat harvest was the Festival of Weeks (Pentecost), and the fruit harvest was the Festival of Booths or Ingathering (Sukkoth).

Land and Land Use 1200 to 587 BCE

In 1200 BCE the area later occupied by the northern kingdom, Israel, consisted of villages and small towns in the Bethel hills, the Samaria hills and Lower Galilee. To what extent the area later occupied by the southern kingdom, Judah, was populated at this time is uncertain. The Philistines occupied the coastal plain level with the Shephelah, while in parts of the region later occupied by the northern kingdom were cities such as Beth Shean, that can, for the sake of simplicity, be called Canaanite. We must not think that the whole of the land was occupied. In fact, large parts of it were covered with forests, some of which had reached the peak of their growth, others of which were in various stages of degeneration because of fires, or because of partial clearing for the purposes of settlement. The social and political organisation of life will be discussed in detail in Chapter 2. The main point that needs to be made here is that there was no central or local government that required the villages to produce a surplus which could be taken as a form of taxation.

If the book of Judges reflects conditions in the period 1150–1050 BCE, the situation changed for those settlements that were closest to main routes. Judges 3 records that a coalition of Moabites, Ammonites, and Amalekites captured Jericho and forced the tribe of Benjamin to pay tribute for eighteen years. This would take the form of agricultural products and entail the production and delivery of surplus grain and fruit. In Judges 6 the Midianites, a nomadic people from the Negev region, are said to have invaded the land at harvest time for seven years, in order to take the harvest for themselves. These raids would be restricted to areas near the main routes, for Judges 6:2 records that the Israelites tried to withdraw into the less accessible regions. Nonetheless, a considerable disruption of normal agricultural life is indicated. If these texts reflect later periods, they still describe realities that would make sense to the writers and hearers/readers.

The most serious and successful threat to the agricultural life of the land in this period came from the Philistines, who occupied parts of the Shephelah. From a geographical point of view, it makes sense that the Philistines should first expand at the expense of the tribes of Dan and Judah, and this is what we find in Judges 13–16. The story of the Danite hero Samson implies that the people of Dan were under Philistine control, and this would certainly mean the payment of tribute in the form of agricultural surpluses. Judges 15:9-13 also claims that the people of Judah (probably those in the Shephelah) had lost their independence to the Philistines. Following the defeat of the combined Israelite forces by the Philistines at the battles of Aphek, the Philistines are said to have established garrisons in Israelite territory. A passage in 1 Samuel (13:16-18) mentions a garrison in Michmash, and says that three parties of Philistines left the garrison, going in different directions to collect produce. The following verses, 19-22 (a passage whose Hebrew text may be partly corrupt), say that there was no smith in Israel and that the Israelites had to go to the Philistines to get their agricultural implements sharpened.

This passage has often been interpreted to mean that the Philistines had a monopoly of iron and that this gave them a technological advantage over the Israelites, an advantage that the Philistines exploited to the point where they let the Israelites have iron agricultural tools to increase the surpluses that the Philistines could then take. In fact, the passage says nothing about iron; and recent research (summarised by Frick 1985: 173-89) suggests that the Philistines did not have a monopoly of iron and that, in any case, iron was not initially superior to bronze. Also, both bronze and iron plough-points were used in settlements after iron became more widely available.

In fact, 1 Samuel 13:19-22 is concerned mainly with a Philistine strategy, designed to prevent the Israelites from having military weapons. To this end, the Philistines restricted the activities of travelling groups of metal-workers, with the result that, whatever the metal involved, the Israelites could get agricultural tools sharpened and repaired only on Philistine terms. However, this indicates a vastly different situation in Israelite life compared with the period when villages were mostly independent and self-supporting. Agricultural surpluses had to be produced for the Philistine overlords, and in bad years this almost certainly meant that the villages did not have enough for their own needs.

A new situation is implied in the narratives in which Saul is appointed to lead the Israelites against the Philistines. Saul needed some kind of standing army, and this would mean that men had to be taken from villages and that surpluses had to be organised to feed the army. 1 Samuel 14:52 says that whenever Saul saw a strong man fit for war he took him into his service. Light is further thrown on the new situation by 1 Samuel 17:12-18, which recounts how David's three eldest brothers joined Saul's army. Whatever may be the difficulty of reconciling 1 Samuel 17 with the fact that, in 1 Samuel 16:22, David is already Saul's armour-bearer, verses 12-18 indicate the problems of recruitment and supplies that an army such as Saul's would need. The departure of David's brothers for the army would reduce the man-power available for agricultural production. David is told by his father to go to the scene of battle to deliver parched corn (wheat) and bread to his brothers, and cheese to the commanders. The implication is that each family or village is responsible for supplying food for those of its members in Saul's army. This would depend, of course, on how far away the fighting was from the homes of the soldiers. In the story of 1 Samuel 17, the fighting is some 20 miles (32 km) from David's home, Bethle-hem.

The length and character of Saul's reign will be discussed in Chapter 4, but if we assume that Saul initially defeated the Philistines and gave relief to his people, this does not mean that conditions returned to the tranquillity that we have assumed for 1200 BCE. When, in 1 Samuel 8:5, the elders of Israel ask Samuel to appoint a king over them he replies (verses 11-17):

> [a king] will take your sons and appoint them to his chariots and to be his horsemen, and to run before his chariots; and he will appoint for himself commanders of thou-sands and commanders of fifties, and some to plough his ground and to reap his harvest, and to make his implements of war and the equipment of his chariots... He will take the best of your fields and vineyards and olive orchards and give them to his courtiers. He will take one-tenth of your grain and your vineyards and will give it to his officers and his courtiers... He will take one-tenth of your flocks, and you shall be his slaves.

Although this passage in its present form was written much later than the time of Saul, it spells out the implications of having power located at a central point, even if this power affected only a small part of the land.

The narrative of David's reign implies an increased concentration of land in the hands of people close to the king. David acquires Jerusalem by right of conquest, and also inherits Saul's possessions. 2 Samuel 9:7 records that David summons Saul's grandson Mephibosheth and promises to restore to him the property of Saul. David also orders Siba, Saul's servant, to administer the property, and to give enough of its produce to Mephibosheth to enable the latter to live at David's court (2 Samuel 9:10). Siba apparently has fifteen sons and twenty servants. The latter are not necessarily slaves, but probably men who had freely entered the service of Saul. Nonetheless, they had to be supported or they had to work, and the implication is that Saul had acquired property.

It is in the narrative of Solomon's reign, however, that the agricultural implications of a centre of power reach their climax. In 1 Kings 4:7-19 twelve officials are named, who are put in charge of twelve regions, each of which has to provide for the king and his court for a month. 1 Kings 5:2-3 lists what is required daily to maintain the luxury of the king and his household. It is noticeable that some of the officials in charge of the districts are Solomon's sons-in-law, for example, the son of Abinadab (1 Kings 4:11) and Ahimaaz (1 Kings 4:15).

The building works attributed by the narrative to Solomon would have placed additional burdens upon the agricultural population. According to 1 Kings 5:13-16,

Solomon conscripted 30,000 workers who worked a shift system whereby in any month 10,000 worked in Lebanon, presumably preparing timber, and the other 20,000 were at home. This pattern of one month on duty and two months at home would be designed to minimise the effect of such programmes upon the manpower needed to produce agricultural goods. No such shift arrangements are recorded, however, for the 70,000 porters, 80,000 quarriers, and 3600 supervisors mentioned in 2 Chronicles 2:2. Although these numbers are, of course, enormously inflated, they indicate the obvious fact that extensive building projects involve the recruiting of workers, and that even if these are paid for their work, they are absent from the land, and have to be fed from central resources while they were away from home.

The loss of the northern kingdom, Israel, to the Assyrians in 734–721 BCE would have brought changes to land ownership and use in the Samaria and Bethel hills. The prominent families were taken to Assyria and were replaced by clients of the Assyrian king. The land given to them was probably a reward for services rendered (2 Kings 17:6, 24). We are not to think of the wholesale transfer of populations to and from Assyria; many ordinary Israelites remained, but they were now the servants of foreign landowners. In the southern kingdom, Judah, it is recorded of King Uzziah (c. 767–739 BCE) that he loved the land, and that he sponsored agriculture in the Negev region, besides possessing herds of cattle in the coastal plain and the Shephelah and fields and vineyards in the hill country (2 Chronicles 26:10).

How did the kings acquire land? Whenever possible, they bought it or acquired it by exchange. According to 2 Samuel 24:18-25 David purchased a threshing floor in Jerusalem for the site of the Temple. Omri purchased a site from Shemer, on which to build his capital, Samaria (1 Kings 16:24). Ahab, though regarded as a particularly evil king by the Old Testament writers, tried initially to acquire a vineyard belonging to his neighbour Naboth by purchase or exchange (1 Kings 21:2). When he failed he resorted to another method: that of taking possession of the land of anyone put to death for a capital offence. This was the fate of Naboth's vineyard, after Queen Jezebel had arranged for Naboth to be wrongly accused, tried, and executed (1 Kings 21:14-16). Also, all land conquered by the king—for example the coastal plain occupied by the Philistines—or land which was not otherwise owned—became the property of the crown. As was indicated earlier, many parts of the Samaria, Bethel, and Hebron hills were forested and unoccupied at the beginning of the monarchy and such areas could be given to royal servants, or might become royal estates, to be cleared and developed by royal officials.

What about the Old Testament ideal that a family's land should not be disposed of? Naboth's refusal to sell or exchange his vineyard is based on the conviction that he should not dispose of the 'inheritance of the fathers' (1 Kings 21:3). Jeremiah, while he is detained in Jerusalem in the year of its destruction (587 BCE), buys a field from his cousin Hanamel in accordance with his duty as nearest relative to keep the land in the family, Jeremiah 32:6-13). In the book of Ruth, the land still belonging to Naomi, in spite of her ten-year absence from her home, Bethlehem, is purchased by Boaz after Naomi's closest relative refuses to carry out his duty (Ruth 4:1-12).

These passages indicate that during the monarchy land was owned by individual families, and that it was the duty of relatives to help any members of the family that found themselves in difficulties. In the case of Jeremiah's cousin Hanamel, we can suppose that he had been unable to produce sufficient grain and fruit to feed his family and to provide surpluses required as taxation. In this situation he sold his land to his nearest relative, Jeremiah. This did not mean that Hanamel would now vacate the land and that Jeremiah would work it. Rather, Hanamel would use the purchase price to pay off his debts, and Jeremiah would become Hanamel's landlord, entitled to some of the surplus. As soon as possible, Hanamel would re-purchase the land.

In principle, this was an excellent social mechanism, designed to preserve the independence of families on their own landholdings. In practice, it sometimes worked out differently. Isaiah 5:8 attacks those who join house to house, and field to field until there is nowhere left in the land for anyone else's property. Amos (8:4-6) condemns those who exploit the poor by selling grain at exorbitant prices and who force the poor to sell themselves into slavery. What do such passages imply?

In social terms, the situation that existed, and which was criticised by Isaiah and Amos, was one in which there were two classes, the landed and the landless. Among the landed were those who exploited the landless poor by hiring them as day-labourers for low wages, by selling them food at inflated prices, and by charging exorbitant interest if they made a loan. The wealth accumulated by these exploiters was spent on luxury items. Amos mentions that such people had winter houses (probably in the warmer zones of the Jordan valley) and summer houses, and rooms or furniture inlaid with ivory (Amos 3:15). Their women were well-fed and fat (apparently a desirable physical attribute in that society) like Bashan cows (Amos 4:1). Their days were spent feasting, drinking wine, and singing songs (Amos 6:4-6). Isaiah 3:16-23 lists the luxury ornaments and clothes possessed by the women of well-to-do families in Jerusalem.

This exploitation, which resulted in a landed wealthy class and an impoverished landless class, has been called rent capitalism (Lang 1985: 93-99). It is interesting that none of the prophets' criticism of these abuses was directed specifically at the monarchy. However, the development of rent capitalism had been made possible by the rise of the monarchy, which brought about changes in land ownership and use compared with the situation around 1200 BCE (Alt 1970: 367-91).

Land and Land Use 587 to 63 BCE

In 587 BCE Jerusalem fell to the Babylonians for the second time in ten years, and the king and other prominent Judahites joined those who had been taken into exile in Babylon in 597 (2 Kings 24:14-16; 25:18-21, cp. Jeremiah 52:28-30). Gedaliah was appointed governor of Judah by the Babylonians in Mizpah in the territory of Benjamin, and he encouraged the people remaining in the land, as well as those who had fled for safety across the Jordan valley, to get on with the harvest (Jeremiah 40:10-12). Jerusalem had fallen in the month of March, and there was an abundant harvest of grapes and figs that year (Jeremiah 40:12). With Babylonian armies in the land, there would have been little possibility of planting grain in the previous winter whereas mature vines and fig trees would need little attention.

Jeremiah 41–42 records the murder of Gedaliah by Ishmael and the flight of many of the people to Egypt. Further, the southern part of Judah was occupied by the Edomites, who probably appropriated the land for themselves. We know nothing about the situation in Judah between 582 and 539 BCE, but we can guess that many of the wealthy landowners had been deported, and that the poorer people who remained may have been able to repossess their own land, or land that was abandoned.

According to Ezra 1:1ff., a decree of Cyrus, king of Persia, in 539 allowed the Jews to return from Babylon to Judah in order to rebuild the Temple. We do not know how many people returned. The list of returning Jews in Ezra 2:1-70 does not date from that period, as the same passage is connected with the situation in 445 in Nehemiah 7:6-72; in any case, it is difficult to see how more than 50,000 people (Ezra 2:64-65) could have been received, accommodated, and provided for in a land that probably barely met the needs of the existing inhabitants. Much more plausible is the picture presented in Haggai 2:10 and Zechariah 1–8, in prophecies dating around 520 BCE. It is one of massive agricultural failure, with disappointing yields caused by poor weather (Haggai 2:16-17). The prophets attribute these disasters to the failure of the people to rebuild the Temple, and they promise that when this has been done, the fertility of the land will be restored (Haggai 2:19; Zechariah 8:12).

Hans Kippenberg (1982: 47) has suggested that in the period beginning in 539 BCE, when Judah was administered as a Persian province, agriculture was diverted from cereals to vines and olives. Judah certainly was now confined, territorially, to a small area roughly 30 by 30 miles (48 by 48 km) comprising the southern part of the Bethel hills, the Jerusalem Saddle, and the northern part of the Hebron hills, together with a small part of the Shephelah. This was not an area especially suited for cereals, and it certainly is plausible that the population intensified their production of wine and olive oil so as to make surpluses that could be sold in return for cereals.

Only at the time of Nehemiah (445–420 BCE) do we get detailed information about the situation in Judah. Nehemiah 5 records the complaints brought by some of the people against their relatives. One group complains that they have to pledge their children in order to get cereals to eat. Another group has to pledge fields, vineyards, and houses in order to get cereals. A third group complains about the taxes that they pay to the king. This probably means that they have to produce surpluses to trade for coinage in which the taxes are paid.

The culprits in this situation are the wealthier Jews and officials. Indeed, Nehemiah 5:8 implies that Nehemiah has been purchasing the freedom of Jews who have become the slaves of foreigners, while wealthy people are actually selling fellow Jews to foreigners. Nehemiah calls a meeting of the culprits and confronts them with what they were doing. They agree to his demand that they should cancel the debts owed to them, and that they should return the fields, houses, and vineyards that they had acquired to their former owners. Nehemiah himself agrees to cancel the debts owed to him.

This reform raises the question of the origin of Leviticus 25. The chapter begins with the Sabbath year law, according to which the land must lie fallow once every seven years. Recent research (Hopkins 1985: 200-202) indicates that the agricultural practice of fallowing was actually much more frequent than this, even as frequent as every other year, at any rate in the Iron Age. The chapter then introduces the custom of the Jubilee year, that is, every fiftieth year, in which all land must revert to its original owners. The year is announced by the blowing of a trumpet, or *yovel*, from which the word 'jubilee' is derived. The chapter further enjoins that no interest may be charged on loans (verses 35-38). In the Jubilee year, those who have been forced to sell themselves into slavery not only become free, together with their wives and children, but can return and take possession of their lands (verses 39-43).

Were these laws formulated in order to confirm Nehemiah's reform? Clearly, if they existed before Nehemiah's time, they were disregarded; and it is strange that Nehemiah does not appeal to these laws—for example the law forbidding the charging of interest—when confronting those who have exploited their kin. It is probably safe to say that, in its present form, Leviticus 25 is later than Nehemiah's reforms and represents an attempt to subordinate economic interests to theological convictions. The land must be allowed to rest in the seventh year as a reminder to the Jews that they are Yhwh's people, and that it was he who gave them the land in the first place (Leviticus 25:38). He did not give it to his people so that they could exploit those who had fallen on hard times; and slavery was an unacceptable permanent situation for Jews to be in, because God had delivered his people from slavery in Egypt (Leviticus 25:55).

These noble ideas were practised only so long as they could be enforced by someone in authority. In the late fourth century BCE Judah became part of the Egyptian empire of the successors of Alexander the Great, and then, about 200 BCE, became part of the Syrian empire of Alexander's successors. Although these events have left little trace in the Old Testament (cp. Daniel 11) and will not be discussed in detail here, the new rulers of Judah exacted taxes, which were collected by powerful members of the Jewish aristocracy, and permitted slavery (Kippenberg 1982: 79-81). Although the revolt of the Jews led by the Maccabees in 167 BCE was, among other things, an attempt to throw off foreign domination so that Jewish laws could be obeyed, the Hasmonean dynasty that thus became established took on the form of an oriental despotic monarchy. It was as a protest against such government that groups such as those at Qumran (who were responsible for some of the Dead Sea scrolls) were established as an attempt to re-establish the people of God on the basis of his laws.

Borders and Boundaries

An important point to bear in mind when reading about countries in the Old Testament is that traditional states did not have borders in the way that modern states do (see Giddens 1985: 49-53). Modern states have borders defined both on maps and on the ground, and claim total authority within those borders. In the world of the Old Testament countries were defined by border towns often sited near natural boundaries such as mountain ranges. Possession of a border town by a small garrison of soldiers enabled a monarch to claim to rule the whole country. In practice, very little actual control was exercised. This fact explains why the account of the 'conquest' of Palestine by Joshua is so incomplete; for even if one doubts the historicity of the account, it will have made political sense to the writers and readers/ hearers. It was necessary only for border towns such as Hazor and Lachish (Joshua 10:31-32; 11:10-13) to have been captured in order to claim that the whole land had been taken into possession, even though other conquests are also claimed in Joshua. Similarly, the heated arguments about whether or not David created a small empire may be seen in a different light if it is realised that it was necessary to capture and minimally garrison only a handful of border towns in order to claim to control a number of surrounding nations. It is true that the book of Joshua contains descriptions of some of the tribal boundaries of an idealised Israel, but these are literary creations obtained by imagining lines running between towns claimed to belong to different tribes. These boundaries did not exist on maps (there were no maps in the modern sense) and were not boundaries in the modern sense (see Rogerson 1999: 116-26).

The Theological Significance of the Land

The aim of this chapter has been to sketch the appearance of ancient Palestine, and to give an outline of how it was used in Old Testament times. Up to this point we have presented a social and historical view. But there is another direction from which this subject can be approached: the theological direction. For whatever the social realities may have been in Old Testament times, when the Old Testament is read as a whole, the land is an important symbol, in terms of which Israel's understanding of God is expressed (see Brueggemann 1977).

The story of the Hebrews begins in Genesis 12:1-8, with the story of Abraham, who became landless in response to the call of God to leave his present home in Haran, north Mesopotamia, and to the promise of God that he will be given a new home. That new home, the land of Canaan, will not be for Abraham only, but also for his descendants (Genesis 13:14-18). Between the promise and its fulfilment, however, there are many stumbling blocks. His grandson Jacob flees to Haran, because of Esau's anger (Genesis 27:42-45), although on the way he also is promised the land of Canaan (Genesis 28:13-14). Later, Jacob and all his family go down to Egypt at the beginning of a sojourn that lasts, according to the story, for 430 years (Exodus 12:40).

The Exodus from Egypt is the movement of a landless people towards a land of their own, although again, there are many hazards involved, not least some of the people's despairing belief that slavery in Egypt was preferable to freedom in the wilderness (Exodus 16:2-3). When the goal is finally reached, two new dangers arise. The first is that the Israelites will become self-sufficient in their land and will forget God (Deuteronomy 8:7-18). The second is that they will forsake their God in favour of the gods of the peoples already in Canaan (Deuteronomy 7:1-5).

The land as the place where Israel lives in the presence of God now becomes a testing ground. Will Israel be faithful to God's commandments or not? According to the prophetic witness, the people do not live faithfully, and so a new element appears: that of the threat of deportation. There will be a movement from possessing the land to being once more landless. This idea is found particularly strongly in the book of Jeremiah, who lived through the period of the destruction of the Temple and the deportations of 597 and 587 (Jeremiah 25). Jeremiah also proclaimed, however, that there would be a return (Jeremiah 32:14-5), and in the words of the prophet of the return (Isaiah 40–55), the movement back to the land is seen as a new exodus and a return across the desert (Isaiah 43:14-21).

Yet the return to the land was, in fact, a time of disappointment. One of the most moving passages in the whole of the Old Testament is the prayer of the people in Nehemiah 9. This ends with the words:

> You gave this land to our fathers so that we could enjoy its fruits and its riches; but now we live in it as slaves. Its rich produce goes to the kings, whom you have set up over us because of our sins. They rule over us and our cattle according to their desires: therefore we are in great need.

In view of such a sentiment, it is no surprise that in the years that followed Nehemiah there were attempts to regain full control over the land and hopes that God would intervene to restore the land fully in accordance with his ancient promises.

The Old Testament cannot be fully understood without an appreciation of ancient Palestine. Geography, social history, and theology combine to assist our reading and to stimulate our imagination.

References and Further Reading

Alt, A.
    1970   'Der Anteil des Königtums an den sozialen Entwicklungen in den Reichen Israel und Juda', in S. Herrmann (ed.), *Zur Geschichte des Volkes Israel* (Munich: C.H. Beck): 367-91. Also published in vol. III of Alt's *Kleine Schriften zur Geschichte des Volkes Israel* (Munich: C.H. Beck, 1959): 348-72.
Borowski, O.
    1987   *Agriculture in Ancient Israel: The Evidence from Archaeology and the Bible* (Winona Lake, IN: Eisenbrauns).
Brueggemann, W.
    1977   *The Land: Place as Gift, Promise and Challenge in Biblical Faith* (Philadelphia: Fortress Press; London: SPCK).
Giddens, A.
    1985   *A Contemporary Critique of Historical Materialism*. II. *The Nation-State and Violence* (Cambridge: Polity Press).
Hopkins, D.C.
    1985   *The Highlands of Canaan: Agricultural Life in the Early Iron Age* (The Social World of Biblical Antiquity, 3; Sheffield: Almond Press).
Kippenberg, H.G.
    1982   *Religion und Klassenbildung im antiken Judäa* (Göttingen: Vandenhoeck & Ruprecht, 2nd edn).
Rogerson, J.W.
    1989   *Atlas of the Bible* (Oxford/New York: Phaidon/Facts on File). (This work gives a geographical and historical overview of the different regions. See also the article by Frank S. Frick, 'Palestine, Climate of', in the *Anchor Bible Dictionary*: V, 119-26.)
    1999   'Frontiers and Borders in the Old Testament', in E. Ball (ed.), *In Search of True Wisdom: Essays in Old Testament Interpretation in Honour of Ronald E. Clements* (JSOTSup, 300; Sheffield: Sheffield Academic Press): 116-26.

Chapter 2

SOCIAL ORGANISATION

Anyone who reads the Old Testament soon comes across a phrase such as 'X the son of Y'. Normally we pass over such information without paying too much attention to it. Most of us do not know very much about our families farther back than our grandparents; nor would it make much difference to our lives, although it might be interesting, if we could trace our ancestry back over many generations. In the Old Testament, the situation is different, and if we can think ourselves into the Old Testament way of viewing social relationships, this will certainly assist our reading.

In Britain and North America men identify themselves by a surname, such as Smith, and a forename, such as John. Women either adopt their husband's surname or retain their own or, increasingly, combine their maiden name with their husband's surname. In our society, with its focus upon the individual, a person tends to think of his or her surname as something belonging to him- or herself. Even though a surname is a family name, that fact does not mean very much to most of us. There are, of course, a few family names that convey, first and foremost, the idea of a family; one example is Kennedy; another is Windsor; but these are the exceptions.

In the Old Testament there is no such thing as a surname. However, this does not mean that families cannot be identified or that they lack importance. On the contrary, the Old Testament way of identifying a person allows his (the word is used deliberately) family connections to be established in a more comprehensive fashion than the British or North American system allows.

Blood Ties

In 1 Samuel 9:1 Saul is introduced as the son of Kish, the son of Abiel, the son of Zeror, the son of Bechorath, the son of Aphiah. What we have in 1 Samuel 9:1 is a maximal lineage—that is, a quick way of linking Saul back to Aphiah, whom we can take to be the person after whom the maximal lineage is named. However, Saul not only has a maximal lineage; he has an ordinary lineage as well—that is, one that links him to his immediate family. We can deduce from 1 Samuel 14:49-51 that Saul's grandfather Abiel had another son, named Ner, whose son Abner (Saul's cousin) was Saul's commander-in-chief:

However, Abiel may well have had brothers, and so may have Zeror, Bechorath, and Aphiah. Saul's maximal lineage might therefore be set out as follows:

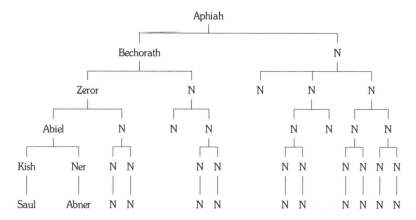

Although this reconstruction is purely artificial, it will help to make the point that each of the persons named in Saul's maximal lineage had descendants, who were therefore Saul's relatives; and the farther back the maximal lineage goes, the greater the number of relatives becomes.

In the world of the Old Testament it was important to know who one's relatives were. There was no centrally organised police force to maintain law and order and to punish wrongdoers. A person's safety was a function of the group to which he or she belonged, and in times of war it was the duty of those who were related to each other to stand together. There are two illustrations of this in the Old Testament, both dealing with Saul's tribe, that of Benjamin. Whether or not we think that these, and other incidents referred to in these narratives, actually happened, their account of social organisation in ancient Israel and Judah and its practical consequences are part of the shared assumptions of the authors and presumed readers/hearers of the stories, and to that extent a guide to the social organisation of those nations.

The first incident concerns Saul himself. In 1 Samuel 11, it is recorded that the Ammonite king Nahash threatens the inhabitants of Jabesh-gilead, a village in Transjordan to the north of Ammon. The villagers send messengers to Israel requesting help, and when they reach Saul, he immediately springs into action; he organises an army of Israelites and defeats the Ammonite king. We may say that he does this because he is king and needs to defend his people. From the point of view of the narrative, however, it is also likely that Saul is distantly related to the people of Jabesh-gilead. According to Judges 21:10-14, four hundred virgins had once been taken from Jabesh-gilead and given as wives to the men of Benjamin, following a vow by the rest of the tribes that they would not give their women to the Benjaminites as wives. Admittedly, we have only one instance in the Old Testament of a descent group based on the female line (Judges 9:1); but unless a woman was expected to sever all ties with her family when she married, we can suppose that links established through marriages also had social implications. Thus, Saul may well have been going to the aid of relatives.

The other incident precedes that in which the virgins of Jabesh-gilead are given to the Benjaminites. It is the account in Judges 20 of a violent confrontation between Benjamin and the eleven other tribes, in which the latter gain the upper hand only with some difficulty. The reason for the confrontation is that the tribes want to punish the Benjaminite town of Gibeah for an outrage that it has committed against a traveller's concubine (Judges 19). The Benjaminites refuse to allow the other tribes to punish Gibeah, and stand by their fellow tribesmen, at considerable cost to themselves.

So far, we have stressed the importance of blood ties between families for the purposes of mutual defence. Two other social mechanisms that depend on blood ties in the Old Testament are blood revenge and the redemption of land and persons.

In the absence of a central authority with a police force and powers of arrest and trial, justice was organised on a local basis through social groups and their representatives. Some crimes, however—and, in particular, homicide—called for drastic and immediate action against the wrongdoer. In the world of the Old Testament this action was taken by the 'avenger of blood', a close relative of the murdered person, whose duty it was to find and kill the murderer. It would appear from the Old Testament that originally the avenger of blood was entitled to pursue a killer even if the killing had been accidental. In Numbers 35:9-29 certain 'cities of refuge' are designated, to which persons can flee if they have accidentally killed someone. If such a killer gets to the 'city of refuge' without being killed by the 'avenger of blood', and the inhabitants of that city accept that the killing was an accident, the killer can remain there in safety. However, the 'avenger of blood' is entitled to take the killer's life if the latter leaves the 'city of refuge'. This state of affairs lasts until the death of the high priest, after which the killer can leave the 'city of refuge' and return to a normal life. As a social mechanism, the law of blood revenge was not peculiar to Israel, and has been found among many peoples (Bohanan 1967: 303ff.). It was not only a device for punishing murderers; it was also a powerful sanction. Anyone contemplating a murder would have to reckon with the fact that the intended victim's relatives had the duty to avenge the killing.

We have already touched, in the previous chapter, upon the redemption of land and persons. If a man fell onto hard times, and was forced to sell either himself or his family in order to pay his debts, it was the duty of his relatives to come to his aid, and to buy the land or the man and his family, with a view to the situation being reversed as soon as possible (cp. Leviticus 25:14-31, 35-43, 47-55). Of course, this ideal, as we have noted, often did not work out in practice. Quarrels between members of a family were as common in ancient Israel as in any other society. Two familiar stories in the Old Testament tell of the conflict between the brothers Cain and Abel (Genesis 4:1-16) and between Jacob and Esau (Genesis 27). Even if these characters belong more to the realm of legend than to history, the stories reflect something of filial rivalry in Old Testament times. Such lapses from the ideal, however, do not diminish the importance of kinship networks as powerful social mechanisms in ancient Israel.

Conflicting Loyalties

We have already seen in the story of Saul that his cousin, Abner, is his commander. In the story of David, this patronage within the family is also apparent (see 1 Chronicles 2:13-17).

Joab, who is David's commander, is also his nephew. Moreover, Joab and David's son Absalom are first cousins. Thus, when we read about a certain amount of collusion between Joab and Absalom in 2 Samuel 14, when the latter had been banished from court, we are not dealing merely with relations between a royal prince and the top-ranking professional soldier but with members of the same family. When Absalom rebels against David and forces him to flee from Jerusalem (2 Samuel 15–18), Absalom appoints another first cousin, Amasa, as commander-in-chief in Joab's place (2 Samuel 17:25). In the battle between the forces of David and Absalom, Absalom is deliberately killed by Joab (2 Samuel 18:14-15), despite David forbidding this; Joab also later kills Amasa (2 Samuel 20:8-10). We read the narrative in a new light when we realise that his victims are his first cousins.

Family relationships also shed light on David's apparent inability to control Joab. Repeatedly, Joab disobeys David and gets away with it, at least during David's lifetime. For example, David disapproves of Joab's murder of Abner, even though this is in revenge for Abner's killing of Joab's brother Asahel (2 Samuel 2:19-23; 3:22-27). David sings a lament at Abner's funeral about the stupidity and waste of Abner's murder, and then speaks the astonishing words:

> Today I am powerless, even though anointed king; these men, the
> sons of Zeruiah, are too violent for me (2 Samuel 3:39).

As we have seen, Joab even kills Absalom against David's instructions, as well as Amasa, whom David has confirmed as commander-in-chief after Absalom's death. In trying to understand how the narrative portrays the relationship between David and Joab we may think that David is unwilling to punish a close relative, even though Joab evidently has no such scruples. If we probe more deeply, we are struck by the fact that Joab's father is never named. Joab and his brothers are always called the sons of Zeruiah, their mother. Who is Joab's father? All that we are told is that he is a Bethlehemite (2 Samuel 2:32). A fragment of genealogy in 2 Samuel 17:25 suggests that his grandfather may have been the Ammonite king Nahash:

On the face of it, this seems absurd, because Zeruiah is David's sister, or half-sister, and we can only reconcile 2 Samuel 17:25 with 1 Chronicles 2:13-17 by supposing either (a) that Abigail's mother was married to Nahash before she married Jesse, or (b) that this same woman was the mother of both Abigail and Zeruiah by Nahash before she married Jesse:

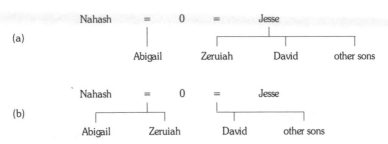

The mention of Nahash in the text could be rejected as a corruption of the text were it not for indications elsewhere in the narrative that David is in fact on good terms with Nahash the Ammonite king. When Nahash dies, David sends messengers to his son to console him: 'I will deal loyally with Hanun son of Nahash, just as his father dealt loyally with me' (2 Samuel 10:2). The fact that Hanun misinterprets this action and insults David's messengers gives David an excuse to attack Ammon, and may be a literary device; but it also implies a genealogical relationship:

Again, when David flees from Absalom, he crosses the River Jordan to the west of Ammonite territory, and there is supplied with food by Shobi the son of Nahash (2 Samuel 17:27). A close connection between David and Nahash is indicated by the narrative, and it suggests an explanation for Joab's power over David, namely, his Ammonite connections. It also puts the relationship between David and Saul into a new perspective. Saul, after all, had delivered the people of Jabesh-gilead from Nahash (1 Samuel 11)!

Another narrative in which it helps to work out who was related to whom is that of Jeremiah 36–41. A good starting-point is 2 Kings 22:3-13, the account of the finding of the book of the law in the reign of king Josiah (622/21 BCE). Two of the people involved with the discovery are the state-secretary Shaphan and his son Ahikam. Also mentioned is Achbor. Jeremiah 26 records events that are dated in the narrative to the beginning of the reign of Josiah's son, Jehoiakim (around 608 BCE)—that is, about fourteen years after the discovery of the law book. Here we find that the son of Achbor, namely Elnathan, is entrusted with pursuing the prophet Uriah to Egypt and bringing him back to Jerusalem to be executed (Jeremiah 26:20-23). We are also told that Jeremiah himself escapes a similar fate, being protected by Ahikam, son of Shaphan.

Jeremiah's support by the family of Shaphan is further indicated by the fact that Jeremiah's letter to the exiles in Babylon (Jeremiah 29) is conveyed by another son of Shaphan, Elasah (verse 3). In Jeremiah 36, which is dated in the narrative to Jehoiakim's fourth year (around 605 BCE), we find that when Jeremiah's secretary, Baruch, reads from the scroll that Jeremiah has dictated, he does it in a chamber that another son of Shaphan, Gemariah, has in the Temple. Among the officials to whom is brought the news that Baruch has read the scroll are the state-secretary Elishamah; Gemariah, son of Shaphan; and Elnathan, son of Achbor. In Jeremiah

39, dated in the narrative to King Zedekiah's ninth year (around 587 BCE), we find that Gedaliah, to whom is entrusted the administration of Judah by the Babylonians, is the son of Ahikam (who protected Jeremiah) son of Shaphan; and it is to Gedaliah's charge that Jeremiah is committed (Jeremiah 39:13-14; 40:6). Gedaliah is murdered, however, by Ishmael, son of Nethaniah, son of Elishamah—presumably the Elishamah who was presiding as state-secretary when the scroll was read by Baruch eighteen years earlier. We can represent some of these relationships as follows:

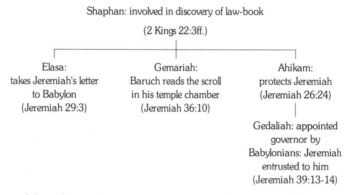

Shaphan: involved in discovery of law-book

(2 Kings 22:3ff.)

Elasa:	Gemariah:	Ahikam:
takes Jeremiah's letter	Baruch reads the scroll	protects Jeremiah
to Babylon	in his temple chamber	(Jeremiah 26:24)
(Jeremiah 29:3)	(Jeremiah 36:10)	

Gedaliah: appointed
governor by
Babylonians: Jeremiah
entrusted to him
(Jeremiah 39:13-14)

On the basis of this, the narrative wishes to convey the view that within the ranks of the officials who run the administration of Judah—at any rate from the reign of Josiah to that of Zedekiah and the early days after Jerusalem's destruction—there are powerful families with conflicting interests. The family of Shaphan is supportive of Jeremiah, and may, therefore, have agreed with his policy, which favoured submission to Babylon. The family of Elishamah, on the other hand, takes a different view, and after the fall of Jerusalem, the grandson of Elishamah assassinates the grandson of Shaphan. This is, perhaps, in the eyes of the Elishamah family, a way of punishing the Shaphan family for its pro-Babylonian sympathies. Such a reading of the text helps to make sense of the lists of names with which Jeremiah 36–41 abounds.

The Function of Genealogies

We have already noted that in the Old Testament a person is defined in terms of the group to which he or she belongs. This is an indication of a desire to construct an orderly social world in which each individual and each larger social unit can be plotted and therefore classified. It is the social equivalent to the mapping and classifying of the objects of the natural world which will be discussed below in Chapters 8 and 11, which deal with creation and sacrifice. Without such classifying, the world would be a chaos of unrelated phenomena; classifying brings the chaos into order and helps a society and its members to locate themselves within a meaningful framework.

This is the function of the genealogies in Genesis chapters 5, 10, and 11:10-31. They place the family of Abraham on a genealogical map that indicates how the whole of the human race had grown and divided since the days of Adam and Eve, the supposed first human beings. These parts of Genesis, greatly abbreviated and simplified, can be represented as follows:

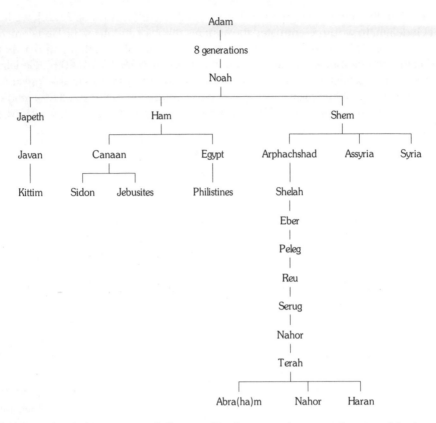

This genealogical map not only locates Abraham in relation to the rest of the human race; it expresses the affinities and distances in relation to other peoples that were felt by the Old Testament writers. There is a closer affinity with Assyria and Syria than with Egypt; and it is noticeable that peoples such as the Jebusites and the Philistines, with whom the peoples of Judah and Israel competed for the land of Palestine, are perceived as belonging to a different branch of the human race from the family of Abraham.

As the narrative of Genesis proceeds, further genealogies express perceived relationships with Israel's immediate neighbours:

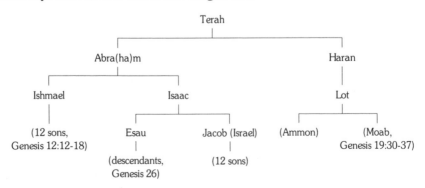

The peoples of Ammon and Moab are seen as 'Israel's' second cousins, whereas the Edomites are brothers, and the Ishmaelites (inhabitants of the Negev, to the south of Judah) are first cousins. Along with these perceived affinities are elements in the narrative that serve to stress the 'purity' of 'Israel' as against the 'mixed' or 'impure' origins of the adjacent peoples. Thus, Ishmael is Abraham's son by Sarah's Egyptian maidservant Hagar (Genesis 16:1-4); Esau marries various foreign women (Genesis 26:34-35); and Lot's children are born of an incestuous relationship between him and his two daughters (Genesis 19:30-37). 'Israel' is related to the neighbouring peoples, but it alone has preserved the 'purity' of the family of Terah.

This point brings us to a consideration of the genealogies of Isaac and Jacob. They can be shown as follows:

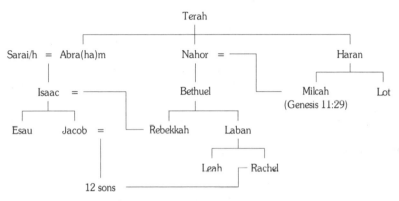

An interesting feature of the genealogy is a tendency to marry across the generations. Nahor marries his niece; Isaac marries his cousin's daughter; and although Jacob marries his uncle's daughters, they are a generation farther away from the common ancestor than Jacob. In fact, the genealogy is probably a 'fiction' designed to link the families of Abraham and Jacob to a common ancestor via the shadowy figure of Isaac. Although the matter cannot be discussed here, it has long been recognised that the Abraham and Jacob cycles of stories developed independently of each other—a fact re-emphasised by the most recent research on the origins of the Pentateuch. The genealogies and stories of Abraham and Jacob may not have originated until the late monarchy (eighth–seventh centuries BCE), whereas the genealogies in the early chapters of Genesis did not reach their present form until probably the fifth century BCE. This does not mean, however, that this material was simply invented at those times. What we now have almost certainly contains earlier attempts to map the genealogical relationships of the peoples of Judah and Israel. In their present and final form the genealogies reflect the social realities of the time of their final redaction.

The genealogies in 1 Chronicles 1–9 reproduce much of the material in Genesis, adding to them genealogies of eleven tribes. In one case, that of Naphthali, the information is very sparse, and simply lists four sons of Naphthali, the information being taken from Genesis 46:24. In the case of the tribe of Dan, 1 Chronicles had no information at all. Probably, the compiler did not think that it was worthwhile listing the one son of Dan recorded in Genesis 46:23! There is also no mention of Zebulon. The reason probably is that these tribes, which occupied Upper Galilee, had been absorbed into the kingdom of Syria since the ninth century, and little or no information about their families had been preserved.

If some tribes have no mention or scant mention, other groups are treated at length. This is especially true of the tribe of Judah, the family of David, and the tribe of Levi, and this is exactly what we would expect. The writer of Chronicles lived in Jerusalem round about 350 BCE, in a community dominated by the Temple and its clergy. There was no longer a Davidic king on the throne. However, the family of David still existed, and its maximal lineage is recorded in 1 Chronicles 3:10-24. There are seven generations following King Jehoiachin (deported to Babylon early in the sixth century BCE) which probably brings the family down into the early part of the fourth century. The Chronicler made links with the past by listing David's descendants down to his own time, and by depicting the Temple worship of his day as worship that had been initiated by David himself (1 Chronicles 23–26).

Social Groupings

As we now turn to discuss actual social organisation in ancient Israel, it is necessary to appreciate that the evidence contained in the Old Testament is not easy to interpret. The Hebrew terms for various social groupings are not the precise language of a modern social anthropologist but terms in the natural language of the people, and they often lack precision. For example the Hebrew *bet av* literally means 'father's house' and is usually held to be a smaller social unit than Hebrew *mishpahah*, which is often translated as 'clan'. The actual usage of the terms is not so straight forward, however. In Judges 17:7 the tribe of Judah is described as a *mishpahah*; but in Amos 3:1 the whole people of Israel is called a *mishpahah* (see further Rogerson 1978: 94-96). The reconstruction that follows is presented with caution.

The *Bet Av*
We begin with the smallest unit, the *bet av*, or 'father's house'. This probably had two senses in Judah and Israel before the deportations of 597–582. First, it denoted a family residing together. The families numbered around five or six persons, even allowing for the fact that more children would be born than survived into adulthood. The *bet av* of an unmarried man or woman would be that of their father, and in this case the term would refer to a nuclear family. A good example would be Genesis 50:8, where Joseph's 'house' can refer only to the nuclear family of which he is head. Lemche (1985: 231-32, 250-51) suggests that nuclear families were more frequent than extended families—that is, groups consisting of a father and mother and married sons and their children living together and acting as a single unit. Such an extended family is that of Noah, in Genesis 7:1. Noah enters the ark with his entire 'house' (Hebrew *bayit*), which includes three married sons.

The second main use of *bet av* is to denote descent. A good example is Genesis 24:38, where Abraham's servant is instructed to travel to Mesopotamia to Abraham's 'father's house' to seek a wife for Isaac. Obviously *bet av* here refers not to a residential group but to a descent group. It is probably best understood as a lineage, from which Abraham had separated but within which he wished his son to marry.

The *Mishpahah*
Mishpahah is usually translated as 'clan' in recent versions of the Bible. This is probably not helpful, because 'clan' has a number of meanings in anthropological literature (Fox 1967: 49-50, 59, 134-36). Non-specialists are probably most familiar

with Scottish clans, which are groups sharing a common surname on either their father's or mother's side. This does not fit very well with the Old Testament, where there are no surnames. Indeed, the Hebrew tribe, sharing a common name such as Judah or Benjamin, was probably closer to clans sharing a common name, such as Cameron. A *mishpahah* was probably a maximal lineage—that is, a descent group which established ties of kinship between families through a common ancestor who was no longer living. However, maximal lineages, unlike Scottish clans, could divide to form new maximal lineages, which would then bear different names from those they had borne earlier. *Mishpahah* is best thought of as a descent group. This explains references such as Judges 17:7:

> There was a man from Bethlehem of the *mishpahah* of Judah...

and Amos 3:1:

> Hear this word which the Lord has spoken against you, children of Israel,
> against the whole *mishpahah* which I brought up from the land of Egypt...

In the first case, the whole of the tribe of Judah is seen as a group descended from its ancestor, Judah. In the second case, Amos addresses the people of the northern kingdom, Israel, as descended from their ancestor Jacob.

The *Shevet*

The *shevet*, or tribe, is the most difficult term to define (see further Rogerson 1978: 36-89), because social groups can be bound together in so many different ways; by descent, by residence, by a common dialect, or by a common religion. In the Old Testament, tribes were certainly groups bound by residence and descent, and also, if we are to believe Judges 12:6, according to which Ephraimites could not pronounce the word 'shibboleth', by common dialects. There is much that we do not know about the Israelite tribes, simply because we do not have sufficient evidence to work on. A minimal definition of *shevet* would be: the largest social unit for mutual defence against other Israelite social units. This would explain the fact that in the book of Judges, tribes fight against each other on at least two occasions (Judges 12, 20, and 21).

If we test out these tentative definitions against Joshua 7:14-17, we shall see how they work in practice. In this passage, the people are assembled so that the culprit who has taken some of the spoils of Jericho can be discovered. This will be done by the manipulation of a 'lot' (perhaps the casting of stones onto the ground), which will identify which tribe (*shevet*) is to be taken, then which *mishpahah*, then which family (*bet av*) and then which man (Joshua 7:14). It is important that the sequel be read in the Revised Version, for it accurately represents what the Hebrew text states, whereas many more recent translations do not:

> So Joshua rose up early in the morning, and brought Israel near by their tribes; and the tribe (*shevet*) of Judah was taken; and he brought near the family (*mishpahah*) of Judah; and he took the family (*mishpahah*) of the Zerahites; and he brought near the family (*mishpahah*) of the Zerahites man by man; and Zabdi was taken; And he brought near his household (*bayit*) man by man; and Achan, the son of Carmi, the son of Zabdi, the son of Zerah, of the tribe of Judah was taken.

We notice first of all the fluidity of the terminology. Judah is called both a tribe and a *mishpahah*. This is best explained by assuming that when Judah is called a tribe (*shevet*) it is viewed as a residential group, and when it is called a *mishpahah* it is viewed as a descent group. We next note that after the maximal lineage of the Zerahites is taken (Zerah is one of the two sons of Judah; see Genesis 38:30) the living heads of the lineages that composed this maximal lineage are brought forward. Zabdi, the grandfather of the culprit Achan, is taken. The next step is important. It is not Zabdi's sons who are next brought forward, but the heads of all the nuclear families that belong to his lineage, including his sons and his grandsons. This is why the text says that Achan was taken, without recording that his father Carmi was taken first. Thus, in this passage, *bayit* (house) means lineage in the case of Zabdi, and the traditional Hebrew text makes perfect sense once we recognise that terms such as *bayit* and *bet av* have more than one meaning.

The Nation

It is important to recognise that names of nations are used in different ways. Much depends on whether they are used by 'insiders' or 'outsiders'. Germans usually refer to Britain as England (to the annoyance of Scots and the Welsh) whereas most English people say Britain (including England, Scotland, and Wales) if that is what they mean. The name 'America' can similarly be used in different ways. Canadians are North Americans, but not Americans! Failure to appreciate this fact can lead to difficulties. When the name 'Israel' is found in inscriptions such as the Merneptah stele or the Mesha Inscription, it must not be assumed that the authors of those texts understood by it precisely what we, or indeed what the biblical writers, might understand. Within the Old Testament itself various names are used to designate the kingdoms of Israel and Judah. In the book of Hosea the most common name used for the northern kingdom is Ephraim, and the same name is used in Isaiah 7:2 where it is reported that 'Aram had allied itself with Ephraim'. The northern kingdom is also referred to as Jacob in the visions of Amos 7:2, 5, but in chapters 40 to 49 of Isaiah, the name Jacob is used to address the deportees from Judah and Jerusalem who are in Babylon. The northern kingdom is called Joseph at Amos 5:15. A rare, poetic name for the nation is Jeshurun used at Deuteronomy 32:15, 33:5, 26 to refer to the whole nation, and Isaiah 44:2, where it refers to the southern deportees. At Micah 3:9-10, a passage usually held to represent the words of the eighth-century prophet, Micah, the 'rulers of the house of Jacob and chiefs of the house of Israel' are charged with having built 'Zion with blood and Jerusalem with wrong'. Why does the prophet accuse the rulers of the northern kingdom of using injustice to build the capital of the southern kingdom? Is he being sarcastic by deliberately getting it wrong or is he, as a man from the provinces of Judah, saying in effect to the rulers of both kingdoms 'a plague on both your houses'? Whatever the answer, modern readers need to be alert to the many terms and nuances that operate when the nation is being addressed or described.

The Power Structure

So far, we have considered social networks, but have not asked how power was exercised in them. This has become an important question, especially in the wake of Gottwald's massive and important book on the origins of Israel (Gottwald 1979). He argues that in the period 1250 to 1050 BCE the Israelite tribes emerged as egalitarian social units, consciously opposed to the oppressive rule of the Canaanite city-states.

Other studies (Wilson 1977) have compared Israelite tribes to the segmentary societies found in parts of present-day Africa—that is, societies made up of groups in which power is shared equally among its members.

It must be said that the evidence for the nature of Israelite social organisation before the monarchy in the eleventh century BCE is very sparse indeed, and that what evidence there is seems to point in a different direction from that of egalitarian segmentary societies. In what has been said above about *bet av* and *mishpahah*, with examples taken from Genesis and Joshua, the assumption has been that these narratives reflect the social realities of the times of the writers, that is, the period of the later monarchy. If it is possible to rely on parts of Judges for information about social organisation prior to the monarchy, the picture that emerges is one in which the tribes are led by men who belong to dominant lineages, and who enjoyed a higher-than-average level of prosperity. Judges 8:30 records of Gideon that he has seventy sons, born to him by many wives. This suggests that he was a powerful member of a dominant lineage, and that his protestation of belonging to an insignificant lineage (Judges 6:15; note the similar disclaimer by Saul in 1 Samuel 9:21) is not to be taken literally. In Judges 10:3-4 we are told that Jair has thirty sons (and by implication, more than one wife), that they ride on asses and possess thirty cities named after their father. Ibzan (Judges 12:8-10) also has thirty sons, and Abdon (Judges 12:13-14) has forty. Whatever we make of these figures, the text means us to understand that these 'Judges' of Israel are men of power and influence. Scanty as our information therefore is, it seems safer to conclude that prior to the monarchy, Israelite tribes had dominant lineages which provided judges and military leaders when necessary. There is no evidence that Israel at this period was a segmentary society (Rogerson 1986). Certainly, with the rise of the monarchy, powerful families and lineages established themselves in the court, as we saw above when discussing the background to Jeremiah 36–41.

The *Bet Avot*

The deportations of 597–582 brought about far-reaching changes in the social organisation of Judah. In texts that can be dated with certainty to the Second Temple period, such as the books of Chronicles, a new term is found: *bet avot*. This is not simply the plural of *bet av* but a term literally meaning 'house of fathers'. In practice it is a descent group similar or identical to a *mishpahah*, but with the difference that it bears a name, and to that extent can be compared with a Scottish clan.

In Nehemiah 7:7-38 (paralleled in Ezra 2:2-35) there is a list of the people who returned from exile. It takes the following form:

> sons of Parosh, 2172
> sons of Shephatiah, 372
> sons of Arach, 652
> sons of Pahat-Moab belonging
> to the sons of Joshua and Joab, 2818

The list gives eighteen such units, whose sizes range from 95 to 2818, the average size being between 600 and 800. Then follow ten geographical units of the form:

> men of Bethlehem and Netopha, 188
> men of Anathoth, 128
> men of Beth-asmaweth, 42

At the end of the list are two or three more groups of the form:

> sons of Harim, 320.

This list is probably to be dated in the first half of the fifth century BCE, and it gives the numbers of the lay persons who belonged to the community in Judah at that time. Other lists in the same chapter record the numbers of priests, Levites, and temple servants. The lay people who are listed under place names are probably those who were not deported by the Babylonians. The rest were descended from deportees, and had developed a type of social organisation that bound groups together by allegiance to or descent from the men, such as Parosh, Shephatiah, and Arach, who are named in Nehemiah 7. We do not know anything about Parosh, Shephatiah, and Arach, and so on, apart from having their names in Nehemiah and Ezra. We can hazard the guess that, while in exile, extended families were broken up and settled in different parts of Babylon, thus necessitating new social groupings, which named themselves after men such as Parosh and Shephatiah. The purpose of these new social groupings was to maintain the identity of the people of Judah, who were living in an alien culture. Nehemiah 7:61-62 records that some of those who returned to Judah could not prove that they belonged to such a *bet avot*, although it is not clear how this affected them. Priestly descendants who were in the same position (Nehemiah 7:63-65) were excluded from the priesthood.

Whatever the origins of these groups, it is clear that they were the basic units of social organisation in the post-exilic community, a community whose centre was the Jerusalem Temple, and of whose population perhaps over a third were priests, Levites, and temple servants. We find these same units occurring, with minor variations, in the account of the rebuilding of Jerusalem in Nehemiah 3, and the dissolution of mixed marriages in Ezra 10:18-44. No doubt these units were each responsible for the collecting and payments of dues to the Persian government (the new masters, following Persia's conquest of Babylon). It may also be that the leaders of these units were the people responsible for making their fellow Jews debtors and slaves, as described in Nehemiah 5. We may suppose that the creation of new social units had weakened the duties of mutual support that had been characteristic of the *mishpahah*, and we may interpret Nehemiah's action, described in that chapter, as an attempt to reassert those duties. At the same time, we find in Leviticus 25 a new basis for this duty of mutual support. It is a religious basis, grounded in God's redemption of his people from slavery in Egypt (Leviticus 25:55). The old social ties are reinforced by a religious ideology appropriate to a community whose life is focused around the Jerusalem Temple. As we shall see in the remainder of this chapter, the history of Judah from 400 to 63 BCE was, to a great extent, a struggle between the demands of authoritarian rulers and the ideals of this religious community.

Other Post-Exilic Groups

In 332 BCE Alexander the Great brought Persian rule in Judah to an end, and from 323 to 198 BCE the country was part of the Egyptian empire established by one of Alexander's generals, Ptolemy. Under the Ptolemies, the selling of people into slavery for debt was legalised (Kippenberg: 79-80) and towards the end of the third century a certain Joseph, of the family of the Tobiads (see Nehemiah 6:1, 17-19; 13:4), gained the right to collect taxes. Joseph doubled the amount collected. In order to meet these new demands, the peasants in Judah had either to sell some of their family into slavery or to switch their production to crops that earned greater income, such as olive orchards. Under the Seleucids, the successors of Alexander who ruled Syria, and who became the overlords of Judah in 198 BCE, there arose in Judah a new aristocracy, who wished to change the basis of the life of the people. Jerusalem became a polis based upon Greek models, whose name was Antiocheia and of which only the aristocracy could become citizens. A gymnasium was built, and Greek sports were encouraged (2 Maccabees 4:1-17). Whatever else may have been the reasons for the banning of Judaism by the Seleucid king Antiochus IV in 168/67 BCE, he only brought to a logical conclusion an attack upon Judaism that had been mounted from within its own ranks. The subsequent Maccabean revolt can be seen as an attempt by the ordinary peasants not only to defend their religion but also to defend the freedom from slavery and impoverishment that was enshrined in its laws.

The revolt, led by the Maccabean family, liberated the Temple in 164 BCE, and after many ups and downs struggled to a final victory. However, the dynasty of rulers that emerged appropriated the high-priesthood (142 BCE), took the title of king (103–102 BCE), enlarged the territory of Judah, so as to include Galilee once more, and generally turned into despotic rulers little better than those whom the revolt had overthrown. In 63 BCE, with two rival claimants to the throne locked in a bitter struggle, Rome took over the rule and administration of the province.

Against this background there were formed religious parties who sought in different ways to practise and preserve the ideology of Judaism. One such group was the community known to us from the so-called Damascus Document, whose ideology owed much to that of the immediate post-exilic community (Davies 1982). The aim of the group was to found a new type of social and religious life based not upon kinship but upon free acceptance of a new covenant made with God. The group had 'camps' in various towns, whose members were households, including servants and day labourers. The organisation of each 'camp' was based upon the leadership of priests and Levites, and Israelites had precedence over proselytes. Mutual responsibilities included the support of orphans and the poor, and the redemption of those threatened with or fallen into slavery. Thus we see here the attempt to form an alternative society to that which prevailed in Judah and to achieve by means of acceptance of a religious covenant what, in earlier times, kinship ties through the *mishpahah* had been intended to achieve. Some members of this group later formed the community known to us from the discoveries at Qumran (Dead Sea Scrolls).

Another group that must be briefly mentioned is the Pharisees. Although little is known about their origins, they became what can best be described as a movement for the education of the people in the knowledge and practice of the Jewish law. This became all the more important after the conquests of the Maccabean kings had greatly enlarged the territory that was ruled from Jerusalem. Although the Pharisees had their own fellowship groups, they did not attempt to be a self-contained community after the fashion of the covenanters of the Damascus Document.

It is also important to mention the Samaritans for, whatever may have been their origins, they represent another attempt to maintain a religious community, free if at all possible from the depredations of tyrannical government. In the Judean-influenced documents that are preserved in the Old Testament and the Apocrypha, the Samaritans are viewed unfavourably, no doubt because their existence was a threat to Judean claims to be exclusive heirs of the religion of Moses. From the social point of view, however, they constituted a temple-based community in the heartland of the old northern kingdom; an alternative temple-based community to that in Jerusalem. Given that their scriptures were the first five books of the Old Testament, we can say that their religious ideology, too, was based upon God's election of his people, an election that had profound implications for how social organisation should support the poor and prevent their degradation into slavery.

When we read the Old Testament and encounter genealogies or find people introduced by means of specifying their descent, we must remember the two features of ancient Israelite life that may seem foreign to us today. The first is a feeling of solidarity between individuals and their social group, in which the group has obligations to protect individuals from harm, injustice, and poverty. The second is a religious ideology which established links of mutual responsibility on the basis of common membership of a covenant community. Both conceptions were, in the periods before and after the deportations of 597–582, attacked by those who wished to use power for their own ends. The resultant conflicts gave rise to new forms of social and religious organisation, as well as being the soil from which grew the messianic hopes and expectations of the people.

References

Davies, P.R.
  1982   *The Damascus Covenant: An Interpretation of the 'Damascus Document'* (JSOTSup, 25; Sheffield: JSOT Press).
Fox, R.
  1967   *Kinship and Marriage* (Harmondsworth: Penguin Books).
Gottwald, N.K.
  1979   *The Tribes of Yahweh: A Scoiology of the Religion of Liberated Israel, 1250–1050 B.C.E.* (Maryknoll, NY: Orbis Books; London: SCM Press).
Kippenberg, H.G.
  1978   *Religion und Klassenbildung im antiken Judäa* (Göttingen: Vandenhoeck & Ruprecht, 2nd edn).
Lemche, N.P.
  1985   *Early Israel: Anthropological and Historical Studies on the Israelite Society Before the Monarchy* (SVT, 37; Leiden: E.J. Brill).
Rogerson, J.W.
  1978   *Anthropology and the Old Testament* (Oxford: Basil Blackwell; repr., Sheffield: JSOT Press, 1984).
  1986   'Was Early Israel a Segmentary Society?', *JSOT* 36: 17-26; reprinted in D.J. Chalcraft (ed.), *Social-Scientific Old Testament Criticism: A Sheffield Reader* (The Biblical Seminar, 47; Sheffield: Sheffield Academic Press, 1997): 162-71.
Wilson, R.R.
  1977   *Genealogy and History in the Biblical World* (New Haven and London: Yale University Press).

Chapter 3

THE PEOPLES OF THE OLD
TESTAMENT WORLD

The nations and peoples that surrounded ancient Israel and Judah helped to shape their origins, history and culture. They also play roles in the 'world' of the biblical literature. We shall look at their character on both the stage of history and in the texts of the Old Testament, trying to demonstrate the relationship between the two portraits.

We shall not find in the Old Testament any disinterested profile of other nations. Immediate neighbours are defined largely in terms of kinship to the biblical Israel (personified as Jacob); others are treated as agents of either punishment or rescue in a divine plan that always focuses on Israel. This egocentricity is a feature of most national ideologies in the ancient Near East: historically these neighbours were not just as the Old Testament shows them, though we should understand why they are depicted as they are.

A common way to represent the relationship between peoples in the ancient world was through kinship and ancestry. Geneaologies often *did* reflect a recognition of ethnic affinity, but also represented political relationships. So, for example, Ammon and Moab sprang, according to Genesis 19, from an incestuous union between Lot and his daughters, while Esau, Jacob's brother, is the ancestor of Edom (Genesis 36). Ammon, Moab and Esau/Edom, each personified by their ancestor, were part of 'Abraham's family', and so 'related' to the 'original' Jacob/Israel (though not of Yhwh's 'chosen people'). From Genesis 9, where this 'kinship' matrix is extended to all the nations of the known world, descended from the family of Noah, comes the category of 'Semitic' (from Shem) and 'Hamitic' (north-eastern Africa). Canaan's place in the line of Ham thus makes sense in terms of Egypt's *political* involvement in Palestine.

We shall consider the neighbours of Israel and Judah in three groups: those which in fact shared the same territory as Israel and Judah; their immediate neighbours; and those more distant whose empires embraced Israel and Judah at some point. However, a word of caution is needed: nowadays we tend to think of nation-states with fixed borders. In reality, however, 'territory' in the political sense was defined by power and influence. The city of Dan, for example, appears in the Bible as a once-'Canaanite' city, Laish, taken over by a tribe of 'Israel' (Judges 18) and later established as a royal sanctuary (1 Kings 12:29). But in the ninth century BCE it fell to Damascus (according to an inscription found there), and any reader of 1 Kings will learn that Israel and Syria were often at war over adjacent territory. An Egyptian map would probably represent Palestine as part of Egypt (as it was in the Late Bronze Age and again during the third century BCE!). 'Map is not territory': how many people think of Masada as in Edom?

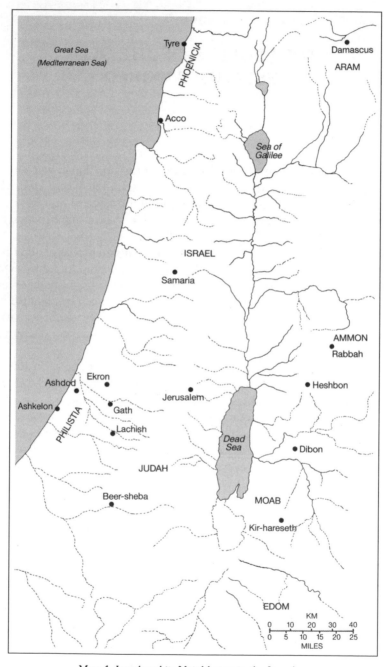

Map 4. *Israel and its Neighbours in the Iron Age*

Peoples within the Borders of Israel and Judah

Most archaeologists and historians now think that the name 'Israel' belonged to groups that settled in the central highlands in the thirteenth century BCE as part of a wider movement including the Transjordanian plateau. But other groups were of course present in Palestine and many were later included within the kingdoms of Israel and Judah.

Again, during the Greco-Roman period (late second century BCE onwards) non-Jewish populations in Idumea (Edom), Galilee and Transjordan were absorbed into Judah, while other Greek cities remained outside Judah but within Palestine. These circumstances created a severe identity crisis. Israel and Judah, then, were always included populations that, according to the ideology of the Old Testament were not 'Israelite' or 'Jewish'.

'Canaanites'

The Old Testament deals most harshly with those populations who, along with the 'people of Israel' made up the kingdoms of Israel and Judah. The 'Deuteronomistic' literature—the book of Deuteronomy and other books influenced by its ideas and vocabulary (including Joshua and Judges)—regards these other indigenous peoples as dispossessed by Yhwh, though that decree was not fully executed, and 'Canaanites' lived among 'Israelites' thereafter. Although these biblical texts (and some modern textbooks too!) treat 'Israel' as a distinct nation, the kingdom of Israel (Judah perhaps less so) embraced several population elements. In the Old Testament 'Canaanite' often designates the culture of Palestine, with its gods and goddesses, mostly related to fertility, and its numerous local shrines, a culture threatening to the religion of Yhwh. But as we now know from archaeology, and also from the Bible, most Israelites and Judahites habitually followed this culture, making themselves indistinguishable from 'Canaanites'.

Yet not all of the Old Testament follows Deuteronomy's lead in demonizing 'Canaanites'. In Genesis 12–36, Abraham's family occupy the land under a divine promise, but live as *gerim* ('resident aliens') among the indigenous population. In Ezekiel 47:21-22, when 'Israel' is reconstituted in the province of Judah after resettlement, non-Israelites in the 'land of Israel' will not be dispossessed, but 'you shall regard them as native-born children of Israel; with you they shall be allotted an inheritance among the tribes of Israel'. Here we see the reality of mixed populations in a land theoretically, or theologically, 'Israel' but shared with many non-'Israelite' peoples.

In the light of recent historical and archaeological research, the general opinion now is that the 'Israelites' were originally indigenous to Palestine. The older chronological distinction (before the Iron Age Palestine was inhabited by Canaanites, and during the Iron Age [c. 1250–500] by Israelites) supposing a kind of population replacement, is misleading. The book of Ezekiel seems to reflect this situation: 'This is what the Lord Yhwh says to Jerusalem: "Your origin and your birth were in the land of the Canaanites; your father was an Amorite and your mother a Hittite"' (Ezekiel 16:3).

The Old Testament identifies different ethnic 'Canaanite' groups. In Deuteronomy and its associated literature, 'seven nations' of Canaan are named (of which one, according to Joshua 3:10, is 'Canaanites'!). Elsewhere we find ten—including both

Canaanites and Amorites (e.g. Genesis 10:15; 15:19)! Of most of these, we know either little or nothing. Girgashites and Perizzites, for instance, are found nowhere outside the Bible; Jebusites (identified in Joshua 15:8 as inhabitants of Jerusalem) likewise. Hivites *may* be Hurrians (see below); Hittites may be linked or not with the Hittite nation of Asia Minor (see below). The biblical terminology is confusing, the identity often dubious: we cannot say if any of the 'seven nations' corresponds to known ancient populations. Possibly the biblical writers wished to define 'Canaanites' as peoples who had already disappeared, who could not therefore be identified with anyone within Israel or Judah or subsequent 'Jewish' populations.

Amorites

Behind the name 'Amorite' is *Amurru*, applied in Mesopotamian texts to Semitic groups who emerged at the end of the third millennium BCE, distinguishable to modern scholars by distinctive personal names. A group of *Amurru* entered Mesopotamia in 2100–1900 BCE, and spread westward; in the fourteenth–thirteenth centuries a kingdom called 'Amurru' existed in what is now Lebanon. But the relationship of these *Amurru* to the biblical 'Amorites' is unclear. For example, 'Amorite' is used for the kingdom of Sihon in Transjordan (Numbers 21:21-34; 32:33; but see below on Ammonites) but can also refer to the population of Palestine as a whole (Genesis 15:16).

Phoenicians

'Phoenician' is the Greek name of the people living on the Lebanese and Syrian coast, north of Acco, mainly in city-states such as Byblos, Tyre and Sidon. In the Amarna letters (written in the fourteenth century BCE to the pharaoh by Palestinian rulers), it is regarded as part of 'Canaan'. Its location facilitated trade with Egypt, Cyprus and Greece, giving it a major role in the Levantine economy. In Genesis 10:15-19 the land of the Canaanites includes Sidon, and texts such as Isaiah 23:8. Proverbs 31:24; Zephaniah 1:11; and Zechariah 11:7, 11, in depicting Canaanites as *traders*, must have the Phoenicians in mind. Since the discovery of the texts from Ras Shamra (ancient Ugarit: fifteenth–thirteenth century BCE), the myths and practices recorded in them have been used by scholars as evidence of 'Canaanite' religion (see more below).

The Phoenicians both absorbed and passed on a variety of cultural influences. They are credited, for example, with disseminating the alphabet, a system of representing individual consonants by signs that underlies both the Hebrew and Greek alphabets. They founded colonies in North Africa and Spain, including Carthage, which became a major Mediterranean power. They also possessed raw materials, especially wood from the forests of the Lebanon range (widely in demand for temple-building); and their craftsmanship in wood, stone, and metalwork was of a high standard (as the story of Solomon's temple illustrates).

Philistines

'Philistine' is strictly the name of one of several groups who were repulsed from Egypt by Ramses III and settled in the Palestinian coastal plain in about 1200 BCE (others are Sikina, Sherdani). They came from Crete (according to Amos 9:7) or the Aegean or Asia Minor. In Palestine they served as agents of Egyptian imperial control (Genesis 10:13-14 refers to them as 'Caphtorim' [Cretans], descended from Egypt).

In this capacity, perhaps, they sought to subdue the populations of the highlands. Like the Phoenicians, they formed not a territorial state but a number of city-states. Three of these—Ashkelon, Ashdod and Gaza—already existed; Gath and possibly Ekron were new foundations. The Philistines expanded along the coastal plain, and, via the Jezreel valley, established a presence at Beth Shean, a former Egyptian garrison city on the edge of the Jordan valley. Near here the Bible narrates that they defeated Saul on Mt Gilboa. Their threat to the southern highlands, where the kingdom of Judah was to emerge, is reflected in the Samson stories, where Judeans seem to be subservient to them. Judges 18 also narrates that because of Philistine pressure the tribe of Dan had to move from a southern location to the foothills of Mt Hermon. David is portrayed as a one-time Philistine vassal, operating from Ziklag, a town given him by the Philistine 'king' Achish. Philistine influence in the highlands waned as the kingdoms of Israel and Judah were established.

Religion and Culture in Palestine

Much of our information about the culture of Canaan is drawn from Ugarit (see above). From its artefacts we can discover the extent of its trade and the wealth that it engendered, but more significant for most biblical scholars are its libraries, from which we learn of its system of writing, its cult and its myths. Many of the texts are Babylonian in language and in content, others are written in the local language, using a cuneiform alphabet and offer a primary source of knowledge about the religion of the regions, including cultic terms and divine names found in the Old Testament.

The religions of Ugarit contained many elements that the Bible vehemently censures as 'abominations'. Its senior deity was El, used in the Bible as a general term for 'God': several divine titles compounded with El (e.g. El Elyon in Psalm 78:35; El Shaddai in Genesis 17:1; El Bethel in Genesis 31:13) refer to Yhwh. El's consort, Asherah, also appears in the Bible, but transformed into a Canaanite cult object (e.g. Judges 6:25). It seems from some inscriptions that she was also once the consort of Yhwh. Hadad, the storm god, was the most important deity in Ugarit; he is better known to us by his title 'Baal' ('lord': sometimes in the plural 'baals', e.g. Judges 2.11). The Ugaritic 'Baal Epic' (or Epics; the reconstruction is uncertain) tells how he overcame Death (Mot), a myth reflecting the cycle of rain and drought, seed and harvest, death and life (*ANET*: 129-42). His struggle with Yamm (the Sea) may betray the concerns of a maritime people. The corn god Dagon was sometimes identified with him and his consort was Ashtart, the goddess of war (and love). There were also gods of the underworld, Reshef and Horon, and numerous other gods, some with duplicate functions and similar names. The importance of fertility, both for crops and humans, in Canaanite religion, private as well as public, is understandable, the latter vividly attested by the large number of nude female figurines found throughout Palestine. The temples of Canaan contained altars, sacred pillars (Hebrew *masseboth),* and statues, and were often located on raised mounds ('high places'; cf. 1 Kings 14:23). Here, sacrifices of many different kinds were conducted (*shelamim*, for example, or 'peace-offerings', are mentioned; cf. Exodus 20:24). The examination of entrails for divination is also mentioned in the Ugaritic texts, too, though only once referred to in the Old Testament (Ezekiel 21:21).

The Philistine apparently adopted local gods: Ashtoreth, Dagon, Baal-Zebul. The only extant Philistine inscription, written in Phoenician, was discovered in 1996 at

Tel Miqneh (Ekron), commemorating a temple built by a king called Achish (see 1 Samuel 21; but there king of Gath). One feature of this inscription is a goddess PTYGH, as yet unidentified, and not indigenous to Palestine. The best-known Philistine material remains are clay coffins with faces moulded on the heads, discovered at Beth Shean and elsewhere. Even here Egyptian influence is strongly suspected, and the coffins tell us little of distinctive Philistine beliefs about the dead. Philistine decorated pottery survived for about two centuries before the local varieties entirely took over. But there is much about Philistine culture we do not know.

Political and Social Organisation in Palestine

During the Late Bronze Age (1550–1200 BCE) Palestine consisted of city-states. These were under greater or lesser Egyptian control, but during the fourteenth century the system collapsed. The reason was probably mainly economic, but helped by weak Egyptian policy, conflict between the cities and struggles with groups outside the system. The cities were dominated by a ruling elite, employing a specialised warrior caste, supported by taxes on the farmers. Groups outside the orbit of the city-states included nomads and *habiru*. The latter, according to the Amarna letters, were a military threat and some scholars have seen in their activity a social revolution against a feudal society. Their connection to the biblical 'Hebrews' is a matter of scholarly disagreement. But the origins of ancient Israel almost certainly derive from this period or shortly after.

Egyptian control over Palestine in the early Iron Age was exercised predominantly over the cities of the plains and lowlands, for the highlands were economically less valuable and more difficult to dominate. The collapse of the city-state system at the end of the Late Bronze Age saw many farmers migrating into the highlands. There are signs that some other cities revived, until the incursion at the end of the tenth century of the pharaoh Sheshonq (Shishak). Despite 1 Kings 14:25, Sheshonq does not record attacking the highlands, and the kingdoms of Israel and Judah may not even have been established at this time. But the weakening of the city-state system opened the way for *territorial* states, covering a wider area and with a stronger ethnic cohesion, to grow.

Peoples on the Borders of Palestine

These neighbours included the Transjordanian kingdoms and several nomadic groups, some with similar origins to Israel and Judah and with ties of kinship. The same may be true of the Aramean kingdoms that stretched into Syria. Other Palestinian inhabitants were the Philistines, who arrived from outside, and the Phoenicians, who were settled there before Israel was formed and whose territory extended into what is now Lebanon.

Transjordan

Ammon, Moab, and Edom were among the territorial 'nation-states' that formed around the ninth century BCE. It is unfortunate that we know so little of these nations, because their origins and social and religious development were similar to Israel's in many respects. Amalekites and Midianites cannot be geographically defined so precisely, though they lived and roamed in Transjordan. We know a little of the Midianites from their material remains and can perhaps deduce some details from biblical tradition, but we have no data on the Amalekites or the Ishmaelites beyond their mention in the Bible.

The kingdoms of Ammon, Moab, and Edom arose from the same, or similar processes as those that formed Israel and Judah. Egyptian control in Palestine weakened at the end of the Late Bronze Age, the Philistines began to arrive and Aramean migration into the region around Damascus resulted in the establishing of other states in the region. The Bible views some of these nations as having had kings before Israel. Genesis 36:31ff. gives a list of 'kings who reigned in the land of Edom, before any king reigned over the Israelites', while the kings Sihon and Og appear in Transjordan in the story of Israel's 'wilderness' trek (Numbers 21:21-35), Eglon king of Moab is the villain in Judges 3, and Jephthah fights with the king of the Ammonites in Judges 11:1-28. These details (or some of them) may well be anachronistic, however.

The attitude towards Ammon and Moab in the Bible is ambivalent. They are represented as kin, yet dubbed inferior, the products of incest; they intermarry with Israelites, possibly include worshippers of Yhwh, but are excluded from membership of Israel's 'congregation'. Edom's ancestor is given as Esau, elder brother of 'Israel' (Jacob), but deprived of his birthright. The reconciliation between Jacob and Esau in Genesis 33 contrasts with the hatred expressed against Edom in, for example, Obadiah and Jeremiah 49. This ambiguity is not necessarily perplexing: the phenomenon is known to anthropologists who have studied 'segmentary societies', among which the most frequent conflicts can take place between those groups most closely related genealogically. Almost certainly Israelites and their Transjordanian neighbours recognised a real kinship, though the case of Edom is more problematic (see below).

Ammonites

The Ammonites settled between the Jabbok and Arnon rivers. Their capital, Rabbath-Ammon (where Amman the capital of Jordan is now sited) lies about 25 miles (40 km) east of the Dead Sea. Their rightful territory, according to the Bible, included only the eastern part, while the western part was settled by Israel, forming with the region north of the Jabbok what the Bible calls 'Gilead'. Israelite claims to Gilead begin in Numbers 21 with the *Amorite* kingdom ruled by Sihon from Heshbon and given by Yhwh to Israel because of that king's intransigence (it is just possible that 'Amorite' here is an error for 'Ammonite', though the 'error' occurs more than once). The territory is detailed in Joshua 12 and 13 and forms the basis of the dispute between Ammon and Israelite Gilead in Judges 10-12. By the end of the eighth century this 'Israelite' territory was part of Ammon—now already, like Judah, an Assyrian vassal.

Israel and Ammon shared origins and probably kinship ties, as well as territory. The Old Testament relates that David headed there during Absalom's revolt, while one of the cults admitted by Solomon (1 Kings 11) was that of 'Milcom' or Molech, the 'abomination of the Ammonites'. The mother of Rehoboam was said to be from Ammon (1 Kings 14:21, 31). 2 Kings 24:2 claims that Ammonites assisted Nebuchadrezzar of Babylon against Judah, and the prophetic books express resentment at Ammonite benefits from his destruction—for example, Jeremiah 27:3; Ezekiel 21:20; and Zephaniah 2:8-9. But many Judeans sought refuge in Ammon, since, after Nebuchadrezzar had departed, they are reported as having returned from there

(Jeremiah 40:11), while a royal claimant, Ishmael, seems to have tried to promote his cause in Ammon (Jeremiah 41:10).

During the Babylonian period, Judeans intermarried with Ammonites (and Moabites), and according to Ezra 9:1 they had not, a century later, separated from these 'abominations'. Nehemiah's enemy, Tobiah, though called an Ammonite, bore a Yahwistic name (a name containing the element '-yah'), and a later Tobias who lived in Ammon participated in Judean politics under the Ptolemies and Seleucids. Around 250 BCE the Egyptian king Ptolemy II changed the name of Rabbath-Ammon to Philadelphia, converting it into a Greek city (a *polis*, a largely self-administering corporation). It resisted the siege of the Judean king Alexander Jannaeus who had conquered most of its territory, but in 63 BCE the Roman general Pompey added it to the league of ten cities called the Decapolis and granted it independence from Jewish rule. The area between the Arnon and Jabbok rivers was now known as Perea; disputes between Jews and non-Jews in this Hellenistic 'development' were not uncommon.

Moabites

Moab was Ammon's southern neighbour, lying between the Arnon and the Zered rivers, though often stretching farther north. Several Moabite settlements are mentioned in the Bible, but scarcely a half have so far been identified. Moab's wealth lay in its sheep breeding (see 2 Kings 3:4) and its position on the 'King's Highway' from Syria to the Red Sea. The Old Testament claims that David conquered Moab. But according to the inscription of the Moabite king Mesha' (the 'Moabite Stone', *ANET*: 320-21), left at the capital, Dibon, and dated to about 830 BCE, Moab had been 'oppressed' by *Omri of Israel* (a king of Omri's dynasty could well be meant). Mesha' celebrates liberating his land as well as recapturing 'Gad' ('Gilead') and using Israelite labour to rebuild many cities. The inscription reveals the script of Moab to have been the same as that used by Israelites, and the language to be only dialectally different. Moab was placed under Assyrian tribute during the eighth century, and is mentioned in the reign of Nabonidus (mid-sixth century). How it fared in the Persian period we do not know, but it later formed part of the territory of the Nabateans (see below).

Moabite religion was apparently similar to that of Palestine generally. Some place names contain 'Baal', while the Mesha' inscription refers to a 'high place' for Chemosh, a god who also appears in many personal names. The language Mesha' uses of Chemosh and of divine control of history and responsibility for warfare resembles that found in the Old Testament: 'Chemosh was angry with his land...' (cf. Deuteronomy 29:24); there is also reference to the *herem*, the 'ban' or wholesale slaughter of a defeated population, as described in the book of Joshua.

Much of what was said above about the racial, religious, and linguistic affinity of Israelites and Ammonites applies to Moab as well: descended from offspring of Lot's incest, Moab is hostile to Israel in the wilderness and Moabites are excluded, like Ammonites, from the 'congregation of Israel' (Deuteronomy 23:3). It is from Moabite territory that the Israelites are depicted as crossing into Canaan; and the stories in the book of Judges open with Ehud's assassination of Eglon, king of Moab. But on the other hand, the story of Ruth has a Moabite heroine and traces her descendants to David. According to 1 Samuel 22, David's parents sought refuge in Moab.

Edom

During the Iron Age the territory of Edom lay to the south of Moab, from the Zered River to the Gulf of Aqaba; but it also crossed the Wadi Arabah, or Rift Valley, though the earliest Edomite sites lie to the east. Archaeological evidence places Edomite origins in the early Iron Age, like Ammon, Moab and Israel, and although it is possible that their emergence is connected with that of Ammon and Moab, they may have come from northern Arabia, and developed into a kingdom slightly later. According to the Bible, Edom was suppressed under David, and Solomon built the port of Ezion-Geber at Aqaba, in its territory. Whether Edom was in fact subjected to Judah at this time we cannot really say, but it certainly became an Assyrian vassal in the eighth century. In the Babylonian and Second Temple periods (587 BCE–70 CE) Edomites moved west and north, while their original homelands were occupied by Arabs and Nabateans. Their new territory—better known in the Greek form Idumea—lay on Judah's southern border. In the Hasmonean period Idumeans were incorporated into the new Jewish nation by the Hasmonean king John Hyrcanus— though it is likely that the two nations were already to some extent culturally and religiously close. That it was the Idumean Herod the Great who finally exterminated the Hasmonean line (see Chapter 7) is therefore rather ironic!

The Edomites have left no substantial literary remains. Their location, and some of the sites excavated, suggest wide trade contacts, for their capital Bozrah (modern Buseirah) lay on the 'King's Highway'. But its lands also contained copper mines. The mine smelters of Edom were a source of copper in antiquity. The name of the major deity was Qaus, probably Arabian in origin, appears on jar-handles from two major Edomite sites at Umm el-Biyara (near Petra) and Tell el-Kheleifeh (ancient Ezion-geber, near modern Aqaba), and in Edomite personal names attested in Assyria and Egypt.

What of relations between Edom and Israel and Judah? The identification of Edom with Esau, the elder brother of Jacob/Israel, whose birthright was usurped (Genesis 25), suggests a close relationship between Edom and Israel. Amos's reference to a 'covenant of brothers' (1:11) might allude to this story and surely reveals a felt proximity between Israel and Edom. Even if the traditions of Israel's journey through Edom on the way to the Promised Land are apparently unhistorical, there are biblical texts connecting Yhwh with the Edomite region of Mt Seir (e.g. the 'Song of Deborah', Judges 5:4). Deuteronomy 2:5 has Yhwh say of Edom: 'Do not interfere with them; for I will not give you their land…because I have given Mt Seir unto Esau for a possession'. This statement makes two interesting points: Edom's land is a gift from Yhwh; but Edom's *original* land, not the Negev that they later occupied! But an ancient connection between Edom in its earlier homeland and Israel remains elusive and hard to reconstruct.

The Arabah and the Negev

Various other nations—sometimes hard to pin down geographically and often little known through literary or archaeological remains—inhabited the territory to the south and east of Palestine, from the fringes of the Arabian desert, across the Arabah (the Rift Valley south of the Dead Sea) and the Negev, the southern part of Palestine. This is the territory in which the books of Exodus–Deuteronomy depict the migration of the Israelites from Egypt towards their Promised Land.

Amalekites

The territory covered by the Amalekites seems extensive. The geographically scat-
tered references, if accurate, suggest a nomadic or semi-nomadic lifestyle. We have
no extra-biblical data about them, though the site of Tel Masos (usually thought to
be Kadesh-barnea) has tentatively been identified with the Hormah and the 'city of
Amalek' of 1 Samuel 15:5 (see also Numbers 14:5). Genesis 36:12, 16 (see also
1 Chronicles 1:36) traces Amalek from Esau (= Edom), while verse 12 names his
mother as Timnah, which was a copper-mining city 25 miles north of Aqaba/Eilat, in
the Sinai Peninsula, in Midianite territory (not to be confused with Timnah in
Judah). Exodus 17 tells of Israel's fight with Amalekites en route to Canaan from
Egypt. 1 Samuel 14–15 states that the Kenites, who also inhabited the Negev, lived
among them, and according to 1 Samuel 30 David fought them near Ziklag. Genesis
14 also seems to locate them in this general region. There are, however, allusions to
Amalekite presence elsewhere: Numbers 14:45 links them with Canaanites in the
'hill country'; Saul's encounter with them (1 Samuel 15) makes better sense in this
region; and the judge Abdon (Judges 12:15) is buried 'in the hill country of the
Amalekites, in the land of Ephraim'. There are, finally, accounts of Amalekites in
league with Moabites (Judges 3) and Midianites (Judges 6 and 7). The Bible mentions them from the time of Abraham (Genesis 14) to Hezekiah (1 Chronicles 4:43,
which tells of fugitive Amalekites slaughtered near Mt Seir).

Amalekites are abhorred in the Bible, threatened with eternal divine hostility (Exodus 17), ultimate destruction (Numbers 24:20), and with a blotting-out of their
memory (Deuteronomy 25) for an unprovoked attack on Israel in the wilderness
(Exodus 17). Yet Balaam's oracle (Numbers 24:20) inexplicably calls them the
'earliest' or 'greatest' of the nations (but predicts their destruction)! The name of the
Amalekite king Agag (1 Samuel 15) becomes a tribal name in Esther, where
Israelite–Amalekite hatred is revived: Haman is an 'Agagite' and Mordecai a
descendant of Saul (son of Kish).

Midianites

The Midianites occupied territory southeast of Moab and Edom, where they can first
be traced archaeologically from about the twelfth century BCE. The most important
site connected with them is Timnah (see above), where, on the site of an older Egyptian shrine to Hathor, stood a tent-shrine containing in its sanctum a copper snake.
This suggests an intriguing parallel with the life of Moses (see below). In Genesis 37
and Judges 6 they are described as living in tents and travelling.

Little else is known of the Midianites. According to Genesis 25:18, they dwelt in
Arabia, and they are traced to Abraham (Genesis 25:1-2). Moses married the daughter of a Midianite priest, Jethro. It is interesting to speculate on the link between this
Midianite connection and the connections with Edom. Both Edomites and Midianites occupied the same general area—where, in fact, the Sinai of the biblical
accounts is often placed by scholars, rather than in the Sinai peninsula. (In Numbers
22 and 25 Midian is located farther north, with Moab; but this may be in fact a
confusion between Moab and Midian.) In Numbers 31 Midian is massacred by Israel;
in Judges it is the oppressor of Israel, vanquished by Gideon. To pin down any firm
historical connection from these traditions is tricky; an early struggle between Israel
and Midian for control over Transjordan is a possibility. But when the biblical

accounts were written, the identity and character of the Midianites, like those of the Amalekites, were perhaps no longer clearly remembered.

Another neighbour worth mentioning is the tribe of the Ishmaelites. However, despite the importance of Ishmael as the firstborn of Abraham, these people play no role in the Old Testament other than a mention in the Joseph story (Genesis 37:25-28; but see also verse 36) and a reference along with other neighbours in Psalm 83:6.

Nabateans

Although situated in the same area as Moab and Edom (and even Aram) had earlier been, the Nabateans deserve a separate treatment, because although they are not mentioned in the Old Testament, they play an important role in the history of Judah/Judea, during the period in which the literature of the Old Testament was still being developed.

The beginnings of the Nabateans as a nation cannot be traced; possibly Asshur-banipal's inscriptions refer to them (c. 650 BCE). But they emerge clearly as a tribe of Arab nomads at the time of Alexander the Great. They settled down where Edom had been in earlier times, in lower Transjordan and south of the Dead Sea. Their empire, as it came to be, was built on trade, including the trading of others who passed through their region—which lay across the major caravan route from the Mediterranean to Arabia and the Red Sea. Their capital city was Petra, about 50 miles (80 km) south of the Dead Sea where the trade routes from both east and west of the Jordan converged towards Aqaba. The Nabateans also practised agriculture, thanks to irrigation systems; their stout fortifications against the Arabs can still be seen, and they were powerful enough to repel the forces of the Macedonian king of Syria, Antigonus, in 312 BCE.

The first Nabatean king known to us is Aretas 1 (c. 170 BCE), under whom they first showed an interest in the politics of the region. He attempted to gain control of the trade routes farther north, to Damascus, and west, to Gaza. However, the Hasmonean kings of Judea had territory in Transjordan, and Alexander Jannaeus came into conflict with Aretas, provoking a Nabatean invasion of Judea, which had to be bought off. Dealings with the Hasmoneans continued as Aretas looked for territory in Transjordan in return for aid to Hyrcanus II in regaining power. Aretas defeated Hyrcanus's brother Aristobulus and besieged Jerusalem. Only the arrival of the Roman general Pompey saved the situation. Later, Herod was obliged by the Romans to fight the Nabateans; his son Antipas, having married a Nabatean princess, then wished to replace her with Herodias (see Luke 3:19). The incident led to war with the Nabateans, and a Roman force had to be sent. It was not until the time of Trajan that the Romans conquered Nabatea, when their capital (now Bostra) became the centre of the Roman province of Arabia.

The most famous Nabatean relic is Petra, whose impressive remains are largely of Greco-Roman style, dating from the second century CE. Like many other trading nations, they produced notable artistic achievements, especially pottery. Their language was a dialect of Aramaic, written in a script that may be an ancestor of the classical Arabic one. Their deities, Dusharat and his consort Allat, were deities of weather and fertility.

Aramean Kingdoms

In Genesis 10:22-23 Aram is listed, with Elam and Asshur, as a descendant of Shem; and Amos asserts that they came from Qir—an unknown region, but linked in Isaiah 22:6 with Assyria and Elam. At the beginning of the Iron Age, the Arameans—mostly Amorite, with some Hurrian elements as well—established states in Syria and northwest Mesopotamia (e.g. Aram-Zobah, whose king, Hadadezer, is mentioned in 2 Samuel 8:10). The kingdom of 'Aram' in the Bible is Damascus, which warred with Israel over territory and local supremacy when Assyria was weak (the background of the reigns of Ahab to Jehoash: 1 Kings 20–2 Kings 13); when Assyria was relatively strong, Aram was distracted, and Israel could flourish; when Assyria was a threat to the region, Aram and Israel could form an alliance, as in the mid-eighth century, when they pressed Judah to participate. But Ahaz of Judah brought in Tiglath-Pileser, who defeated Rezin of Damascus in 732 BCE (2 Kings 16:5-9; see also Isaiah 7). There was a deportation, and Damascus lost its independent status, being included in the Assyrian province of Hamath. But the city remained an important economic centre during the Babylonian and Persian periods, then passed to the Seleucids, then Nabateans, Armenians, and finally Romans. From at least the sixth century onwards, it contained a Judean community.

The Arameans occupied an important area, controlling trade routes between Mesopotamia and both Anatolia and Egypt. The Assyrians thus sought control over this area, and in their empire Aramean culture played a large role. In particular, Aramaic was widely used alongside Akkadian, as it was under the Babylonians and Persians, when it was the recognised *lingua franca* of the western part of their empire. In 2 Kings 18:26 the Assyrian general (*rab-shakeh*) who is besieging Jerusalem, is implored to speak in Aramaic rather than Hebrew, since Judean officials could speak it, but not the rest of the people. It increasingly became the language of Palestine from the sixth century BCE.

We have several inscriptions from Aramean kings, including Zakkur, Kilamuwa, Bar-rakib, Panammuwa, and Azitawadda. These mainly recite the king's deeds and give us little insight into the material culture of these states; however, they occasionally reveal the existence of dynastic and personal gods worshipped alongside major deities like El, Baal-Hadad, Reshep, Baal-Shamem (Lord of heaven), Baalat, Atar/Athar and Atta (Anat).

In Deuteronomy 26:5 Israel is described as descended from a 'wandering Aramean' (or an 'Aramean about to perish')—probably a reference to Jacob. According to Genesis 24, Jacob was sent to Abraham's 'country and family', to 'Aram Naharaim' ('Aram of the two rivers'), to the 'city of Nahor', probably Haran (Genesis 27:43), where lived Laban 'the Aramean'. Genesis 28 calls the territory 'Paddan-Aram'. It lay between the rivers Habor and Euphrates, bounded on the west by the cities of Carchemish and Aleppo, an area occupied by the Aramean state of Bit-adini (2 Kings 19:12; Amos 1:5), which was absorbed into Assyria in 855 BCE. It was from Haran that, according to Genesis 12, Abraham travelled to Canaan, and the close kinship portrayed between Israelite and Aramaean ancestors may suggest a tradition of common descent, or at least a strong cultural affinity. Although the stories of Elijah and Elisha (1 Kings 17–2 Kings 9) are set against the background of war between the two nations, Elijah comes from Gilead and Elisha anoints an Aramean king, while the Aramean Na'aman seeks help from Yhwh.

Occupying Empires

Lying between Egypt, Asia Minor and Mesopotamia, Palestine lay at the mercy of more powerful kingdoms on every side. Israel and Judah both succumbed to Assyria, while Judah continued under the Neo-Babylonians, Persians, Macedonians (Ptolemies and Seleucids) and Romans. Throughout much of the second millennium, Mesopotamia exerted a wide cultural influence, but Egypt had political control of Palestine. During the Iron Age political dominance came from Mesopotamia, afterwards passing to Persia, to the Macedonian/Greek kingdoms, and thereafter to Rome.

The cultural influence of the imperial nations upon Israel and Judah is rarely considered in the Bible. Their main role is as agents of Yhwh or as his opponents or rivals; whether exploited to execute his plans for Israel, or offering a challenge to his ordering of world affairs, these empires are often treated disdainfully. The biblical writings naturally have a Judah-centred view of the world, in which these empires are almost peripheral to history. But Palestine was unavoidably the victim of imperial ambitions for most of the period covered in this book, since it lay in the path of trade and military routes.

Egypt regarded Palestine as part of its sphere of influence—its own territory, even. On the eve of Israel's appearance, Palestine was under Egyptian control. During the early Iron Age, between the wane of Egyptian power and the rise of Assyria, a number of small kingdoms—Israel, Judah, Aram, Ammon, Moab and others—briefly flourished. These were tribal or territorially based, unlike the city-states of the Bronze Age. But as Assyria grew more powerful, one part after another of Syria-Palestine fell under its vassalage or became absorbed into its empire. From the Assyrian yoke Judah passed briefly under the Neo-Babylonian, then Persian. It then formed part of the Hellenistic kingdoms of the Ptolemies (Egypt), then Seleucids (Syria). After a glorious century of Jewish independence, when its boundaries exceeded even those claimed for David. Judah/Judea became a tributary kingdom before being broken up, with Judea proper a directly ruled province.

Egypt

Egypt enjoyed a stable political structure, based on a reliable economy, good internal communications along the Nile, a strong monarchic ideology and an elaborate bureaucracy. A secure geographical location protected it from easy invasion. At the end of the Late Bronze Age (c. 1250 BCE) it still had control of Palestine, thanks to a peace treaty with the Hittites, concluded under Ramses II. His successor, Merneptah, repelled the 'Sea Peoples' and in celebration of a military campaign in Palestine erected a stela on which the earliest mention of an 'Israel' occurs. In the mid-tenth century, Sheshonk I, to whose court Jeroboam I is said to have fled (1 Kings 11:40), invaded Palestine (1 Kings 14:25-26 places this in the time of Rehoboam).

Egypt itself was later invaded by the Assyrian kings Esarhaddon and Asshurbanipal between 670 and 660 BCE. It regained independence, and during the death-throes of Assyria, the pharaoh Necho took his army through Palestine to confront the Babylonians and Medes and lay his claim to Palestine. According to 2 Kings 23:29 Josiah was killed by Necho at Megiddo. But Egypt won nothing: Nebuchadrezzar's victory at Carchemish in 605 opened up Palestine to a new imperial master. Egypt itself remained independent until the Persian king Cambyses invaded in 525 BCE. Occasional revolts during the Persian period were unsuccessful, except for a spell of independence in 404–341. The arrival of Alexander the Great in 332 led eventually to a Macedonian dynasty, founded by Alexander's general Ptolemy, which administered Palestine until 199 BCE, when the kingdom named after another of Alexander's generals, Seleucus, wrested it from the Ptolemies. In 30 BCE Egypt became a province of the Roman Empire. But whether under Persians, Macedonians, or Romans, Egypt's culture remained recognisably Egyptian.

Four dominant factors in Egypt's culture were the Nile, the sun, the king and bureaucracy. The economy depended on the reliable annual flooding of the Nile, which inundated a strip of land beyond its banks. Another regular phenomenon, which caught the Egyptian imagination, was the daily passage of the sun: across the sky, down through the underworld, and back up the other side, travelling (naturally) on a boat, the obvious means of travel in Egypt. The chief gods were represented by the sun—Re, Atum, Aten, and the underworld (Osiris Horus, Isis). Absolute power was vested in the divine king, son of the sun god. Egyptian bureaucracy is manifested in actual records, but also in paintings of everyday scenes and, most memorably the judgment of the dead, in which the deeds of the soul are recorded and weighed by divine bureaucrats. (There was, of course, a god of bureaucracy, called Thoth.) Texts of instruction for bureaucrats abound, too; and there was a goddess of justice, truth, and order (Ma'at), personifying royal and scribal ideals— one might say the goddess of order. The obsession of Egyptian culture with the afterlife is well-known; the afterlife was taken for granted, and elaborate care taken to preserve the bodies of the illustrious.

Egypt figures in the Old Testament as a place of slavery, of course. Although we cannot locate the Exodus historically, and it does not fit into current archaeological reconstructions, expulsions of Semites from Egypt were recorded in Egyptian sources. The influence of Egyptian religion on Israel is difficult to assess. The Bible betrays no interest in Egyptian religion and mentions none of its gods. Some cases of cultural influence can, however, be cited. Akhenaten's hymn to Aten (fourteenth century: see *ANET*: 369-70) is quite similar to Psalm 104, while the 'Instruction of Amenemopet' (*ANET*: 421-24) probably inspired Proverbs 22:17-24; the influence of Egyptian books of Instructions, which gave advice on how to behave and succeed in life may be seen in Proverbs, where the retributionary principle may reflect the order represented by Ma'at. The story of Ahiqar was also widely known, and is alluded to in Tobit 1:21-23. Egyptian influence on Judea in the Greco-Roman period must also be taken into consideration; but such influence—as, for example, upon Jewish apocalyptic literature and upon the Wisdom of Solomon, 2 Maccabees, and (possibly) Tobit—stems not from indigenous but Hellenised Egyptian culture. The large Jewish population in Alexandria was open to the Greek culture vigorously promoted in that city, but close contacts between the Jews of Judea and Alexandria are also widely attested. While amicable relations between Egypt and Judah are reflected in the apocryphal books of Aristeas and 3 Maccabees, the Wisdom of Solomon displays deep contempt for Egypt.

Hittites and Hurrians

The Hittites and Hurrians both established empires in the vicinity of Syria during the Middle Bronze and Late Bronze periods, though neither played a direct role in the history of Israel or Judah. The Hittite 'New Kingdom', which just preceded the emergence of Israel, was really Hittite–Hurrian; the dynasty was Hurrian, as were the major deities, and the Hurrian language was widely used. The Hittites were people of the central Anatolian plain, whose state developed between 2000 and 1700 BCE, centred on Hattusa (modern Boghazköy, in Turkey), and after 1700 grew into a network of states extending into Syria and beyond. Hittite control in Syria later gave way to the Hurrian kingdom of Mitanni, until about 1450, when a period of Hittite, or Hittite–Hurrian, power ensued, reaching its zenith under Suppiluliumas (c. 1380– 1350). The treaty of 1284 between Hatti (as their nation was called) and Egypt set the boundary between them just south of Damascus. But Hattusa was overrun in 1190, and since no written record of the event survives, we do not know by whom. Seven Hittite city-states (such as Hamath and Carchemish) remained in Syria along-side Aramean states; the Assyrians knew the region as 'Hatti-land'. These cities are often called Neo-Hittite, and their language (Luvian) differed from that of the earlier Hittite empire.

At the summit of the patriarchal, agricultural Hittite society was the king, the effective proprietor of the land, in place of the storm god. In war, the king was the commander; in religion, the chief priest. Many Hittite deities were attached to particular cities, according to the typical Near Eastern pattern, while others, such as the weather god, Taru, and his consort Wurusimut were absorbed by their Hurrian counterparts (Tesup and Hebat). Hittite laws are of special interest, since like the Hurrian texts from Nuzi they reflect Indo-European, rather than Semitic principles— in particular that of compensation, rather than of talion, or punishment in kind ('an eye for an eye…'). There are also numerous treaty texts, royal annals and proclamations. Many extant Hittite texts are in Akkadian, the language of Mesopotamia used throughout the ancient Near East in the second and early first millennium; and both the covenant treaties and annals conform broadly to the ancient Near Eastern pattern exemplified in numerous Assyrian texts.

The Bible does not allude to Hittite empire, but, as mentioned earlier, mentions Palestinian 'Hittites', including Uriah, the husband of Bathsheba (2 Samuel 11), while 1 Kings 10:29 and 2 Kings 7:6 refer to the Hittite states of Syria. Some cultural influence upon Israel from the Anatolian Hittites has been claimed: the vassal treaty form underlying the Sinai covenant and the book of Deuteronomy, and individual laws (e.g. the heifer-sacrifice of Deuteronomy 21:1-9; the scapegoat ceremony of Leviticus 16, the removing of a sandal to indicate non-discharge of responsibility, as in Ruth 4 and Deuteronomy 25:5-10). Other biblical phenomena may also be explained from the Hittites, for example, the *obot* ('mediums'?), available, according to 1 Samuel 28:3, to enquirers of God (the Hittite *aybi* was a pit which served as access to or for a spirit of the lower world). Also, *teraphim,* apparently devices for predicting the future, are probably related to the Hittite *tarpi,* or 'demon'. Yet it is hard to see any general cultural Hittite influence on the Old Testament, and many of the detailed instances remain hypothetical.

The Hurrians, who can be traced in Mesopotamia from about 2100 BCE, spread into northern Mesopotamia and northern Syria between 1700 and 1600. In Mitanni, upper Mesopotamia, early in the fifteenth century, a brief empire was established, which dominated Syria. After Mitanni had fallen to Assyrians and Hittites in 1350, the Hurrian language, and culture, remained influential. The most important Hurrian archive is from Nuzi, on the upper Tigris, from whose legal texts parallels have been suggested to episodes in the Genesis stories, including the adoption of slaves by childless couples (Genesis 15:2-3), the giving of a concubine by a childless wife, and the selling of a birthright. These parallels, if genuine, would attest the survival of Hurrian practices in Canaan well into the Iron Age.

Assyria

More than any other foreign nation, Assyria defined the political shape of the ancient Near East during the Iron age. The city of Asshur lay on the Tigris about 200 miles (320 km) north of Babylon, in the northern Mesopotamian plain. Assyria was bordered on the west by the Syrian desert and on the north and east by mountains separating it from the ancient kingdoms of Urartu and Media respectively. Genesis 10:11 derives Assyrian from Babylonia: and certainly, its Akkadian language was virtually a dialect of Babylonian, many of its gods were also Babylonian. Assyria appears first around 2000 BCE, when we find it trading with Asia Minor, an economic necessity that was always paramount in Assyrian imperial policy.

Assyria emerged as a military power in the fourteenth century BCE under Asshur-uballit I and his immediate successors. In the ninth century Assyria again pushed towards the Mediterranean under Asshurnasirpal II, in a series of vicious campaigns, celebrated in contemporary Assyrian accounts. His successor Shalmaneser III developed a more consistent policy of annual campaigns in all directions. In 853 he fought at Qarqar a coalition led by Damascus and including other Aramean states, Israel, some Phoenician ports, Egyptians, Arabians, and Ammonites. The battle was inconclusive, but in 841 Shalmaneser defeated Hazael of Damascus and received tribute from Tyre, Sidon, and Jehu of Israel, as depicted on the 'Black Obelisk', which he erected in his own honour.

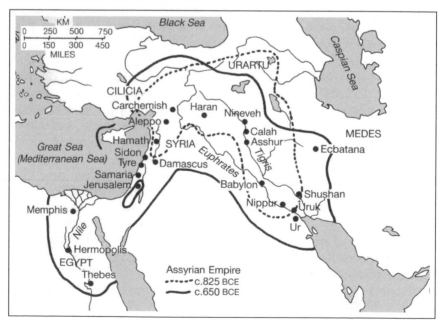

Map 5. *The Assyrian Empire, c. 825 BCE and c. 650 BCE*

Shalmaneser's annals stress the economic and material gains of his campaigns—in particular raw materials, luxury items, and manpower for building projects. Assyria consolidated its access to the Mediterranean coast, and especially to Cilicia, a source of iron and silver. These and other goods accrued from yearly tribute and from (one-sided) trade agreements. Assyrian colonies began to be established in distant places, obviating the need for annual campaigns for tribute, as well as providing potential military bases. Assyrian deportations were not solely punitive, but also served a policy of providing manpower in the heartland. The Assyrians drafted defeated soldiers into their ranks and imported craftsmen: these then assimilated. The names of officials called *limmu*, by whose terms of office years were dated, contain many foreign names; Israelites do not appear here, but many of these will also have become Assyrian. Sennacherib had Nineveh rebuilt, and, indeed, prisoners and deportees from his campaigns (perhaps including Israelites) are depicted at work there.

In 672 BCE Esarhaddon conquered part of Egypt—a victory reasserted by his successor, Asshurbanipal, under whom the Assyrian empire reached its greatest extent. But within a few years it was dismantled by an alliance of Media and Babylon from the south and east, and Scythians from the north. Asshur fell in 614, Nineveh in 612, and finally Haran in 610. Assyria no longer existed, except as a geographical region.

The Assyrians have earned for themselves a warlike and vicious reputation, one that their own graphic art seems to confirm. The Lachish frieze, for instance shows an efficient and cruel war machine at work besieging the Judean city. Assyrian kings took trouble in their annals to record in self-glorifying detail their military exploits. Other favoured subjects of Assyrian friezes are hunting, in which the slaughter of animals (as well as their muscular strength) is emphasised. Nevertheless, the cruelty and militarism of Assyria form only part of the picture. Assyria's geographical position made it vulnerable: it was surrounded by powerful states (Mitanni, Urartu, Mari, Babylon) and with few economic resources. One aim of expansion was in fact trade, of which Syria was the hub and the Arameans the proprietors. Assyria subdued its empire by an ideology of terror, with exemplary ruthlessness and exaggerated accounts of exploits. But if at first its rulers were content to extract tribute, they learned how to administer an empire, converting client kingdoms into provinces and (as in the case of Ekron in Philistia) constructing huge installations for the processing of olive oil from the region.

There were also impressive cultural achievements. Assyria's role in the transmission of Mesopotamian civilization was considerable, although distinctive characteristics are not easy to isolate. Magnificent building programmes adorned cities such as Calah (Nimrud), where, for example, Asshurnasirpal created botanical and zoological gardens. The different kinds of sculpture and relief work include glazed panels, ivory carvings, metalwork, and murals. Asshurbanipal created a library, collecting and copying texts from Assyrian and non-Assyrian archives, as a result of which many otherwise unknown texts have been preserved. Assyrian administration and culture is extensively recorded here in royal annals, building inscriptions, letters, legal texts, myths and legends, hymns, proverbs, as well as records of observations of entrails, astronomical bodies, and omens, from which arose the sciences of anatomy, astronomy, botany and mathematics.

The king, the religious and military leader and regent for the god Asshur, collected tribute through local governors, where these were appointed (e.g. the *rab-shakeh*, 2 Kings 18). Territories ruled by vassal kings were expected to pay tribute but little else. There is no evidence of Assyrian interference in their cult. In territories formally annexed, however, it seems that the population, regarded as citizens of Assyria, were obliged to support the Assyrian cult. Thus there would have been no official imposition of Assyrian religion in either Israel or Judah under Assyrian vassalage. Even after the annexation of Samaria in 722/21, although the worship of other gods entered with the colonists, the worship of Yhwh continued alongside these cults. Syncretism between Asshur and local deities often took place in annexed territories, but the cultural influence was not all in one direction. The Assyrian empire, in destroying the political power of the Aramean states nevertheless acquired a degree of Aramaic character, at least in the areas to the west of its own heartland. Aramaic became the *lingua franca of* most of the region between the Tigris and the Mediterranean, and Arameans the traders who provided the economic blood-supply, while Aramean scribes were drafted into the Assyrian administration. In the eighth and seventh centuries we should speak of an Assyrian–Aramaic culture, and this is no doubt how Israel and Judah experienced it, as far as religion and language were concerned. Such a state of affairs may be reflected in Genesis 10:22 where Aram is presented as the brother of Asshur.

Assyrian religion expressed a strong allegiance to the national deity Asshur, by whom enemies were overcome. Assyrian wars were holy wars. Yet the Assyrians claimed their victories not as triumphs of Asshur over other gods but as the result of support for Assyria by those gods. The speech of the *rab-shakeh in* 2 Kings 18:25 reflects plausible Assyrian propaganda in this respect—Yhwh, he claims, is on Assyria's side. Other Assyrian gods were associated with certain cities, as in Babylonia, where their cult was celebrated in temples and ziggurats. Many deities—for example, Anu, Hadad, Ishtar, Nabu, and Sin—were also worshipped by Babylonians and Arameans. It has been suggested that these deities were assimilated to Asshur to the point of virtual monotheism—a possible view if we recognise that a Mesopotmaian pantheon often reflects political configurations, with the heavenly world projected as a mirror of the earthly: a strong unitary state has its counterpart in a strong unitary divine kingdom.

The Assyrians appeared to Israel and Judah not as a foreign culture or religion but as a military predator to be feared (see Isaiah 10:13-14). Hatred of them is expressed in Nahum's jubilation over the fall of Nineveh (Nahum 3). By the time much of the Old Testament was being written, Assyria had passed into history, though its memory remained, for Assyria had definitively shaped that part of the world. In Jonah's mission, Nineveh serves as an ironic example of repentance from a hated nation stirring Yhwh's love for humans and his autonomy in deciding matters of forgiveness and punishment.

Babylon

In the Tigris-Euphrates basin, the site of one of the oldest civilizations on earth, a number of city-states vied for supremacy but shared a common culture. The most famous and enduring was Babylon (in Akkadian 'gate of God')—so much so that southern Mesopotamia is also known as 'Babylonia'. A site open to invasion on all sides, it aspired only briefly to widespread military conquest, but remained an important cultural centre throughout its history. Because of its geographical and cultural proximity, it was treated respectfully by Assyrian, despite its frequent revolts. The city may go back to the third millennium BCE, but came to prominence in the eighteenth century BCE with the Amorite dynasty of Hammurabi. Between the sixteenth and sixth centuries, Babylon enjoyed independence intermittently. It became a major power at the end of the seventh century BCE with the rise of the Chaldean (or Neo-Babylonian) dynasty under Nabopolassar, when it overthrew Assyria. This is the only period in which Babylon exercised control over Palestine. It was soon captured by Cyrus, but remained an important city of the Persian empire until captured by Alexander the Great, who died there in 323. It then belonged to the Seleucids until 64 BCE, when it passed to the Parthians.

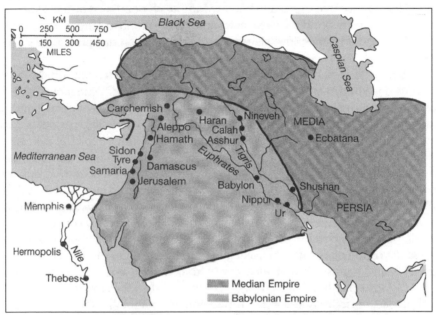

Map 6. *The Median and Babylonian Empires, Sixth Century BCE*

We know a good deal about Babylonian culture from its own archives and those of other ancient cities. In religion, the king was supreme, and under him were numerous priestly castes, whose activities ranged from temple maintenance, sacrifice, and liturgy to the casting of spells, diagnosis of medical complaints, and the reading of various omens. The major cities had their own festivals and sacred days, the best known being the *akitu* festival, which, in local variations, featured the ritual re-enthronement of the king by the god, possibly accompanied by a ritual combat celebrating the creation of the world and a 'sacred marriage' celebrating fertility. Babylonian religion (like Assyrian) operated at three levels: national, city and private. At the national level is the supreme triad of Anu, the heaven god (principal temple at Uruk); Enlil (chief temple at Nippur), the wind and air god; and Ea, the god of wisdom (chief temple at Eridu). Their consorts were Inanna, Ninlil and Damgal-nunna respectively, gods borrowed from the earlier Sumerian civilization. Others making up the pantheon included Marduk (of Babylon); Ishtar, the fertility goddess; Sin, the moon god (Ur and Haran, consort Ningal); Shamash, the sun god (Sippar and Larsa, consort Aya); and Nebo, the god of science, who was also popular in Assyria. The god of war and hunt was Ninurta; Nergal (consort Ereshki-gal) ruled the underworld. Gods of foreign origin included the storm god Adad,

Dagon and Dumuzi (Tammuz), a god of vegetation. Syncretism took place: Marduk (the god of Babylon) replaced Enlil in some versions of the pantheon, and Ishtar could be identified with Inanna. Although each of the major gods was patron of a different city, there was little overlap, and some rationalisation between cults of the city-states apparently occurred.

At the city level, the local god was paramount in the cult; its temple would be the focus of religious life and festivities, supporting a large priesthood and playing a central role in the city's economy, owning most of the land. Babylonian cosmology divided the cosmos into upper and lower worlds, each populated by a host of minor deities; in the upper world the *Igigu*, in the lower the *Anunaku*. These, together with numerous good and evil spirits, played a larger part in everyday private life than the major gods.

The language of Babylonia, Akkadian, was Semitic, and written usually on clay with a wedge-shaped stylus (Latin cuneus = 'wedge', hence 'cuneiform' writing). Literary remains include grammar books, love songs, fables, incantations, omen lists and myths. The Babylonian Chronicle, from the Neo-Babylonian period, is a contemporary, and regarded as remarkably objective, account of political events.

Babylon's dealings with Judah were brief but highly consequential. 2 Kings 20 (paralleled in Isaiah 39) tells of an attempt by Merodach-Baladan (*Marduk-apla-iddina*) to achieve independence from Assyria with help from Hezekiah of Judah. A century later, Nebuchadrezzar captured Jerusalem, destroying the Temple and deporting the leaders to Babylonia. Most remained there, forming communities that grew large and important over the following centuries (Babylonian academies formed the centre of rabbinic Judaism from the third century CE onwards). Babylonian laws and myths, disseminated throughout the ancient Near East from well before the advent of Israel and Judah, recur in the Bible: the stories of creation and flood parallel episodes and themes in Babylonian mythology; the literature about Enoch (collected in 1 Enoch; see Chapter 14) also betrays Babylonian influence, as do parts of Daniel. The influence is hard to date: during the monarchic era, or the Neo-Babylonian period, or via the Judean communities in Babylonia that presumably remained in close contact with Judah; perhaps all of these.

The influence of the Babylonian deportations upon the development of Judean religion has been exaggerated. Attention needs rather to be focussed on Judah itself at this time, and on the subsequent revival of Jerusalem under the Persians. The increased importance of law and its interpretation, the political and economic power of the priesthood, and the universalizing of Yhwh into a cosmic creator god may have some roots among Judean communities Babylonia but the situation in Persian period Judah after repatriation and the restoration of Jerusalem is perhaps a more likely context.

Persians and Medes

The arrival of the Persians in the land now called Iran was the result of that Indo-European migration late in the second millennium that also introduced the Hurrians. Some of these groups settled east of the Tigris, and are referred to in the annals of Shalmaneser III around 836 BCE as paying tribute to him. Their territory, called Parsua, was also 'visited' (in the words of the Assyrian scribe) by Tiglath-Pileser III, who paid a similar 'visit' to a related and neighbouring tribe, the Medes. Some years before the fall of Nineveh, both became fully independent. At this time, the Medes were the more powerful, and in alliance with the Babylonians they sacked Nineveh under their king Cyaxares, whose son Astyages gave his daughter in marriage to the son of the Persian king, Anshan. This son, Cyrus, united the two tribes, waging war against his father-in-law and sacking the Median capital of Ecbatana. Media became the first satrapy of the Persian empire, and henceforth Medes and Persians constituted one empire (though the book of Daniel keeps them as separate and chronologically successive kingdoms).

Cyrus' empire spread westwards into Armenia and Asia Minor, and eastwards towards India, before he turned his attention to Babylon, to whose subjects he presented himself as the legitimate successor of the old dynasty. The innovation and liberalism of his policy of allowing previously deported groups to return to their homelands and sponsoring local religion have been overemphasised, for this practice was neither new nor disinterested. But it signalled a concern for the restoration of national cultures that was utilised in the maintenance of a large and culturally varied empire. Cyrus' successor, Cambyses, added Egypt to the empire. But on his death in 522 BCE occurred the first of the palace revolutions that were to plague the history of the empire. Darius won this struggle and imposed his rule over the empire, including Egypt. He then began the 200-year struggle with Greece, and was defeated at the battle of Marathon (490 BCE). His successor Xerxes (485–465) sustained this policy but was again repulsed, after briefly taking Athens. Darius II (335–330) had to face the revenge of the Greeks, now united under Alexander the Great. But the conquest of the entire Persian empire by Alexander was not the end of Persia. Another Persian empire rose under the Parthians.

Map 7. *The Persian Empire, Sixth to Fourth Centuries* BCE

The Persians were a relatively small warrior society, whose members belonged to guilds, each of which had a master. The army was based, like the Roman army later, upon units of fifty and multiples. The famous Persian road system was designed especially for military movement—again, like the Romans; there were stores at intervals on the route, and of course, they also facilitated trade, which the Persians vigorously promoted as a means of imperial income. The empire was divided into satrapies, usually about twenty at any given period after Darius, and each was subdivided into provinces and then into districts. Each satrap had an elaborate financial and military administrative system at his disposal. Although the satrap was

Persian, his subordinates would be local, for the Persians were too small a nation to run the empire, except by allowing local structures and personnel to govern under Persian control. This arrangement was of course conducive to nationalistic revolt. Satraps often treated their areas as minor domains of their own, and satrapies often became hereditary. An empire-wide system of scrutiny was maintained by the 'king's eyes', agents who visited parts of the empire unannounced, yet the cohesion of the empire was frequently strained.

It is probable that from the time of Cyrus, or at least Darius, the Persian royal family was Zoroastrian (Zoroaster/Zarathustra's dates vary widely: the 'traditional' date is c. 600 BCE; but 1000–1200 BCE is just as likely). His teachings proclaimed Ahura Mazda as the begetter of two spirits, one good and one evil. But he later became identified with the good spirit in a more formally dualistic system. Importantly, Zoroastrianism was not a nationalistic religion and did not play a role in imperialistic ideology. Ahura Mazda is the deity most often mentioned by Darius in his inscriptions, and the god's principal ministers were the Median tribe of Magi. In the religion of Mazda the king played a major part as supreme priest and warrior (though the latter title was honorary; the king did not always engage in combat). Other known Persian deities were Ahita and Mithra, who was especially venerated by soldiers. In the late Roman Empire the cult of Mithra was widely followed, especially by soldiers, and was a serious rival to Christianity.

The Persians are portrayed rather favourably in the Bible. Cyrus is named Yhwh's agent in Isaiah 44:28–45:7. Nehemiah, the royal cupbearer, is given a commission to rebuild Jerusalem; and the Temple is rebuilt by Persian decree. In Daniel 6, set in the reign of Darius ('the Mede'), the king is on the side of Daniel. Most remarkably, perhaps, Esther marries a Persian king—a circumstance presented as quite natural. Does all this indicate some kind of respect for Persian culture? Many features of Judaism—angels, eschatology, heaven and hell, a ban on images and messianism—have been thought to derive from Persian religion. One rather striking borrowing may be in Isaiah 44 and 45, in which Yhwh is called creator not only of light and darkness but also good and evil, a typically Zoroastrian formulation. There can also be little doubt of the presence of Persian dualism in the Dead Sea Scrolls—less probably a (later) borrowing from the Parthians.

Greece

The long struggle between Persia and Greece ended when Alexander the Great (died 323) marched victorious through its empire. He was an agent of Greek culture, having been a pupil of Aristotle, and sought revenge for Persian aggression. But he created no single political empire. The semi-autonomous Persian satrapies, often old kingdoms in new forms, became Greek kingdoms; after decades of fighting between Alexander's successors (his generals), two realms emerged in the Near East: the kingdom of Ptolemy, which comprised Egypt and Palestine, and that of Seleucus, including Mesopotamia and Syria. Each king ruled from a newly built Hellenistic city (Alexandria and Antioch, respectively). Many other cities were founded throughout these kingdoms as settlements for Greek soldiers and traders; but in the spirit of Hellenism they embraced many of the local populace, too; and many older cities became Greek-type self-governing cities (Greek *polis*), including Samaria and Beth-Shean and briefly Jerusalem itself.

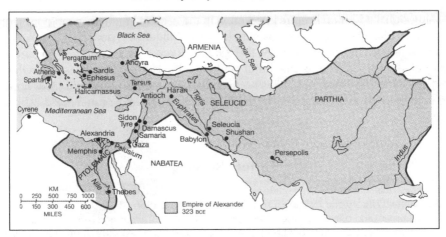

Map 8. *The Empire of Alexander the Great and his Successors,*
Fourth to First Centuries BCE

There are essential differences between the Greek and the preceding Oriental empires. The earlier empires were monarchic and reinforced by divine sanction. Assyria, Babylon, and Persia were essentially a product of Oriental feudalism, with the conquering nations ruling over vassal states. Although the Persians introduced a measure of concern for the cultural autonomy of all their subjects, the satraps' essential function was the gathering of taxes and, even more than its predecessors, this empire maintained a strict distinction between the ruling aristocracy and the ruled nations. The system was different in Greece, where (in the period we are speaking of) cities were the political and social units, ruled by their own citizens (which was not the whole population). No monarchy existed, and neither gods nor priests were involved directly in the political process. As citizenship replaced aristocracy, rational decision-making by equals replaced royal decree. Politics became the responsibility and duty of the individual citizen. Humanism, politics, and justice were enshrined in the Greek system of education, which taught that philosophy was an integral part of political life. Yet the Hellenistic culture that emerged from the 'Greecing' of the ancient Near East offered a new way of urban life. But the Hellenistic monarchies maintained the local tradition of despotism, even divine kingship. Hellenism was a compromise, or mixture, of cultures. Judaism could not resist this new blend entirely, but preserved its cultural autonomy by defining itself as a philosophy superior to but not entirely different from the Greeks (as with Philo of Alexandria), and by promoting a distinctive set of practices (circumcision, abstinence from certain foods, sabbath observance). Other nations resisted too, but with less vigour and less success.

Hellenism is not explicitly addressed in the Old Testament, though it looms in the books of 1 and 2 Maccabees in the Apocrypha. Greece (Yawan, 'Ionia') is, however, mentioned—for example, in Genesis 10 (1 Chronicles 1), Joel 3:6 (Greeks as traders alongside Phoenicians), and Isaiah 66:19 (as a place far off). In the book of Daniel Greece is the world empire succeeding Persia. Antiochus IV, the Seleucid 'king of the north' who issues the final challenge to the 'Most High', is portrayed as a horn growing on the head of the Greek beast, but not as the beast itself. Since both Ptolemies and Seleucids had previously administered Palestine tolerantly, no condemnation of Greece itself is implied.

Although the Roman Empire intervened in the eastern Mediterranean during our period, its direct cultural, as opposed to political, influence is not considerable, and many scholars choose to speak of the 'Greco-Roman' as a period of continuous cultural identity. Since, too, the major centres of the Roman Empire lay elsewhere, and since the Old Testament takes no account of it, the Roman world most appropriately belongs in a discussion of the New Testament and of early and rabbinic Judaism.

Further Reading

Reference in this chapter has been made to Albrecht Alt, 'The God of the Fathers', in his *Essays on Old Testament History and Religion* (Oxford: Basil Blackwell, 1966): 1-77.

On the history and culture of ancient Palestine, see K.L. Noll, *Canaan and Israel in Antiquity: An Introduction* (Biblical Seminar, 83; London: Sheffield Academic Press, 2001). An older survey is D.J. Wiseman (ed.), *Peoples of Old Testament Times* (Oxford: Clarendon Press, 1973). The various deities are well covered in John Day, *Yahweh and the Gods and Goddesses of Canaan* (JSOTSup, 265; Sheffield: Sheffield Academic Press, 2000). For Ugarit, see Adrian Curtis, *Ugarit (Ras Shamra)* (Cambridge: Lutterworth Press, 1985); its religious texts are conveniently collected in N. Wyatt, *Religious Texts from Ugarit* (Biblical Seminar, 53; Sheffield: Sheffield Academic Press, 2nd, edn, 2002). Transjordan is covered in John F.A. Sawyer and David J.A. Clines (eds.), *Midian, Moab and Edom: The History and Archaeology of Late Bronze and Iron Age Jordan and North-West Arabia* (JSOTSup, 24; Sheffield: JSOT Press, 1983); more recently on Ammon, see Burton MacDonald and Randall W. Younker (eds.), *Ancient Ammon* (Leiden: E.J. Brill, 1999), and for the Edomites, D.V. Edelman (ed.), *You Shall Not Abhor an Edomite for He is your Brother: Edom and Seir in History and Tradition* (Atlanta: Scholars Press, 1995).

The empires (especially Syria-Mesopotamia) are conveniently covered in Wolfram von Soden, *The Ancient Orient: An Introduction to the Study of the Ancient Near East* (Grand Rapids: Eerdmans; London: Gracewing, 1994); for Egypt, the classic introduction is still John Wilson, *The Culture of Ancient Egypt* (Chicago: University of Chicago Press, 1951), and for the Hittites, O.R. Gurney, *The Hittites* (London: Allen Lane, 1975). On the Persians, see P. Briant, *From Cyrus to Alexander: A History of the Persian Empire* (Winona Lake, IN: Eisenbrauns, 2002). On Hellenism, see John Marks, *Visions of One World: Legacy of Alexander* (Guildford, CN: Four Quarters Publishing House, 1985).

Part II

THE HISTORY AND RELIGION OF ISRAEL

Reconstruction of Herod's Temple and Antonia

Chapter 4

UNTIL THE TIME OF SOLOMON

When does the history of Israel begin? Forty years ago there were clear, if not unanimous, answers to this question. Two books that appeared in English at roughly the same time gave clear, but divergent answers. John Bright's *A History of Israel*, first published in 1960, began Israel's history with the Patriarchs (Abraham, Isaac, and Jacob), who were placed between the twentieth and sixteenth centuries BCE (Bright 1960: 76). Even so, Bright described the Patriarchs as the Hebrew Ancestors, and looked to the experience of the Israelites in slavery in Egypt and to what he called the Tribal League (Israel in Canaan in the period roughly 1200–1050 BCE) as the formative factors in the constitution of Israel, as well as to the fact that Israel as a dynastic state was formally somewhat different from Israel as a tribal confederacy. Bright's history followed a well-established model, that of using the Bible as the primary source, and supplementing it from archaeology and from the historical records of Egypt, Assyria, and Babylon.

Martin Noth's *The History of Israel* was published in German in 1950, and an English translation of the second, 1955 edition, appeared in 1958. Noth's approach was more radical than that of Bright. He began, not with the Patriarchs, but with Israel as an amphictyony, that is, a twelve-tribe confederation living in Canaan around 1200 BCE, and bound together by sacred and other laws. The chapters in the Bible dealing with the Patriarchs and the Exodus were treated as 'traditions of the sacred confederacy'. On one matter Bright and Noth disagreed fundamentally. Bright accepted the view of the book of Joshua that there had been a violent, if incomplete, assault on Western Palestine which had enabled the Israelites to transfer their tribal centre there (Bright 1960: 126). Noth believed that the Israelite occupation of Canaan had been peaceful, and part of a process of sedentarisation (i.e. the movement from a 'semi-nomadic' to a settled form of existence).

When the first edition of *The Old Testament World* was published in 1989, it sided with Noth rather than Bright. The view that Israel was an amphictyony was rejected, but it was accepted that the occupation of the land had been peaceful. This was based upon the researches of Finkelstein (1988), according to which there had been a gradual movement of population back into Western Palestine in the second half of the thirteenth century following an abandonment of villages and settlements there at the end of the fourteenth century BCE. However, the first edition of *The Old Testament World* agreed with both Bright and Noth in using the traditions in the books of Judges, Samuel, and Kings to reconstruct the period of the Judges, the rise of the monarchy and the reigns of David and Solomon. The first edition (p. 347) also agreed with Bright and Noth (Bright 1960: 198; Noth 1958: 219-20) that the reign of Solomon was the most likely setting for the beginning of Israel's history writing. David and Solomon, it was assumed, had created a dynastic state and a small 'empire'. They needed a bureaucracy to help administer it. The creation of a professional administration, possibly with Egyptian help, provided the right conditions for an historian (the so-called Yahwist) to begin to collect traditions about the ancestors, the Exodus, and the time of the Judges, and to compose a history that showed how the divine promises made to Abraham, that his offspring would inherit the land of Canaan, had been fulfilled in the achievements of David. The dating of the beginnings of Israel's history writing to the tenth century brought this activity sufficiently close to the time of the Judges, Samuel, and Saul, to vouch for the general accuracy of the traditions, while it was accepted that they had been edited into something like their final form by deuteronomists in the seventh–sixth centuries.

It is now necessary to indicate how the identification of the reigns of David and Solomon as the time when Israel's history writing most likely began has become problematic, and to work out the consequences of this for reconstructing the history of Israel to the time of Solomon. The first factor is that archaeological discoveries and sociological and economic comparisons have led some experts to conclude either that David and Solomon did not establish a small 'empire', or that if they did conquer and control small neighbouring countries, this did not require a large or elaborate administration. Excavations in southern Jordan (Bienkowski 1992) have indicated that Edom and Moab did not become 'states' until the ninth century BCE at the earliest. They could not have been part of a Davidic 'empire' as small 'states'. Further, recent excavations at sites in Israel such as Hazor have questioned whether the Solomonic gates and walls that have been cited as evidence for an Israelite state under Solomon, do in fact date from that time. Again, studies of the development of Judah suggest that it was not until the eighth century BCE that it became anything like a state (Jamieson-Drake 1991), while Auld and Steiner (1996) have questioned whether Jerusalem was, in fact, inhabited at the time when the Bible states that it was conquered by David. Some of these findings are currently bitterly contested in the scholarly world, but from various angles the reign of Hezekiah (c.727–698 BCE) is increasingly being seen as the earliest time for the beginning of Israel's history writing. With the destruction of the northern kingdom, Israel, in 722/21 by the Assyrians, and a large influx of refugees into Judah from the north, Judah took over the role of Israel. Indeed, Hezekiah's ultimately abortive attempt to resist Assyria and to extend his power to parts of the former northern kingdom required him to claim that Jerusalem had once been the capital of a united Israel. The biblical accounts of the united monarchy of David and Solomon may therefore reflect the political realities of the eighth or later centuries rather than those of the tenth century; and they raise acutely the question of what can be known about the times of David and Solomon, and earlier. In what follows, the reconstruction will begin with Solomon, and work backwards to the traditions about the patriarchs.

Solomon

The most recent investigation of the biblical traditions concerning Solomon (Wälchli 1999) dates the composition of a 'history of Solomon' to the time of Hezekiah (Wälchli 1999: 198). Of texts that come from Solomon's time, only various lists in 1 Kings 4, documents concerning the building of the temple in 1 Kings 5–7, and a few particulars in 1 Kings 9–10 come into the reckoning. Walchli warns against concluding too much about the functions of the officials who are listed in 1 Kings 4:7-19 as presiding over twelve districts, each of which was responsible for provisioning the court for one month in each year. Whatever their role might have been (the recruitment of labour for building the temple and the royal palace?) the rapid demise of Solomon's kingdom following his death does not suggest that he had succeeded in establishing a centralised, administered state (Wälchli 1999: 200), and the three administrators listed at 1 Kings 4:3 would be adequate for a small court, but hardly for a small empire (cp. Wälchli 1999: 199). The eighth-century 'history of Solomon' grossly exaggerates the realities. What is likely is that Solomon presided over a small administrative base with a very modest court, whose temple served as a private shrine. His claim to territory was probably secured by small garrisons of a hundred men or so in strategic border towns such as Hazor in the far north and Arad in the far south. If his rule extended further it was, again, through small garrisons in strategic towns. Jerusalem may have made economic demands upon the immediately surrounding villages, as would, to a lesser extent, the garrisons (cp. 1 Samuel 13:17-18); but many villages would have continued their subsistence farming life, with little need to be aware of Solomon and his rule.

David

The time of David is a different matter. If the reign of Solomon has been romanticised and its achievements exaggerated in the tradition, that of David has become a focus for much theological reflection in the course of the growth of the biblical tradition. A man after his [God's] own heart (1 Samuel 13:14), and one who 'did not turn aside from anything that [God] commanded him…except in the matter of Uriah the Hittite' (1 Kings 15:5), David is credited in the books of Chronicles with being the founder, if not the actual builder, of the temple in Jerusalem and the organiser of its worship, and is regarded in the titles added to many of the psalms as the author of these compositions. At the same time, the account of the 'matter of Uriah the Hittite', a somewhat under-stated way of describing David's adultery with Uriah's wife Bathsheba, and the subsequent 'disposal' of Uriah by placing him in the most dangerous part of a battle (cp. 2 Samuel 11), allows the tradition to show that even the greatest of Old Testament kings is only human, and subject to failings and to divine judgment. Is it possible to penetrate back to an historical David? The detailed literary analysis of Kratz (2000), finds old traditions embedded in 1 Samuel 9–11, 13–14, 16, 18–19, 21–29, which most likely come from northern sources and concern the origins of Saul's kingship, David's activities as a rebel, and his eventual desertion to the Philistines. These traditions would either have been brought south following the collapse of the northern kingdom in 722/21 or were preserved among members of the tribe of Benjamin which became part of Judah. They became the basis for the earliest history writing of the Old Testament that began to take shape at that time. As they were adapted and reinterpreted, they were used to put Saul in a bad light and David in a good light, that is, they came to reflect the political realities of the situation post-722/21, when Judah, in effect, became Israel.

If we can rely on these old traditions, David cannot be considered apart from Saul and Samuel, and the Philistines. The presence of the latter in the southern coastal plain and the Shephelah from around 1200 BCE, is well attested. That they should have come into conflict with the tribes of Dan and Judah, as indicated in the stories about Samson (Judges 14–16), is quite plausible. It is also a plausible guess that, having subdued Dan and Judah (their nearest neighbours), the Philistines would turn their attention northwards, and initially to the area occupied by Benjamin, precipitating Saul into a leadership role in organising the resistance, certainly of his own, and possibly other, Israelite 'tribes'. The traditions place Samuel and Saul in Benjamin (there is an odd reference in 1 Samuel 8:2 to Samuel's sons being judges in Beersheba in Judah's remote south), and also indicate that opposition to the Philistines came particularly from prophetic groups, ones that had embraced a zealous and strongly national devotion to Yhwh. The proverb 'is Saul also among the prophets?' (1 Samuel 10:12; 19:24) suggests that Saul was either propelled into leadership against the Philistines by the prophetic groups led by Samuel, or that he enlisted the aid of these groups. The nature and extent of Saul's 'reign' (it has been rightly observed that the term 'king' must be used with caution) is not known to us. There is probably no reason to doubt, however, that David became first, an ally of Saul and later, an enemy. We can only speculate on the reasons. The biblical account attributes the breach to 'an evil spirit from God' (1 Samuel 18:10), perhaps a way of describing suspicion and depression on Saul's part. David's ambitions cannot be ruled out, either. After the breach, David seems to have lived as a kind of brigand, leading a motley band of discontents, which he expected local villages and landholders in Judah to support. The traditions about Saul's attempts to pursue and capture David (for example in 1 Samuel 23) may indicate that Saul was temporarily able to gain sufficient respite from Philistine pressure to be able to try to deal with dissent within his own jurisdiction. 2 Samuel 23:9-39 contains a list of David's 'mighty men' together with some brief accounts of their doings. The text is corrupt and difficult to interpret; but its account of 'the three' and 'the thirty' heroes most likely describes David's private 'army' that was formed from the region around Bethlehem, and was active during the time when he was on the run from Saul, a vassal of the Philistines, and an opponent of the Philistines after their defeat of Saul.

It is to this same group of warriors that David's 'conquests' of small, neighbouring peoples, can be ascribed. It is important to realise that the conquest and occupation of territory was conceived of totally differently in traditional societies as compared with modern societies (Giddens 1995: 102-103; Rogerson 1999; see also above, p. 21). In the twentieth century, lines drawn on maps have established areas within which states have claimed to exercise total authority. It is quite otherwise with traditional societies, where the occupation of key border towns can justify a claim to rulership over a territory, but where there is nothing remotely approaching central-ised control over that territory. In the case of ancient Judah and Israel, this is borne out by strategic sites such as Hazor or Arad. In both cases, the occupation of these sites from the tenth century amounted to tiny fortresses on what had earlier been large Canaanite cities. The Israelite and Judahite garrisons of a couple of hundred men served to establish a claim to sovereignty over the areas bordered by these frontier settlements. However, as Niemann (1993) has shown, very little centralised control was enjoyed in territories thus enclosed. Returning to David, we cannot rule out the possibility that his highly efficient army captured, and then garrisoned, towns such as Rabbah (in Ammon) and Damascus (cp. 2 Samuel 8:6 for the mention of a garrison in Damascus). Such victories would make possible the claim to sovereignty over the countries with which they were associated, and their former rulers would be required to raid their treasuries to pay tribute. It would be entirely wrong, however, to suppose that David thereby exercised control over anything other than the garrisoned towns, and also misleading to speak of him creating an empire. The Judahite source for David's reign (2 Samuel 9–20), which in its present form is an apology for the divine right of the davidic dynasty to rule over 'Israel', and which cannot be earlier than the time of Hezekiah, records two rebellions against David's rule. The first is led by his son Absalom, the second by a distant relative of Saul. While the narrative in its present form shows how these setbacks are both divine judgement (for the matter of Uriah the Hittite) and the fulfilment of the divine promise to uphold the dynasty of David, the rebellions are unlikely to be inventions of the tradition. David's reign was therefore one of mixed fortunes. He delivered the Israelite and Judahite 'tribes' from Philistine domination, and set up garrisons in strategic towns of neighbouring peoples. He did not retain the undivided loyalty of either his own people Judah, or that of the northern tribes that made up Israel.

The Period of the Judges

If we disengage the editorial and redactional frameworks from the book of Judges (Kratz 2000: 193-216) we are left with stories about heroes and a heroine who are located principally in the areas of Benjamin and Ephraim. They are therefore of a northern, Israelite provenance and were presumably brought south to Judah after 722/21 or preserved in the tribe of Benjamin. We cannot be certain about the date or dates in which the principals lived. It was pointed out in Chapter 2 (p. 35) that some of the so-called minor judges (Judges 10:1-5; 12:7-15) have many sons (and, presumably, wives) and that they are local rulers; but a major 'judge', Gideon is also credited with seventy sons and many wives (Judges 8:30). Also many of the religious practices found in these stories (e.g. Jephthah's vow that compels him to sacrifice his daughter, Judges 11:30-31) are strange from the standpoint of later Yahwism. However, it would be perilous to conclude from these facts that the heroes and heroine who feature in the book of Judges must be dated to the period 1200–1050 BCE. This is where the redactional framework of the book of Judges places them; but this is an artificial device. What was said above about borders and centralised control must also be borne in mind. It must not be thought that the establishment of monarchy in the northern kingdom, Israel, after the death of Solomon, automatically disposed of the existence of local powerful rulers such as are described in the stories in Judges. Further, recent research on the popular religious practices in Israel during the monarchy has indicated how varied they were. The strangeness of some of the religious practices in Judges does not necessarily, therefore, indicate that the stories antedate the time of Saul and David. The evidence available enables no conclusion to be drawn about the 'period of the Judges' except, perhaps, in two instances, the stories about Samson, and the traditions of Deborah and Barak. Both deal with struggles within the land of Israel against non-Israelite enemies: the Philistines in the case of Samson and the 'Canaanites' in the case of Deborah and Barak.

The Samson stories have an extra-biblical point of reference. Unfortunately, they tell us little more than that the Philistines oppressed the Danites, and that an individual hero, Samson, resisted valiantly, before being taken prisoner by them. How far the details of the story, for example Samson's fatal attraction to women, can be regarded as historical is anyone's guess.

In the case of Deborah and Barak there is no extra-biblical point of reference and any reconstruction rests on plausibility only. That there would have been a decisive confrontation between the people who regarded themselves as Israelites and those called in the tradition 'Canaanites' seems likely. Whether this involved an 'all- Israelite' coalition as implied in the poem in Judges 5 is less likely, and the restriction of the Israelite combatants to the tribes of Zebulun and Naphtali as in Judges 4 seems more plausible.

'Conquest' and Exodus

The mention of Israelites in conflict with 'Canaanites' brings us to the biblical themes of the 'Conquest' and the Exodus. It was noted earlier that the occupation of the land seems to have been a process of the gradual movement of population from northern Transjordan to Western Palestine in the thirteenth century. It cannot be supposed that all of the people involved regarded themselves as 'Israelites' or that Western Palestine had become entirely depopulated in the fourteenth century. The question that has to be answered is how the Israelites came to see themselves as a distinct people, one that became locked in a struggle with the non-Israelite inhabitants of the land for the type of mastery that was consistent with the dynamics of a traditional state.

The simplest answer to this question is in genealogical terms. The Israelites shared maximal lineages that bound them together for mutual defence against other occupants of the land. The names of some of the principal members of these maximal lineages no doubt occur in the patriarchal traditions about Jacob and his sons. Yet there is also an unsolved mystery, that of the origin and meaning (if it has a meaning) of the name 'Israel'. There is no ancestor of this name in the biblical traditions and the story in Genesis 32:22-32 in which Jacob's name is changed to Israel only reinforces this point. It is also important to notice that the name 'IsraEL' carries not the divine name Yhwh, but the general Semitic designation for God, El. Yet there is no doubt that an entity named 'Israel' existed in Canaan at the end of thirteenth century. The victory stele of the Egyptian pharaoh Merneptah, dated to 1207 BCE claims:

> Plundered is Canaan with every evil;
> Carried off is Ashkelon;
> Seized upon is Gezer;
> Yanoam is made as that which does not exists;
> Israel is laid waste, his seed is not (*ANET*: 378).

How this designation relates to later manifestations of Israel in the biblical and extra-biblical materials is impossible to say. It does provide evidence, however, for the existence of a group that could be recognised and named by an invader.

Leaving this mystery aside, the next problem is that of the origin of the worship of Yhwh among the Israelites. Recent research has linked the name Yhwh with the southern Negev and with groups of nomads known in Egyptian sources as *shasu* (Staubli 1991; see also Görg 1997). It is possible that Israel's belief in Yhwh has its origins in a group of *shasu* that escaped from Egypt and linked up with proto-Israelite families in northern Transjordan in the early thirteenth century. The biblical tradition that Yhwh came from Edom in the south would be consonant with this (cp. Judges 5:4). We would then presume that the proto-Israelite families in northern

Transjordan placed themselves under the protection of Yhwh as they moved to settle in Western Palestine. Elements of the Passover ritual, such as the daubing of blood on the entrance to tents and houses to ward off evil, may derive from this transition. Following, and as part of, the gradual occupation of Western Palestine, the Israelites clashed with their neighbours locally. Joshua may have been a local leader of Israelite groups against such opposition, as may have been some of the 'judges' although, as was pointed out above, both the major and the 'minor judges' could just as well have lived in the monarchic period as in the time before Samuel and Saul. The final, and decisive, confrontation was with the Philistines at the close of the twelfth century.

The Patriarchs

The stories of the Patriarchs, Abraham, Isaac, and Jacob reflect the political realities of the time of their initial compilation, that is, following the destruction of the northern kingdom, Israel, in 722/21 BCE. Because Judah had now taken over the role of Israel, the Judahite ancestors Abraham and Isaac, precede the Israelite ancestor, Jacob. The names were doubtless preserved among the local communities where these figures had founded maximal lineages: Hebron in the case of Abraham, Beersheba in the case of Isaac, and Bethel in the case of Jacob. In their present form, the patriarchal narratives, like those of the Exodus and law giving at Sinai, provide little or no information for modern historians. They function as 'founding stories' traditions that define the people and its (ideal) religion. They are full of many profound theological insights, and that is their chief value, as was emphasised as long ago as 1806 by W.M.L. de Wette.

A final word must be said about the religion of Israel at this time. Because the traditions in their present form are at least seven hundred to five hundred years later than the period under consideration, and have been subjected to continuous addition and supplementation, not to mention theological reflection, they can be used only with the greatest caution for the purposes of historical reconstruction. The factor that stands out most clearly is the importance of ecstatic prophetic groups in the struggle to free the Israelites from outside interference. This would be consonant with the belief of *shasu* groups that they had been freed from slavery by Yhwh, who was seen principally as a God of battles. Such belief would also have appealed to the soldier's soldier, David. However, the development of the distinctive insights of the religion of the Old Testament was still a long way off.

References

Auld, A.G., and M. Steiner
    1996   *Jerusalem. I. From the Bronze Age to the Maccabees* (Cambridge: Lutterworth Press).
Bienkowski, P.
    1992   *Early Edom and Moab: The Beginning of the Iron Age in Southern Jordan* (Sheffield: J.R. Collis Publications).
Bright, J.
    1981   *A History of Israel* (Philadelphia: Westminster Press; London: SCM Press, 3rd edn).
Giddens, A.
    1985   *A Contemporary Critique of Historical Materialism. II. The Nation State and Violence* (Cambridge: Polity Press).

Görg, M.
    1997   Die Beziehungen zwischen dem Alten Israel und Ägypten von den Anfängen bis zum Exil
               (Erträge der Forschung 290) (Darmstadt: Wissenschaftliche Buchgesellschaft).
Jamieson-Drake, D.W.
    1991   Scribes and Schools in Monarchic Judah: A Socio-Archaeological Approach (JSOTSup,
               109; Sheffield: Almond Press).
Kratz, R.
    2000   Die Komposition der erzählender Bücher des Alten Testaments (Göttingen: Vandenhoeck
               & Ruprecht).
Niemann, H.M.
    1993   Herrschaft, Königtum und Staat. Skizzen zur soziokulturellen Entwicklung im
               monarchischen Israel (FAT, 6; Tübingen: J.C.B. Mohr).
Noth, M.
    1958   The History of Israel (trans. S. Godman; London: A. & C. Black).
Rogerson, J.W.
    1999   'Frontiers and Borders in the Old Testament', in E. Ball (ed.), In Search of True Wisdom:
               Essays in Old Testament Interpretation in Honour of Ronald E. Clement (JSOTSup, 300;
               Sheffield: Sheffield Academic Press): 116-26.
Staubli, T.
    1991   Das Image der Nomaden im Alten Israel und in der Ikonographie seiner sesshaften
               Nachbarn (OBO, 197; Freiburg Schweiz: Universitäts Verlag; Göttingen: Vandenhoeck &
               Ruprecht).
Wälchli, S.
    1999   Der Weise König Salomo. Eine Studie zu den Erzählungen von der Weisheit Salomos in
               ihrem alttestamentlichen und altorientalischen Kontext (BWANT, 141; Stuttgart: Kohl-
               hammer Verlag).

Chapter 5

FROM THE DEATH OF SOLOMON
TO THE BABYLONIAN DEPORTATIONS

There are two ways of tackling the history of Israel and Judah from the death of Solomon to the Babylonian deportations. The first method—which was largely followed in the first edition of *The Old Testament World*—is to follow the biblical story (albeit not uncritically) and to supplement it with information from archaeology, especially extra-biblical texts. The other method is to give primacy to archaeology, especially to those aspects of the discipline that reconstruct the economic and social history of the land on the basis of material finds and large or small-scale surveys. This approach has tended to put large question marks against the accuracy of the biblical record, which in turn has divided scholars between those that are supposedly 'for' the Bible by adopting the first method and those that are 'against', following the second method. It is most unfortunate that the discussion has taken this almost theological turn, as though the side one takes indicates whether or not one is a 'believer'.

In fact, both methods contain some truth. On the one hand, the biblical writers had access to archival material and to traditional stories about past heroes and incidents. On the other hand, like any ancient historian (and some modern ones!) in using these materials to describe the past they were profoundly affected by the concerns and interests of the time in which their accounts received their principal form. This was almost certainly the era (from the late eighth century or the late seventh century) when the southern kingdom, Judah, was laying claim to the history and identity of the former northern kingdom, Israel. This profoundly affected the way in which the history of the two kingdoms was presented. Given this, one of the main roles of archaeology is to give critical assistance to biblical scholars when they are working with biblical material. At the end of the day, it is not a matter of always deciding for the Bible or always deciding for archaeology, but a critical and sensitive use of both sources. One can go much of the way with Dever (2003: 226) when he says that 'the basic traditions about ancient Israel now enshrined in the books of Exodus–Numbers and Joshua through Kings cannot be read uncritically as a satisfactory history, but neither can they be discarded as lacking any credible historical information. The challenge for critical scholarship…is to sort out fact from fiction; and it is only modern archaeology, as an independent witness to the events of the past, that may enable us to do that.' We would want to add that traditional historical and literary criticism of the text also has a part to play.

The Revolt of Jeroboam

This last point becomes immediately pertinent when the revolt of Jeroboam against Solomon's son Rehoboam is considered; for there are two conflicting accounts, one in the Hebrew text of 1 Kings 12:1-24 and another in the ancient Greek version of 3 Kingdoms 12:24a-z (= 1 Kings 12:24). In the Hebrew version Jeroboam is one of Solomon's overseers (1 Kings 11:28) who is encouraged by Ahijah, a prophet of Shiloh, to revolt against Solomon (1 Kings 11:29-40). He seeks refuge from Solomon in Egypt and returns to lead the assembly of the people of the north when they meet Rehoboam at Shechem to demand a lightening of their burdens. When Rehoboam declines to do so, Jeroboam is made king of the northern tribes and leads their revolt. In the Greek version Jeroboam carries out the work of fortifying Jerusalem and building the Millo (work ascribed to Solomon in the other account). He flees to Egypt and marries the daughter of the pharaoh Shishak. After Solomon's death, Jeroboam rallies the tribes to Shechem, at which point the prophet Shemaiah (see 1 Kings 12:22) encourages the revolt by tearing his garment into twelve pieces and giving ten to Jeroboam.

Scholars are almost unanimous in regarding the account found in the Greek Bible as a 'Midrashic' expansion (originally in Hebrew) of the Hebrew version of 1 Kings 12:1-24 and 14:1-9 with the aim of putting Jeroboam in a unworthy light; but this verdict creates a problem. If a Hebrew writer was prepared to 'expand' an already existing version of events in order to make an ideological point, what does this tell us about the process of the composition of the books of the Old Testament? It indicates at the very least that the materials in the possession of editors or redactors were not regarded as sacrosanct. Suppose, however, that the majority scholarly view is incorrect, and that the Greek version is an alternative tradition about the events. It could be argued that the tradition had preserved some key points: that Jeroboam was encouraged to rebel by a prophet and that there had been a gathering of tribes at Shechem to air certain grievances. The exact order of events and the exact name of the prophet had become confused; but the story of a garment being torn into pieces as a prophetic sign is the kind of incident that would be long remembered, certainly as a kind of justification for the existence of a northern kingdom claiming allegiance to Yhwh. Whether the garment was torn into *twelve* pieces depends on whether, at the time of Jeroboam, there had been *twelve* tribes. It has been argued recently that the twelve-tribe idea is a late, and literary concept (Schorn 1997)

A constant theme running through the books of Kings from 1 Kings 12 onwards is that the northern kingdom, Israel, was a bad thing and that Jeroboam the son of Nebat was responsible for it. Also, that its main shrine at Bethel was an affront to Yhwh. These objections must have had some grounding in reality. The accounts of Jeroboam's revolt are intended, written from the standpoint of Judah, to present the northern kingdom as a rebellious and idolatrous institution from its foundation. Perhaps the truth is that Jeroboam was a tribal leader whose actions in opposition to those of the rulers of Jerusalem, and encouraged by local prophets, became in the tradition shaped by Judah, a figure who could be credited with 'founding' a breakaway kingdom. However, that 'kingdom' probably had none of the appurtenances of a small state, namely a standing army, public buildings, limited fiscal control over some areas, and a bureaucracy to administer it. This was to change, if we follow the suggestion of Finkelstein and Silberman (2001: 160-62) about the significance of the invasion of Palestine by the Egyptian pharaoh Seshonq I. This happened near the end of the tenth century and is mentioned in 1 Kings 14:25-28. Shishak (as the pharaoh is called) is said to have taken away the treasures and golden shields of the temple and palace in Jerusalem. Sheshonq's own account, in the form of a depiction of prisoners each of whom bears the name of a captured city (see Kitchen 1973: 432-47), indicates that he destroyed cities such as Rehov, Beth-shean, Taanach and Megiddo as well as sites in the central hill country, the Jezreel valley, and the coastal plain. There is no mention of Jerusalem, which could mean that it was not sufficiently important to warrant an attack. According to Finkelstein and Silberman, Sheshonq's campaign brought to an end the situation in which the area of the northern kingdom had been largely controlled by Canaanite city states. The resultant vacuum enabled Israel as a small state to emerge under the leadership of Omri, towards the end of the first quarter of the ninth century BCE.

The Rise of Omri

The books of Kings (1 Kings 15–16) describe a situation of near anarchy following Sheshonq's invasion, with a 'coup d'état' in the 'northern kingdom', warfare between 'Israel' and 'Judah', and the involvement of the king of Damascus. There is no objection to taking these accounts at face value, provided it is recognised that we are not dealing with wars between states, but encounters between powerful dynastic families and their supporters. One such leader, Baasha of the house (or tribe?) of Issachar (a group located in the eastern portion of the Jezreel valley, according to Joshua 19:17-23), is credited with a rule of twenty-four years following his 'coup d'état' against Jeroboam's son Nadab (1 Kings 15:25-33). Following Baasha's death, a 'coup d'état' against his son Elah by Zimri, one of his commanders, led to civil war between a certain Tibni and another commander, Omri, until the triumph of the latter (1 Kings 16:8-24).

The reigns of Omri and his son Ahab (c. 884–852) bring the Bible into sharp contrast with the findings of archaeology. On the one hand these findings add greatly to the sparse account of Omri's rule, and on the other they clash with the fulsome account of Ahab's rule. Omri's reign is described in only one verse (2 Kings 16:24) if the standard formulae about a king's reign are disregarded. The account of Ahab's rule extends from 1 Kings 16:29 to 22:40, the longest account for any ruler in the books of Kings except Solomon. This is partly because it incorporates the cycle of stories about Elijah.

The Dynasty of Omri

The one biblical verse that mentions Omri's achievements (1 Kings 16:24) says that he purchased a hill from a certain Shemer and built upon it a city named Samaria after the name of its former owner. Excavations there in the first half of the twentieth century revealed a royal acropolis of some five acres crowned by a royal palace whose interior furnishings included exquisitely carved ivory plaques (see Parrot 1958, and cp. Amos 3:15). Samaria was not the only building project of Omri. Excavations at Megiddo, Hazor, Gezer, and Jezreel have revealed gates and walls increasingly ascribed to Omri or his son, Ahab (see Finkelstein and Silberman 2001: 180-91), although the view that Solomon was responsible for these buildings is still held (for example by Mazar 1990: 380-87).

Not only do archaeological artefacts shed light on Omri's reign. There are several references to him in extra-biblical texts. The most explicit is in the Inscription of Mesha, a ruler of Moab, and dated around 840 BCE. It reads:

> Omri, king of Israel...humbled Moab many days. Omri had occupied the whole land of Medeba and he dwelt in it during his days (*ANET*: 320).

It has been pointed out that 'Omri' is used in two senses here: as the name of the king and as the name of the kingdom, for Omri obviously did not spend his days living in Moab. Nor is it likely that he controlled the whole land in the sense of a modern occupation, but rather garrisoned key points. Omri is also named in Assyrian texts, and as late as the second part of the following century 'Israel' was still being referred to by the Assyrians as the land, or house of Omri. The one biblical verse (1 Kings 16:24) conceals the fact that Omri established a viable small state that exercised some control over surrounding peoples, probably also including Jerusalem.

The Reign of Ahab

Omri's son Ahab, who succeeded him, was also a great builder and fortifier of cities, as he sought to consolidate the small state bequeathed by his father. It is probable that during Ahab's reign, Jehoshaphat, king of Judah, was a vassal of the king of Israel, and that Ahab's hold over Moab was retained. The reigns of Omri and Ahab were, from the material point of view, a period of peace and prosperity, at least so far as the wealthy were concerned.

This picture in fact contradicts the biblical record, which claims that the reigns of Omri and Ahab were characterised by setbacks at the hands of the king of Damascus. We are expected to infer, first, that the king of Syria conquered some of the territory held by Omri, and that he set up trading outlets for Syrian merchants in Omri's capital, Samaria (1 Kings 20:34). Furthermore, the biblical narrative records three campaigns of the Syrian king against Ahab. In the first (1 Kings 20:1-21), Ahab won a victory, but only after his opponent had penetrated as far south as Samaria and laid siege to the capital. On the second occasion battle was joined at Aphek, and the Syrian king was forced to give himself up to Ahab. This was the occasion on which he promised to give back to Ahab the cities that had been taken from Omri (1 Kings 20:22-34). The third campaign led to the death of Ahab at the battle of Ramoth-gilead (1 Kings 22:1-40). In the light of these narratives, the reigns of both Omri and Ahab were characterised by defeats at the hands of Syria, one of which lead to the death of Ahab.

While it is possible to defend the order of events as they are presented in 1 Kings 20 to 2 Kings 8, in our view there are insuperable difficulties that tell against accepting the narratives at face value. The difficulties are fully set out by Miller and Hayes (1986: 259-64, 290-91, 297-302) and will be briefly indicated here. First, the king of Syria who was Ahab's foe is given in 1 Kings 20 and 22 as Ben-Hadad, whereas Assyrian records indicate that the Syrian king was Hadadezer. The same problem occurs with regard to Ahab's son Jehoram. His foe also is Ben-Hadad (2 Kings 6:24; 8:7), whereas according to Assyrian records Hadadezer was still the Syrian king. Moreover, 2 Kings 8:7-15 reports that Elisha encouraged Hazael to rebel against Ben-Hadad. An Assyrian account strongly indicates that it was Hadadezer who was overthrown by Hazael (*ANET*: 280). The second main difficulty is that Ahab is said to have 'slept with his fathers' (1 Kings 22:40), normally the description of a peaceful death, although according to 1 Kings 22:37, Ahab died in battle. Thirdly, the account of the death of Ahab in battle at Ramoth-gilead is very closely paralleled by the account of his son fighting a battle at Ramoth-gilead and receiving severe wounds in the fighting (2 Kings 8:25-29). Finally, there was a Ben-Hadad, king of Syria, who was a contemporary of Jehoahaz (813–797 BCE). This king was the son of the Jehu who led a prophetically inspired revolt against the house of Omri and Ahab. The mention of the prophets who were on the side of the king of Israel in passages such as 1 Kings 20:13, 28 would fit in better with a member of Jehu's dynasty than with Ahab, who was bitterly opposed by the prophetic groups.

This leads us to the conclusion that 1 Kings 17–22 gives a largely misleading account of the reign of Ahab and that material from a later reign, that of his grandson Jehoram, has been mistakenly attributed to Ahab. The account of the death of Ahab who, according to 1 Kings 22:1-40, dies in fighting against the king of Damascus at Ramoth-gilead, has been based upon the story of Jehoram who is badly wounded when fighting the king of Damascus at Ramoth-gilead (2 Kings 8:28-29).

In adopting here a reconstruction of Israel's history that is at variance with the surface reading of the text we would stress a point that has been made earlier, that these narratives are theological rather than historical, and that they must therefore be evaluated by different criteria, as they are in Chapter 9. For the moment, we can say simply that the biblical writers had to do the best they could with the traditions available to them, without having Assyrian records and archaeological investigations to help them (see Rogerson 1998: 49-57).

Internal and External Conflicts

We return then, to Omri and Ahab, and to the view that their reigns enabled Israel to enjoy a spell of material prosperity and with some control over their immediate neighbours. This tranquillity was spoiled by only two features. The first was the appearance on the scene of the Assyrian king Shalmaneser III. In 853 BCE, he fought a coalition of kings from Syria, Israel, and neighbouring countries at Qarqar on the river Orontes. The Old Testament says nothing about this battle, whose outcome was indecisive, but which probably indicated to Shalmaneser that he should go no farther south on this occasion. His opponents included Hadadezer, the Syrian king, who provided 1200 chariots and 20,000 foot soldiers, and Ahab, who provided 2000 chariots and 10,000 foot soldiers. Ahab's total may well have included the forces of Judah, which are not separately mentioned in the Assyrian records (*ANET*: 279).

The second negative factor, according to the biblical account, was bitter opposition to the house of Omri by prophetic groups. What provoked special opposition was the ardent championing of the fertility god Baal by Ahab's foreign wife Jezebel. 1 Kings 18:4 says that Jezebel tried to destroy the prophets of Yhwh, some of whom were hidden from her by one of Ahab's officials. In their place were put prophets of Baal. Elijah, the leader of the Yhwh prophets, used a prolonged drought as an occasion to proclaim that Yhwh was opposed to Ahab, and he also succeeded in defeating the Baal prophets at a confrontation to see who could call down fire on a sacrifice (1 Kings 18). Elijah's victory, however, was short-lived, and he was forced to flee from Jezebel's wrath (1 Kings 19). In the story of Naboth's vineyard (1 Kings 21) the values of the two sides are encapsulated. Jezebel abused royal power in deceitfully depriving Naboth of his vineyard; Elijah proclaimed that such behaviour was condemned by Yhwh.

Events during the years immediately following the death of Ahab are unclear, owing to contradictions in the biblical material itself. This can best be illustrated by the problematical succession of J(eh)oram. There are two dates for the accession of Joram (Jehoram), king of Israel: either Jehoshaphat's eighteenth year (2 Kings 3:1) or the second year of the reign of Jehoshaphat's son Joram (2 Kings 1:17) that is, nine years later. Joram, son of Jehoshaphat, is said at 2 Kings 8:16 to have acceded in the fifth year of Joram, son of Ahab. It is not possible here to discuss the problems of these figures (see Miller and Hayes 1986: 280-81). It will be noticed that, for a period, the name of the kings of Judah and Israel was identical. This raises the question whether one and the same man ruled both kingdoms. Hayes and Miller argue that this was so, suggesting that Joram, king of Judah, also became the king of Israel on the death of Ahaziah.

There is, however, another possibility: 2 Kings 8:16 says that Joram, son of Jehoshaphat, became king of Judah while Jehoshaphat was still on the throne. This could, of course, indicate a co-regency between Jehoshaphat and his son; but if there was one and not two Jorams this text might indicate that Jehoshaphat was deposed by Joram, king of Israel:

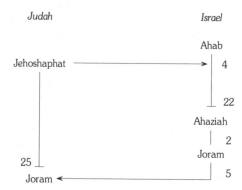

Thus Jehoshaphat's reign of twenty-five years tallies exactly with the eighteen remaining years of Ahab, two of Ahaziah, and five of Joram. It makes more sense to suppose that the dominant house of Omri usurped the throne of Jerusalem than that a relatively weak Judean king acceded also in Samaria. All this, of course, assumes that there was only one Joram.

The End of the House of Omri

The dynasty of Omri lasted for a little over forty years, from roughly 885 to 841 BCE. It ended when Joram was badly wounded in the battle of Ramoth-gilead against the Syrian king Hazael (2 Kings 8:25-29). Jehu, a commander, used this opportunity to kill both him and Ahaziah, king of Judah, at the instigation of a prophet sent by Elisha (2 Kings 9) while Joram lay recovering from his wounds in Jezreel. Jehu shot Joram with an arrow as the latter tried to flee; Ahaziah was killed, also in flight, by one of Jehu's servants. Jehu now killed Jezebel, forced the officials in Samaria to destroy Ahab's lineage, and also killed the relatives of Ahaziah and all of the prophets of Baal (2 Kings 10). There remained of the family of Omri only his (grand-) daughter Athaliah, who succeeded in consolidating her power in Jerusalem.

The dynasty of Jehu was destined to last for almost 100 years, from roughly 841 to 747 BCE. For the first half of its existence, it was to suffer badly at the hands of its neighbours. Jehu was forced to pay tribute to the Assyrian Shalmaneser III in 841; and a few years later, the Syrian king Hazael began to humiliate Israel (2 Kings 10:32-33). It is in this period (c. 830–805 BCE) that narratives such as those of 2 Kings 6, which describe Samaria's frequent sieges and consequent famine, are probably to be set. Excavations at Jezreel indicate that the palace built there by Omri or Ahab was destroyed at this time (Finkelstein and Silberman 202) and if the so-called 'house of David' inscription found at Dan is genuine (see Lemche 2003: 46-67) it may attest to the destruction of that city at this time by Hazael.

In the reign of Joash (c. 797–782) things began to turn in Israel's favour. Joash was able to defeat Hazael's son Ben-Hadad and regain some of the cities that had been lost (2 Kings 13:25; cp. 1 Kings 20, which may belong to this period). He was no doubt helped by the pressure on Syria which was exerted by the Assyrian Adad-nirari III. From about 796 BCE, Syria ceased to be a menace, and for 50 years both Israel and Judah enjoyed a spell of peace.

Kings of Judah

Judah figures only incidentally in the biblical narrative from 1 Kings 17 to 2 Kings 10. The probability is that during most of the ninth century BCE Judah was at most a small newly established state with Jerusalem as a small administrative capital (Steiner 2001: 280-88). It had probably been a vassal nation to Israel of the house of Omri. Omri's (grand-)daughter, Queen Athaliah, held on to power in Jerusalem when Jehu overthrew the Omride dynasty in the north. Her reign lasted for seven years, before she was ousted by a revolt led by the Jerusalem priesthood. The aim of this revolt was simple: to restore the family of David to the throne of Judah and to establish Judah's independence once more. Athaliah was replaced by the boy king Joash, who was no doubt subject to the wishes of the priesthood, except that he, not they, took the initiative in making repairs to the Temple (2 Kings 12:5-17). During his reign, the rampant King Hazael of Syria made a raid against him, appropriating the temple and palace treasures as tribute (2 Kings 12:18-19).

Joash was assassinated by two of his servants around about 796 BCE and was succeeded by Amaziah (2 Kings 12:21; 14:1-2). Amaziah enjoyed military success against Edom (2 Kings 14:7) and was then unwise enough to challenge Joash, king of Israel, to a battle (2 Kings 14:8). It was this Joash who had begun to turn the tide of Israel's fortunes against Hazael's son Ben-Hadad, and he defeated Amaziah, proceeded to Jerusalem, and tore down part of the wall. He also raided the treasuries and took hostages (2 Kings 14:12-14). There is certainly something to be said for the suggestion (Miller and Hayes 1986: 307) that Judah was, in fact, again reduced to vassal status, and that this situation lasted for the next forty years or so. On the other hand, it is possible to argue from 2 Kings 14:17-21 that Judah's vassal status lasted for only fifteen years. At the end of this period, Amaziah was assassinated, and replaced on the throne by Uzziah, in a gesture of independence by the people of Judah.

Time Chart: Israel and Judah				
961–931 Solomon				
		Israel	Judah	
		931–910 Jeroboam	931–914	Rehoboam
924	Invasion by Shishak	914–912 Abijah		
		911–871 Asa		
		909 Nadab		
		909–886 Baasha		
		885 Elah		
		885 Zimri		
		885–874 Omri		
		873–853 Ahab		
859–824	Shalmaneser III of Assyria		871–848	Jehoshaphat
		853–852 Ahaziah		
		852–841 Joram	848–841	Joram (probably the Israelite king)
		841–813 Jehu	841	Ahaziah
			840–835	Athaliah
			835–796	Joash
		813–797 Jehoahaz		
		797–782 Joash		
			796–767	Amaziah
		782–747 Jeroboam II		
			767–739	Uzziah
		747 Zechariah		
		747 Shallum		
745–727	Tiglath-Pileser III of Assyria	747–742 Menahem		
		742–740 Pekahiah		
		740–731 Pekah		
			739–734	Jotham
			734–728	Ahaz
722–705	Sargon II of Assyria	731–722 Hoshea		
705–681	Sennacherib of Assyria	(Fall of Northern Kingdom 722/21)	728–699	Hezekiah
			699–643	Manasseh
			642–640	Amen
			640–609	Josiah
605–562	Nebuchadrezzar of Babylon		609	Jehoahaz
			609–598	Jehoiakim
			597	Jehoiachin
			597–587	Zedekiah (Destruction of Jerusalem 587/76)

Of the long reigns of Uzziah (he is credited with fifty-two years at 2 Kings 15:2) and Joash's successor in Israel, Jeroboam II, little is known. The biblical narrative claims that Jeroboam greatly enlarged Israel's borders (2 Kings 14:25; but see Miller and Hayes 1986: 307-309), and Uzziah is said, at 2 Chronicles 26:1-15, to have fortified Jerusalem, to have built up the army, and to have waged successful campaigns against Ammon and the Philistines. The end of the reigns of these two kings is the period of the prophetic activity of Hosea and Amos, which was directed against the luxury of the rich, the oppression of the poor, and the insincerity of the religion of the people.

Assyrian Aggression

From 745 BCE there was a sharp decline in the fortunes of Israel and Judah, brought about by the Assyrian king Tiglath-Pileser III (744–727). He strengthened his kingdom and embarked upon a policy of expansion that was to bring under his dominion the whole of Syria, Israel, Philistia, Judah, and Transjordan. The events of the years 745–721 BCE, which saw a rapid succession of kings in Israel (six of them in the fifteen years between 747 and 732) present some of the most difficult problems for historical reconstruction in the whole of the Old Testament (for a detailed discussion see Miller and Hayes 1986: 322-37). Coup was followed by counter-coup, as parties opposed to, or prepared to accept, Assyrian dominance struggled for the upper hand. According to Isaiah 7:1-14, the Israelite king Pekah and the king of Syria, Rezon, formed an alliance against Ahaz, the king of Judah, perhaps in an attempt to force Ahaz to join a coalition against Assyria. This happened in about 734 BCE. 2 Chronicles 28:5-8, 16-18 reports that Ahaz suffered greatly at the hands of Pekah and the Philistines, the latter capturing parts of the Shephelah. Ahaz appealed to Tiglath-Pileser for help, and paid him tribute. In campaigns in 734–732, the Assyrian king conquered Syria, annexed the territory of Israel from the Jezreel valley northwards, and reduced Israel to a client kingdom ruled by Hoshea. In 725 BCE, Hoshea rebelled against Shalmaneser V, whereupon the Assyrians besieged Samaria. It fell in 722 or 721 to Shalmaneser's successor, Sargon II, thus bringing to an end the history of the northern kingdom.

It is arguable that the fall of Israel to the Assyrians was one of the most important events for the development of the religion of the Old Testament. Here again, however, widely differing reconstructions are possible, given the meagre evidence. We know from archaeological investigations that the population of Jerusalem grew noticeably in the latter part of the eighth century BCE, and one explanation is that this was because of immigration from the former northern kingdom. Among these arrivals from the north may have been levitical or prophetic groups who brought with them traditions, written and oral, arising from their Exodus-based faith. This made possible the beginnings of a fusion between the northern Exodus-based religion and the southern Jerusalem and house-of-David-oriented religion. Much depends on how the reign of Hezekiah (728–699 BCE) is interpreted.

A passage in 2 Kings (18:3-8) presents Hezekiah as a religious reformer who destroyed the sanctuaries other than the Temple in Jerusalem. 2 Chronicles 29–30 goes into much more detail about the religious reforms, and gives an account of Hezekiah sending messengers to parts of the northern kingdom inviting its people to celebrate the Passover in Jerusalem. In the account of that celebration, the narrative gives the impression that it was carried out in spite of uncertainties and irregularities; for example, it was held in the wrong month (2 Chronicles 30:2, 15). It is necessary, of course, to use this material from Chronicles with a good deal of caution. The narrative is certainly strongly coloured by the theological bias of Chronicles; but there may be more than a grain of truth in its claim that Hezekiah ordered the Passover to be celebrated in Judah—probably for the first time in the south. If this is correct, then the influence of the arrivals from the north on the religion of Judah is evident. It is, of course, possible to interpret Hezekiah's actions mainly in political terms, with religious reforms being merely a way of achieving national unity (Miller and Hayes 1986: 357).

Hezekiah was bent on achieving independence for Judah from the Assyrian rule under which it had existed since his father Ahaz appealed for help to Tiglath-Pileser III. Revolt was not easy, however. In 713–711 BCE, Hezekiah seems to have joined a revolt against Sargon, together with Philistia, Edom, and Moab; but this seems to have fizzled out (cp. Miller and Hayes 1986: 352). With the death of Sargon in 705 Hezekiah made a determined effort at revolt, backed by careful preparations, which included the fortification of Jerusalem and other cities. In 701 BCE, Judah was invaded by Sennacherib.

The Invasion

The course of events during the invasion presents another body of evidence, which is far from easy to interpret. Scholars are divided over the dates of Hezekiah's reign, there being two possibilities, based upon 2 Kings 18:1 and 2 Kings 18:13. According to the first passage, Hezekiah became king in the third year of Hoshea, that is, c. 728 BCE. According to the second passage, Sennacherib's invasion (of 701) took place in Hezekiah's fourteenth year. This would place his accession in 715 BCE. Moreover, some scholars have strongly championed the view (see Bright 1981: 298 ff.) that 2 Kings 18:13 and 19:37 telescope two campaigns of Sennacherib against Hezekiah, one in 701 and the other in 689 BCE. If the higher chronology that makes Hezekiah's reign from c. 728 to 699 is correct, he would have been dead nine years before the second campaign. The view taken here is that the higher chronology is more likely to be correct and that there was only one campaign of Sennacherib. In any case, its effects were sufficiently drastic to teach Hezekiah a lesson he was not likely to forget. Judah was occupied by the Assyrian army and Jerusalem was besieged. The fortified city of Lachish was forced to surrender, an event commemorated in the famous reliefs now in the British Museum. Hezekiah was forced to pay heavy tribute (2 Kings 18:13-16); yet Jerusalem itself remained unconquered, a fact that gave rise to legends about its inviolability.

In reality, Judah had become once more an Assyrian vassal state, but in what sense it was a state is an interesting question. Steiner (2003: 76-78) believes that by destroying all the main towns of Judah except Jerusalem, Sennacherib radically altered the balance of affairs between Jerusalem and the other provincial centres of Judah, leaving Jerusalem as the only town in the land and opening the way for it to assume a completely dominant position. At any rate, Judah remained an Assyrian vassal for the 55-year reign of Hezekiah's son Manasseh, who probably acceded soon after the debacle of his father's rebellion. Of Manasseh's reign we know very little. The assessment of him in 2 Kings 21:1-9 is entirely in theological terms. He is said to have reversed his father's religious reforms, to have allowed child sacrifice, and to have encouraged occult practices such as communication with the dead. A passage in 2 Chronicles (33:11-20) implies that at some point Manasseh rebelled against Assyria, was taken captive to Babylon (*sic*), turned in desperation to God, and on returning to Jerusalem carried out a reform of the cult. Scholars are divided over whether or not this is a reliable piece of information.

As Manasseh's reign wore on, so Assyrian power began to decline. Manasseh's son Amon, who acceded in 642 BCE, ruled for only two years before being assassinated. The 'people of the land' now installed the boy Josiah on the throne. He was to enable Judah to enjoy its last spell of independence before the deportations.

Josiah's reign, from 640/39 to 609 BCE, was probably the most important of any reign of a king of Israel or Judah for the development of the religion of the Old Testament. In 2 Kings 22:8-20 we find the famous story of the discovery of the 'book of law' in the Temple in 622 BCE. As a result of this 'discovery', Josiah implemented a religious reform directed against the 'high places' (the local sanctuaries) that were to be found in his kingdom, as well as involving a thoroughgoing purge of the personnel and fittings of the Jerusalem Temple. The reform culminated in a celebration of the Passover, of which 2 Kings 23:22 records:

> Such a Passover had not been celebrated since the days of the Judges who ruled Israel, and not in the whole period of the kings of Israel and Judah.

This could mean no more than that this was the first Passover celebrated at the command of the king (in which case we must discount Hezekiah's observance of the feast). More radically, it may record the fact that this was the first Passover ever to be celebrated in Judah.

Whatever the truth is, we can detect behind the reform a victory of the bearers of the northern Exodus-based traditions who had fled from the north a century earlier and who had kept faith with their convictions during the difficult years of Manasseh's reign. They had probably put the 'law book' into the possession of Hilkiah, the high priest of the Temple—the 'law book' itself being part of, or an earlier draft of, what we now know as Deuteronomy. The book itself is dealt with in Chapter 10; here, the important point to note is that it represented the final fusion of the Exodus and Jerusalem traditions. Deuteronomy speaks of a single sanctuary, at which alone sacrifice can be offered to Yhwh. Although never named in Deuteronomy, this place was accepted by its writers and by King Josiah to be Jerusalem. In regard to the concept of kingship, however, the book is most explicit (Deuteronomy 17:14-20). The king must not accumulate wealth or a harem, but must devote his life to studying God's law so that he may better perform the duties of kingship.

Because of Assyrian weakness (Nineveh, the Assyrian capital, fell in 612 BCE), the latter part of Josiah's reign saw Judah enjoying a spell of independence and an extension of its territory. Josiah, however, was killed, when he went to meet or to fight the Egyptian pharaoh, Neco II, in 609 BCE, at Megiddo (2 Kings 23:28-29). Of this incident, we know almost nothing. It is usually assumed that Josiah set out to prevent Neco from going to the assistance of the remnants of the Assyrian army, who were making a last stand at Haran against the Babylonians; and most modern translations of 2 Kings 23:29 imply this, although the traditional Hebrew text (which may, of course, be corrupt) indicates that Josiah was going to Neco's aid. The result of the encounter was tragic for Judah, and initiated a brief period in which it was subservient to Egypt (2 Kings 23:33). For the few remaining years of Judah's existence, the tiny state was a helpless spectator of the power struggle between Egypt and Babylon.

In 605 BCE the Babylonians, under the leadership of Nebuchadrezzar, defeated the Egyptians at the battle of Carchemish, and a year later he moved into Syria and Israel. The prophet Jeremiah saw in this movement the hand of God, and he declared the impending downfall of the state (Jeremiah 25:1-14). The Judahite king

Jehoiakim, who had been put on the throne by Neco, transferred his allegiance to Nebuchadrezzar (2 Kings 24:1), but following a setback for Nebuchadrezzar in a battle against Egypt in 601 BCE, Jehoiakim rebelled. In 597 Nebuchadrezzar captured Jerusalem, and deported to Babylon King Jehoiachin, who had meanwhile acceded to the throne, along with a number of important officials (2 Kings 24:8-17). The last king to rule in Jerusalem was the exiled Jehoiachin's uncle, who remained a loyal vassal for ten years before attempting another rebellion. This time, the Babylonian response resulted in the destruction of Jerusalem and its Temple, and the end of the southern kingdom of Judah.

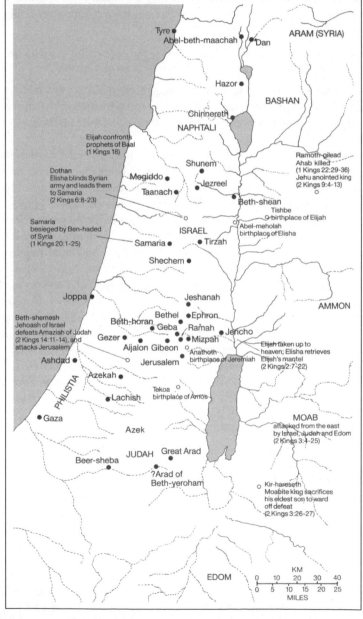

Map 9. *Events of the Divided Monarchy*

References and Further Reading

Bright, J.
   1981   *A History of Israel* (London: SCM Press, 3rd edn).
Dever, W.G.
   2003   *Who Were the Early Israelites and Where Did They Come From?* (Grand Rapids: Eerdmans).
Finkelstein, I., and N.A. Silberman
   2001   *The Bible Unearthed: Archaeology's New Vision of Ancient Israel and the Origin of its Sacred Texts* (New York: Free Press).
Kitchen, K.A.
   1973   *The Third Intermediate Period in Egypt (1100–650 BC)* (Warminster: Aris & Phillips).
Lemche, N.P.
   2003   ' "House of David": The Tell Dan Inscription(s)', in Thompson (ed.) 2003: 46-67.
Mazar, A.
   1990   *Archaeology of the Land of the Bible, 10,000–586 B.C.E.* (New York: Doubleday).
Miller, J.M., and J.H. Hayes
   1986   *A History of Ancient Israel and Judah* (Philadelphia: Westminster Press).
Parrot, A.
   1958   *Samaria, The Capital of the Kingdom of Israel* (London: SCM Press).
Rogerson, J.W.
   1999   *Chronicle of the Old Testament Kings: The Reign-by-Reign Record of the Rulers of Ancient Israel* (London: Thames & Hudson). (This work gives a popular but critical account of the kings of Judah and Israel with reference to the biblical material and archaeological findings.)
Rogerson, J.W. (ed.)
   1998   *Beginning Old Testament Study* (London: SPCK, 2nd edn).
Schorn, U.
   1997   *Ruben und das System der zwölf Stämme Israels. Redaktionsgeschichtliche Untersuchungen zur Bedeutung des Erstgeborenen Jakobs* (Berlin: W. de Gruyter).
Steiner, M.
   2001   'Jerusalem in the Tenth and Seventh Centuries BCE: From Administrative Town to Commercial City', in A. Mazar (ed.), *Studies in the Archaeology of the Iron Age in Israel and Jordan* (JSOT, 331; Sheffield: Sheffield Academic Press): 280-88.
   2003   'Expanding Borders: The Development of Jerusalem in the Iron Age', in Thompson (ed.) 2003: 68-79.
Thompson, T.L. (ed.)
   2003   *Jerusalem in Ancient History and Tradition* (JSOT, 381; London: T&T Clark International).

Chapter 6

JUDAH UNDER THE PERSIANS AND PTOLEMIES AND THE JUDEANS IN BABYLONIA

After thirty-seven years of confinement in Babylon, Jehoiachin and his sons were released by the Babylonian king, as attested in 2 Kings 25:27-30 and cuneiform ration lists. The other deported Judeans (mostly, Jerusalemites) were located in certain sites rather than being dispersed; apparently, many of these were ruined cities, called *tels* (cp. Ezra 2:59; Ezekiel 1:3). Thus, some independent social organisation was achievable. It is often assumed by historians and biblical scholars that these Judeans expected to return one day, but such an outcome was unusual and therefore probably not anticipated. Jeremiah 29:5-7 recommends that the deportees build homes and farm the land. Verses 10-14 admittedly promise a repatriation after seventy years, but the Deuteronomistic language of this passage makes it look suspiciously like a later insertion (after the event?).

According to the book of Ezra, many of those who did return were wealthy, with slaves (Ezra 1:6; 2:65). Life in Babylonia, for most, did not mean 'captivity', and for many it brought prosperity. From a century later we have the archives of a firm from Nippur run by the Murashu family, containing names of Jewish business clients, showing Jewish ownership of land and housing, and their employment as officials and administrators. Although the stories of Daniel 1–6 and Esther are not to be taken as historical or literal in their details, they attest the attainment of high office by some of the Jews, at least under the Persians, and Nehemiah's position of royal cup-bearer offers a further example. Aspiration to political influence is endorsed, not condemned, and we may infer a Babylonian Judean population generally positively disposed to their situation.

Nevertheless, the impression of Babylon in the Bible is as hostile as Assyria (more so, if we take Jonah's positive view of Nineveh into account). Psalm 137 imparts a longing to return home, and the allusion to the 'waters of Babylon' points up the differences in terrain between the highlands of Judah and the flat Tigris–Euphrates basin, with its higher rainfall, wide rivers, and canals (but verse 1 says '*there* we sat down', not '*here* we sat down'—so presumably an imaginative poem written after returning to Judah?). Second Isaiah (chapters 40–55) denounces the Babylonian gods and their statues, made by hands and carried about on the backs of animals (44:9ff; 46:1). Jeremiah 50:36-38 sums up a Judean impression of Babylon: diviners, warriors, horses and chariots, treasures, waters, images, and idols. The feeling of political inferiority was countered by an assertion of religious superiority.

Living in communities meant that social or religious assimilation could be resisted. Two developments that may have occurred are the political and economic power of the priesthood (without a temple the priesthood may have become *more* important) and the absorption of the culture of manticism (see Chapter 14). The influence of the priesthood in Babylonia, for whatever reasons, persisted and even expanded in Judah after the return of many priests to Jerusalem; manticism (divination) was a fundamental dimension of Babylonian religion, which purveyed an interpretation of things unseen by reading signs. But how much Babylonian cultural, literary, and religious influence was exerted during the sixth century is uncertain: it could have been borrowed at almost any time, so widely disseminated was it.

Judah

Upon the fall of Samaria, the Assyrians had divided the territory of Israel into the three provinces of Megiddo (including most of Galilee), Dor (the Shephelah), and Samaria (the highlands). Samaria, despite repopulation by Assyria from elsewhere, remained essentially Yahwistic, although defined (at some stage) as being outside 'Israel' by Judeans and their Bible, for whom the ten tribes were 'lost'. What is very important is the status of the territory of Benjamin; having been part of Israel, it subsequently seems to have been absorbed into Judah. The territory of Judah— though the precise boundaries are not certain— thereafter probably extended as far as the Dead Sea, more or less from Bethel in the north to Bethzur in the south and from Jericho in the northeast to Azekah (mentioned as a Judean city in the Lachish letters during the Babylonian invasion of 589) in the southwest (see the map on p. 84).

The majority of Judeans, of course, were not taken to Babylon. These, called the 'poor people of the land', were given vineyards and fields (2 Kings 25:12; Jeremiah 39:10), presumably those once owned by the deportees. No foreign populations were deliberately introduced, but some Ammonites, Moabites, Edomites, and Samarians probably settled there. Judah was perhaps already divided by the Neo-Babylonians into six districts (as under the Persians, according to Nehemiah 3). But it was into *Benjaminite* territory that the political and religious focus of Judah was transferred until Jerusalem was restored as capital and chief sanctuary, probably in the latter half of the fifth century. Most likely, during this period a number of Israelite traditions centred on the old Israelite sanctuaries (especially Bethel, but also Gibeon and Mizpah, the provincial capital) were adopted as Judean. The reverberations of the rivalry between Benjamin and Judah, between Bethel and Jerusalem, resound throughout the Old Testament. In particular, the stories of Saul and David, the ark, the 'conquest' and many of the judges make better sense as Israelite (specifically Benjaminite) stories revised (sometimes in the opposite direction) by Judeans. At all events, while Bethel was the major sanctuary of Judah, Jacob became the ancestor of Judeans as well, and Judah a 'tribe' of a greater 'Israel'.

Perhaps here was written or edited some of the literature often ascribed to the Judeans in Babylonia—Jeremiah, Ezekiel, the Pentateuch, and the Deuteronomistic history. But if literature was being produced at this time, it was most likely at Mizpah and Bethel, not Jerusalem, and therefore it would have been strongly influenced by Benjaminite ('Israelite') traditions, not Judean ones, and especially not those centred on Jerusalem! We must not be surprised if, either, the population remaining in Judah (including the governors in Benjamin) opposed the 'returnees', for many of these were rich, were claiming land, apparently had imperial support (and even patronage) for their return, and wished to reinstate Jerusalem as the capital and religious centre.

Resettlement in Judah

The biblical version of Israel's history asserts or implies that 'Israel' went into 'exile'; the majority who remained are of little or no interest or significance. This is the reverse of the view adopted in several prophetic books that saw the removal from the land as punishment on *wicked* Israel—yet we find those deported claiming to be the *preserved* line of the 'righteous'! Behind this opposition may lie an important historical-social factor: tension between those returning to Judah from Babylonia and those who had remained in Judah. The claim to be the true 'Israel' (or 'Judah') justified the 'returnees' in claiming control of the Temple, of the government, of the land, excluding the 'people of the land' who were assumed to have abandoned heir 'Israelite' status and, among other things, intermarried with non-Judeans. For genealogy (as Chronicles, Ezra, and Nehemiah all clearly reflect) emerges as an important definition of who is 'Israel' and who is not.

The Ezra and Nehemiah stories present a swift and organised 'return', but also speak of local opposition, from Samaria and other neighbouring peoples and 'people of the land' (Ezra 3:3), who thus become 'Canaanites'—an evil influence which will, unless strenuously rejected, corrupt the 'people of God' (called 'children of the exile': Ezra 6:16, 19-21; 10:7, 16). That the 'people of the land' had any rights or grievances against the incomers is not acknowledged.

The biblical account of the 'return' is unreliable not only because it is highly partisan but also because the accounts were probably compiled much later than the events. The starting point of the story (found only in the book of Ezra) is an edict of Cyrus allowing Judeans to 'return' (Ezra 1:2-4 in Hebrew; 6:3-5 in Aramaic). The authenticity of the Aramaic decree was once widely accepted; more recently it has come under suspicion, like the Hebrew version. That Cyrus would bother himself with the details of the Judean temple (given that despite such powerful support it was not accomplished until much later) does not seem likely. The authenticity of further letters in Aramaic in Ezra 4:11-16, 17-22; 5:7-17; 6:6-12; and 7:12-26 is still disputed (on this see Grabbe 1998).

But Ezra and Nehemiah both make it clear that the 'return' was a Persian initiative: both characters have a royal commission. In the famous inscription known as the 'Cyrus Cylinder', Cyrus presents himself as a restorer of local gods and temples and a repatriator of dispersed peoples. Cyrus announces how Marduk, the god of Babylon, looked through all the earth to find the righteous ruler to liberate Babylon. Another tablet, from Nippur, attributes this commission to the god Sin, and Second Isaiah (chapters 40–55) attributes it to Yhwh. Although often contrasted with that of Assyrian and Babylonian rulers, this claim is very much in their tradition, but it is hard to see how the Bible would credit the Persians if the 'return' had been a Judean initiative. Persian policy was in any case to administer a politically passive but economically productive empire. There is evidence of a consistent Persian policy to create religious communities rather than political ones—which in the case of Judah worked extremely well. An additional factor in Judah's case is probably the need for a strong and loyal province close to the sensitive border with Egypt.

The process of 'restoration' comprised three objectives: the building of the Temple (cultic), the building of city walls (political-economic), and membership of a religious community (social). All these objectives had economic implications. The two decrees in Ezra nevertheless focus on the rebuilding of the Temple, making *that* the purpose of the return. But the building of the Temple is a rather confusing story. First, at the beginning of Cyrus's reign, the Temple vessels are said to have been handed over to Sheshbazzar, the 'prince' (Hebrew *nasi*) of Judah (Ezra 1:7), and he is later said— this time bearing the title *pehah* ('governor')—to have laid the foundation, as decreed (Ezra 5:14-16). The returnees gather in Jerusalem to rededicate the altar (Ezra 3:1-6). A little later (Ezra 3:7-13) Zerubbabel lays the Temple foundations. However, there is now a further delay, for Ezra 4:4–6.12 says the building was stopped for seventeen years until Darius reaffirmed it and Zerubbabel proceeded (see also Haggai 1:12-15, which makes no mention of the earlier start).

When did these returnees actually make the journey? Ezra 1:11 implies that this happened in the time of Cyrus, with Sheshbazzar, but Nehemiah 7:6-7 gives a list of those who came with Zerubbabel (and the list is reproduced more or less in Ezra 2, including Zerubbabel but not Sheshbazzar!). In fact, we cannot say when work really started on the Temple, or when and how the 'return' took place. The complications in the biblical story seem to derive from a wish to insist that the 'restoration' began immediately. However, the great cultic ceremony recorded in Nehemiah 8–9 suggests that the Temple was only just completed *then*, a century after Cyrus's conquest of Babylon. How far should we base our understanding of events on these accounts?

Ezra and Nehemiah's Commissions

Besides confusion over the rebuilding of the Temple, further literary and historical problems in Ezra and Nehemiah need to be unravelled. The most obvious one is that we cannot be sure of the date assigned to Ezra, though he is presented alongside Nehemiah (Nehemiah 8–9; 12:36). And yet, although they seem to be doing similar things, at the same time—such as dissolving mixed marriages—they do not actually cooperate at all except for one episode (Nehemiah 8–9)!

The date of Ezra's arrival in Jerusalem—and thus his relationship to Nehemiah— is the most notorious problem of biblical chronology. Nehemiah's arrival is clearly dated in the twentieth year of Artaxerxes: this must be Artaxerxes I, which means 445 BCE. He finished in 433 (Nehemiah 5:14), but soon after came back (13:6). Ezra is commissioned in Artaxerxes' seventh year (Ezra 7:8). If this is also Artaxerxes I, then Ezra precedes Nehemiah by thirteen years. Many scholars think that Ezra's king was Artaxerxes II, and that Ezra thus came much later than Nehemiah, in 398. But this means that Ezra and Nehemiah did not meet, as Nehemiah 8 claims. A third proposal, then, is that for the seventh year (of Artaxerxes I) we should read the thirty-seventh year, that is 428, perhaps during Nehemiah's second stint. There is a problem with the relationship of the two men and their mandates, since either they are working on similar reforms, apparently at the same time or almost, and both personally authorised by the same king, or Nehemiah's reforms failed and Ezra went to put this right. The problem becomes clear (though is hardly solved) if we recognise that the juxtaposition of Ezra and Nehemiah in Nehemiah 8 is an editorial device associated with the joining of the two books. (The same explanation can be given of Nehemiah 12:36: see below.) In fact, the entire ceremony in Nehemiah 8–10 is more appropriate to the book of Ezra and his religious mission than to Nehemiah's political and economic one. It may therefore be Nehemiah who is the 'intruder' here. Disentangling the two characters may seem to make their relationship even more problematic, but if we assume that originally the Ezra and Nehemiah stories were independent, and were brought together by an editor who joined the characters (and the books), the historical difficulty disappears.

The possible correlations of events in Nehemiah and Ezra with the sequence of Persian kings can be summarised like this:

Time Chart: Persian King and the Main Events in Judah			
Persian Kings		Events in Ezra–Nehemiah	
559–529	CYRUS (539–538 capture of Babylon)	538–522	Various returns from Babylonia (Ezra 1–2)
		538–537	Altar dedication (Ezra 3:1-2)
529–522	CAMBYSES		
522–486	DARIUS I (Hystaspes)	520–512	Building of Second Temple (Ezra 5–6)
486–465	XERXES I		
465–425	ARTAXERXES I (Longimanus)	458	Ezra's mission, first conjecture (Ezra 7–10; Nehemiah 8)
		448	Abortive attempt to rebuild the walls (Ezra 4:7-23)
		445–433	Nehemiah's first term as governor(?) (Nehemiah 1–7)
		438/428	Ezra's mission, second conjecture
		430(?)	Nehemiah's second term as governor(?) (Nehemiah 13)
425–424	XERXES II		
424	SOGDIANUS		
424–405	DARIUS II (Ochus)		
405–359	ARTAXERXES II (Memnon)	398	Ezra's mission, third conjecture
359–338	ARTAXERXES III (Ochus)		
338–336	ARSES		
336–331	DARIUS III (Codommanus)	332	

Nehemiah

Nehemiah's mission is not without problems. Apparently given full royal permission to rebuild the walls of Jerusalem, he returned to Judah accompanied by Persian troops, bearing official letters and a provision of wood from the royal estates (Nehemiah 2:7-8). But he conceals his commission from the officials and local population (Nehemiah 2:16), and meets powerful opposition from the Persian-appointed officials Sanballat and Tobiah (probably of Samaria and Ammon respectively)— would this occur if he had such authority? Another reform was to increase the population of the city (Nehemiah 11:1-2). In Nehemiah's second phase, a certain Tobiah the Ammonite (a different Tobiah this time?) was removed from the Temple, levites who had no Temple status or income were given a role and provided with a tithe (more taxes!), a curfew on Sabbath trading in Jerusalem was imposed and mixed marriages banned. On this occasion, Nehemiah's power seems greater, for some of these are cultic matters, and the measures were also said to be unpopular (Nehemiah 13:25). Is Nehemiah's story as straightforward as it ought to be for a reliable historical account?

A final problem to raise here (there are several others that could be mentioned) is why the Persian king would wish to have Jerusalem re-established as the main city and sanctuary of Judah. True, this is nowhere said to be his aim, but clearly that is what Nehemiah accomplished, and if he really was governor, he regarded Jerusalem as the capital of Judah. Yet, Mizpah had been functioning for well over a century as the capital. Why should the Persians be prepared to move it, and back to the place where Judean kings had once reigned? A decision to allow a temple to be built there is understandable, but why would the Persians support what could well appear as a nationalistic programme? And why in the middle of the fifth century? To these questions the books of Ezra and Nehemiah are not giving answers!

Ezra

The mission of Ezra is even more difficult to understand than Nehemiah's. Ezra himself appears only in Ezra 7–10, plus the reference in Nehemiah 8, which, as mentioned earlier, may be an editorial manufacture, and some incidental references in Nehemiah 12 (see below). Ezra is described as a priest and a scribe skilled in the 'law of Moses which Yhwh, the God of Israel, had given' (Ezra 7:6)—a written, religious code. He was not sent as a governor, or to rebuild Temple or walls, but specifically to bring home fellow Jews, take gifts and grants for the national-ethnic cult, investigate the status of the law, and appoint judges of the law—not just in Judah, but *over the entire satrapy of 'Beyond the River'*, that is west of the Euphrates. If Ezra's mission did include regularisation of law throughout the satrapy, that law must have been seen as religious law, binding only on those who acknowledged Judean ethnicity, and not a law by which the province of Judah should be ruled politically. However, if he were a kind of 'minister for Judean affairs' in the satrapy, it is strange that he had no successors. Yet if the figure of Ezra is an invention of a later period, the idea of a law governing ethnic Jews over a more dispersed area (the 'diaspora', including Babylon itself) would make a different kind of sense.

Perhaps the nature of Ezra's mission is clarified by a hieroglyphic inscription relating the activities of another scribe, a certain Udjahorresne, a priest who sided with the Persians during the invasion of Egypt by Cambyses. Later, he was sent from the imperial court to Egypt to reorganise the 'house of life' at the sanctuary in Sais, and part of this mission involved the codifying of religious laws. The relevance of Udjahorresne's account is that it might reveal a Persian policy of encouraging the codification of native laws as an essential instrument for legal order in a multicultural empire. But we do not have other clear examples of such commissions.

What, then, did Ezra achieve? The biblical account concentrates on his reading of the law, celebration of the Feast of Tabernacles, and institution of a covenant (Nehemiah 8), which included the putting away of foreign wives—a course of action that was said not to have been carried through (Ezra 10:4-44). He fulfilled the task of bringing returnees and gifts, but the parts of the commission relating to the law correspond only partly and vaguely to what Ezra did.

Perhaps all these difficulties have a different explanation. There are some indications that the figure of Ezra may be a literary creation. First, the Jerusalem scribe Ben Sira (c. 200 BCE), while mentioning Nehemiah, omits to mention Ezra, who should have been much more important to him. In addition, 2 Maccabees 1:18-36 describes how *Nehemiah* offered sacrifices at the feast of Booths (= Nehemiah 8); nowhere is Ezra mentioned. Finally, Nehemiah 12 contains a list of twenty-three 'priestly leaders' who 'came up with Zerubbabel', which includes the name 'Ezra' without further elaboration. In Nehemiah 12:36 we find a list of priests leading the dedication of the city wall: 'and the *scribe* Ezra went in front of them' which looks rather like an afterthought (leaders are usually named first!), and so may be a later editorial attempt to bring Ezra again into the sphere of Nehemiah's activity.

Nevertheless, if Ezra is a literary creation, is he based on a historical personage? According to Nehemiah 12:1 there *was* a priest called Ezra among the returnees *with Zerubbabel*. The hero of the book of Ezra was perhaps fashioned from a minor character in Nehemiah. Several aspects of Nehemiah's commission and behaviour also look suspicious, and the first-person narrative is not necessarily a genuine 'memoir', but the evidence is hardly strong enough to indicate that he is an invented figure.

But we must at least allow that what Ezra is said to have done conforms to how we know Judaism developed—as a religious community defined by a covenant and governed by the 'law of Moses'. Ezra's story may be a dramatisation of how that state of affairs came about in one short period and under a great leader: that is quite a common phenomenon in cultural traditions. If Ezra and Nehemiah at one time represented alternative stories of this kind (perhaps favoured by different Jewish groups), their combination into a single book (and their contrived meeting), would 'unite' the origins of Judaism, providing a single narrative combining both traditions.

Elephantine

Our main non-biblical literary sources relating to the early Persian period are documents from a Judean colony in Egypt. Babylonia was not the only site of Jewish settlement outside Judea: Jeremiah (chapters 43–44) is said to have gone with a number of refugees to Egypt, possibly before the end of the Judean monarchy. We know in particular of a Jewish military garrison which was stationed at Elephantine on the upper Nile (modern Asswan) as early as the seventh or sixth century BCE, and which has left papyri written towards the end of the fifth century. From these papyri we learn that this colony had a temple in which they worshipped Yahu, Bethel, Harambethel, Ashambethel, and Anat. The temple had been recently destroyed by Egyptians, and a letter was written, presumably to the satrap, requesting permission to rebuild it. A further letter went to Bagohi, the Persian governor of Judah, repeating the request, and also to Johanan and other priests in Jerusalem. This request to Bagohi was also repeated, while yet another went to the sons of Sanballat, governor of Samaria and opponent of Nehemiah. These bore Yahwistic names—that is names containing the element Yah (Yhwh)—Delayah and Shemayah, and they had advised the satrap to permit use of the altar except for burnt offerings. The interesting point here is that authority over Judean religious practice in the entire satrapy was apparently vested in Jerusalem. Another papyrus regulates observance of the Feast of Unleavened Bread, claiming that the 'Great King' had ordered the satrap in Egypt concerning the observance of this feast. The interest of the Persian king in matters of Jewish cult seems confirmed. On the other hand, the local practices of this presumably Judean cult do not conform to the prescriptions of the biblical law presumably now being enforced in Judah.

The Establishment of the Religious Community in Jerusalem

The problems of Ezra and Nehemiah make it difficult to describe the events of fifth century Judah. From our knowledge about later times we can infer the developments that must have taken place, but not exactly how or when, or to what extent. How did a community of returnees from Babylon establish itself as the new 'Israel' in Judah, governed by the 'law of Moses' and centred on the Jerusalem temple and with priestly leadership? One model, proposed by Joel Weinberg, is of a 'temple-community', a well-known social-economic model in the ancient Near East. The book of Deuteronomy (which may derive from this period) insists on a single sanctuary, and requires the Passover to be celebrated at this sanctuary. Its ideology certainly fits the scenario in Nehemiah. However, its interests are largely social rather than cultic. The Holiness Code in Leviticus 17–26, which dates from some time in the Persian period (see Leviticus 26:43), enhances, above all, the economic interests and the ideology of the priesthood. It prohibits, for example, animal slaughter unless offered as a sacrifice (effectively a Temple tax on meat), and emphasises the holiness of priests. The Temple thrived, then, by exacting tithes and by serving as a major customer for wood and oil, perhaps granting franchises—not to mention that the Persian empire probably used the Temple as its tax-collecting agent. Whether or not Weinberg's model is applicable, the new 'Israel' was founded on law, temple, priesthood, and Jerusalem. But that this development occurred without significant protest or resistance is unlikely. A good deal of Old Testament literature (especially in the Prophets, and above all Isaiah 56–66 and Malachi) expresses very strong opposition to the political and religious leadership of the time. Indeed, the tumultuous events of the second century BCE might well be seen as evidence of one or more basic fault lines in the economic and religious structure of Judah.

Of the developments between the time of Ezra and Nehemiah and Alexander the Great we learn very little from biblical sources. We know from elsewhere that Egypt revolted against Persian rule and was finally subdued and that there was a widespread revolt of satraps. It has been suggested that in a further revolt of Phoenician cities Judah was involved, and this may be supported by evidence of the destruction of cities in Palestine; but the case is not impressive. The Jewish historian Josephus (first century CE) relates that—in the time of Artaxerxes II or III?—the high priest Johanan killed his brother, who had tried to secure the high priesthood for himself with the connivance of a high Persian official, Bagoas. This, if true, foreshadows a similar conflict in the reign of Antiochus IV (see below). Since the high priest was controller of the Temple, and hence the treasury, the office was worth trying to buy. By the second century BCE we find the high priest ruling together with a council of elders (Greek *gerousia*), a development that may date from the late Persian period. We also know that during the fourth century, the province of Yehud (=the Aramaic form of Judah) minted its own coins, several of which have been preserved, as have jar handles stamped with *yh(w)d* or *yrshlym*. Coins had been introduced into the Persian empire from Lydia, and their introduction stimulated the growth in trade during the Persian period, especially with Greece—though Judah does not seem to have participated very much in this.

Alexander and the Ptolemies

In 333 BCE Syria–Palestine fell into the hands of Alexander, who, taking Tyre and Gaza en route, marched to Egypt, back through Palestine, and on to Mesopotamia. A story of Josephus (Antiquities 11.336-39) relating that Alexander visited Jerusalem is improbable. However, although the Samaritans were permitted to build a temple on their sacred mountain, Gerizim, Samaria was converted into a military colony because of a rebellion against their local governor. With this episode, most probably, are connected the Wadi Daliyeh papyri, legal texts found in a cave in the Jordan Valley along with several skeletons, and referring to the family of a certain Sanballat, probably descended from the Sanballat represented as Nehemiah's opponent.

The sudden death of Alexander in 323 BCE threw the entire empire into confusion, as his generals fought for their territories. Ptolemy, governor of Egypt, seized Syria and Palestine, which he retained, after losing it twice, from shortly after 301. From this period onwards Judean loyalties were to be divided between the Hellenistic kingdoms of Egypt (Ptolemaic) and of North Syria–Mesopotamia (Seleucid). During the struggle for control of Palestine, many Jews, according to Josephus, were taken to Egypt, enlarging the Egyptian communities that were already settled there, especially in the newly founded city of Alexandria.

In accordance with ancient Egyptian tradition, the Ptolemaic kingdom was tightly organised under the exalted king, with considerable power in the hands of his chief minister of finance. Syria and Palestine together (including Samaria and Judah) were integrated into the Egyptian system of land allotment, in which the king nominally owned all, requiring leases and taxes. From the Zenon papyri we learn of a visit to Palestine, undertaken at the instruction of the Egyptian finance minister, Apollonius, by Zenon, reaching as far as the military colony of Tobias (Tobiah) in Transjordan, and to the vineyard owned by Apollonius himself in Galilee. The papyri also contain letters to Apollonius from Tobias, which attest the pro-Ptolemaic attitude, and the enterprise, of Tobias's family—one that was destined to play a major role in the politics of Judea. In Jerusalem, however, there were pro-Seleucid sympathies, encouraged by Seleucid attempts to regain control of Palestine. As part of this pro-Seleucid resistance, the high priest Onias II at some point withheld the taxes due. His nephew, Tobias's son Joseph, then moved to Jerusalem, successfully opposed this anti-Ptolemaic stand, and in return replaced the high priest as the people's political representative (Greek *prostates*) before the Egyptian king. He used this position to secure the rights to collect the taxes in Syria and Palestine, a lucrative sinecure which he held for a long while. Under this scheme, non-payment of taxes led to forfeiture of lands, and the personal wealth thus accumulated by the tax gatherer no doubt stimulated the economy of Jerusalem, a process which would also have widened further the gap between rich and poor.

However, as the possibility of Seleucid take-over of Palestine increased, Joseph's sympathies wavered. The Seleucid Antiochus III took twenty years to acquire Palestine, and the tension split the Tobiad family. Joseph's youngest son Hyrcanus was sent to Egypt, where he tried to usurp his father as official representative. But he ended up, opposed by his family, back in the family estate in Transjordan at Araq el-Emir. Excavations here have uncovered a very well fortified dwelling, possibly including a Jewish sanctuary. If this identification is correct, the sanctuary may have been a substitute for the one at Jerusalem or a family shrine: in either case, biblically 'unorthodox'. Hyrcanus finally committed suicide during the beginning of the troubles that soon began in Jerusalem. Antiochus III, in an inscription found at Hephzibah near Beth-Shean (later rebuilt by Pompey as Scythopolis), had granted generous benefits and religious freedom to the Jerusalem community, and Seleucid sympathies in Jerusalem presumably intensified, led by both the Tobiad family and the high-priestly family, the Oniads. However, tensions built up between them, as the high priest Onias III and the Tobiads vied for influence at the Seleucid court. Even within the priestly dynasty, Onias and his brother Jeshua (Jason) disagreed about the adaptation of the Jewish state economically and religiously to its Hellenistic environment.

The defeat of Antiochus III in Asia Minor by the Romans in 190 BCE was a serious setback to the Seleucid kingdom. The resulting loss of territory in Asia Minor (hence also loss of revenue), and the cash payments to Rome initiated a process of financial crisis and political instability. This development, coupled with the internal struggles in Jerusalem, led to a crisis within Judea that was to have enormous repercussions, both religious and political. Among the consequences was a brief revival of Jewish independence, and an enforced expansion of the 'Jewish' presence on Palestine. The scale of Jewish fortunes, both high and low, in the period following was far to exceed anything previously experienced.

Further Reading

Lester L. Grabbe (*Judaism from Cyrus to Hadrian* [2 vols.; Minneapolis: Fortress Press, 1991]), discusses all the sources and historical issues; equally valuable is his *A History of the Jews and Judaism in the Second Temple Period* (Library of Second Temple Studies, 47; London: T&T Clark International, 2004). The most up-to-date account of the Persian empire is Pierre Briant, *From Cyrus to Alexander: a History of the Persian Empire* (Winona Lake, IN: Eisenbrauns, 2002). Paolo Sacchi, *The History of the Second Temple Period* (JSOTSup, 285; Sheffield: Sheffield Academic Press, 2000), gives a good account of internal as well as external developments, while Philip R. Davies (ed.), *Second Temple Studies 1: Persian Period* (JSOTSup, 117; Sheffield: JSOT Press, 1991) contains a number of very useful essays on important aspects of Judah under the Persians.

On Ezra and Nehemiah, a good recent review of the issues is Lester L. Grabbe, *Ezra–Nehemiah* (London: Routledge, 1998). Joel Weinberg, *The Citizen-Temple Community* (JSOTSup, 151; Sheffield: JSOT Press, 1992) develops a fruitful model for understanding the structure early Judean community of Judean returnees from Babylonia.

Udjahorresne(t) is discussed by J. Blenkinsopp, 'The Mission of Udjahorresnet and Those of Ezra and Nehemiah', *JBL* 106 (1987): 409-21.

The Elephantine colony and its archives are presented by B. Porten, *Archives from Elephantine: The Life of an Ancient Jewish Military Colony* (Berkeley and Los Angeles: University of California Press, 1968). For the Ptolemaic period, see M. Hengel, *Judaism and Hellenism: Studies in their Encounter in Palestine during the Early Hellenistic Period* (London: SCM Press, 2nd edn, 1974).

Chapter 7

FROM THE MACCABEES
TO HEROD THE GREAT

Only one biblical book has an evident background in the period covered by this chapter. This is the book of Daniel, apparently written around 165 BCE during the three-year period in which the Jewish religion was banned (see also Chapters 9 and 14). Two accounts of these events are found in the deutero-canonical (Apocryphal) books of 1 and 2 Maccabees. The first-century CE Jewish historian Josephus gives a history of this period, too (partly using 1 Maccabees), while other Greek sources, Jewish and non-Jewish, afford us a much better knowledge of this period than exists for the preceding three centuries. Our information, however, relates mostly to external, political events; about internal religious and social developments we have little direct information. We can, however, guess that important changes were taking place. The existence, in the first century CE, of religious groups such as the Pharisees, Sadducees, and Essenes, a number of apocalyptic writings from the Hellenistic, Hasmonean, and Herodian periods, and the discovery of the Dead Sea Scrolls suggest a religious pluralism within Palestine (let alone in the Diaspora, or Jewish communities abroad), which must have accelerated under the impact of the political and religious crises from 175 onwards with hardly a break. In this chapter we shall sketch the relatively well known (if less well understood) political events. The main (and often the only) source is Josephus, who is not to be relied on consistently but whose account can be verified in general—and who was usually in a position to tell the truth even when he chose not to; he himself regularly consulted other sources, reliable and otherwise.

The 'Hellenistic Crisis' (175 to 140 BCE)

'Hellenism' is the term for that culture produced by the spread of Greek influence throughout the eastern Mediterranean, an area already politically and economically interlocked for several centuries. What emerged was a fusion, in which the Greek language, Greek institutions, and Greek customs predominated, but in which Oriental elements (e.g. divine kingship) were also present, and, in turn, influenced Greek and Roman culture and religion (as Christianity was to do). The Greek empire, of which the Romans were heirs, was a cultural rather than a political empire. As a single domain it hardly survived the death of Alexander the Great (323 BCE), but its effect on the subsequent history of the Western world, at least, was deep and permanent. The impact of Hellenism on Judah/Judea, however, occurred gradually and on many levels. The province found itself increasingly surrounded by Hellenistic cities, its priestly and scribal classes confronted by Hellenistic ideas, its administrators and traders challenged in their affairs by the Greek language, and the whole society affected by its Hellenistic rulers.

The meeting of Hellenistic culture and traditional Jewish customs was not, on the whole, violent. Judaism was able to survive in fairly profoundly Hellenised forms, as we know very well from the Jewish literature from Alexandria and from archaeological evidence over a wide area. But in Judea, during the reign of the Seleucid king Antiochus IV ('Epiphanes'), a bitter conflict erupted, which is often referred to as the 'Hellenistic crisis'. This term, however, is a simplification.

The Ptolemaic kingdom in Egypt was—as Egypt had always been—a united, relatively homogeneous, and organised realm. The Seleucid kingdom, by contrast, covered an area that had never been united and consisted of different nations and religions, held together to some extent by the person of the king. However, there was no policy (at least until the reign of Antiochus IV) of interfering in the autonomy of the local cults, including that of Judea. Administration was essentially economic, with the king authorising the minting of coins, the control of trade, the collection of taxes, and the granting of charters to cities.

It was not the Seleucid monarchy but Hellenism, as embodied in the institution of the Greek city or *polis*, that was to have a profound impact on Jewish culture. Alexander himself had founded a number of cities in Palestine, and many existing cities were reformed into Greek-style cities. These were concentrated along the Mediterranean coast and in Transjordan, with the exception of Samaria (later renamed Sebaste by Herod the Great) in the highlands, not too distant from Jerusalem itself. The Greek city (*polis*), with its semi-autonomous economy, its (limited) democracy, its gymnasium, arena, hippodrome, and schools (teaching Greek literature and philosophy), implanted a radically different culture into the conservative, religion-centred society of Palestine. The Greek and Macedonian soldiers and traders who settled in these cities mingled with the indigenous population. Gradually the two populations became integrated—at least at the levels of the artisan, merchant, and aristocratic classes. Palestinian citizens even tended to dress according to Greek fashion. The ethos was somewhat hedonistic, tolerant; religion was social and private rather than bound up with the political structure, and condescending towards rigidly traditional cults such as that of Judea, where customs like circumcision, abstinence from pork, and adherence to ancient rituals were seen as quaint, amusing, or annoying.

Many of the native population of Judea viewed the introduction of Greek attitudes with alarm and hostility; and this cultural-religious difference was to be a central factor in the conflict here. But there were several more immediate causes of this crisis. On the Seleucid side, one factor was the financial crisis of the Seleucid kingdom. Seleucus IV inherited this problem, which obliged him, among other things, to try to ransack the Jerusalem Temple treasury. It also prompted his successor, Antiochus IV, to invade Egypt. The humiliating rebuff he received there from the Roman legate may have provoked him to deal more harshly with unrest in Jerusalem than he might have otherwise. This brings us to another oft-cited Seleucid factor, the character of Antiochus IV. Even in contemporary reports he is sometimes described as arrogant and greedy, even insane. He is also said to have wanted to unify his kingdom under a single cult. These explanations for the crisis are now generally held to be at best partial.

Time Chart: Syria and Judea			
Syria		**Judea**	
223–187	Antiochus III (the Great)	198	Judea comes under Seleucid rule
187–175	Seleucus IV		
175–164	Antiochus IV (Epiphanes)	167	Edict and onset of revolt
		166–160	Judas Maccabee
162–150	Demetrius I Soter	160–142	Jonathan
150–145	Alexander Balas	152	Jonathan becomes high priest
		150	Jonathan made military and civil governor by Alexander Balas
145–138	Demetrius II		
(145–142	Antiochus VI)	c. 145	Jonathan made governor of Syria by Antiochus
		143–134	Simon appointed high priest and ethnarch by Dimetrius
138–129	Antiochus VII (Sidetes)	134–104	John Hyrcanus I
129–95	Demetrius II	104–103	Aristobulus I assumes title of king in addition to that of high priest
		103–76	Alexander Jannai
95–78	Demetrius III		
83	Syria conquered by the Armenian king Tigranes	76–67	Alexandra/Shelomzion queen, Hyrcanus II high priest
			Hyrcanus II king
			Aristobulus II
		67	Hyrcanus II king
	Rome	67–63	Aristobulus II
64	Syria becomes a Roman province	63	Pompey captures Jerusalem and enters the Temple
		63–40	Hyrcanus II high priest (again)
		47–43	Antipater procurator of Judea
		40–37	Antigonus
		40–38	Parthian invasion: Hyrcanus II captured
		37–4	Herod the Great appointed king (that Herod appears to have died before the birth of Jesus [1 CE] is due to an error in traditional reckoning. It is probable that Jesus was born in 6 or 4 BCE.)
			Hyrcanus II killed

On the Judean side, we may note two causes for conflict, which are nevertheless closely related. One was the rivalry between the high-priestly family of the Oniads and the non-priestly Tobiads. Under the Seleucids, as previously under the Ptolemies, the political leadership of Judea was vested in the office of the high priest.

Following the death of the high priest Simon II, the struggle between the two families centred on Onias III, his successor. Onias's sympathies with the Ptolemies allowed his Tobiad rivals to undermine his influence at the Seleucid court, while his conservative stance brought him into conflict with his brother Jason (Jeshua). Jason belonged to a large body of priestly and aristocratic Judeans who desired greater official recognition, if not adoption, of Greek fashions already popular within the province.

This Hellenizing trend among the Judean aristocracy is the other, related, cause. The motives of the 'Hellenisers' are widely overlooked or misunderstood. Partisan sources (including a good deal of modern scholarship) tend to regard the 'Hellenisers' as traitors. But these men were Judean, religiously minded, and not—at least in their own eyes—betraying their religion. One suggestion for their motives is that they wished to increase the wealth of their city and province and to make common cause with Jews in Syro-Palestine who had gone further in embracing the Hellenistic way of life than had the Judeans. Whatever the truth, these 'Hellenisers' had a vision of a 'liberated' Judaism that survived and flourished elsewhere. However, the proposal to make a Hellenistic city in Jerusalem, the seat of the cult of the Jewish God, focus of political aspirations, and spiritual home of Jews everywhere, and to exclude from citizenship most of the populace was religiously and socially provocative. We do not know exactly how this new *polis* was intended to relate to the Temple itself, and the proponents of the plan presumably did not intend to interfere with the traditional cult. They may, of course, have believed that ordinary Jews did not need to participate in it. Most Jews, after all, living far from Jerusalem, did not. But a person imbued with Hellenistic ideals might genuinely fail to understand the social, psychological, and religious importance of ancestral forms of worship and their contribution to political stability and national identity. The proposal for a *polis* in Jerusalem was at the very least a serious mistake.

The 'Hellenistic crisis' thus had internal and external causes. It began as a mainly internal struggle between two alternative views of how Judea should develop. Antiochus's intervention forced the issue, but did not in the end, perhaps, make a great difference to the outcome, except that the king himself was always remembered as an arch-persecutor of Jews. The Syrian kingdom, however, was in decline, the traditional high-priesthood had become an office to be bought, and compromise with Hellenism was inevitable. What can be said is that Antiochus's extreme actions provided the Hasmonean family with the opportunity for political leadership.

Development of the Crisis

Seleucus IV's shortage of funds and the Oniad–Tobiad rivalry conspired to start the chain of events. The king needed money, and whoever could provide it in Judea could buy power. Access to the Temple treasury, a key to this power, was controlled by Onias; but the Tobiad Simon, head of the Temple administration, tried to gain some financial leverage of his own. First he tried to get control of the Temple markets, a major source of revenue. Then he informed Seleucid officials that Onias was hoarding vast sums in the Temple. Consequently, Seleucus sent an official named Heliodorus to raid the Temple. Somehow Onias dissuaded him. The only account of this episode, in 2 Maccabees 3:10ff., describes how Heliodorus was scared off by an angelic apparition. Simon then accused Onias of sedition, and the high priest went to Antioch to face the king.

But Seleucus was then assassinated by Heliodorus and succeeded by his brother Antiochus IV. The Tobiads rallied behind Jason, who offered to 'buy' the high-priesthood with a higher tax return and a policy of greater toleration of Hellenistic culture. Antiochus accepted. His appointment of Jason must have been seen by many Judeans not only as a serious intrusion into whatever political autonomy they had previously enjoyed, but as a challenge to their customs. From their point of view the crisis might be seen as religious from the outset, and both of our main sources, 1 and 2 Maccabees, interpret it so, if in different ways.

Jason, the lay aristocracy led by the Tobiads, and no doubt some of the priests also, then proposed to Antiochus to make Jerusalem—or more strictly perhaps, an area within Jerusalem—a Hellenistic city. This city would have an enrolment of citizens, 'Antiocheans in Jerusalem', and would be provided with a *gymnasion* (in which athletics were practised naked) and an *ephebeion*, a sort of Greek 'youth club' in which Greek culture would be absorbed. Yet this does not appear to have satisfied the impulses that had secured it. Jason became himself a victim of the momentum of reforming Hellenism; he was outbid by Menelaus (Menaham), who, unlike Jason, was not Oniad, or even a member of the family of Zadok, from whom the high priest had until then been appointed. War between the rivals broke out; Menelaus plundered the Temple and had Onias III, still in Antioch, murdered.

Returning from his first Egyptian campaign (169 BCE), Antiochus visited Jerusalem, now in revolt against Menelaus, and restored order, killing many people and plundering the Temple. A year later he sent his general Apollonius to repeat the exercise. On this occasion, according to the sources, many of the inhabitants were massacred on the Sabbath or taken as slaves, the city was burned, and the walls torn down. Apollonius then fortified the citadel, which stood on the western hill of the city (near the present Jaffa gate) and placed in it some of his troops and some sympathetic Judeans. This citadel (the *Akra*) became a city within a city, a non-Jewish stronghold in the midst of a defenceless Jewish temple city. Its inhabitants—the Syrian troops at least—even used the temple for the worship of their own deities.

Shortly afterwards, in the winter of 167 BCE, Antiochus issued a decree forbidding the practice of traditional Judean religion, including festivals, circumcision, and the possession of copies of law-scrolls. The crowning act, according to the book of Daniel, was the setting up in the Temple of an abomination that was 'desolating' (*shomem*, a pun on Baal *Shamen*, the Syrian 'lord of heaven'). The cult of the God of Israel, whose chief feature was the morning and evening sacrifice, was terminated. Other festivals, such as the king's birthday, were imposed. The traditional liturgical calendar of Jerusalem was abandoned and time was officially measured but by the Seleucid calendar. At this point the issue obviously ceased to be how far Jewish religion should be 'modernised'; the struggle became seen as between a traditional religion or none at all. Reformers, however tenaciously they continued to hold their convictions, had no ground on which to stand in the struggle. Initiative passed to the 'conservatives', who included, it seems, most of the populace.

The Maccabean Revolt

The story of the beginnings of the armed resistance is told in 1 Maccabees 2:1-26. In the village of Modi'in, 17 miles (27 km) northwest of Jerusalem, an aged priest named Mattathias, of the family of Hashmon, killed a Jew who was about to offer a pagan sacrifice. With his five sons, he then withdrew to the countryside to wage a guerrilla war against any Jews who capitulated to the Syrians. This account, though it may contain some truth, is not only intrinsically improbable (an aged priest doing all that?), but contains many recognisable scriptural elements (Moses, Gideon) and smacks in particular of Numbers 25, where Phinehas, whom Mattathias commends to his sons as a model of the 'zealot' priest, slays an idolatrous Israelite. Finally, 1 Maccabees itself is obviously written to enhance the reputation of the Hasmonean dynasty which sprang from the family of Mattathias, and to justify its leadership of the nation by giving it virtually exclusive credit. What is true is that Mattathias's son Judas was the first great leader of armed resistance to the Syrians. His nickname 'Maccabee' ('Hammer') came to be applied to the entire family.

Under Judas, the struggle progressed from campaigns against compliant fellow-Judeans to attacks on Syrian troops. It seems to have had widespread support, and those who fought in support of their traditional religion called themselves the 'pious' (Hebrew *Hasidim*). The Judean highlands are ideal for guerrilla warfare, and the Judean fighters were able to melt away into their villages and regroup at short notice. Judas inflicted four defeats on four different Syrian generals who had tried four different routes into Judea. Since these routes all followed valleys, the opportunities for ambush were excellent. The Syrian regent, Lysias, in control while Antiochus campaigned against Parthia in the east, brought an army by a roundabout route from the south. He was defeated at Judea's southern border, near Beth-Zur.

At this point, war gave way to negotiation. Three years after the decree had been issued, Antiochus rescinded it, and the Temple was rededicated in December 164, an event now commemorated in the Feast of Hanukkah. The *polis* disappeared, but not the Akra. Most *Hasidim* presumably saw the conflict as won. But the impetus generated over three years drove Judas and his brother Simon to more ambitious ventures, in the direction of political independence, even regional power, and perhaps already in the direction of establishing a dynasty. Military campaigns were conducted outside Judea, and Jewish populations in Galilee and Transjordan were brought safely to Judea (again, this detail is suspicious—why were they in any danger? Is this another case of representing 'foreign' lands as dangerous for Jews?)

Judas went on to capture Hebron and destroy its pagan altars. Hebron had not been Judean territory since the Neo-Babylonian period, and Judas seems already to have been embarked on religio-political imperialism (assuming the facts to be correct, he was no more tolerant of non-Jewish altars in his 'realm' than Antiochus had been of the Jewish one in his!) Judas was testing its power, and the Syrians were uncertain of theirs. Judas's luck held for a while; besieging the Akra, he was attacked by the Seleucid general Lysias, who then had to withdraw because of internal rebellion, leaving the *Hasidim* in a strong position. Menelaus was executed and Alcimus installed as high priest. At this point (if not several years earlier) the 'legitimate' high priest, Onias IV, fled to Egypt and built another temple in Leontopolis.

Judas was not satisfied. He quarrelled with Alcimus, who fled to Antioch, and the fight against Syria continued. The Seleucid king Demetrius sent Nicanor with an army, which was defeated. Later that year he sent Bacchides, who was more successful; Judas was at last defeated, and died in battle. The result was that the upper-class reformers began to reassert themselves: Alcimus seems to have taken some pro-Hellenizing measures.

From here onwards, political developments in Judea were governed by the gradual collapse of the Seleucid kingdom in a series of struggles for the throne. The ability of the Seleucids to retain control over Palestine fluctuated, and with it the opportunities for Judea to assert a degree not only of independence but also of control over neighbouring territories. The Hasmoneans' success in revolt gave a springboard for greater achievements. Impotent in the face of a determined and powerful Syria, they could nevertheless exploit its periods of instability. The issues of Hellenism and religious freedom were quickly overtaken by political independence and dynastic ambition.

The Hasmonean Dynasty

Jonathan and Simon

Resistance by the Hasmonean family to the state of affairs in Jerusalem began to build up very slowly under Judas's brother Jonathan, and the struggle reached a climax again when Bacchides, intervening against Jonathan, was defeated. As Syria was still unstable, Jonathan continued to build his power, playing off contenders to the Syrian throne while fortifying Jerusalem, securing Syrian nomination first as high priest, then as governor of Judea, then as governor of Syria, and extending his territorial control to parts of the coastal plain and Samaria—and, according to Jewish sources, destroying non-Jewish altars. His blatant usurpation of the high-priesthood in 152 BCE may very well have created widespread resentment, for although the family was priestly, it had no close links with the traditional high-priestly family. But no reaction is explicitly recorded. Jonathan's astute dealings with the Syrians finally got the better of him, and he was killed treacherously by a pretender to the Syrian throne named Trypho. His brother Simon succeeded him as high priest, and continued to extend the borders of his realm, finally capturing the Akra. Yet he and two of his sons died at the instigation of his son-in-law Ptolemy, with whom they were feasting near Jericho.

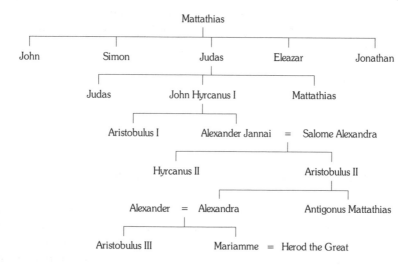

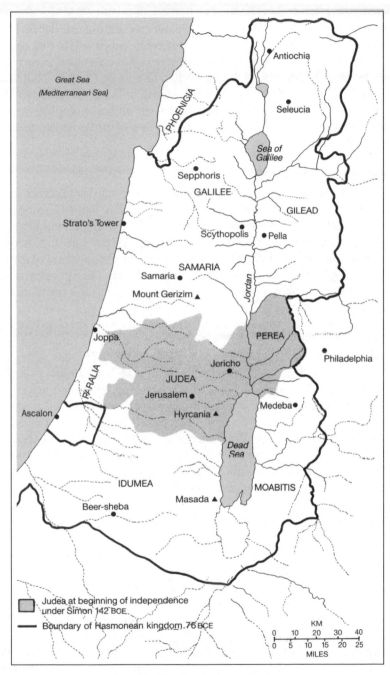

Map 10. *The Hasmonean Kingdom*

John Hyrcanus

John Hyrcanus (Yohanan I), Simon's third son, survived Ptolemy's assault and established himself as his father's successor in Jerusalem, but only to face a siege by the Syrian king Antiochus VII. He had to surrender and disarm, relinquish all territories outside Judea, provide hostages, and pay a large sum of money. Effectively all this re-established Syrian sovereignty. But in the severe disruption into which Syrian affairs promptly fell, Judea could once again assert political independence. Hyrcanus set out to gain control of a realm that was to correspond closely to that ascribed to David. He also enforced circumcision on the conquered Edomites (some may have practised this already), destroyed the Samaritan temple on Gerizim, obliterated the city of Samaria, and plundered the supposed tomb of David in Jerusalem. Hence, before his death in 104 BCE, Hyrcanus had seen Judea triumph over most of (Hellenised) Palestine, though it was hardly a triumph of the traditional Judaism that had inspired the original revolt.

Aristobulus I and Alexander
Hyrcanus's son Aristobulus was high priest for one year only but accomplished three significant things: he took the title of king, he added Galilee to the Hasmonean territories, and turned against members of his family. The assumption of kingship and high-priesthood by one individual is just another symptom of the aspiration of the Hasmoneans to equality with their Hellenistic royal counterparts and of their insensitivity to the religious sentiments of many of their subjects. His successor, Alexander Jannaeus (Yannai), took the further step of minting—with the permission of the Syrian king—his own coins.

Alexander sought, with some limited success, to extend the kingdom further, while encountering opposition within. He had narrow escapes in confrontations with both the Egyptian king Ptolemy Lathyros and the Nabatean king Obodas, while at home he was, according to Josephus, pelted with lemons while officiating as high priest during the festival of Tabernacles (Sukkoth). Josephus, in fact, reports open rebellion against Alexander, resulting in the loss of thousands of lives; and both Josephus and rabbinic sources claim that the Pharisees took an active part in opposition to him. But Alexander survived the rebellion, and celebrated his victory, Josephus tells us, by crucifying 800 of his opponents. The resulting calm enabled him to annex some more territory in Transjordan, so as to bring the Hasmonean kingdom to the largest extent it, or any Israelite kingdom, ever attained.

Salome Alexandra (Shelomzion) and Her Sons
Alexander's widow, Salome, tried to achieve internal tranquillity by appeasing the Pharisees and appointing her son Hyrcanus II, one of their supporters, as high priest. His brother Aristobulus II did not approve. The struggle between them was still unresolved at their mother's death, and although Aristobulus subsequently emerged victorious as king and high priest, the cause of Hyrcanus was taken up by Antipater, the governor of Idumea. Antipater arranged for Hyrcanus to be supported by the Nabatean king Aretas, who laid siege to Aristobulus in Jerusalem.

No sooner was one foreign power established in Judea than another stepped forward. The Romans had already become rulers of Syria, and now their general Pompey intervened. He had a pretext: several sources recount letters of treaty between the Hasmoneans and Rome, going back to Judas Maccabee. Such treaties perhaps constituted, for the Judeans, a plausible, if distant, threat to the Syrians; to the Romans they had provided a 'legitimate interest' in the region and a pretext for future intervention. Pompey adjudicated in favour of Aristobulus; but a few years later he was faced with three delegations from Judea, one from each of the rival Hasmonean brothers plus a third group, possibly Pharisees, asking for the Hasmonean monarchy to be abolished. When Aristobulus pre-empted Pompey's decision and installed himself in Jerusalem, the Roman general lost patience, besieged and captured the city, and even entered the holy of holies, the innermost shrine of the temple. He also took possession of the Hasmonean territory in Palestine except Judea, Idumea, Galilee, and Peraea, and appointed Hyrcanus as a vassal ruler with the title of 'ethnarch' ('chief of the nation'), a powerful title but not as fine as 'king'. Aristobulus and three of his children were taken hostage to Rome. Judea's independence had effectively come to an end after less than a century.

Herod the Great

The rise of Herod the Idumean was prepared by his father Antipater and secured by his combination of charm, astuteness, and ruthlessness. It was also promoted by the behaviour of his rivals. The Hasmoneans did not acknowledge that Rome was there to stay; Herod did. Aristobulus's son Alexander escaped custody and went back to Judea to campaign. He was defeated by the Romans, aided by a Jewish army—led by Antipater, still investing in the future (including making friends with Mark Antony who was among the Roman commanders). Then Aristobulus attempted the same escapade as his son, with similar lack of success. The challenge to Rome presented by Parthians—now in control in Transjordan and threatening Syria and Palestine—made Judea of some importance to Rome, now treating Judea as a Roman possession. However, what might have been a dismal prospect for Judea was redeemed by the ever opportunistic Antipater, who seized a chance to help Caesar when the latter was in Egypt pursuing Pompey. Caesar bestowed on the Jews, inside and outside Judea, exemptions from several obligations to Rome, and in Judea itself appointed the Idumean as procurator. Antipater promptly appointed his sons Phasael governor of Jerusalem and Herod governor of Galilee. The whole family made itself disliked by the Judeans by its complicity in any Roman measures, however unpopular. Not surprisingly, Antipater was assassinated—poisoned by a popular leader named Malichus. But Phasael and Herod remained in firm control, with the support of the new Roman ruler of Syria, Mark Antony.

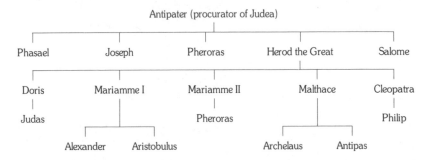

Even so, the Hasmonean line and its hopes were not extinguished. One survivor was Hyrcanus II, high priest though powerless. Antigonus, the remaining son of Aristobulus II, still awaited an opportunity to reassert his claims—an opportunity that presented itself when Antony's liaison with Cleopatra invited the Parthians to invade Palestine. They installed Antigonus as high priest and king, and he took the Jewish name of Mattathias. Hyrcanus and Phasael were captured: Hyrcanus's ears were cut off, invalidating him for the priesthood, while Phasael committed suicide. Herod fled, eventually to Rome, where he somehow won Roman appointment as king of Judea. With Roman military support the Parthians were driven back and Herod eventually forced his way to Jerusalem and had Antigonus beheaded. With the last Hasmonean pretender dead, and Hyrcanus out of the picture, Herod could now play the true successor by marrying the Hasmonean princess Mariamne.

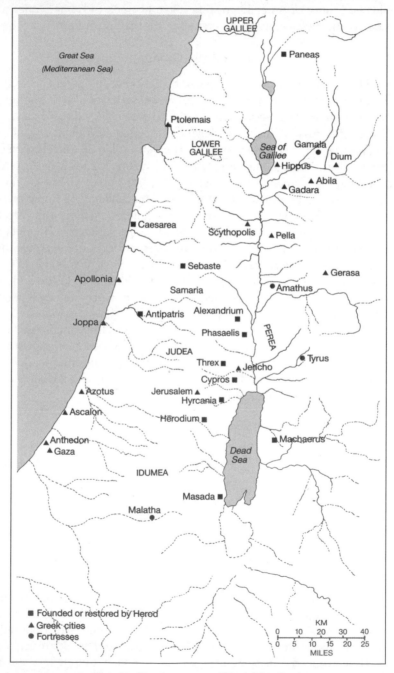

Map 11. *The Conquests of Herod the Great*

In 37 BCE Herod became king of Judea—and of Idumea, Perea, Galilee, and Jaffa. His subjects included Jews and non-Jews and his kingdom seethed with irreconcilable interests, given the history of the previous 150 years. As an Idumean he was disliked by Judeans; as the usurper of the Hasmoneans he was resented. During his reign he created his own 'aristocracy' from those loyal to Rome and appointed by himself. He regularly replaced the high priests, often bringing them in from outside Judea. But he apparently favoured traditional religious groups who did not oppose him, such as Pharisees and Essenes. His own loyalty to Judaism was probably genuine: at all events, he did nothing that indicated the contrary (apart from placing an eagle over the gateway to the Jerusalem temple). Even in his private residences there was nothing to offend Jewish religious scruples. But perhaps the most widespread attitude towards Herod is reflected in the *Psalms of Solomon*, a collection of poems written during his reign. One of these (no. 17) calls for a king of David's line who will reprove the Gentiles and reign justly. No Idumeans, no Hellenisers—but no priests, either!

Apart from pacifying such a mixture of subjects, Herod also had to obey Rome, to whom he was entirely answerable. His kingdom was part of Rome's bulwark against Parthia. At first, 'Rome' meant Antony, an old friend. Antony's defeat by Octavian in 31 BCE threatened to topple Herod. To secure his position, Herod had to meet Octavian, and before he left Jerusalem he took the precaution of having the last Hasmonean figurehead, the earless Hyrcanus, executed on some probably false charge, and placed his own Hasmonean wife and mother-in-law under guard. Only a few years later he had both killed; later still, the remaining members of the Hasmonean family. Perhaps Herod was genuinely suspicious, or perhaps he was being callously pragmatic. We shall not know; possibly Herod did not know—at any rate, he mourned the death of Mariamne for the rest of his life. But Herod went on to dispose of more members of his family, prompting the comment from Octavian that he would sooner be Herod's pig than his son. (Jews did not eat pork.)

Despite Herod's homicidal tendencies, Octavian decided that he was nevertheless the best option for Rome, and not long afterwards gave him large tracts of territory in Palestine and Transjordan. During his reign the inhabitants of his kingdom, and indeed many non-subjects, enjoyed his generosity. Everywhere, he built: he was arguably the greatest architectural patron in the entire Greco-Roman period, in terms of both quantity and quality. He built temples, baths, aqueducts, and other public works throughout the Hellenistic world. The motives behind this probably included personal esteem, though it is arguable that Herod was attempting to project a favourable attitude towards Judea and its religion among its non-Jewish (especially culturally Greek) neighbours. At home, he built for himself several well fortified, lavish, and near-inaccessible residences, such as Herodion and Masada; he rebuilt the port of Strato's Tower and renamed the city Caesarea, which became the largest harbour on the entire Mediterranean. In Jerusalem he built two fortified palaces, the Antonia fortress on the northwest corner of the Temple mound, and another on the western hill of the city, dominated by three towers named after his wife Mariamne, his brother Phasael, and his friend Hippicus. But his most famous building was, of course, the new temple, which was begun in 20 BCE and whose finishing touches were completed only a few years before it was destroyed in 70 CE. Its precincts were twice the area of the previous Temple, being situated on an artificial platform.

Herod also spent on other projects. Outside Palestine he subsidised games and festivals. And everywhere he provided water; his palaces were supplied by aqueducts, as were Caesarea and Jerusalem (impressive remains are still visible at both). Not only cities, but also the countryside benefited from improved water supplies; thanks to improved irrigation, the kingdom became much more productive agriculturally. And when famine struck at home, Herod supplied grain from his own funds.

How was this massive expenditure funded? Some of the funds were personal: income from estates and revenue from commercial concessions; but much of it came from taxes. The prosperity of the land certainly increased through better agriculture (helped by irrigation) and increased trade, thanks to peace secured by Octavian's treaty with Parthia in 20 BCE. But prosperity did not necessarily induce popularity.

Herod is widely depicted as a despotic, cruel, and even insane ruler. But an equally good case can be made for his sensitivity to his Jewish subjects and their religion, his concern for Jews outside Palestine, and his determination to preserve as much independence as possible within the protection of Rome. Because Herod's private life was more interesting to ancient writers—as it is to many modern ones—and because of the legend in Matthew 2 that he slaughtered male children, he has tended to be judged not as a ruler but as a human, on personality rather than policy. As a human he was arguably not much worse than the Hasmoneans. His realm was unstable; he was unpopular, walking a tightrope. In his later years a painful disease may have deranged him. He was also ostentatious. But if one considers what was achieved and what might have otherwise occurred, he does not deserve to be a byword for tyranny. To assess his rule fairly, one needs only to contrast the state of affairs before and after his reign. The chaos in which the Hasmonean dynasty ended was due to the Roman presence but equally to internal, even fratricidal, rivalry. Herod appeased Rome and brutally suppressed even the possibility of rivalry. After his death the enormous tensions were released, and in 74 CE the final conflict between Jewish fanaticism and Roman intransigence was to be played out in one of Herod's own fortress-palaces, Masada.

Further Reading

L.L. Grabbe, *Judaism from Cyrus to Hadrian* (2 vols.; Minneapolis: Fortress Press, 1992) gives a fairly comprehensive review of the sources; also his *A History of the Jews and Judaism in the Second Temple Period* (Library of Second Temple Studies, 47; London: T&T Clark International, 2004). For the impact of Hellenism in Palestine the indispensable study is still M. Hengel, *Judaism and Hellenism: Studies in their Encounter in Palestine during the Early Hellenistic Period* (London: SCM Press, 2nd edn, 1974). E. Bickerman's, *From Ezra to the Last of the Maccabees* (New York: Schocken Books, 1962) is a classic set of studies, including one on the Maccabean conflicts.

On Herod the Great, see Peter Richardson, *Herod: King of the Jews and Friend of the Romans* (Columbia: University of South Carolina Press, 1996).

Part III

LITERATURE AND LIFE

Excavations at Mari, Tell Hariri, Syria

Genesis

Chapter 8

CREATION AND ORIGIN STORIES

No section of the Old Testament has been more fiercely argued about than Genesis 1–11. Because the Bible was held to be inspired by God, Jews and Christians believed for many centuries that the content of Genesis 1 to 11 was accurate science, history, and geography. This did not, however, prevent thinkers from discussing some of the difficulties raised by the narratives. For example, the creation of light before the creation of the sun (Genesis 1:3, 16) worried interpreters from at least the fifth to the nineteenth century. The fact that the moon is not a light-emitting but a light-reflecting body was accepted by Calvin in the sixteenth century. Calvin also acknowledged that—against Genesis 1:16, where the moon is identified as one of the 'two great lights'—there are in fact planets much larger than the moon. His solution was that Genesis 1 described the world as it would have been seen with the naked eye by Moses and his contemporaries, not as it was seen through the telescopes of his own time. Despite such concessions, however, Genesis 1–11 continued to be regarded as the prime authority regarding the origins of the world and humankind until the end of the eighteenth century.

In the 1820s, Old Testament interpreters were challenged by the findings of geologists, who argued that the world was thousands (sic) of years older than was implied by the Old Testament figures. (According to Archbishop Ussher's very influential interpretation of these figures the world had been created in 4004 BCE.) The response of orthodox interpreters to the geologists was that the Flood had destroyed and distorted the original layers of the earth. The geologists were therefore being misled by their findings. The next challenge came from the publication of Darwin's *Origin of Species* in 1859. This was a challenge to Genesis 2–3, for if it was true that humankind had gradually evolved from elementary life forms, what was one to make of the biblical story that a once perfect human couple had 'fallen'?

The most interesting challenge to the interpretation of Genesis 1–11, however— and the one that will concern us here—came towards the end of the nineteenth century with the discovery of ancient Babylonian texts that contained material similar to that in Genesis 1–11. On 3 December 1872 a young scholar on the staff of the British Museum, George Smith, gave a lecture entitled 'The Chaldean Account of the Deluge'. It dealt with what is now known to be part of Tablet XI of the *Epic of Gilgamesh*. In 1875 Smith announced, in a letter to a London newspaper, the discovery of a Babylonian account of creation, part of the text now known as *Enuma Elish*. These discoveries aroused a great deal of interest, and within a few years Old Testament scholars began to argue that the material in Genesis was in fact dependent upon Babylonian material.

An important point was reached with the publication in 1895 of H. Gunkel's *Creation and Chaos at the Beginning and End of Time*. Gunkel argued that the Genesis creation story was dependent upon the Babylonian text *Enuma Elish*; but he also went further than this. In *Enuma Elish* the universe is recreated by the god Marduk, after he has met and killed in battle the goddess Tiamat; he creates it from parts of her dismembered carcass. Now there is no hint in Genesis 1 that God created the world after having vanquished another god; but there are hints elsewhere in the Old Testament of a conflict between Yhwh and some kind of monster, which preceded the creation, for example in Psalm 89:9-12. Other examples are Isaiah 51:9-13 and Job 26:12, where God is said to have defeated not only Rahab but also a 'fleeing serpent'. It will be noticed that, as well as, or as part of, defeating Rahab, God overcame the raging of the sea; and this is an immediate reminder that according to Genesis 1:2 there was a watery chaos present before God began to create an ordered world. Gunkel argued that passages such as Psalm 89:10-12 showed that a myth of God's defeat of the forces of chaos was known in ancient Israel, and that the Genesis creation story was directly or indirectly dependent on *Enuma Elish*.

For a long time after the appearance of Gunkel's book it was commonly accepted that *Enuma Elish* was the source behind Genesis 1. When, for example, the order in which things were made was extracted from *Enuma Elish* and compared with Genesis 1, the correspondences were striking:

Enuma Elish	*Genesis 1:1–2:3*
• Divine spirit and cosmic matter are coexistent and coeternal	Divine matter creates cosmic matter and exists independently of it
• Primeval chaos: Tiamat enveloped in darkness	The earth a desolate waste with darkness covering the deep (*tehom*)
• [Light emanating from the gods]	Light created
• The creation of the firmament	The creation of the firmament
• The creation of dry land	The creation of dry land
• The creation of the luminaries	The creation of the luminaries
• The creation of man	The creation of man
• The gods rest and celebrate	God rests and sanctifies the seventh day

This table is taken from Heidel (1963a: 129), who in fact was doubtful whether Genesis was dependent on *Enuma Elish*; and it is vital that readers should read *Enuma Elish* for themselves in order to see to what extent it is similar to Genesis 1. With regard to the Flood, there can be no argument. The biblical account is only one of a number of flood stories.

Sumerian and Akkadian Texts

The situation today with regard to Genesis 1–11 and other texts from the ancient Near East is much more diverse and complicated than it was in Gunkel's day. The object of the summary that now follows is not to try to prove or disprove the dependence of Genesis on other traditions. It is, rather, to indicate what themes are treated in the texts that have been discovered. This will give a range of possibilities in the light of which Genesis 1–11 can then be read.

First of all, a distinction must be made between the Sumerian texts, and the Akkadian texts of the Semites who founded the later empires of Assyria and Babylon. In the Sumerian texts about creation there is no reference to a battle between gods preceding the creation. In fact, creation by division of things into classes, as we also find it in Genesis 1, seems to be indicated by the admittedly partly fragmentary evidence (Pettinato 1971: 31; *ANET*: 43). It is only in Akkadian texts that a conflict precedes creation; but there are also Akkadian texts in which the conflict is absent (Heidel 1963: 62-66).

Regarding the creation of man, there is again a difference between Sumerian and Akkadian texts. One of the former allows that man may have grown spontaneously from the ground, rather in the way that the earth generates plants and trees in Genesis 1:11-12 (Pettinato 1971: 31). Humankind was like a wild beast, eating grass and going on all fours, and it was necessary for the gods to introduce civilisation in order to complete the creation of humankind. Akkadian texts, together with other Sumerian compositions, know only of the forming of humankind from clay, in some cases, mixed with the blood of a god, or, in the case of *Enuma Elish*, from the blood of a traitor god (*ANET*: 68). Both Sumerian and Akkadian texts are agreed that the reason why the gods created humankind was so that the human race could perform manual labour for the gods, such as building canals or cities. However, there is apparently a difference between Sumerian and Akkadian texts about the dignity or otherwise of this work (Pettinato 1971: 25-30). Sumerian texts have a high view of the value of civilisation, and therefore regard it as a privilege for humankind to be allowed by the gods to share its benefits. Akkadian texts, on the other hand, regard the work imposed by the gods as a heavy burden.

On the question of the destiny of humankind there is also a difference between Sumerian and Akkadian texts, a difference pointed up by the existence of Sumerian and Akkadian stories about Gilgamesh. In the Sumerian story *The Death of Gilgamesh* (*ANET*: 50-51), Gilgamesh is told to be content with the fact that he is to die. After all, he has enjoyed great privileges in his life and has been a mighty and victorious king. His reputation will live on after him. The Akkadian *Epic of Gilgamesh*, which is based upon some of the Sumerian stories (Tigay 1982), is far more pessimistic. The death of Gilgamesh's companion Enkidu (*ANET*: 87-88) plunges Gilgamesh into despair, and into a quest for immortality that remains unsatisfied (see generally George 2000).

The Problem of Sources

These, and other themes, will be picked up as Genesis 1–11 is examined in more detail. Before this is done, however, we must briefly consider two questions: the use of sources in the biblical material and the term 'myth'. The opening chapters of Genesis were the first parts of the Old Testament to be subjected to source criticism. This was because in Genesis 1:1–2:4a, the divine name *'elohim* (God) is used throughout, whereas in Genesis 2:4b–3:24 the divine name is consistently *Yhwh 'elohim*, rendered in the standard English translations as 'the LORD God'. Already in the eighteenth century it was suggested that Moses (the presumed author according to eighteenth-century opinion) had used two different documents in compiling chapters 1–3. The search for sources was then extended further, and it was argued (still in the eighteenth century) that the Flood narrative could be attributed to two sources, one of which used the divine name *'elohim*, and the other of which used Yhwh (Rogerson 1984: 19).

However, this is not the end of the matter of sources. Genesis 1:1–2:4a and Genesis 2:4b–3:24 have both been further broken down into possible components used by their authors. It has long been recognised, for example, that Genesis 1 combines eight creative actions into six days of creation, necessitating two acts of creation on two days, the third and the sixth (Genesis 1:9-13, 24-31). It has also been suggested that Genesis 1 combines two versions of creation, one in which God created by uttering commands and another in which he created by working like a craftsman. (See further Rogerson 1991.) The stories of the creation of humankind in Genesis 2:4b-25 and of the Fall in Genesis 3 have been held to be originally separate stories that were later joined together to produce a unified narrative.

In the following detailed comments on Genesis 1–11, sources and sources within the sources will be largely ignored. This is not because we reject the validity of source criticism; in fact, we accept its validity. At the same time it is not clear to us that the best way to understand what Genesis 1–11 is trying to convey is to divide it into sources. We are much more interested in identifying the motifs and questions contained in the final form of Genesis 1–11 and in seeing how the text wrestles with these ideas. In this connection, it is interesting to compare the Genesis material with Sumerian and Akkadian texts, as already mentioned. We know, from the history of the composition of *the Epic of Gilgamesh*, that ancient writers did indeed adapt and re-use older stories, and that once a new, lengthy composition had been established it could still be revised and added to (Tigay 1982). This is, indeed, the justification for investigating the sources behind Genesis 1–11. But because we cannot identify the basic units used by the biblical writers, it is safer to content ourselves with comparing the motifs of themes of Genesis 1–11 with those of other ancient Near Eastern texts. In this way we acknowledge our belief that the biblical writers took over and adapted popular existing stories, while we confess our ignorance about the form and content of the actual stories that the biblical writers used.

The Meaning of 'Myth'

This leads us to the problem of 'myth'. Genesis 1–11 is often described as myth; what does this mean? If we define a myth as a story about the gods, Genesis 1–11 is not myth. It is true that these chapters tell of the involvement of the God of Israel with the origin and earliest history of the world and humankind, but there is nothing comparable here to what we find in Sumerian, Akkadian, and Greek myths, where many gods are present, often in conflict and disagreement, and struggling for ascendancy. If, however, we mean by myth a story set in the beginning of time—a time different from that of the storyteller but one in which the conditions of the storyteller's own time were established once and for all—then Genesis 1–11 can be described as myth. There are clear indications in the text that the time of the stories is different from that of the storyteller. Take, for example, Genesis 6:4:

> There were giants in the earth *in those days.*

The promise of God to humankind, in Genesis 8:22, that he will never again destroy all that lives marks off the storyteller's time from a time when such destruction was nearly accomplished. Also, the storyteller of Genesis was quite aware that in his time the nations did *not* have a common language, and that the presumed existence of a universal tongue, before the attempt to build the Tower of Babel, therefore took place in a different era. The same would be true of the claim that before the Flood people lived to be hundreds of years old.

If we accept that Genesis 1–11 is myth in the sense just defined, we must also say that we reject the popular understanding of myth as something that is not true. The stories of all the peoples of the ancient world that wrestled with questions of life, death, and origins were true for at least some of those who wrote and heard them. This was not so much an intellectual truth as a truth that enabled the world to be coped with and lived in. Faced with overwhelming manifestations of power in the natural world in storms, floods, droughts, and burning heat, and faced also with death, the inhabitants of the ancient world had to domesticate the world of nature in order somehow to feel at home in it. This was done by giving things names, by classifying them into groups, by devising strategies that might cope with floods and droughts, and by telling stories that set humankind within some sort of cosmic framework. The truth of these stories was their effectiveness in enabling those who heard and told them to cope with the world.

And so it is with Genesis 1–11. The truth of these stories is not to be measured by their agreement with modern astronomy, biology, geography, history, and linguistics. Their truth is bound up with their effectiveness in explaining for the Old Testament writers the origin and destiny of the world and humanity in the light of their belief in God.

Genesis 1:1–2:4a

The key to understanding creation in the Old Testament is the word 'order'. To say that the world is created is to say that it is ordered: divided into various sectors to each of which belong appropriate life forms.

This can be seen from the following diagram:

Sector	Life forms
Heavens	luminaries (i.e. sun and moon); birds humans
Earth	animals
	plants and trees
Waters	fishes and sea creatures

This may look at first sight to be so obvious that it is hardly worth mentioning. However, in the light of other world-views of antiquity it is quite striking. There is no place in this scheme for the gods that we find in Sumerian and Akkadian stories. The nearest we get to the heavenly beings of those texts is the luminaries, but their role is strictly limited to that of giving light. Nor do we find any place for chaos monsters of the seas: the seas and their life forms in Genesis 1 belong entirely to this world and have no supernatural powers. Thus the rather obvious (to us) order implied in Genesis 1 is significant in what it omits. It portrays an order of things entirely subordinate to one God.

Genesis 1 not only speaks of order but exemplifies it, in the construction of its narrative. The first three days balance days four to six:

Day 1	Creation of light	Day 4	Creation of lights
Day 2	Creation of the firmament separates waters from waters, resulting in the heavens and the seas	Day 5	Creation of the sea creatures and birds
Day 3	Creation of dry land and plants and trees	Day 6	Creation of animals and humans

But this carefully constructed narrative has a further aim: to order time as well as life-forms and their sectors. The ordering of time into blocks of seven days, of which one is a day of rest, while so familiar to us, was unique in the ancient world, so far as we know. Even if it was not unique, it was an important way of organising time into manageable blocks, and it was a further way of asserting God's sovereignty over the created world. By observing the Sabbath commandment, Israelites would both imitate God and remember that he was the author of time.

The climax of the creation story in Genesis 1 is the creation of male and female. The meaning of the statement that humanity is made in the image and likeness of God (Genesis 1:26-27) has caused more discussion and disagreement than any other passage in the chapter. Whatever it means, it at least indicates that the relationship between God and humanity is one of dignity, responsibility, and intimacy. Compared with Sumerian and Akkadian texts, which agree that humankind was created to perform manual tasks for the gods, Genesis 1:26-27 is breathtaking in the way it accords dignity to the human race. It is true that the command to multiply and to subdue the earth (Genesis 1.28ff.) is a command that will entail work; and the text implies that this work will be carried out by humankind as God's representative. But there is a great difference between the gods making humans to serve as their lackeys and God entrusting to humanity a world that has been carefully ordered.

It has often been pointed out that prior to the Flood, only plants, not meat, are allowed to humanity as well as to the animals. This 'vegetarianism' is reminiscent of the Sumerian story that humankind originally went on all fours and ate grass. Within the narrative structure of Genesis 1–11, however, the contrast between the vegetarianism of Genesis 1 and the concession that meat can be eaten after the flood (Genesis 9:3-6) indicates that, for the final editors of these chapters, the world described in Genesis 1 is not the world of human experience. The world of human experience is the post-Flood world of a meat-eating humanity and meat-eating animals. In the vegetarian world of Genesis 1 that conflict is not part of the created order. It is noteworthy that the vegetarian world reappears in visions of the time when God recreates the heavens and the earth (Isaiah 65:17-25; see further Rogerson 1991).

Genesis 1, then, has taken the idea of creation as ordering the world and setting limits to its powers, and has given us a comprehensive and artistic statement of how humankind is to conceive of its place and duties in the world, albeit a world which does not entirely correspond to the world of human experience. One further aspect must be mentioned. In passages such as Leviticus 26 creation is linked to morality and obedience. Israel is promised that if it obeys the commandments God will give the rain at its proper times, and the earth will be fruitful and abundant. If Israel is disobedient the opposite will happen. The earth will produce no food, and the trees will be bare of fruit. It is legitimate to take this theme back to Genesis 1 and to the narrative contrast between the vegetarian world of Genesis 1 and the meat-eating world of Genesis 9, which results from human disobedience. If we do not, we may be left with the idea that God has entrusted an ordered world to humankind, but will not be bothered about how humanity discharges this trust. Nothing could be further from the truth. Genesis 1 bestows upon humankind a dignity that comes from God's graciousness. The world is not, or should not be thought of, as a place of interplay between overwhelming forces in whose presence humankind is merely a plaything. The world is subject to the will of a power who deals personally and graciously with humankind but who is not indifferent to human wickedness. This is a moral view of the world and carries moral consequences. However strange it may sound to us today that natural disasters have moral causes, this was certainly an integral part of the Old Testament understanding of creation.

Genesis 2:4b-25

The second chapter of Genesis is often called the second or alternative account of creation. In fact, it says little about creation compared to Genesis 1. It says nothing about the creation of the sun and the moon, or the seas or sea creatures. The setting is a part of the earth rather than the whole universe, and the dominant figure is the first male. The theme of his creation out of the dust invites comparison with other ancient Near Eastern texts. In the epic of Atra-hasis (Lambert and Millard 1969: 59), man is created from a mixture of clay and blood:

> Let one god be slaughtered
> So that all the gods may be cleansed in a dipping,
> From his flesh and blood
> Let Nintu mix clay,
> That god and man
> May be thoroughly mixed in the clay.

What is interesting about this passage is that it implies that humans somehow share something of the life of the gods. The blood that was necessary to create human life belonged to a god.

The Genesis account (Genesis 2:7) allows for no possibility that the human race could have originated from a divine being. It comes from the earth and is enlivened not by divine blood but by divine breath. (The Hebrew word here, *neshamah* ['breath'], does not mean spirit [*ruah*], as is sometimes asserted in student essays.)

The reason why the human race is created is in order to tend the earth (Genesis 2:15). We are again reminded of the Sumerian and Akkadian texts which say that humans are created in order to work for the gods, but again we find that Genesis stresses the graciousness of this arrangement. God goes out of his way to find companionship for the first man. The naming of the animals recalls the theme of creation as order. If things are to be classified, they must have names. In this case, the order is imposed by the man upon the natural world, as he gives names to the animals and living things as he sees them (Genesis 2:19-20).

The creation of woman (Genesis 2:21-3) indicates, as does Genesis 1:27, that complete humanity consists of male and female. But Genesis 2 goes further by stressing the social dimension of the male–female relationship. They are to become as one person (Hebrew *basar*, 'flesh') by setting up home together. That this is not to be understood in a physical sexual sense is indicated by the statement that they knew no shame in spite of being naked.

Genesis 3

Of all the chapters of Genesis 1–11, chapter 3, which relates the events surrounding the Fall, is the most difficult to understand. First, it has played such an important role in Christian theology that it is difficult to read it as though this use had never existed. The point is not whether Christian theology has validly used Genesis 3; it is simply what was the writer trying to convey? Second, there are no direct parallels with Genesis 3 in ancient Near Eastern literature which might shed light on it (although individual motifs occur also in other writings). Third, there is the puzzling fact that Genesis 3 is not alluded to anywhere else in the Old Testament. This may, of course, be simply an accident; or it may be that Genesis 3 serves to symbolise and dramatise ideas that *are* common in the Old Testament. It is also possible that it is a very late text.

The closest parallel to Genesis 3 in other ancient Near Eastern writings is also found in the Old Testament, in Ezekiel 28:11-19's poem about the prince of Tyre. Here, the king of Tyre, who presumably personifies the rich trading city itself, is described as having been in Eden, the garden of God, and of having been perfect until the day that he committed evil and was expelled to the earth from the mountain of God by a protecting cherub. The cause of his downfall was pride at his great beauty and riches. Although we must not overlook the differences between Ezekiel 28 and Genesis 3—the former has no serpent, no woman, no tree of good and evil or of life—there are sufficient similarities (Eden, expulsion, guardian cherub) to suggest that both of these chapters are based upon some other, yet undiscovered story.

When we turn to ancient Near Eastern literature, we find a number of distant parallels. The Sumerian *Enki and Ninhursag* (*ANET*: 37-41) is set in the land of Dilmun, which is 'pure, clean and bright' and where

> The lion kills not,
> The wolf snatches not the lamb,
> Unknown is the kid-devouring *wild dog*,
> …Its old woman [says] not 'I am an old woman';
> Its old man [says] not 'I am an old man'.

This situation seems to be disturbed when Enki, the divine ruler of Dilmun, cuts down and eats eight plants created by the goddess Ninhursag. Ninhursag now curses Enki, saying that she will not look upon him until he dies. He presumably (though the text does not say this explicitly) begins to experience pains. The Sumerian gods, the Anunnaki, assemble; a fox brings Ninhursag to the assembly, and she creates eight deities from eight parts of Enki's body where he experiences pain. We are not told that Enki is now cured or that he does not die, although these things might be inferred from the text. The motifs in common with Genesis 3 are, first, the existence of a place where the animals are tame and there is no death (cp. also Isaiah 11:6-9); second, the coming of sickness and death as a result of the cutting down and eating of plants; and, third, the birth of offspring as a result of bodily pains—albeit male, and not female.

A central role in Genesis 3 is that played by the serpent. The closest parallel found in other ancient Near Eastern literature comes from the flood story in the *Epic of Gilgamesh* (Heidel 1963b: 91-92). Gilgamesh has travelled to visit Utnapishtim, the hero of the flood in this text, who gained immortality by building a ship and surviving the flood. Utnapishtim tells Gilgamesh of a plant that restores people's youth. Gilgamesh gets it by diving to the bottom of the sea. He means to keep it until he is an old man and then to eat it. Unfortunately on the return journey from visiting Utnapishtim, a serpent snatches it, and then sloughs its skin.

The text contains the theme of a serpent depriving man of rejuvenation. Von Soden (1985: 181) has suggested an Egyptian source for the serpent in Genesis 3, referring to a story of an island paradise guarded by a divine serpent.

Genesis 3 itself is best understood in terms of a 'before' and 'after': The 'after' is the world familiar to the writer. Men and women die and the human race is continued by the painful female experience of childbirth. Serpents slither on their bellies and arouse revulsion in human beings. The earth is not wholly benign, but produces thorns and thistles as well as food. Tending the land is hard work. This 'after', the world known to the writer, is the result of what was done in the 'before', a world no longer available to human experience. That earlier world is envisaged as full of wonders—epitomised by a serpent that can speak and go upright, and that arouses no revulsion. Contact between God and the man and woman was immediate. All this changed because the man and woman proved to be unworthy of the trust that was placed in their hands. Thus, in contrast to the Sumerian and Akkadian texts, humankind's hard lot in the world is the result not of a decree of lazy gods, but of the violation by humans themselves of a trust that was part of a favoured, blessed situation in which God had placed them.

But we must go a little further than this. We have already noted that passages such as Isaiah 65:17-25 envisage a world restored by God to what we have called the 'before'; and it is legitimate to ask whether such a restoration was envisaged by the writer of Genesis 3. If it was not, then humans, not God, would have the final word about the destiny of the world and humankind. A comment is also necessary about the serpent. It is worthwhile noting that the idea of doing wrong does not originate with humankind but comes from another creature—even though humankind is fully responsible for actually doing what is wrong. This means that we should not read Genesis 3 to mean that wrong is simply something within human beings. In the real world it is much more complex than that. Wrongdoing is socially transmitted from generation to generation, and becomes almost demonic when a situation presents someone who is trying to do what is right only with a choice of wrongs. We do not know, of course, whether these thoughts were in the mind of the writer of Genesis 3; but they are certainly explored elsewhere in the Old Testament. The story of Moses, for example, shows the dilemmas faced by someone responsible both to God and to an unwilling and reluctant people. Jeremiah, in advocating submission to Babylon, as penance for the erring Judeans, was branded a traitor. Whatever the writer of Genesis 3 had in mind we may legitimately interpret this chapter as an embodiment of the idea that the present world is not what God intended, and that this is somehow bound up with human betrayal of a divine trust.

Genesis 4

The motif of quarrelling brothers is found in the literature of many nations (see Gaster 1969: 51-55). In the Old Testament such conflicts occur between Jacob and Esau (Genesis 25:29-34; 27:1-41) and between Amnon and Absalom (2 Samuel

13:22-33). Such stories may, of course, reflect the facts of life in some families; however, they also have a symbolic dimension. The quarrel between a shepherd and a farmer is contained in the Sumerian text *Dumuzi and Enkimdu* (*ANET*: 41-42). Here, the shepherd-god Dumuzi is rejected by the goddess Inanna. She favours the farmer-god Enkimdu and intends to marry him. Dumuzi argues his superiority in what he can produce as a shepherd, compared to that offered by a farmer, and begins a quarrel with Enkimdu, in which he appears to be victorious and to win over Inanna. We can detect behind this story the competing strategies of using land for agriculture, as against using it to graze animals.

In the story of Cain and Abel it is the shepherd Abel who has the initial advantage, when God favours his offerings. The farmer, Cain, seems to have the last word when he kills Abel. However, this is not the end of the matter, because the blood of the murdered Abel cries out for justice, and God declares that because of this blood Cain will get no return from the land if he tries to work it. There may be a hint here of the moral interpretation of the reason for agricultural failures. More striking, however, is what we might call an anti-civilisation theme. Cain is the founder of the first city to be mentioned in Genesis (4:17); and the development of civilised skills seems to bring more strife and killing in its train (Genesis 4:19-24). If this reading is correct, then Genesis views the rise of civilisation more negatively than the Sumerian texts. It must be added that, in its form in Genesis 4, the story is a highly artistic composition expressing hope. The repeated use of the word 'brother' (in verses 8 to 11) contrasts with Cain's unbrotherly behaviour, and the chapter ends on a note of hope, with people beginning to call upon the name of God. In the darkness of human wickedness vividly portrayed in this chapter, God is still at work.

Genesis 5

The list of the long-lived men (and presumably women) who lived prior to the Flood invites comparison with the Sumerian King Lists, although the men named in Genesis were not kings. The Sumerian list (*ANET*: 265-66) gives figures for lengths of reigns compared to which the Genesis longevity figures of 900-plus years seem insignificant! The first two kings, for example, are claimed to have ruled (between them) for 64,800 years! After the flood, reigns were shorter. Twenty-three kings reigned for 24,510 years, three months and three-and-a-half days. We can assume that the Sumerian lists and the Genesis material shared the same function: to mark off present time from the time before the Flood. What is being said is that the world of the time of the writers is not the same as the world as it once was, when life expectancy was far greater.

Genesis 6–9

The story of a universal flood is attested in some ancient Near Eastern literature. As we have seen, it is alluded to in the Sumerian king lists. There is also a Sumerian flood story, in which the hero, Ziusudra, survives by building a boat after being warned by a god of the impending flood. The flood lasts seven days and nights, after which Ziusudra leaves the ark, prostrates himself before the sun-god Utu, and is finally granted life 'like that of a god' (*ANET*: 42-44). The reason for the flood, however, is not clear from this fragmentary text.

In Akkadian texts there is a flood story preserved in various versions whose hero is Atra-hasis. The reason for the flood, according to this story, is that humans have become numerous, and their noise has become more than the gods can bear. The hero is again informed, as in the Sumerian story, by one of the gods, that a flood is to occur. Atra-hasis is instructed not only to build a ship, but to take into it his family and animals (Lambert and Millard 1969: 93). This, then, is a rescue operation not only for humankind, but for other living creatures also, as in the case of Genesis 6–9.

In Tablet XI of the *Epic of Gilgamesh* we find probably the closest parallel to the biblical story (Heidel 1963b: 80-88). The gods decide to destroy humankind, although no reason is given for this at the beginning of the account. The hero, Utnapishtim, learns of this via one of the gods, and proceeds to build a ship and to make preparations, which are described in some detail. When the time comes to enter the ship, he takes animals and craftsmen on board, as well as his family. The flood turns out to be so violent that it frightens even the gods.

When the ship grounds as the flood subsides, Utnapishtim releases a dove and then a swallow, both of which return. A raven, however, does not return—an implication that the earth is once again fruitful. The party leaves the ship and offers sacrifices, which, when the gods smell them, cause them to gather 'like flies over the sacrificer'. For saving humankind and human civilisation, Utnapishtim and his wife are made to be like gods and to live in a far district.

In the Genesis Flood story there is no suggestion that the punishment to be inflicted is too severe. The thoughts and intentions of human hearts are, or have become, evil (Genesis 6:5), and humans (and possibly animals) have corrupted the earth (Genesis 6:11-22). Moreover, because Genesis has one God, as opposed to many, the biblical account necessarily lacks the motifs that one of the gods secretly informed a human about what was to happen, and that the gods were themselves terrified when the flood came. In Genesis, God intends that a righteous man (Genesis 6:9) and his family should enable a new start to be made. Noah is, to be sure, rewarded, but not with immortality. The Genesis story is concerned with God's justice and with his mercy.

After the waters have subsided, and Noah has discovered, by sending out birds, that some land is dry, and has also offered a pleasing sacrifice to God, there is a renewal of creation, but not exactly of the creation described in Genesis 1. The language of Genesis 9:1-7 refers to Genesis 1:28-30, with the addition that humans can now eat meat. This is preceded by a puzzling, perhaps significant, statement that God will never again curse the earth; and the reason why he will not do so is that the inclination of humankind is evil from his youth (Genesis 8:21-22). But this was why the Flood happened in the first place! We may therefore have, after all, a hint of the motif that the effect of the flood was terrifying to the gods themselves—and that it was this, and not any softening of Yhwh's feelings towards humanity, that caused him to relent. At any rate, in Genesis God has deliberately discarded one way of punishing humankind, and seed-time and harvest, summer and winter continue, not because of, but perhaps in spite of, human nature. The natural world has been blessed. What happens to humans depends to some extent on what they do; and as if to point this up, Genesis 9 ends with the incident in which Noah gets drunk and Ham, the father of Canaan, sees his father naked. Noah's cursing of Canaan because of this is no doubt an Israelite justification for driving out the Canaanites from their land, or enslaving them within it. In the context of Genesis 6–9 it is a sign that, although the earth will never again be punished, the same is not necessarily true of humankind.

Genesis 11:1-9

The first nine verses of Genesis 11 (Genesis 10 was discussed in Chapter 2) tell the story of the Tower of Babel. No other ancient Near Eastern text offers a parallel to this narrative, although it may be possible to link the story with the Etemenanki Temple in Babylon, an enormous ziggurat which may have stayed in an unfinished condition for some centuries (Von Soden 1985: 134-47). The implication of Genesis 11:4, that the city later to be called Babylon (verse 9) was the first great city to be built, does not correspond with history, but indicates the success of the propaganda of the priests of Babylon. Other Mesopotamian cities, including Ur and Kish, were much older than Babylon. However, it is stated—for example in *Enuma Elish*—that Babylon was the first city to be built after the creation of the universe and humankind (Tablet VI line 57, *ANET*: 68).

It has been suggested by Von Soden that the separate Etemenanki Temple in Babylon, whose height when finally built by Nebuchadrezzar II (605–562 BCE) was about 280 ft (85 m), was begun by Nebuchadrezzar I (1123–1101), and not completed. According to this view, stories about an uncompleted massive ziggurat in Babylon could be the origin of the Genesis account of a tower in Babylon whose unfinished state suggested divine intervention—in this case to confuse the speech of humankind. Genesis 11:9 contains a word-play on 'Babylon' (Hebrew *babel*) and 'confuse (speech)' (Hebrew *balal*). Von Soden believed that the biblical story had been written down between 950 and 800 BCE, and commented on the irony that the temple had been destroyed by Xerxes, king of Persia, following a rebellion of Babylon in 484–482, and while deportees from Judah were there. Witte (1998: 321), however, draws attention to this destruction and thinks that the biblical story may be linked to that incident via Alexander the Great's unfulfilled plan to rebuild the temple and to make Babylon the capital of the Macedonian kingdom. Another suggestion has linked the story with the attempt of Sargon II to build an enormous capital at Dur-Sharrukin (see Witte 1998: 320 n. 24).

As a story in itself, Genesis 11:1-9 is about the attempt of humankind to preserve its unity and perhaps gain everlasting reputation by building a mighty tower. The meaning of verse 4 is not altogether clear:

> Let us build a city, and a tower with its top in the heavens; and let us make a name for ourselves unless we are (? so that we are not) scattered on the face of all the world.

This action is seen, however, as a challenge to God. Humanity wishes to define itself in terms of its own achievements, and to this extent wants to do without God. We may also detect here the anti-civilisation theme noted in Genesis 4, as well as the theme that humankind wishes to subvert the order that maintains a division between the human and the divine. The divine punishment in this case is the division of humankind into groups separated by the barrier of language. Humankind, as a unified whole, has rejected God. From now on in Genesis the story will concern God's dealings not with humankind but with one people. These dealings will, however, have as their goal the blessing of all the nations (Genesis 12:3).

Conclusions

Nothing has been said above about the date of composition of Genesis 1–11. Readers are referred to the discussions in Chapters 16 and 17. Our aim has been to show how motifs common in ancient literature were used by the biblical writers to describe the realities of their times in terms of their belief in the God of Israel. They wanted to show that the world in which they lived was an ordered reality dependent on the power of God, who had placed humankind in a position of great trust. That there were divisions and hostilities between human beings, that some of them enslaved others, that producing food to eat was hard and precarious work, that humankind was faced with the final uncertainty of death—none of these facts counted against the belief of the writers that God had bestowed dignity and trust upon humanity. The story of Israel, to which Genesis 1–11 was the prelude, was the story of God's attempt, through Israel's co-operation, to realise something of the creation as it had once been. The fact that Israel was unwilling to cooperate only showed that it understood God's gracious purposes as little as did the humans that God had first created. He had embarked upon an enterprise which would cause him, looking at it from a human angle, disappointment, frustration, regret, anger, and pain.

References and Further Reading

George, A.R.

2000 *The Epic of Gilgamesh: The Babylonian Epic Poem and other Texts in Akkadian and Sumerian* (London: Penguin).

Heidel, A.

1963a *The Babylonian Genesis* (Chicago and London: University of Chicago Press, 2nd edn).

1963b *The Gilgamesh Epic and Old Testament Parallels* (Chicago and London: University of Chicago Press, 2nd edn).

Lambert, W.G., and A.R. Milllard

1969 *Atra-Hasīs: The Babylonian Story of the Flood* (Oxford: Clarendon Press).

Pettinato, G.

1971 *Das altorientalische Menschenbild und die sumerischen und akkadischen Schöpfungsmythen* (Heidelberg: Abhandlungen der Heidelberger Akademie der Wissenschaften, Phil.-Hist. Klasse).

Rogerson, J.W.

1984 *Old Testament Criticism in the Nineteenth Century: England and Germany* (London: SPCK).

1991 *Genesis 1–11* (Old Testament Study Guides; Sheffield: Sheffield Academic Press).

Soden, W. von

1985 *Bibel und Alter Orient. Altorientalische Beiträge zum Alten Testament* (Berlin: W. de Gruyter).

Tigay, J.H.

1982 *The Evolution of the Gilgamesh Epic* (Philadelphia: University of Philadelphia Press).

Witte, M.

1998 *Die Biblische Urgeschichte. Redaktions- und theologiegeschichtliche Beobachtungen zu Genesis 1,1–11,26* (Berlin: W. de Gruyter).

Chronicles
1 Maccabees
2 Maccabees
Genesis
Ruth
Jonah
Apocrypha

Chapter 9

NARRATIVES

What is a narrative? It is a story, whether long or short, in poetry or in prose. A great deal of the Old Testament is narrative, and it is through stories that its writers conveyed their ideas about God, humanity, and the world. In this chapter we shall examine the more important kinds of narrative in the Old Testament and consider where they have their roots and how they functioned in Israelite and Judean society.

'Factual' Versus 'Fictional' Narratives

Scholars have long been fond of dividing biblical narratives into two kinds: those which in the words of Otto Eissfeldt, are 'shaped with an imaginative or a purposeful attitude to the world and to life' and those which 'adhere in a more scientific manner to what has happened, and set out to tell how things actually took place' (Eissfeldt 1966: 32). That may now seem a very simplistic distinction, but it still deeply affects the way we approach the narratives of the Old Testament. For while the word 'story' is readily applied to the former, the latter are often called 'historical' (in English Bibles Joshua to Esther are traditionally known as the 'Historical Books').

It is doubtful how far such a distinction between 'story' and 'history' was made (or *could* be made) in the ancient world. In any case, all narratives, including those we call 'historical' are 'stories'. This is because all narratives employ a plot, have a beginning, middle, and end, a shape, a purpose or moral. They also feature selected characters, who have not only their own traits, but also often specific functions, such as hero, helper, and villain. Stories employ devices such as suspense, surprise and ambiguity to engage the reader, as well as being constructed in such a way that the hearer or reader will become emotionally engaged, liking some characters and not others, wanting some to succeed, others to fail. What biblical stories do not have artistic merit, or employ the recognisable marks of the teller of tales? Think of Jonah's lucky escape from the great fish; or of the dramatic contest between Elijah and the worshippers of Baal on Mt Carmel (1 Kings 18); of Daniel in the furnace; of the Tower of Babel; or of the deeds of Samson. The story of Joseph (from pit to palace; family finally reunited) and of David's family drama (full of sex, violence, and wayward children) are further examples. These stories have settings in the real world, with a precise geographical location, they concern supposedly real people, and often the exploits are reasonably credible, too. But even if the people are events correspond to history (and we very often cannot tell) we recognise them as players in a constructed story. This means that there is no biblical narrative in which 'fact' can be neatly separated from 'fiction', 'plain truth' from embellishment. Storytelling in ancient Israel was a major part of popular (and learned) culture, and it conveyed a large part of the real and imagined world in which the hearers lived. Modern studies of professional story-telling also make it completely clear how each teller and each telling is a combination of traditional content and individual ingenuity and original- ity. A story is a telling, not a text. Of course, the story shape and all the elements were expected to be recognisable; but whether the 'events' were 'true' or 'history' is quite another issue.

Story and History

Why were stories told? First of all, to entertain; but also to instruct or instil certain feelings, or stir the hearers to action; and very often to reinforce in the hearers a sense of *identity*, as individuals and communities. The idea of a story that sets out purely to give scientifically accurate information about the past does not belong the world of the Old Testament. However, there is a genre of writing that tells a lengthy story about the collective, social past of a city or people as distinct from tales about individuals or families or places, which we call 'historiography'. Historiography does not differ from other stories in its factuality or truthfulness: it differs in its content, style, and conventions. In the continuous story from creation to the Babylonian deportation (Genesis to Kings) we have myth, legend, historical memory, historical record, and sheer invention rolled in together. Together with political events that we know happened (invasions, sieges, battles) and real historical persons (kings of Israel and Judah), we have incidents of an incredibly strong man carrying off city gates (Samson: Judges 16), a prophet making axe-heads float (Elisha: 2 Kings 6), and an angel killing 185,000 Assyrian troops overnight (2 Kings 19:35)—let alone stories of paradisal gardens, a universal flood, or a woman turning into a salt pillar (Lot's wife: Genesis 19:26). We have private conversations and scenes that are almost certainly dramatically imagined. Whether historiographies are factually reliable or not is, to their original hearers and readers, immaterial, since they could not *know* what had happened. For us, to whom historicity *does* matter, the answers are given on the basis of the sources used and their proximity to the events, the identity, time and place of the story-teller, the intended audience, and the existence of other corrobo- rating data. Nevertheless, many biblical historiographies speak of matters that cannot be checked against other sources. If we want to understand and appreciate them for what they are, we should pay more attention to their narrative features, because *these* tell us what the story is really *about*.

In short, then, recognizing a particular genre of narrative as historiography is not turning it into 'history', not the same as separating 'true' from 'fictional', or even discerning a scientific or truth-telling motive on the part of the narrator. Even ancient forms of 'historical' writing such as annals, campaign reports, and dedication inscrip- tions, found among the neighbours of Israel and Judah, are also shaped by conven- tional styles and formats, by aesthetic and rhetorical considerations, and they often take conscious liberties with the facts by telescoping, rearranging, omitting, and exaggerating. That, simply, was the way of ancient Near Eastern societies: from the court to the village, stories were told for various purposes: conveying what 'really happened' was not the main purpose—indeed, 'what really happened' may have been a meaningless conception in a society without a reliable collective memory.

Simple and Complex Narratives

The Old Testament contains many narratives, but the majority of them are connected together to form larger ones. So it is probably helpful to start by distinguishing between these extended narratives and the shorter ones from which they are largely made up.

The books of Chronicles and the Samson or Elisha story-cycles, to give two examples of biblical narrative, differ not in their factuality (both have elements of 'fact' and 'fiction' as explained above) but in their length and complexity. The Samson cycle, though a small 'complex' narrative, has the form of a sequence of individual tales, though furnished with a rather rudimentary overall plot. The Elisha cycle is likewise a collection of individual tales, but with hardly any overall plot. The Chronicler, however, strings episodes together into an extended and coherent narrative involving many persons over a long period and with a consistent ideological position that the individual episodes generally illustrate. There is also an important difference in background: the Samson stories are folk tales in form, a popular oral genre and the actual stories probably originated in oral telling (though in the end we can never, by its very nature, retrieve an 'oral story' from the ancient world). The book of Chronicles was *composed* as a literary text. The Joseph story (Genesis 37–47) and the story of David's family (2 Samuel 2–20; 1 Kings 1–2) are examples of something else: they constitute a single story (not a cycle), and exhibit many features of oral story-telling, but also may have been composed in a written form, possibly to contribute to a more complex narrative.

But it would be wrong to assume that oral=folk=simple, that 'shorter'='earlier' = 'more primitive'. Oral storytellers can recite very long stories, while short stories can be written and clearly fanciful. The distinctions are useful for analysis, but do not translate into some kind of sliding scale of 'realism' or 'historicity'. There are certain forms of literature that require to be written down, because they require an identical text to be read and re-read (certain kinds of prophetic oracle or liturgical text). In the case of extended narratives, certain patterns and meanings can also emerge more clearly when the reader can repeat and move around the written text. In an oral recitation the listener hears once, and may not ever hear *exactly* the same story twice. However, many written stories in the Bible replicate the style and character of oral stories, especially if they were written to be read out publicly—though *why* a story to be recited should need to be first written is a good question. Presumably, it has something to do with control of knowledge. For writing does not preserve knowledge or facilitate communication: it rather restricts and controls it (especially where the literacy rate is about 5 per cent and confined to an elite group).

Relatively simple stories, like those of Ruth or Jonah, are by no means necessarily oral or popular in origin, but quite possibly literary compositions by professional authors. It was once thought that the cycle of tales of the ancestors (Genesis 12–36) originated in a series of short oral anecdotes, which were later assembled into longer, written narratives. However, the linking together of loosely related episodes without any solid structural shape is quite characteristic of oral composition too, and individual episodes could have been originally written down in a style imitating oral tales. Just as oral storytelling often contains inconsistencies, gaps, and awkward transition, so might an extended written narrative: such features are not *necessarily* an indication of clumsy editing. Consistent *ideological* differences, on the other hand, may well point to such things. For while oral stories are always essentially performance and can be varied in the telling, written stories can also be 'performed' by the copyist as he (it will almost certainly be a male) emends the text he is transcribing. That texts were regularly changed in the process of being copied is beyond doubt from the large amount of evidence we have (compare Kings and Chronicles!).

Complex Narratives

Historiography

The Old Testament contains only one predominant form of complex narrative, which we have already met: historiography. This genre of writing is not found else-where in the ancient world until the fifth century BCE, with Herodotus (c. 480–425), and there are good reasons to think it appeared in Judah no earlier (the story from Genesis to Kings ends in the sixth century; Chronicles ends in the fifth). Earlier sources of information, whether oral or written, are obviously to be taken for granted, but not earlier editions of the historiography we have, or even extended parts of it. Historiography did not develop naturally out of oral epics. According to Van Seters, its origins lie in the ancient Near East, in various kinds of records that deal with monarchs: king-lists, which consist of continuous, if fictive, chronologies, often going back to the beginning of the world; royal inscriptions reporting contemporary events; and, most important of all, chronicles, which combined both chronology and reportage of recent or contemporary events and which reached their zenith in the Neo-Babylonian period. The *Histories* of Herodotus (the 'father of history'), which recount how Persia and Greece came into conflict, draw on earlier quasi-historiographical writings in the form of rationalised myths and genealogies. Closer to Judah, the Babylonian Chronicles, from the end of the seventh century BCE, offer a contemporary or near contemporary account of important political events. With the accelerated spread of Greek culture from the fifth century onwards, and especially with the rise of Hellenistic kingdoms in the early fourth century, historiography became more common throughout the ancient world. We can accept a definition of 'historiography' as an account of a nation, or a civilization or a society that by means of a connected story of the past defines its identity. Put another way, 'who "we" are' is defined by any number of stories we tell about ourselves—as individuals, members of families and professions. But the nation also has its own defining story, though this national story is normally not a matter of 'folk memory' but the product of domi-nant classes. It is through historiography that the scribes of ancient Judah created the nation 'Israel', not as a now defunct kingdom but as a *nation* that was especially created and chosen by the supreme and only God.

It is a matter of debate how the great biblical historiographical narratives achieved their final shape (see more below and Chapter 17). Most scholars speak of a 'Deuter-onomistic History', a single work that ran from Joshua's conquest of the land to the loss of the land—this might correspond most closely to the scope and plot of Herodo-tus' *Histories*—and of a separate Pentateuchal narrative, composed from various drafts, that took Israel from its ancestor Abraham to the edge of Canaan where Moses died—with the story of human origins in Genesis 1–11 possibly a further addition. It was also thought until recently that Chronicles, Ezra, and Nehemiah also formed a single historiographical work; nowadays the consensus has vanished. Other scholars speak of a 'Primary History', the story from Creation to Deportation

(Genesis–Kings), corresponding in scope to the historiographies of Babylonia, Egypt, and Phoenicia written respectively by Berossus, Manetho, and Philo of Byblos, all in the Hellenistic period. Yet, these were works composed by individual authors, and written in Greek. The biblical historiography is different in both respects, a unique and in some ways mysterious but magnificent literary achievement.

Tracing the history of a *nation* from the beginning implies an audience, a purpose and a role for the finished work. In the case of the other historiographies just mentioned, the motive may have been the advent of a new Hellenistic world culture (linguistic, literary, philosophical, political) that prompted nations with their own ancient traditions to generate a written account of their own people and civilization. It is possible that the biblical historiography was prompted by a similar need— to affirm their own identity, extending back from the new world of an imperial province to an earlier era of native monarchy and free possession of a land. Scholars do not agree on the purpose of Old Testament historiography, and many see no need even to ask, assuming naively that 'writing down the past' was a natural and obvious thing—which it was not!

Did ancient historiographers genuinely seek to describe what they *thought* had happened in the past? If so, should we not call them 'historians'? This is not just a tricky question, but also a trick question, because it presupposes that the ancient mindset corresponds to the modern one. 'What had happened' cannot be distinguished from 'what we believe happened' or 'what we have always been told had happened', because there was no evidence or data on which to base such a reconstruction. Moreover, in a society with a rich store of stories about the past, what is served by a single rationalised, cumulative account? In the ancient world virtually all literature was propaganda: writing was used in the exercise of royal or priestly power, controlling knowledge and belief. It was natural that any account of the past would have in mind what was needing to be known or believed rather than disinterestedly 'what had been the case'. Ancient historiographers *did* of course use sources, sometimes critically (though not before Herodotus), and sometimes faithfully, in the sense that they simply recorded what they found, without questioning alternative versions. This 'faithfulness' may explain why we sometimes have two versions of the same incident—such as how Saul was chosen king (1 Samuel 9 and 10:17-24), or how David met Saul (1 Samuel 16:14-23 and 17:12-58). How could an ancient historiographer tell which version was 'true'? The books of Kings imply some knowledge of a sequence of rulers in Israel and Judah and some major events of their reigns (though there are still gaps and mistakes).

The 'Primary History'

It is now time to consider the making of the Old Testament historiographies. The first, from Genesis to Kings, is conventionally divided into Pentateuch/Torah (Genesis–Deuteronomy) and 'Deuteronomistic History' (Joshua–Kings minus Ruth). This historiographical narrative ends with the Babylonian exile, and thus was written during or after it. Discussion over the composition of the Pentateuch has been vigorous for the last two centuries and more. Some think of parallel accounts being merged, others of different episodes, era, and topics being juxtaposed at a relatively late stage into a coherent sequence. A similar difference of view exists over the 'Deuteronomistic History'. Although it is usually thought to have been conceived as a single work, under the influence of the book of Deuteronomy, some scholars feel that the individual character of each book points to independent origins, with the books being edited into a consecutive account later. Equally uncertain is the connection *between* the Pentateuch and the 'Deuteronomistic History'. The prehistory of this long narrative is a topic we shall reserve for Chapters 16 and 17. The narrative begins, at any rate, with the origins of the world, explains how a rift between God and humanity developed and—once the possibility of ending creation has been disposed of—narrates the division of humanity focusing upon one particular family. From this family derive a number of nations, all living in, or in the vicinity of, Palestine (Ammonites, Moabites, Edomites, Ishmaelites, Israelites). By the end of Genesis the story has become a story about Israel. Exodus–Deuteronomy describes the creation of a nation, its laws, and its cult before any land is given to it. In Joshua this nation then displaces the inhabitants of the land promised to the ancestors, and the land is apportioned among the tribes. From Judges to 2 Kings runs the story of Israel in its land, ending with the removal of political independence.

This narrative is a tragic one. A tragic narrative or drama is driven by one or more of the following: fate—humans are at the mercy of forces which are either indifferent or hostile to them, and human ambition and effort is ultimately futile; flaw—humans bring themselves to ruin through some defect in their character; and divine hostility—the tragic hero arouses the anger of one or other deity who decides to punish the presumed offence. These three plots are not necessarily alternatives; many tragedies portray a hero who is brought to grief by a combination of a personal flaw and inexorable forces or an offended deity. The Old Testament narrative as a whole does not emphasise fate. Although the movement of history is directed by Yhwh, it is humanity's decisions that govern their destiny. Hence Adam and Eve choose and are subsequently expelled from the Garden; later, Israel chooses to disobey Yhwh and is expelled from its own land flowing with milk and honey.

Nevertheless, historiography is about the nation, not the individual. The juxtaposition of the Eden story with the history of the kingdoms of Israel and Judah gives the latter a cosmic, mythic dimension. At the same time, however, it subsumes the destiny of Israel under the destiny of all humans (just as the Creation in six days underlines the universal value of the Sabbath). The Eden story internalises the relationship of God and humanity, since toil and childbirth, ambition and death, are personal as well as social experiences. The exile to Babylon is, in a sense, a reversal of the Tower of Babel story (Genesis 11), in which the peoples were dispersed *from* Mesopotamia; Abraham's ancestors now return to his birthplace. From these illustrations we can see that the biblical history is no mere recital of a chain of events, but a thoughtful theological narrative constructed to carry many meanings. Seen in the broader perspective, the biblical historiography from Genesis to Kings stands as a monument to the intellectual power of the Jewish scribes in the Persian period, but no less to the storytellers of earlier times who provided some of the material on which they drew.

One question to ask, of course, is: why the tragic plot? Why does this story end in exile? The answer may be that the writers wished to show two things: that under a native monarchy Israel and Judah were led astray, whereas the present political regime under the Persians was preferable; and that only absolute obedience to the demands of Yhwh's law would secure his benevolence towards his people. These two lessons would plausibly reflect the interests of the Judean elite, and are clearly displayed in the books of Ezra and Nehemiah who are shown, under Persian patronage, as enforcing the Deuteronomic law and covenant on the population.

The Chronicler

It is generally thought that the Chronicler substantially rewrites the corresponding sections of Samuel and Kings, adjusting the material to his own viewpoint. However some recent studies have re-argued an older suggestion that both historiographies derive from a common source. It was until fairly recently thought that the Chronicler's work included the books of Ezra and Nehemiah, but this is now doubtful for several reasons, though there are close ideological patterns in the three books, and at some point a scribe has linked the two by recapitulating 2 Chronicles 36:22ff. at the beginning of Ezra, presumably to underline that the works fall into a chronological sequence. Still, in the Hebrew Bible, Chronicles, for some reason, comes *after* Ezra–Nehemiah, making the link even more important!

Chronicles does not narrate the events between creation and the death of Saul, listing instead a set of genealogies: from Adam to Israel/Jacob (1 Chronicles 1:1–2:20), then the tribes, with Judah first place (chapters 2–4) followed by the others (chapters 5–8). Then come lists of priestly and levitical families and the family of Saul (chapters 9–10). But this last section in fact opens (1 Chronicles 9:1-9) with a list of those 'were first to dwell again in their possessions in their towns' after Judah's exile to Babylon. Thus, the newly reconstituted community in the Persian period is given more than an historical continuity with all that precedes; using the code of kinship and descent, the 'Israel' of Chronicles is identified with that of the ancestral Israel. The narrative proper commences with the death of Saul and runs as far as the edict of Cyrus repatriating the Judeans in exile. The story, then, is not a tragedy, but an affirmation of an Israel restored through Judah.

If the history of Joshua–Kings describes an Israel (and Judah) very different from its own time, Chronicles is concerned to stress the fundamental continuity. Accordingly, the history of the kingdom of Israel is not related; the kingdom of Judah represents 'all Israel'. That other kingdom, after all, had been a dead end, and the history of 'all Israel' lay in the Davidic monarchy of Judah that had once embraced the totality of tribes. That monarchy is of course defunct; but it is still symbolised by the Temple; the promise to David of a 'house' in 2 Samuel 7:11 represents there a dynasty: Yhwh does not want David to build a temple house, but will instead build for David a ruling 'house'. In Chronicles that promise is turned upside-down. In 1 Chronicles 22:8 (and 28:3) David is not allowed to *build* the house but he is responsible for the project (including its personnel and its liturgy), which Solomon merely carries out. The temple is the 'house of David' and still stands in the Chronicler's day in Jerusalem.

When and by whom was Chronicles written? It is generally suspected that the author was a levite; the text gives prominence to this caste, who were, according to Chronicles, the administrators of the Temple and its worship. The date of composition is usually placed in the late fifth or in the fourth century BCE.

The First and Second Books of Maccabees

1 Maccabees was probably written at the end of the second century BCE, and originally in Hebrew, though it is now preserved only in Greek. It reads like a sober

account of events from the edict of the Seleucid king Antiochus IV against the Jews (167 BCE) until the reign of John Hyrcanus (died 104 BCE). But, in fact, it is cast in such a way that it presents its story as a re-run of events of biblical history, especially those found in Judges and Kings. The Jewish renegades who build the Hellenistic gymnasium are said to want to make a league with the 'nations round about' (1 Maccabees 1:12), an allusion to the warnings of Deuteronomy about associating with the Canaanites; and according to 1 Maccabees 5:1, these 'nations round about' want to destroy Israel. The story of Mattathias's assault (see Chapter 7) recapitulates the act of Phinehas in Numbers 25 in slaying an apostate and winning for himself an 'eternal priesthood'. The assembly at Mizpah (1 Maccabees 3:46ff.) is also modelled on biblical reports of assemblies there (especially Judges 21:1), while Judas Maccabee executes a 'ban' in 1 Maccabees 5:51, killing the inhabitants in the manner of Joshua. Two military leaders meet defeat because they are not 'from those to whom the deliverance of Israel was given' (i.e. the Maccabees, latter-day 'judges'). To reinforce that parallel with Judges, the land of Judah 'has peace' after the defeat of Nicanor (1 Maccabees 7:50), as it did after the victories of the judges. At the end of 1 Maccabees, the words 'the rest of John's acts…are found recorded in the chronicles of his high priesthood…' recall the formula used of the kings of Israel and Judah in the books of Kings. The aim of the book, then, is quite obviously to glorify the ruling Maccabean (Hasmonean) family and to justify their right to rule over Israel by dint of military prowess, given by God.

2 Maccabees, on the other hand, was probably written in Alexandra, and its style is that of the Greek 'pathetic history', a rhetorical use of the past designed to entertain, instruct, and move the reader—as the writer explicitly announces (2 Maccabees 2:19-32). The story aims to demonstrate that the afflictions of Israel were the result of sinfulness, and that only after due atonement on behalf of the people by righteous martyrs could military victory (still with the aid of God, of course) be achieved. This plot allows the author to depict harrowing scenes of torture alongside the daring exploits of military valour and permits a much more colourful narrative than that of the first book.

Beyond these biblical examples, we know of several other historiographical writings by Jews in the Greco-Roman period. But unfortunately little of their work remains beyond fragments in other writers (see Holladay 1983).

Simple Narratives

Folk Narrative
Folk narratives, though constructed for the purpose of live performance with an audience, retain much of their oral characteristics even when transcribed, or imitated, in literary format, often as episodes or elements in larger narratives. Hence to identify a narrative as a 'folk narrative' does not necessarily imply that it originated with popular storytellers, but only that it follows the conventions set down by these storytellers. The four types of 'poetic narrative' defined by Hermann Gunkel, and still largely recognised, are myth, saga, legend, and folk tale.

Saga
The category of the 'saga' has been introduced into Old Testament studies from two directions. On the one hand, it became an issue with the work of Gunkel, who applied it to the stories in Genesis. *Sagen*, according to Gunkel and many since, are

originally oral; deal with personal and private matters rather than public or political ones; are part traditional but part conscious invention; contain miraculous or fantastic events; and have aesthetic qualities which inspire, move, or at least gratify the listener. According to Gunkel's approach the saga is an individual story, which at a secondary stage may be combined into a cycle. Another approach derives from the work of André Jolles, the pioneer of this approach to the biblical stories, who studied Icelandic sagas, whose essential theme (and structure) he described as determined by the idea of 'family'. The subject of saga is not the state, nation, or society but the ongoing clan or family, and the relationships between the characters in a saga are familial. The Icelandic saga is, unlike Gunkel's *Sage*, a sequence of family tales, given in chronological order, with several minor characters, most of whom are provided with a genealogy when they appear. The style is factual and the action swift, with a minimum of background description or digression. The characters are not fully drawn, being described mainly in terms of their actions. Two or more versions of the same story may also appear in the sequence.

The clearest examples of this type of saga or family story in the Old Testament are the ancestral narratives in Genesis 12–36. They make up a cycle—possibly more than one cycle originally—which is in turn made up of individual narratives. The ancestry of Israel is traced back to a family, which remains the centre of interest. All the main characters are related, and there is scarcely any concern with events or characters outside the family circle. This is one reason why attempts to relate the ancestral stories to ancient history are doomed; the stories simply are not interested in history, only in ancestry. The narratives in their present form, nonetheless, are held together, sometimes loosely, by the theme of Yhwh's promise of land, heirs, and other blessings to his family/people.

The Genesis ancestral saga cycle, incidentally, affords an interesting perspective on the varieties of' telling one story. There are three accounts *of* a patriarch passing off his wife as his sister, in Genesis 12, 20, and 26. It is easy for us to imagine that all three are the same simply folk-story with minor modifications; but a careful comparison will show meaningful differences. All three play a different role in the larger complex narrative to which they now belong. All the same, we can surely presume that behind each of them *is* a story originally narrating how a wily old ancestor gained wealth by deceiving the king of a lustful foreign nation and exploiting the beauty of his bride. The bowdlerised version of chapter 26 definitely suggests a scribal revision, whereas chapter 12 conceals little of the hero's lack of scruple and, no doubt, reveals a prejudicial attitude to foreigners and women typical of small conservative and patriarchal groups.

Legend

Gunkel believed that legend was a degenerate offspring of saga. In English, the German *Sage* is often rendered as 'legend' (Gunkel's *Legends of Genesis* being really *Sagas of Genesis*). Among the many definitions offered, however one can see a tendency to regard legends as stories about great individuals rather than families (as with sagas). Jolles's classification of 'legend' was 'a virtue embodied in a deed', offering an example for the reader/hearer to follow. If the genre 'legend' *is* to be distinguished from 'saga' and 'folk-tale (see below), it therefore is probably best seen as focusing on an individual hero, sometimes as an archetype or a paragon; though not always to be imitated rather than admired (Samson comes to mind).

This doubt is well illustrated in a good example of a cycle of prophetic legends clustering round the figures of Elijah and Elisha in 1 Kings 17–2 Kings 9, where we find, alongside religiously appropriate prophetic legends, like that of the Shunammite widow or Naaman, stories about poisoned soup (all in 2 Kings 4–5) and bears killing cheeky children (2 Kings 2:23-24), which appear to be legends in a fairly unrefined state (and hardly exemplary). In the Samson cycle, too, are motifs about an amoral man of great strength who is presented as a Nazirite who saves the whole of Israel.

A characteristic feature of legends is that originally anonymous stories tend to become associated with known figures. A legend that may have gravitated from a lesser-known to a better-known figure is the slaying of Goliath by David. In 2 Samuel 21:19 this feat is ascribed to Elhanan—a discrepancy which the Chronicler has resolved: Elhanan is described in 2 Samuel as a *beth-halahmi* (probably 'Bethlehemite'), and in 1 Chronicles 20:5 Elhanan is said to have slain 'Lahmi the *brother* of Goliath...' The implication is that the more famous David has been given credit for another Bethlehemite's exploit.

In many cases we have to infer this process; but in one case we have proof. In a fragment from Qumran (4QPrNab), Nabonidus, a king of Babylon, relates how an unnamed Jewish exorcist cured him of an ulcer. Almost certainly this is a version of the story in Daniel 4, where the unknown Jew has become Daniel, and the virtually unknown Nabonidus has become the famous Babylonian king Nebuchadrezzar.

Folk-Tale

The term 'folk-tale' (or sometimes 'fairy-tale', though this is for obvious reasons never used in biblical studies) is the approximate translation of Gunkel's category *Märchen*, which embraces a number of different kinds of relatively simple folk narrative. Gunkel himself was unable to define the form of the *Märchen* very precisely, and subdivided it into many types. Its essential features as he saw them, were fantasy and credulity: magical events are treated as a matter of course and people of lowly stock rise to thrones, animals talk, miracles are commonplace and so on. The *Märchen* is not meant to be taken as a story from the real world; it projects a world of imagination, where different rules apply. In modern literature the word 'romance' also carries something of Gunkel's definition—a make-believe narrative, a fantasy. *Märchen* are not necessarily only about humans: they can involve nature and animals, demons, fairies, giants, and everyday objects that acquire magical characteristics. In the Old Testament the most common examples tend to be aetiological, explaining how things came to be as they are. One example is in Genesis 19, the destruction of Sodom and Gomorrah, which includes explanations of the sulphurous smell of the Dead Sea and the salt crystal formations on its shores.

The classifications given above, though by now long-established, and quite useful in illustrating the variety of folk narratives, are not necessarily the most appropriate ones. Ongoing research into folklore does not uniformly support such distinctions. The folk tale, for example, can be subdivided into many different types, such as fables, trickster tales, tall tales and trove tales (finding treasure), and these categories embrace what Gunkel would have defined as 'legends'. The important point to bear in mind in connection with the Old Testament is that literary narrative did not lose touch with its older, or contemporary, oral matrix. Writing, in short, did not replace talking, and ancient Israel and Judah remained mainly oral cultures.

Non-Folk Forms

To illustrate simple non-folk forms let us consider royal inscriptions and didactic narratives. The former include commemorative inscriptions, which recount royal deeds and are inscribed on statues, cylinders, or tablets and record building activities or campaigns. A particular class of these, known from Assyria and Hatti, are annals, which record individual campaigns or campaign series and are inscribed on a stela or a rock. These texts generally conform to fairly strict conventions of style, language, and motif, and serve not simply to record events but to inspire confidence or (more usually) fear in the readers. Another type is the king-list, which sets out the reigns of kings with the length of the reign given and occasionally details of major works or deeds. The Sumerian king-list, perhaps the most famous, and also rather exceptional, begins 'When kingship was first lowered from heaven', and gives reigns of thousands of years for earliest rulers, including events associated with these kings (compare the extended lifespans of the earliest humans in Genesis). Chronicles, which we find in Assyria and Babylonia, recount political (i.e. military) events, precisely dated, of the recent past. Curiously, we have no royal inscriptions from ancient Israel or Judah. Did such inscriptions exist? If they did, where are they?

The relatively modern term 'novella' has come to be applied by scholars to a literary type of story found in the ancient Near East and in the Old Testament. According to Gunkel, the 'novella' developed from the *Sage*. Novellas are artistic fictions, but all of them are given historical settings, and they sometimes include historically identifiable characters. Many are set in or around a royal court, and may also be classified as 'court-tales', a quite distinct genre in itself. A very early example of such a tale is the Egyptian story of Sinuhe which dates from at least as early as 1800 BCE (*ANET*: 18ff.). It relates the travels and adventures of a courtier before he finally returns to Egypt. From about the eleventh century BCE, another Egyptian novella tells of a certain Wen-Amon—not a courtier but a temple administrator—who goes to Phoenicia on business. Like Sinuhe's story, its appeal seems to lie very much in its 'travelogue' quality. But later court tales tell also of rivalry between courtiers, of individual courtiers who achieve their ambitions by cunning, and of disgraced courtiers who eventually achieve restoration. Ahikar, whose story was known all over the ancient Near East and in Greece, is a courtier of Sennacherib. He adopted a son, who repaid him by denouncing him to the king. After many vicissitudes, the hero is restored and chastens his son by teaching him parables and proverbs. Many of the motifs contained in this story are echoed in Esther, where the courtier Mordecai is made the victim of a plot by a fellow courtier, a plot foiled by Queen Esther. Daniel contains several court-tales, in which he and his friends are also the victims of plots by kings or courtiers. But Daniel has two other attributes: he is able to interpret dreams, and he is cunning. His cunning is demonstrated in the stories called 'Susannah' and 'Bel and the Dragon' (found in the ancient Greek version of the book, now usually located in the Apocrypha). Joseph uses his interpretative powers to elevate himself in the Egyptian court and his cunning to get even with his brothers, though only part of the Joseph story is comparable to a court-tale.

Not all biblical novellas are court tales. One of the best-known biblical novellas is the story of Ruth, a Moabite girl married to a Judahite Boaz. The book is very hard to date, and the search for a theological message in it seems futile. It is a happy little story, and the information that this couple are the ancestors of King David hardly

adds much to its quality. It is economical, neat, and simple but also quite sophisticated in its characterization and construction (for an excellent commentary with
folkloristic analysis, see Sasson 1979). It is less obviously didactic than the Joseph
story, which is a novella embedded in historiography. But the story of Joseph likewise has no supernatural dimension, yet conveys the notion that events are guided
by a providential God. The same can be said of the story of David's family (often
called the 'Succession Narrative' because it seems to deal with problem of who will
succeed David) in 2 Samuel 9–20, and Esther. The ethos of all these novellas is
humanistic, and their heroes and heroines behave as recipients of divine favour,
though (unlike the great historiographies) there is no overt divine motivation.

The book of Jonah, which dates probably from the Persian period, might be
classed as a folk-tale or a novella (showing how hard it is to maintain fixed boundaries between the types), but is probably in a category of its own. It, too, is superficially
simple—naive, even—but more openly didactic, and placing the character of God as
much as the character of Jonah himself in the limelight. In this story, unlike the
novellas, God is to a supreme extent the architect of historical and natural events.
Here we also see the first sign of the obsession with foreign capitals that characterises
novellas from this period and onwards. Jonah is probably best understood as a satire
on Deuteronomistic prophecy, featuring a prophet who preaches repentance with
astounding success, then laments his success; a God who 'appoints' things to
happen at a stroke, a hypocritical psalm, and an element of incredibility in a
man-swallowing fish. It is entertaining not only for its story line but for its flashes of
wit: Jonah is commissioned to 'arise' and he 'descends'—first to the coast, then into
the boat, into the bottom of the boat, into the sea, and then into the fish. The king of
Nineveh, in an excess of penitence, but characteristically of totalitarian rulers, orders
sackcloth for the animals; a plant springs up immediately and a worm eats it immediately; the prophet sulks because a city has repented. The great fish is indeed the least
of the miracles in this tale, which, though certainly not humanistic, yet pokes fun at
many theological conventions.

From the third or second century BCE comes the story of Tobit, found in the
Apocrypha. It tells of an exceptionally pious exile in Nineveh who becomes blind
and falls from prosperity to destitution. In Ecbatana (the Median capital) lives a
woman named Sarah who has been married seven times, but lost each husband on
the wedding night to a jealous demon called Asmodeus. Both Tobit and Sarah pray
and Raphael is sent to cure them. Tobit's son Tobias goes to Media, meets Raphael
in disguise, and is nearly eaten by a fish. Instead, he catches the fish and keeps parts
of it. Then he meets Sarah and marries her; when Asmodeus appears, Tobit repels
him with the magical remains of the fish. On their return to Nineveh, Tobias applies
another part of the fish to his father's eyes and so cures his blindness.

The story of Judith is also found in the Apocrypha. It shares with Esther and with
Ruth a heroine rather than a hero (are we to think of original female authors and
readers here?), and with Esther it features a Jewish massacre of enemies—but the
resemblances end there. Like many stories from the Greco-Roman period, it centres
on Mesopotamia, but mixes up Assyria and Babylon in having Nebuchadrezzar as
king of Assyria! The Jews, lately returned from exile, are faced by Holofernes, sent
by Nebuchadrezzar to conquer Syria and Palestine. The core of the story tells how
Judith, a very pious widow, insinuates herself into Holofernes' camp, is invited by
him to a banquet, and when they are alone cuts off the drunken general's head.

Probably dating from the first century BCE, it has no obvious purpose unless intended as an oblique comment on the Maccabean wars. Judith can be seen as a combination of the leader Deborah and the widow Jael, who between them dispose of the general Sisera (Judges 4 and 5).

Other forms of narrative, omitted here, include the autobiographical (Nehemiah and Daniel 4), the story of Job, usually seen as a framework for a wisdom poem, the biographical material in the book of Jeremiah, and the sacred historical recital, as in, for example, Psalm 136. But no exhaustive account can really be offered—nor any precise classification. For narrative is really a vehicle of communication that knows no boundaries of form or imagination, of length, scope, or style. Narrative is, in fact, the predominant mode of Old Testament literature, and the vehicle for most of philosophy, theology, and anthropology. Even today, narrative—from the joke via the anecdote, to the novel—remains a favourite and distinctive mode of Jewish expression.

Further Reading

Reference in this chapter has been made to O. Eissfeldt, *The Old Testament. An Introduction* (Oxford: Blackwell, 1966); H. Gunkel, *The Folktale in the Old Testament* (Historic Texts and Interpreters in Biblical Scholarship; Sheffield: Almond Press, 1987); G. von Rad, *Studies in Deuteronomy* (London: SCM Press, 1966); John Van Seters, *In Search of History: Historiography in the Ancient World and the Origins of Biblical History* (New Haven: Yale University Press, 1983). The work by André Jolles referred to has not been translated into English: *Einfache Formen: Legende, Sage, Mythe, Rätsel, Spruch, Kasus, Memorabile, Märchen, Witz* (Halle: M. Niemeyer, 2nd edn, 1956); J.M. Sasson, *Ruth: A New Translation with a Philological Commentary and a Formalist-Folklorist Interpretation* (Baltimore: The Johns Hopkins University Press, 1979 [repr. The Biblical Seminar, 10; Sheffield: Sheffield Academic Press, 1995]).

On orality and literacy, see Susan Niditch, *Oral World and Written Word* (Louisville, KY: Westminster/John Knox Press, 1996); on narrative, S. Bar-Efrat, *Narrative Art in the Bible* (JSOTSup, 70; Sheffield: Almond Press, 1989), and R. Alter, *The Art of Biblical Narrative* (London: Allen & Unwin, 1981). On the Pentateuch, an excellent introduction is Joseph Blenkinsopp, *The Pentateuch: An Introducton to the First Five Books of the Bible* (New York: Doubleday, 1992). Martin Noth's thesis of a 'Deuteronomistic History' is in *The Deuteronomistic History* (JSOTSup, 15; Sheffield: JSOT Press, 1981) and his view of the Chronicler in *The Chronicler's History* (JSOTSup, 50; Sheffield: JSOT Press, 1987).

On Jonah, Jonathan Magonet, *Form and Meaning: Studies in Literary Techniques in the Book of Jonah* (Bible and Literature Series, 8; Sheffield: Almond Press, 1976), and Kenneth Craig, *A Poetics of Jonah: Art in the Service of Ideology* (Columbia: University of South Carolina Press, 1993); on Esther, Michael V. Fox, *Character and Ideology in the Book of Esther* (Columbia: University of South Carolina Press, 1991).

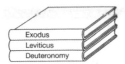
Exodus
Leviticus
Deuteronomy

Chapter 10

LEGAL TEXTS

Is the study of Old Testament legal traditions a study of Israelite law; or is it a study of Israelite ethics, or wisdom, or even religion? This may seem to be a strange question to ask. Surely, the legal traditions of the Old Testament are, in fact, laws, deriving from legal practice and recorded in order to further their observance and enforcement. Surely, this view is confirmed by the parallels that can be drawn between Old Testament law and law codes from elsewhere in the ancient Near East, such as the Babylonian Code of Hammurabi.

In fact things are by no means as simple as this. In the first place, some experts in the study of ancient Near Eastern law have become reluctant to use the word 'code' for collections of laws such as those of Hammurabi. The word 'code' implies an official version of laws, made and promulgated with a view to its observance and enforcement in a given society. Although no scholar wishes to suggest that the laws in Hammurabi's collection have nothing to do with legal practice, it is certainly questioned whether they were gathered together on Hammurabi's instructions in order to be promulgated as a code. Rather, it is suggested that Hammurabi's collection is a text designed to commend the ruler to the gods as one who sought to uphold justice. Thus, the purpose of the *collection* was religious and political, rather than legal, even if that of the individual laws themselves was legal. If this is generally true of ancient Near Eastern collections of law, it may possibly be true also of Old Testament collections of law.

In the second place, the Old Testament collections bring together material that is quite disparate. Some of it is undoubtedly case law; but it is mixed up with cultic regulations and with injunctions of a categorical nature (i.e. applying to all situations and persons regardless of circumstances). For example in the so-called Book of the Covenant (Exodus 21:1-23:19) we find a law that distinguishes between intentional and accidental killing:

> Whoever strikes a man so that he dies shall be put to death. But if he did not lie in wait for him, but God let him fall into his hand, then I will appoint for you a place to which he may flee. But if a man wilfully attacks another to kill him treacherously, you shall take him from my altar, that he may die (Exodus 21:12-14).

However, this is immediately followed by a categorical injunction:

> Whoever strikes his father or his mother shall be put to death (Exodus 21:15).

Nothing is said about the force of the blow, or about its results, and no allowance is made for the fact that a child or young adult might strike a blow in self-defence while being beaten by a parent. In the same collection we find cultic regulations such as the following:

> You shall not offer the blood of my sacrifice with leavened bread, or let the fat of my feast remain until the morning. The first of the first fruits of your ground you shall bring into the house of the LORD your God (Exodus 23:18-19).

To the disparate nature of the material in the Book of the Covenant we can add a third point, the fact that the actual case law in this collection deals with a very limited number of areas of human life: slavery, murder, damages to persons and property, and fornication. There is nothing about marriage, divorce, adoption, the rights of prisoners-of-war, redress against a physician for injuries received during medical treatment, or redress against the builder of a faulty house or defective boat—all of which are treated in the laws of Hammurabi. Although it would be wrong to insist that all of these matters must have been dealt with in Israelite laws in biblical times, it is reasonable to be surprised at the absence of laws about marriage, divorce, and adoption from the Book of the Covenant in view of the fact that marriage and divorce (but not adoption) are dealt with, albeit briefly, elsewhere in the Old Testament.

It is important that we approach the study of Old Testament legal traditions with a certain amount of caution. There is much that we do not know about them, and there are widely differing scholarly approaches and conclusions. This chapter will deal in turn with the development of administration of justice, the Book of the Covenant, the Holiness Code, Deuteronomy, and the Decalogue (Ten Commandments).

Administration of Justice

Michael Fishbane (1985: 234-65) has suggested four categories of legal process: (1) the direct appeal to God, or the use of an oracle or ordeal procedure to decide a case; (2) making an ad-hoc decision in a particular case, perhaps with the help of an arbitrator; (3) laws collected, systematised, and administered by established legal authorities; and (4) law making and law drafting within a professional school of lawyers or scribes. Although these four categories suggest an historical development from the first to the fourth, it is likely that they also overlapped to some extent. The four categories will be briefly outlined here, to provide a framework against which the Old Testament legal traditions can then be discussed.

Direct Appeal to God, or Use of an Oracle, or Ordeal Procedure

The direct appeal to a supernatural being or force was used in a variety of cases: to discover the law; to discover the culprit; and to determine guilt where there were no witnesses.

An example of the first situation can be found in Numbers 15:32-36. A man is gathering sticks on the Sabbath, presumably to light a fire. Does this action constitute 'work', which is prohibited on the Sabbath? As there is no way of knowing the answer to this, Moses seeks a ruling directly from Yhwh. The answer is that the man should be stoned to death. As we have the incident in Numbers, it conforms, of course, to the requirements of the narrative sequence. According to the narrative, Israel has already received the Ten Commandments, one of which forbids work on the Sabbath (Exodus 20:8-10), although nowhere is there a definition of 'work'. Moses therefore has to seek a ruling from God in this case. However, we do not have to accept the historicity of the incident in order to accept the procedure. The narrative, whatever its origins, indicates a method of deciding a case by seeking direct Illumination from God. Since this concerns a cultic matter, we can guess that such rulings were delivered by priests.

The use of an oracle to discover a culprit is instanced in 1 Samuel 14:40-42 (where the fuller Greek text is to be preferred as found in most modern translations). Here the casting of a lot reveals that Jonathan had unwittingly broken the oath that Saul had administered to the people (1 Samuel 14:24).

The establishment of guilt where no witnesses are present can be illustrated from Exodus 22:7 and 10, in which a person entrusted with someone else's property which has then been stolen can take an oath that he is not guilty. Numbers 5:11-31 describes an ordeal ceremony which a man can use if he suspects his wife of unfaithfulness.

Making an Ad-hoc Decision in a Particular Case

The most notable instance of this is in 1 Kings 3:16-28, where Solomon decides the custody of a disputed baby. Fishbane (1985: 239) suggests that judges such as Deborah and Samuel functioned in this manner, and to this suggestion we can add the judges listed in Judges 10:1-5 and 12:8-15. We have already seen above (p. 35) that these judges were people of substance and position, and we can further guess that, as local chieftains, they had the authority and skill to adjudicate cases. The same is implied in the story of David after he became king. One of the reasons why Absalom was able to win over the hearts of the people was that he spread the rumour that David was neither hearing cases brought to him for arbitration (2 Samuel 15:2-4) nor appointing a deputy to do so.

It is probable that before and during the early monarchy, a good deal of family law was decided locally, by heads of families, or by locally convened courts 'in the gate' (of the city), as their meeting place is described in Ruth 4:1-12, which gives an account of such a case. However, it would still be necessary to have to resort to higher authorities in instances where local self-help was insufficient to decide a case, and the refusal of the king (whether real or imagined) to arbitrate would have serious implications for the rule of law in the community.

Laws Collected, Systematised, and Administered by Established Authorities

According to 2 Chronicles 19:4-11, Jehoshaphat (c. 871–848 BCE) established judges in Judah in every fortified city and charged them to administer justice impartially. Deuteronomy 17:8-13 presupposes a system of local justice, with appeal to a central court in the 'place chosen by God' when local justice is unable to cope with a case.

With the establishment of recognised legal authorities in Israel and Judah, whenever that took place, laws were collected together, presumably from oral as well as from written local sources, and formed into official collections. Once this had been done, there began the practice of written interpretation of laws, a process that can be easily discerned within the Old Testament (see, most fully, Fishbane 1985). Examples of this written interpretation include Exodus 23:11b, where the words 'you shall do the same to...' indicate that the law of leaving a field fallow every seventh year is extended to vineyards and olive orchards, and Exodus 22:9, in which the words 'or a garment or any other case' have been added to a law dealing originally with entrusting animals to someone's care to look after them.

Law Making and Drafting by Professional Lawyers or Scribes

Within this process we may distinguish between the practice of law, where legal jurisdiction approaches cases by drawing out principles from particular laws, and what we might call theoretical reflection on the law, where laws or principles may be framed independently of actual practice. As an example of the second type of procedure, Weinfeld (1972) has argued that in its final form, Deuteronomy is the product of a wisdom school of scribes, whose aims lay more in the realm of ideology than of legal practice.

This typology of four legal processes has been freely adapted from Fishbane to provide a framework for our discussion of the main sections of legal tradition in the Old Testament.

The Book of the Covenant

The legal part of the Book of the Covenant begins with a law about the release of Hebrew slaves (Exodus 21:2-11). Such slavery is restricted to six years for a male, unless he wishes to remain permanently in servitude, in which case a publicly attested ceremony is prescribed for this agreement. Female slaves have no such right of release, except that if they become the wife of a master or a member of his family they assume some of the rights of wives. Some of these provisions can be paralleled from Babylonian cuneiform law (Paul 1970: 45-61).

An important question is why the Book of the Covenant should begin with laws about slaves. It has been suggested (Phillips 1984) that since the laws are meant to apply to Israelites who are free, a law enabling slaves to regain their freedom is an appropriate opening for the collection. Another suggestion (not necessarily contradicting that of Phillips) is that in its final form the Book of the Covenant looks back to God's freeing of his people from slavery. The enslavement of people who have been freed by God must thus be regulated at the outset of these laws.

Verses 12-17 deal with four cases: killing a man, striking one's parents, robbing a man of his freedom, and cursing one's parents (for the order see Jackson 1975: 144). We may assume that originally the four cases were simple categorical statements:

> Whoever strikes a man mortally...
> Whoever strikes his father or mother...
> Whoever robs a man (of his freedom)...
> Whoever curses his father or mother...

As such, they may have been religious rather than legal exhortations, for although we know that murderers were proceeded against by the victim's next of kin, and that kidnapping was a capital offence in the laws of Hammurabi (Paul 1970: 65), we do not know whether children who cursed their parents were executed (Paul 1970: 66). The assumption here may be that judgment will be carried out ultimately by God, and that originally the laws dealing with the murder or forcible enslavement of a person were undetected offences, while those concerning parents were not punishable by humans.

Verses 18-27 deal with injuries inflicted upon men, women, and slaves by human agency. They have been the subject of much discussion as they contain the law of talion ('an eye for an eye'), popularly and wrongly supposed to epitomise Old Testament morality, as well as the only passage in the Bible (verse 22) that can be pressed into the current debate about abortion. Verses 18-21 seem to be straightforward. A man who injures another in a fight is required to compensate for the loser's inability to work and to assist his recovery. These are important considerations in an agricultural society. A male or female slave who dies immediately after being beaten by the master can be avenged in the usual way. This is not so, however, if the slave lives for a day or two after being struck. Presumably, the master is given the benefit of the doubt that the beating was not the only cause of death.

With verses 22-24, we encounter difficulties, which may be the result of a complicated process of interpreting and addition (Jackson 1975: 75-107). The case concerns injury done to a pregnant woman who intervenes in a brawl on behalf of her husband, as a result of which she gives birth prematurely. Verse 22 seems to imply that if the only harm is the (successful) premature birth, then the husband can fine the person who struck the blow. An addition at the end of the verse restricts damages to what is decided by arbitrators. Verse 23 then specifies what happens if there is further injury, without making it clear whether the injury is to the child or to the woman. In the case of such injury, the rule is 'life for life'. Jackson has argued that in the form of the law prior to the addition of verses 25-28 ('eye for an eye' etc.), the law meant that a living child was to be substituted by the offender if the premature birth was a miscarriage. With the addition of verses 24-25, however, the remedy for the premature birth was overlooked in favour of providing compensation for the injured woman. Finally, there was added to the passage a provision awarding freedom to slaves who lost an eye or tooth when beaten by their master. Jackson's argument is based partly upon the Middle Assyrian Laws, from which it is clear (Table A line 50: *ANET*: 184) that the penalty for causing a miscarriage by hitting a pregnant woman is the giving of a living child to replace the miscarried one.

Verses 28-32 deal with injury inflicted upon human beings by a goring ox. An ox that gores a man to death is stoned (to death), probably by the local community, to whom it constitutes a threat. Vicious bulls can inflict fatal injuries on farmers even today. If an animal is known to be potentially dangerous, is not restrained by its owner, and then causes fatal injuries, both the animal and the owner are to be killed (verse 29). The Hebrew words rendered 'not kept it in' raise questions about how a vicious animal was to be restrained, and it has been suggested (see Jackson 1975: 123) that a very slight alteration to the Hebrew should be made, producing the meaning 'has not destroyed it', thereby eliminating the danger. Verses 30-32 introduce the possibility of a fine instead of the death of the owner, and this is extended to include compensation if an ox kills a member of another man's family. The death of a slave is to be compensated for by a fine.

Verses 33-36 deal with injuries caused to other animals by a goring ox. We can assume that the passage began originally with verse 35, and that 33-34 were added later to cover injuries caused accidentally to animals by human activities, such as digging pits.

In Exodus 22:1-4 (Hebrew 21:37–22:3) attention is switched to the theft of animals. On the face of it, 22:1 belongs with 22:4, since they both concern this subject, whereas 22:2-3 may be an insertion. As 22:1 and 22:4 stand, two different penalties for theft seem to be envisaged, depending upon whether the thief has disposed of the stolen animal by selling or killing it (in either of which case he must pay compensation of four or five times its value) or whether he still possesses the animal (in which case compensation is to be double its value). However, it may be that 22:4 represents a later stage in biblical law from 22:1, when the penalty for theft became compensation of double the value of what was stolen. Verses 2-3 are usually held to distinguish between intended burglary during the night and during the day. The owner's right to self-defence is implicit in the provision that he can with impunity strike a burglar entering at night, even if the blow is fatal.

Verses 5-6 (Hebrew 4-5) presuppose the practice, well known in modern farming, of burning off a field or vineyard, prior to preparations for new planting. Where the property of another person is damaged, there must be compensation.

In verses 7-15 (Hebrew 6-14) there is a complicated passage dealing with compensation for property entrusted for safekeeping by one person to another, which is then lost or damaged. The main problem is faced by the person who has been entrusted with something to look after. How can he prove that he had not in some way used it for his own purposes? We notice the use of cultic oaths, lots, or oracles (verses 8 and 10) to help establish guilt or innocence.

With verses 16-17 (Hebrew 15-16) we come to the end of the section dealing with damages. This passage concerns damage done to an unbetrothed virgin who is abducted and loses her virginity. The damage is considered to be done to her father, since he will not get the normal bride price for a daughter who is not a virgin. The man responsible must marry her and pay the normal bride price; even if he refuses the marriage, he must still pay it.

From 22:18 to 23:19 we have a mixture of social and cultic laws which have a different tone from the preceding section on damages. The injunctions cover witchcraft, bestiality, and idolatry (verses 18-20); support for foreigners, widows, orphans, and the poor (verses 21-27); due respect to Yhwh and the ruler (verse 28—note that the Hebrew word for ruler is *not* king); the dedication of first-born sons and animals to God; a prohibition against eating dead animals found in the open (verse 31); a call to fair dealing in matters of justice (23:1-3); kindness to one's enemy's domestic animals (verses 4-5), and support for the rights of the poor and foreigners (verses 6-8). The Book of the Covenant ends with specific cultic rules about the Sabbath, the Sabbath (seventh, fallow) year, the three major festivals (note that Passover is not explicitly mentioned), and, finally, rules about sacrifice and first-fruits.

Is it possible to suggest a date and setting for the Book of the Covenant? Any answer to this question has to assume things that we do not know. For example, did the Book of the Covenant (Exodus 21:1–23:19) ever exist separately in substantially its present form? Did the instances of case law (e.g. Exodus 21:18–22:17) exist separately from the rest? Jackson (1972: 225 and *passim*) argues that those parts of the Book of the Covenant dealing with theft do not presuppose the existence of courts or the need for witnesses, but point, rather, to self-help. Other clues that might point to a date for the Book are the fact that the 'ruler' is not described as king and that in 23:14-17 Passover is not included as one of the three major festivals. This might suggest that the Book of the Covenant dates from the time when justice was largely a matter of family and local self-help, with difficult cases being dealt with by special arbitrators. On the other hand, we must guard against thinking that once the northern and southern kingdoms of Israel and Judah began to exist as small states, central judicial authority was exercised in them and that the features just described therefore point to a date before their establishment. The fact is that the Book of the Covenant is made up of materials from different times and social situations, but with particular stress on matters pertaining to the family, property, and the protection of the poor and slaves. Its compilation into its present form was undertaken at a time (or times) and by a circle (or circles) where these interests, and especially that of solidarity with the poor, were important. Presumably, this was in the very late monarchy in Judah, some time in the seventh century BCE.

Leviticus 17–26

Chapters 17–26 of Leviticus are usually called the Holiness Code because of their repeated insistence that Israel should be holy because God is holy (e.g. 19:2). Several instances of repetition and overlap in these chapters (for example between 18:2-18 and 20:11-17, 19-21) argue against this being a formal codification of laws. However, in view of the currency of the term 'Holiness Code', we shall use it here. In its present form the Code probably dates from the fifth century BCE but some of its material may be more ancient. For example, some writers trace the regulations about sexual offences (18:6-18) back to the pre-monarchic period.

Probably the most valuable way to approach these chapters is in terms of their content and ideology. We notice at once a striking contrast with the Book of the Covenant. The central core of the Exodus chapters deals with damages; there is no mention of priests. In Leviticus 17–26, however, there are only six verses (24:17-22) about damages, whereas several large sections deal with priests and the special regulations that govern their lives (e.g. 21:1–22:9). At several points, the Book of the Covenant and the Holiness Code overlap: they both deal with respect for parents, treatment of slaves, and observance of festivals. However, the holiness of God requires a strict separation between priests and the people, and between Israel and other peoples. Within Israel itself, one of the main purposes of regulated order is to allow God's blessing to fall upon the land. The land can be made impure and thus barren by violating the divine order. Our brief discussion of Leviticus 17–26 will cover some of its most important themes.

Sexual Relations

Chapters 18 and 20 prescribe degrees of relatedness within which sexual intercourse is prohibited. We shall not discuss here whether one passage is earlier than the other, or whether the regulations deal with the quite different matters of marriage and incest. It will be assumed that, in its final form, Leviticus 18:6-19 sets down boundaries in regard to both marriage and incest. From the standpoint of a given male (here called 'Ego'; there are no comparable female-oriented regulations) all the women are prohibited except Ego's wife and—apparently—his daughter, who is, for some reason, not mentioned.

The diagram below assumes that the father of Ego will have more than one wife, and that Ego will then have half-sisters. If Ego himself were to have more than one wife, the diagram would be more complex. The nearest relative with whom marriage is allowed is a first cousin on either the father's or mother's side, and marriage with a first cousin was probably quite common in Israel, as it is today in many parts of the world. We do not know to what extent these regulations were enforced or enforceable. The prohibitions against homosexual acts (18:22; 20:13) and against intercourse with an animal (18:23; 20:15-16) are to be seen in terms of preventing the violation of order in which men, women, and animals have specific functions which may not be confused. They are part of an ancient priestly way of envisaging the social and moral order of the world, and have no application to modern discussions about sexual relationships.

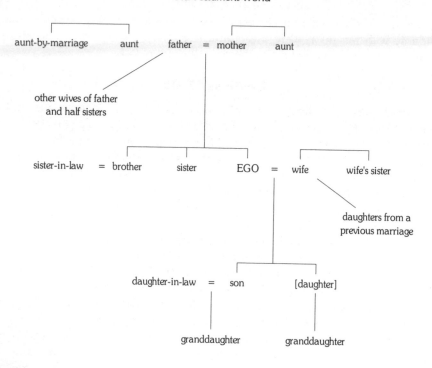

Religious Life

Where the Holiness Code deals with religious festivals it is, not surprisingly, far more detailed than the Book of the Covenant (cp. Exodus 23:14-17 with Leviticus 23:4-8, 15-22, 33-36). It includes the Passover (23:5), and it specifies sacrifices that are to be offered at the major festivals: the New Year Festival (23:23-25) and the Day of Atonement (23:26-32). However, it is not so much in giving fuller details about festivals that the Holiness Code asserts its priestly interest, as in the attempt to bring secular aspects of life into the religious sphere.

Leviticus 17 is concerned with the proper disposal of blood. This is because blood has a religious function from the priestly point of view, that of purifying what has been stained by wrongdoing. Thus blood must be handled properly, even when it comes to the innocent business of killing an animal or bird hunted as food. The blood of the prey must be properly drained from its corpse, and then must be covered over with earth (17:13). The blood of a menstruating woman makes her unclean (18:19), requiring her to undergo purification rituals presumably because it belongs to the sphere of the sacred. A man may not have intercourse with his wife during her periods.

A good example of the different outlook of the Book of the Covenant and the Holiness Code comes from the treatment of an animal corpse found in the open. Exodus 22:31 (Hebrew 22:30) simply says that the flesh of such an animal may not be eaten. Leviticus 17:15-16 prescribes a ritual of cleansing for those who have eaten such flesh. This involves washing the body and the clothes, and waiting until sunset, after which the person becomes clean. This seems to be a clear example of extending to lay people the priestly regulations (22:1-9) about becoming pure following contact with impurity, thus well illustrating the extension of religious ideas of purity into everyday life.

Social Relationships

Regulations governing social matters are confined to two sections, chapters 19 and 25. The latter of these looks like a unified composition, and while chapter 19 seems to be more of a collection of oddments, it can be argued that verses 1-18 are a version of the Decalogue with the addition of humanitarian obligations. The basis of the regulations in 19:11-18 about fair dealing with one's neighbours is not so much social solidarity as mutual religious responsibility. This is even more sharply seen in chapter 25, where regulations about not charging interest on debts and about the freeing of slaves are integrated into the regulations for the jubilee year. The purpose of the Jubilee year is to allow all Israelite slaves to be freed, and all sold land to revert to the traditional owners. Although we are here in the realm of religion, not law, this is a noble religious vision: one in which abuses and inequalities have been set aside so that the social order can reflect the will of a God who acts graciously towards his people and will have them do the same to each other.

The Holiness Code ends (chapter 26) with the stipulations that undergird the preceding laws. Their observance will ensure the fertility of the land; their neglect will result in the loss of it. Leviticus 26:39-45 is clearly addressed to the situation of the exile. Israel has lost the land, and it will be restored only with the passing of a number of Sabbath years equal to those that the people ignored. The restoration of the land will be achieved by virtue of God's covenant with Jacob, Isaac, and Abraham (26:42).

Deuteronomy

In its present form, Deuteronomy dates from after the time of the deportations in the sixth century BCE. Chapter 30 presupposes that the Israelites are already in exile, but promises their restoration to the land if they return to God 'with all their heart and all their soul' (Deuteronomy 30:2). There is an apt parallel between the Israelites about to enter the land of Canaan for the first time (which is the literary setting of the book) and the descendants of deportees about to return to the land where their forbears once dwelt. In both cases, Deuteronomy sets out what God requires of his people.

It is clear, however, that Deuteronomy has had a complex literary history. Some of its provisions may have been preserved in the northern kingdom until its guardians came south to Judah after the fall of Samaria (c. 722 BCE). An important stage in its composition was its reworking probably early in the reign of Josiah (640–609 BCE), after which it became the basis for Josiah's reforms in 622 (2 Kings 22:8ff.). Many interesting suggestions about its purpose in the reign of Josiah have been made. According to Weinfeld (1972: 139) it may be the work of the scribal family of Shaphan, whose members supported Jeremiah. Weinfeld thus sees Deuteronomy as a product of a secular 'wisdom' school of scribes. Frankena (1965) suggests that Deuteronomy took the form of a treaty between God and the people of Judah. Before the reign of Josiah Judah had been a vassal of Assyria, and probably subject to a vassal treaty. With independence from Assyria, Judah now reaffirmed its allegiance to God by means of Deuteronomy, which uses the treaty structure of prologue (chapters 5–11), obligations (chapters 12–26), and blessings and curses (chapter 28).

These matters are dealt with fully in the commentaries (see Mayes 1979). The aim of what follows will be to discuss the central part of Deuteronomy (chapters 12–26) in the light of the Book of the Covenant and the Holiness Code.

The most striking thing about these chapters is that they deal with matters that are treated nowhere else in the Old Testament legal traditions. Rules for the conduct of wars, for example, take up chapter 20; parts of chapter 13 concern an individual or a town that has decided to follow false gods; and the setting up of courts and judges is dealt with in chapters 16 and 17. Chapter 24 contains the only explicit regulation in the Old Testament about divorce, although divorce is actually only incidental to the main point that is being made: namely, that a man may not receive back his divorced wife if she has remarried and re-divorced or been widowed. And this brief selection of what is peculiar to Deuteronomy leaves out what is best known about the book—the insistence that sacrifice may be offered to God only at a single and central sanctuary designated by him.

The main ideology that unites the regulations is the need for unity. There is to be one sanctuary, and individuals or groups who seek other gods must be punished severely. Similarly, false prophets who support other gods are to be eliminated. The decisions of judges are to be accepted unconditionally. Although exemptions from military service are envisaged, the rules about warfare imply the duty of Israelites to serve in the army. However, along with the stress on the unity of the people and their absolute loyalty to God, Deuteronomy contains some of the most humane regulations anywhere in the Old Testament and, as we shall see, is remarkable for its positive attitude to women. If we bring these twin themes of unity and humanitarianism together, we get the essence of Deuteronomy. The former guarantees the latter. Only a people fully united under the God of Israel can be obedient to the calls for fair-dealing and compassion that characterise the book. Even the king himself is part of this unity, and is subject to its regulations. These will now be considered in more detail.

Religious Practice

Weinfeld (1972) has made an interesting attempt to demonstrate the 'secular' nature of Deuteronomy compared with the Holiness Code of Leviticus. Thus, there is little in Deuteronomy about priests; the section on festivals is comparatively short (16:1-17), the animals that may be eaten as food are no longer restricted to those that are hunted (12:20-28); and there is no necessity for the blood of such animals to be covered over by earth (12:24). On the other hand, we must not overlook the book's persistent, if not boldly stated, stress on purity. Deuteronomy 14:3-21 distinguishes carefully between clean and unclean creatures, and 17:1 insists that animals that are to be sacrificed must be perfect. At 21:1-9 there is a description of a ritual to be carried out where there is an unsolved murder. The elders of the town nearest to where the body is found are to take a cow that has not yet been yoked to a cart or plough, and are to bring it to a perpetual stream, where its neck is broken. The elders wash their hands over the animal, asking that the effect of unavenged blood will be set aside. The whole passage is a mixture of the secular (the ceremony is carried out by elders, and although priests appear in verse 5 they are not given a function) and the ritualistic. For example, the precise details about the type of cow and the place where it is to be killed, must be noted.

In Deuteronomy 21:22-23 the regulation requiring the corpses of those executed by hanging to be buried the same day is justified on the grounds of not making the land impure, and avoidance of impurity in the sense of the confusion of things that ought to be kept separate is probably behind the prohibitions of men wearing women's clothes and vice versa (22:5), vineyards being additionally planted with non-vines (22:9), and wool and flax being woven together (22:11). Deuteronomy 23:10-15 indicates that the purity of the army camp can be violated if a man ejects sperm during the night, while proper toilet arrangements in the camp are grounded not in the need for hygiene, but for purity. Finally, as mentioned earlier, the main thrust of the passage about divorce in 24:1-4 is that if a divorced woman has remarried, her sexual intercourse with her second husband will have made her impure, and thus forbidden, to her first husband.

We may detect a move towards theologising purity: to observe it is not to observe an irrational taboo (as would be the case in a 'primitive' society) but to respond responsibly to a God who has given a special land to a special people, and has set down boundaries whose violation will result in the loss of the land.

Women

Of all the legal traditions in the Old Testament, those in Deuteronomy grant the greatest recognition to the rights of women. This is most clearly apparent at Deuteronomy 15:12 and 17, where the right of release of female slaves (denied in Exodus 21:7) is allowed. Women are also protected in 21:10-14, regulations dealing with the treatment of female prisoners-of-war.

In Deuteronomy 22:13-19 safeguards are given to a newly married woman against her husband trying to divorce her on the grounds that she was not a virgin at the time of the nuptials. As evidence of her virginity, she can deposit with her father her stained night-garments from the first night of her marriage. A man who is proved to have accused his wife falsely of not being a virgin may never subsequently divorce her. In another regulation, a man who forces an unbetrothed virgin must pay a fine to her father, must marry her, and may never subsequently divorce her (22:28-29).

Regulations about War

In Deuteronomy 20 we are faced with material that is pure ideology. These regulations can hardly have been carried out in practice, and they exhibit clearly the themes of unity, purity, and humanitarianism that are characteristic of Deuteronomy. In 20:1-9, the humanitarian provisions allow that the following may absent themselves from the field of battle: anyone who has just built a house but not yet dedicated it (verse 5), anyone who has newly laid out a vineyard but not tasted its first vintage (verse 6), and anyone who is betrothed but not yet married (verse 7). In addition, anyone who has the courage to say that he is afraid is excused the battle (verse 8). These concessions, astonishing to a modern reader, can be made because of the certainty of victory when Israel fights with Yhwh on its side (verses 2-4).

In verses 10-17 a distinction is made between conquered enemy cities within the land claimed by Israel and those outside it. Whereas the latter are to be treated relatively fairly, the former are to be utterly destroyed, together with their inhabitants. If we feel that this apparent heartlessness contrasts strangely with the humanitarian provisions for the betrothed, and so on, we must appreciate that here, too, we are in the realm of ideology rather than actual military practice. Verse 18 makes it clear that the need to destroy entirely the non-Israelite inhabitants of the land is to prevent them from leading Israel astray to the worship of other gods. We are thus in the realm of the important themes of purity (no foreign gods) and unity (no foreign peoples).

The regulations about attacking cities outside Israel return to the theme of humanitarian behaviour. The cities must be given the chance to surrender, and only if they do not will all the males be killed following the inevitable Israelite victory (verses 10-15). When cities are besieged, fruit trees may not be used to build siege works (verses 19-20).

Humanitarian Provisions

In addition to those humanitarian measures already discussed, we can note the special tithes every third year for the benefit of Levites and the poor (Deuteronomy 14:28-29), the cancelling of debts every seven years (15:1-2), the respecting of landmarks (19:14), the protection of birds and the young in their nests (eggs or young may be taken, but not the mother (22:6-7), the prohibition against ploughing with an ox and an ass yoked together, the prohibition against taking the tools of a person's livelihood as a pledge (24:6), the payment of a day-labourer's wages on the same day (24:14-15), the leaving in the field for the use of the poor a forgotten harvested sheaf (24:19), and the harvesting of grapes in such a way that some will remain for the poor (24:20-22). Otto (1994: 192) has suggested that the humanitarian laws of Deuteronomy imply a social situation in which the family and kinship networks that normally supported individuals who had fallen on hard times, had broken down. The responsibilities that once fell on family members are now extended to all members of the nation. Deuteronomy 15:7 defines as a person's 'brother' any fellow member of the nation who needs help and who in that regard has a claim on any other member of the nation.

To sum up: if the Holiness Code seeks to bring aspects of everyday life under the influence of priestly ideas of purity and separateness, Deuteronomy understands purity more in ethical terms, and sees its expression as a matter of right dealing and the compassionate treatment of the poor. There is, as we have pointed out, an emphasis in Deuteronomy on details of ritual insofar as they affect purity, but priestly language and ideas are entirely absent from such passages. It is as though the details about ritual are relics of older practices, still adhered to out of a superstitious fear of ignoring them. Whereas in the Holiness Code the land will be restored to Israel when the number of ignored sabbatical years has been made good (and then out of consideration for the covenant with the patriarchs), in Deuteronomy the land will be restored when the nation seeks God with all its heart and soul.

The Decalogue (Ten Commandments)

In the Old Testament the Decalogue exists in two versions, in Exodus 20:1-17 and Deuteronomy 5:6-21. How they are to be numbered is a matter of dispute. Orthodox Jews take the first commandment to be Exodus 20:2, 'I am the LORD your God' and the second to be 20:3, 'You shall have no gods before me'. Christian tradition takes the first commandment to be 'You shall have no gods before me' but disagrees about whether 20:4-6 continues the first commandment (Catholic and Lutheran traditions) or whether verses 4-6 are the second commandment beginning 'You shall not make a graven image' (Reformed Protestant position). The issue is whether the word 'them' in verse 5 ('you shall not bow down to them') refers back to the graven image of verse 4 or the gods of verse 3. In order to make the number of commandments up to ten, the Catholic and Lutheran tradition refers to Deuteronomy 5:21, with the ninth commandment being 'you shall not desire your neighbour's wife' and the tenth being 'neither shall you covet your neighbour's house etc.'. These disagreements about the numbering rest on problems within the text that are the result of the complicated genesis of the Ten Commandments.

The best-known difference between the Exodus and Deuteronomy versions is in the reason given for observing the Sabbath. In Exodus, the Sabbath must be observed because it is the day on which God rested after the creation. In Deuteronomy the Sabbath must be observed because God freed the Israelites from slavery in Egypt, and they must, as a consequence, show compassion to their servants by allowing them to rest on the Sabbath. There are other, smaller differences, such as that in the commandment about honouring one's parents in Exodus 20:2 and Deuteronomy 5:16. Unfortunately it is impossible here to deal with the complex problems that these interrelationships conceal.

When we consider the content of the Decalogue in its final form we see that it covers a number of areas. The absolute claim of Yhwh upon his people is backed up by the practical requirements that no other representatives of gods may be made or placed alongside Yhwh in the sanctuary, that the divine name will not be used for swearing or for magical purposes, and that Yhwh's lordship over time will be recognised by the observance of the Sabbath. In the matter of social relationships, stress is put upon the sanctity of people and their property. Within the family group this entails honouring and supporting one's parents. Between families it upholds the sanctity of life by prohibiting premeditated murder, and in declaring against adultery and theft it protects a man's property from invasion by another. False evidence is prohibited because it undermines the entire workings of justice. The commandment against coveting, together with that against theft, shows that the Old Testament condemns those who plan mischief as much as those who carry it out.

What of the origin and purpose of the Decalogue? The only evidence that we have is its position in the books of Exodus and Deuteronomy, and the date of its final form depends on the date of composition of those books. In both cases, the Decalogue occupies a key position. In Exodus 20 it is the opening statement of what God revealed to Moses on Mt Sinai. In Deuteronomy, it is also the beginning of the 'statutes and ordinances' declared by Moses, and it is possible to see in the immediately following chapters of Deuteronomy a systematic exposition of the Decalogue. The tradition, then, gave to the Decalogue a place of prime importance in the setting out of God's requirements of his people but provided no further clues about the origin of the commandments.

The purpose of the Decalogue was to express the exclusive claim of Yhwh upon his people and to indicate how life was to be lived in the light of this claim. If the commandments were violated, then the party principally aggrieved was God, even if the offence involved wrongdoing against another Israelite. In the course of the development of the administration of justice, the injunctions of the Decalogue were incorporated into the system. We have noticed earlier in this chapter that the Old Testament also contains specifically legal injunctions regarding homicide, adultery, theft, false evidence, and apostasy. But, in spite of its amplifications, the Decalogue seems to have remained as a coherent text which served to express most definitively the exclusive demands of Yhwh upon his people.

We began by asking whether the legal traditions of the Old Testament are to do with law, ethics, wisdom, or religion. We have not really dealt with wisdom; we have hinted at it by suggesting that some material may reflect the activity of scribes rather than the actual practice of lawyers. Of the other categories we have given ample evidence. We have tried to show that it is certainly a mistake to regard the legal sections of the Old Testament simply as collections of laws. Their content is always a mixture of the legal, the ethical, and the religious, and they are certainly as much a source for knowledge of Israelite ethics and theology as they are a source for Israel's legal practice.

References and Further Reading

Crüsemann, F.
    1996   *The Torah: Theology and Social History of Old Testament Law* (Edinburgh: T. & T. Clark, 1996; German original *Die Tora. Theologie und Sozialgeschichte des alttestamentlichen Gesetzes* [Gütersloh: Chr. Kaiser/Gütersloher Verlagshaus, 1992 (2nd edn, 1997)]). (This work offers a detailed study of the theology and history of Old Testament law.)

Fishbane, M.
    1985   *Biblical Interpretation in Ancient Israel* (Oxford: Oxford University Press).

Frankena, R.
    1965   'The Vassal-Treaties of Esarhaddon and the Dating of Deuteronomy', *OTS* 14: 122-54.

Jackson, B.S.
    1972   *Theft in Early Jewish Law* (Oxford: Clarendon Press).

Jackson, B.S.
    1975   *Essays in Jewish and Comparative Legal History* (SJLA, 10; Leiden: E.J. Brill).

Mayes, A.D.H.
    1979   *Deuteronomy* (NCB; Grand Rapids: Eerdmans; London: Oliphants).

Otto, E.
    1994   *Theologische Ethik des Alten Testaments* (Stuttgart: Kohlhammer Verlag).

Paul, S.M.
    1970   *Studies in the Book of the Covenant in the Light of Cuneiform and Biblical Law* (VTSup, 18; Leiden: E.J. Brill).

Phillips, A.J.C.
    1984   'The Laws of Slavery', *JSOT* 30: 51-66.

Weinfeld, M.
    1972   *Deuteronomy and the Deuteronomistic School* (Oxford: Clarendon Press).

Chapter 11

SACRIFICES AND PSALMS

This chapter will deal with Leviticus 1–16, plus other references to sacrifice, and with the book of Psalms. Sacrifices and psalms are two different ways of approaching God. The first involves offering to God something that is a gift, or a substitute for the offerer; this is usually an animal, but sometimes a bird or an offering of grain. The second is an activity in which worshippers offer themselves, using words of praise or petition, and sometimes joining in liturgical movements such as processions. We presume that sacrifices and psalms both had their setting in the Temple in Jerusalem; but this likely assumption is virtually unsupported by any evidence. Sacrifices are only occasionally mentioned in the psalms while we have no idea of what, if anything, was said when sacrifices were offered. In fact, the study of sacrifices and of the psalms presents difficult problems. First of all, there is hardly any evidence in the Old Testament outside of passages such as Leviticus 1–16 that the sacrifices as prescribed were ever offered. Secondly, whatever may have been the use of the psalms in the Temple service, the book of Psalms in its final form is intended to be a collection for private, individual meditation, and not for public use. The exploration of these two problems will be the main concern of this chapter.

Sacrifices

Leviticus 1–16 assumes that the Israelites are in the wilderness. They obviously have no permanent place of worship. Instead, there is the Tent of Meeting, which is a portable shrine standing at the centre of the camp, with an altar of burnt offering at its entrance, an altar of incense within, and a holy of holies separated by a veil from the remainder of the tent. For this portable sanctuary there are regulations about burnt offerings (chapter 1), meal offerings (chapter 2), peace offerings (chapter 3), sin offerings—for involuntary transgression (chapter 4), and offerings for atonement for deliberate offences (chapter 5). Following rules for the consecration of priests and the offerings special to them (chapters 6–10), there follow rules about purity, including clean and unclean animals, and how one deals with 'leprosy' (chapters 11–15). Chapter 16 deals with the Day of Atonement.

Leviticus sets these regulations in the wilderness because they are represented as having been revealed by God to Moses on Mt Sinai. However, if these regulations are as old as this, it is surprising that there is no reference to them in other parts of the Old Testament. The difficulties can be outlined as follows:

First of all, the very existence of the Tent of Meeting is problematical. The Tent is supposed to have contained the Ark of the Covenant. However, according to

1 Samuel 1–3 the Ark was in a temple while it was at Shiloh. Furthermore, according to 2 Samuel 6:17, when David brought the Ark to Jerusalem, the king himself provided a tent for it. What happened to the Tent of Meeting? A widely held scholarly view is that the supposed instructions to Moses for making the tent and its appurtenances (Exodus 36:8ff.) are based upon what was actually the case in the Temple at the time Exodus was written. In other words the description of the tent in Exodus 36 is a fiction.

Another problem is that the history of sacrifice, so far as we can reconstruct it from the narrative traditions of the Old Testament, seems to present a different picture from that in Leviticus 1–16. Manoah (Judges 13:19), Samuel (1 Samuel 7:9), Saul (1 Samuel 13:9), David (2 Samuel 6:17), Solomon (1 Kings 3:4), and Elijah (1 Kings 30–38) all offered sacrifices, whereas none of them was a priest. These sacrifices were primarily burnt offerings. Of sin offerings there is no mention in these traditions. The narrative traditions give the impression that any head of a family could and did offer sacrifice, when occasion demanded it, on behalf of the household or lineage. Thus a widespread scholarly view holds that the sacrifices detailed in Leviticus 1–16 were introduced only after the exile, and that the stress in Leviticus on purity and atonement reflects the mood of the post-exilic community in Judah.

Sacrifice on the Old Testament

Almost every people known to scholarly research engages in, or has engaged in, sacrifice. No doubt the need to sacrifice arises from the need for humankind to make the world intelligible. Where technology cannot help—for example, in situations of sickness, death, danger from enemies, or threats to the production of food because of droughts or floods—the attempt to please, to placate, or to persuade unseen powers believed to be able to help, plays an important role in enabling humans to cope with everyday life. But belief in unseen powers that control the forces of nature and can influence life and death means that the world has to be divided into areas of the sacred and the ordinary. The sacred is where the unseen powers can be approached, and access may be dangerous. Thus, there often arises a professional class of those who alone can have the most immediate access to divinity, and this class determines how and with what offerings divinity may be approached. In particular, divinity may be approached only by what is perfect and pure physically; but the idea of purity can extend widely into the world of the ordinary, so that happenings or objects that are common in everyday life are perceived as potentially dangerous to ordinary people, because they belong to the realm of divinity, or because they blur the boundaries within which the life of a society is ordered.

Within the framework just described, various types of sacrifice can be made. There may be regular offerings of food and drink. It is not necessarily believed that the divinity needs them in order to survive, and they probably function primarily as a reassurance to the worshippers that because they continually remember the divinity, it will not forget them. There may also be regular offerings of what are regarded as the result of blessings from the divinity, for example, first-born sons and animals, and the first-fruits of crops. Second, there may be offerings to placate the divinity when its property has been damaged, or a prohibited boundary has been crossed. For example, eating the flesh of a forbidden animal would be the violating of such a boundary. Third, there may be sacrifices at times of individual or national crisis. As we shall see later, burnt offerings were sometimes made in ancient Israel prior to a battle. Offerings might also be made along with vows in the face of illness. Such offerings, and others, formed part of Old Testament sacrifice.

Regular and Special Offerings
We begin a survey of Old Testament sacrifice with regular offerings of food. Exodus 25:30 commands:

You shall set the bread of the Presence on the table before me always.

This practice of always having the bread of the Presence, or showbread, in the sanctuary is certainly a survival of an ancient custom of offering food to the gods. The same idea is also found in the phrase 'a pleasing odour to the LORD' in Exodus 29:18, where the ancient underlying custom is that of offering to the gods a pleasant smell of incense or burnt flesh. Furthermore, there is a command that there should be each day a morning and an evening sacrifice, consisting of a lamb, together with flour and oil:

It shall be a regular burnt offering throughout your generations at the entrance of the tent of meeting before the LORD (Exodus 29:42).

These are all regular offerings which are made by the priests, but they would have to get the necessary fuel (one tree to burn wholly an ox) and animals from the people.

The people themselves would be responsible for bringing offerings of what God had blessed them with: first-born sons and animals (Exodus 22:28-29) and first-fruits of agricultural produce (Exodus 23:19).

Offerings designed to help restore boundaries that have been violated are dealt with especially in Leviticus 4–6 and 12. To modern readers, these sacrifices seem especially irrational. For example, there is nothing irrational to us about women losing blood during their monthly periods, but for a society in which blood was held to be sacred, not least because it was used to purify sacred things (see below), its loss was regarded as a serious matter. For normal menstrual periods no actual sacrifices were required, but for prolonged menstrual periods, or for abnormal loss of blood, a sin offering and a burnt offering were required eight days after the discharge ceased (Leviticus 15:25-30). Sin offerings will be discussed more fully shortly.

The offering of burnt sacrifices on occasions of national or personal crisis is reasonably well attested in the Old Testament. It has already been noticed that Samuel (1 Samuel 7:9) and Saul (1 Samuel 13:9) offered burnt sacrifices prior to taking part in battle, and that Manoah made a similar offering when confronted by an angel (Judges 13:15-23).

The History of Old Testament Sacrifice
Having briefly examined various types of sacrifice described in the Old Testament, we shall now try to discover something of their history. Earlier scholarship made the mistake of supposing that sacrifice had developed along a single line, and that this could be divided into three periods. In the first period, there had been no established priesthood or rituals, and sacrifices were family or clan celebrations at which the male head of the group carried out the sacrifice and the participants shared the flesh of the animal. In the second period, Josiah's reform, and his centralisation of the cult in Jerusalem in 622 BCE, moved things decisively in favour of greater regulation. In

the third period, after the return from the deportations, the religion of Judah became dominated by the sacrificial rituals of the second temple, with particular emphasis on sin and atonement.

Although this reconstruction is not without its merits, it is too rigid. The Old Testament picture of religion before the monarchy is one in which religion was carried out locally, and that there were communal festivals, especially at harvest-time, and sacrifices offered by male heads of families. There were also many regional sanctuaries: Bethel, Shiloh, Shechem, Gilgal, Beer-Sheba, Mizpah, Gibeon, Nob, to name only some. These were not, of course, necessarily Israelite sanctuaries, and the rituals performed in them were no doubt based upon superstitious notions of religion which were already very ancient. We can guess that at these sanctuaries food offerings were made to their gods (cp. perhaps 1 Samuel 21:4 where David is given holy bread to eat from the sanctuary at Nob), and that they were the places to which offerings of first-born animals and first-fruits were taken. Also, since fears about uncleanness can be deeply rooted, we can assume that it was at these regional sanctuaries that offerings to restore purity were made. Such sanctuaries were also the places where disputes were decided by the swearing of oaths or the undergoing of ordeals (see below). In short, there was not an early period in which priests and purification rituals played no part. Rather, in the early period, religion was based upon the local social group and on the regional sanctuaries, with their priesthoods.

According to the Old Testament, the first important change came with the rise of the monarchy. According to 1 Samuel 28:3, Saul, who is presented as being sympathetic to the prophetic groups, tried to suppress mediums and witchcraft. The beginning of the centralisation of power had consequences for local religion. Saul eliminated the sanctuary at Nob because it assisted David, according to 1 Samuel 22:11-19. Under David's rule, a new cult was established in Jerusalem in which the worship of Yhwh was centred upon the Ark of the Covenant; this was further consolidated by the building of the Temple by Solomon. The Temple was essentially a royal shrine under the control of the king, and hardly affected the lives of ordinary people; but it is likely that regional sanctuaries were gradually brought under the control of the monarchy to some extent.

When the northern tribes rebelled under Jeroboam, it was the Israelite king himself who reorganised the sanctuaries of Bethel and Dan and appointed new priests (1 Kings 12:28-31). Such royal patronage, however, brought doubtful benefits when some later rulers of the northern kingdom, Israel, became supporters of the fertility god Baal, and when some kings of Judah encouraged the pagan practices of their Assyrian overlords.

The reforms of Josiah (and possibly those of Hezekiah before him) involved closing down the regional sanctuaries and centralising worship at Jerusalem. No doubt there were good political reasons for this. Such a move signalled the need for greater national unity; and if Josiah hoped to extend his territory to include the Bethel and Samaria hills, the pressing of the exclusive religious claims of Jerusalem would assist that end. But Josiah's reforms also implied that Jerusalem was no longer simply a royal sanctuary; it was now a national sanctuary, which the people were expected to patronise. Although the reform was short-lived, it paved the way for the situation after the return from the deportations, in which Judah became a community centred upon the Temple.

We must not suppose, however, that in this period Judah was now a devoutly religious community dutifully carrying out the rituals prescribed in Leviticus. The evidence from Ezra and Nehemiah, and for the period before the Maccabean revolt shows otherwise. It was now possible, however, for the priests to rewrite and to re-present ancient rituals in idealistic terms which assumed that the people of God was gathered around one sanctuary, as it had been gathered around the Tent of Meeting in the wilderness period.

The history of Old Testament sacrifice is not, then, a movement from a ritual free-for-all to a total conformity to the rituals of Leviticus. At all periods there existed both freedom from and dependence upon the sanctuaries and their rituals. The changed circumstances of the period after the deportations, however, enabled the priestly writers to describe the rituals in such a way as to express a total world-view, in which an idealised Israel lived its life as the people of God by observing the levitical prescriptions. What this world-view was will be explored below.

The World-View of Leviticus 1–16

So far we have tried to sketch the history of Old Testament sacrifice in order to reject the idea that rituals such as those described in Leviticus were introduced only after the deportations. In fact, many of these rituals may be ancient, although we do not know their origin. In their present form, however, they date from the period after the deportations, and are best read as articulating a distinct world-view that is to be dated in those times. We shall deal with three particular areas: defilement and purification of the sanctuary; rites of passage; and atonement for the whole people.

Defilement and Purification of the Sanctuary

Leviticus 4 deals with the steps to be taken if divine regulations are broken unwittingly. The implication is that such offences defile the sanctuary, which must then be purified. The more senior or important the offender, the greater is the degree of defilement; and therefore more powerful methods of purification are called for. This can be illustrated as follows:

Offender	Animal	Blood	Fats, etc.	Remainder
Priest, or the whole congregation	bull	sprinkled seven times in front of veil of sanctuary; some put on altar of incense, rest poured out at foot of altar of burnt offering	burnt on altar of burnt offering	burnt outside the camp
ruler	male goat	put on horns of altar of burnt offering, rest poured out at foot of altar of burnt offering	burnt on altar of burnt offering	burnt on altar of burnt offering
ordinary Israelite	female goat	as for ruler	as for ruler	as for ruler

An offence by a priest or the whole congregation was held to defile the entrance of the sanctuary, and the altar of incense within it. These were therefore sprinkled with blood, and because the blood had been used for so holy a purpose, the flesh and skin of the animal had to be burnt outside the camp. A ruler or ordinary Israelite was held to have defiled only the altar of burnt offering, and after this had been purified, the fat parts and then the remainder could be burnt on the altar.

Rites of Passage

The rites of passage specified in Leviticus 1–16 assume that there are three spheres: the sacred, the ordinary, and the abnormal; they are rituals designed to enable a person to pass from one sphere to the next and have similar features in quite differing circumstances.

The most striking similarities are in the anointing of the right earlobe, thumb, and big toe in the case of the priest and the 'leper' (the Hebrew term covers a wide variety of skin complaints, some of them curable). This ritual takes place at different points in the ceremony for obvious reasons. The priest is not unclean at the outset of his ceremony, whereas the leper is considered to be so. A noticeable feature of each case is the period of seven days of waiting, which permits the transition from one sphere to the next. The washing or consecrating of clothes also helps to mark the process of transition from one sphere to the next.

Person	Sphere	Destination	Initial	Clothes	Waiting	Final stage
priest (Lev. 8–9)	ordinary	sacred	bull and ram; blood put on right earlobe, thumb, and big toe	consecrated with oil	seven days at door of Tent of Meeting	offers bull
leper (Lev. 14)	abnormal	ordinary	two birds; one released, the other killed and its blood mixed with water and sprinkled on leper seven times	washes clothes	seven days outside his tent: on seventh day shaves off all his hair	offers two male lambs; blood put on right earlobe, thumb, and toe; sprinkled seven times with oil, and oil put on right earlobe, thumb, and toe
male who has a discharge of fluid (other than semen)	abnormal	ordinary	none	washes clothes	counts seven days	offers two turtledoves or young pigeons
female who has unusual discharge (not menstruation)	abnormal	ordinary	none	not specified	counts seven days	offers two turtledoves or young pigeons

Atonement for the Whole People

On the Day of Atonement, the most powerful of the rituals is performed, in order to purify the holiest part of the sanctuary:

> …because of the uncleanness of the people of Israel, and because of their transgressions… (Leviticus 16:6)

Here the divisions between the sacred, the ordinary, and the abnormal are at their sharpest. In order to enter the holiest part of the sanctuary, the priest has to make a sin offering, for himself and his house. Once he has entered the most holy place, he sprinkles the mercy seat (a piece of furniture symbolising God's presence) seven times with the blood of a bullock. He then repeats this with the blood of a goat. When he has completed the purification of the sanctuary, he brings forward a live goat, lays his hands upon its head, and confesses (verse 21):

> all the iniquities of the people of Israel, and all their transgressions, all their sins…

This is one of the very few places in the Old Testament that indicates that there was a liturgy of things spoken which accompanied the ritual of things done. The goat (the original scapegoat) is now led from the sphere of the sacred, through the camp (the sphere of the ordinary), and released into the abnormal and chaotic world outside the camp. Its progress symbolises and effects the removal of the defilement suffered by the sanctuary because of the people's transgressions.

Perhaps one surprising thing about all these ceremonies is that they are directed more towards ritual offences than towards moral ones. It is true that Leviticus 5–6 deals briefly with deliberate offences of a moral kind, such as fraud, robbery, oppressing one's neighbour, and lying; but there is no mention of sacrifice for what we today would call more serious offences such as murder. Yet this should not surprise us. Murder was dealt with by members of the victim's family, and the penalty was the death of the murderer. An unsolved murder raised the problem, dealt with in Deuteronomy 21:1-9 (see Chapter 10, p. 146) of freeing the land from impurity caused by the unavenged shed blood of the victim, but no sacrifice could atone for murder. The very fact that the ceremonies of Leviticus 1–16 and elsewhere concentrate upon ritual rather than moral offences is a testimony to their age; but we should not regard them as quaint or unnecessary. Insofar as they expressed a view of the world, they were an attempt to remind Israelites in many ways that their every-day lives were lived in the presence of God. This reminding was achieved by the marking out of boundaries or the defining of 'taboos', together with offerings for the restoration of normality when there were violations.

If the rituals of Leviticus are looked at purely from an anthropological point of view, they appear to be survivals of primitive ideas about purity. In the context of Genesis to Leviticus, however, they take their meaning from the story as a whole. This story concerns the deliverance of Israelites from slavery in Egypt to freedom in the wilderness, and later in their own land. In the larger context, the rituals concerning purity are in effect theologised, so that they become part of the people's response to a God who deals personally with them. Thus, ancient ceremonies, whose origins and development are largely unknown to us, take their place in the whole story of Israel's witness to God, and express from a priestly point of view what it means to be a people having a special relationship with their God.

The Psalms

In the matter of their interpretation, the psalms present a similar problem to that of the ceremonies described in Leviticus. We know what the whole Psalter in its final form is meant to be: not a collection of pieces for use in public worship, but a manual of private devotion and meditation which encompasses confession (Psalm 51), lament (Psalm 3), adoration (Psalm 8), and praise (Psalm 150), to name only some of the contents. Yet some of the psalms must have been used in the worship of the Temple, and were surely the spoken or sung accompaniment to solemn and festive ceremonies. This is certainly the view of the books of Chronicles (e.g. 2 Chronicles 6:41-42). Even so, whatever these ceremonies were, they have receded so far into the background that they are virtually impossible to recover from the psalms in their present form (Wilson 1985: 170-72 and *passim*). We shall try to deal with these matters in relation to three topics: the royal ceremonies of the psalms, the form-critical study of the psalms, and the collection and editing of the psalms.

The Royal Ceremonies of the Psalms

The Jerusalem Temple was a royal foundation and a royal chapel. Probably until the time of Josiah (640–609 BCE) the ordinary people used other sanctuaries when they needed them. However, it would not be surprising if some of the psalms reflected ceremonies that centred upon the king and his household.

The attempt to identify such psalms and to guess at the underlying ceremonies is quite old in biblical scholarship. The seventeenth-century Puritan commentator Matthew Poole, for all that he saw many references to Christ in the psalms, noted that Psalm 2 had been connected by some scholars with David's inauguration as king. He accepted that Psalms 24, 47, and 68 were composed on the occasion of the bringing of the Ark by David to Jerusalem (2 Samuel 6). He also connected Psalm 132 with the same ceremony, although he believed that 132 was written by Solomon and was used by him as a prayer which reminded God of how David had given the Ark a resting place.

Scholarship in the twentieth century enlarged the scope of so-called royal psalms to include those that may have been used by a king prior to a battle (e.g. Psalm 44) and those that may have been used at an annual ceremony, such as the anniversary of the king's coronation or a New Year Festival. Into this category have come Psalms 93 and 96–99, which celebrate God's universal kingship over the world. There have also been variations upon the view that some of the psalms accompanied royal occasions. One variation suggests that some psalms were composed before David captured Jerusalem, and were used by the northern tribes at a New Year celebration. These psalms were brought to Jerusalem by the attendants of the Ark of the Covenant. Another variation suggests that at the New Year Festival in Jerusalem, the king suffered ritual humiliation, death, and resurrection. We do not believe that either of these variations can be convincingly demonstrated, and we content ourselves with outlining the possible ceremonies that lay behind the so-called royal psalms.

Psalm 2 pictures the nations of the world conspiring together to overthrow the king in Jerusalem. The text asserts, however, that this is useless because God says (verse 6):

I have set my king on Zion, my holy hill.

This is probably the point at which we should say something about 'Zion ideology'. We glimpse something of this ideology in other psalms, most notably Psalm 46. Here, the city of God is built above a river (verse 4), which was probably believed to be a river of paradise. As the place where God dwelt (verse 5), Jerusalem was safe from all its enemies, and this sense of security is expressed in the psalm by the refrain, twice repeated:

> The LORD of hosts is with us;
> The God of Jacob is our refuge.

This refrain, incidentally, possibly indicates the fusion of northern and southern religious ideas. Jacob was the patriarch associated with the northern tribes and 'LORD of hosts' was a title associated with the Ark (see below). These ideas of northern origin have here been located in Jerusalem and fused with the Jerusalem ideology that the city of God, situated above the river of paradise, will endure for ever.

Returning to Psalm 2, we can now see why the psalm expresses so much confidence. Zion is not just any city; it is the dwelling place of the one who (verse 4):

> sits in the heavens...

This is why human plotting against it can never succeed. But the king has a further ground for confidence. At his coronation he is given a scroll which sets out the mutual obligations between the king and God. This scroll contains (verse 7) the words:

> You are my son,
> today I have begotten you.

The king has thus been received on his coronation day into a special relationship with God by adoption. This is guarantee enough that he will withstand assaults upon his power; for such assaults will be against his 'father' also.

Psalm 24 is widely held to have been used, if not on the occasion when David brought the Ark to Jerusalem, then at least annually thereafter. The psalm is thought to consist of two parts: a liturgy of confession for those who are to bear the Ark to its resting place after it has been carried in procession outside Jerusalem, and a question and answer ceremony (verses 7-10) at the city gates. In the latter, the bearers of the Ark demand admittance in the name of the king of glory:

> Lift up your heads, O gates!
> and be lifted up, O ancient doors!
> that the King of glory may come in.

The gatekeepers ask:

> Who is the King of glory?

The bearers of the Ark reply that it is the Lord, strong and mighty, mighty in battle. When the questions and answers are repeated the bearers answer:

> The LORD of Hosts,
> he is the King of glory!

We know from 1 Samuel 4:4 that the full name of the Ark was the Ark of the Covenant of the LORD of Hosts (see also Numbers 10:35-36). This is why the guess is made that Psalm 24 reflects a ceremony in which the Ark was carried in procession, and that the name 'Lord of hosts', so closely associated with the Ark, was the final word of authority which caused the gatekeepers to admit the procession.

Psalm 44 is believed to have been used by the king prior to battle. This is partly because of the sudden switch from the first person plural to the first person singular in verses 5-6 (and in 14-16):

> Through you we push down our foes;
> through your name we tread down our assailants.
> For not in my bow do I trust
> nor can my sword save me.

It is suggested that this surprising change can best be understood if the king is speaking for the people as a whole. He can use both 'we' and 'I' language. From its content, the psalm is clearly a prayer for success in battle.

In Psalm 47 the phrase (verse 5)

> God has gone up with a shout,
> the LORD with the sound of a trumpet

has suggested a sort of coronation festival for God, in which the Ark was carried up the hill of Zion ('God has gone up...'), and trumpets were blown to celebrate this enactment of his kingship. The subject-matter of the psalm celebrates the universal kingship of God.

In Psalms 93 and 96–99 there are no references to anything like processions or removals of the Ark. It is the subject-matter of these psalms that has suggested that they were used at a ceremony to celebrate God's universal kingship. They share certain themes: that the seas or powers of nature roar in defiance of or in obedience to God; that he has founded the world and ensures its stability; and that he has also established moral decrees. He is coming to execute judgment and justice, and this will be welcomed by the powers of nature. These psalms are called 'royal' because it is presumed that the king would have taken an important part in the ceremonies.

Psalm 110 appears to be connected with David's successors' coronation in Jerusalem. It is addressed by a priest to the king, and the priest speaks the words of God (verse 1):

> The LORD [i.e. God] says to my Lord [i.e. the king],
> 'Sit at my right hand, until I make your enemies your footstool'.

We meet again the theme prominent in Psalm 2, that God will give victory to the king. There is here, however (verse 4), a new element:

> The LORD (i.e. God) has sworn
> and will not change his mind,
> 'You are a priest for ever
> according to the order of Melchizedek'.

It has been supposed that the king is here being admitted to the rights and privileges that the priest-kings of Jerusalem had before its capture by David, although this must be seen in the light of the current controversy about whether, and to what degree, Jerusalem was occupied prior to its capture by David (see p. 66). Also, *malki-sedeq* may not be a proper name, but mean 'righteous king'.

Psalm 132 has been held to contain clear traces of a ceremony in which the whole story of David bringing the Ark from Kiriath-jearim to Jerusalem (2 Samuel 6) was re-enacted. Two verses, 6 and 8, are especially pertinent:

> We heard of it in Ephrathah,
> we found it in the fields of Jaar…
> Rise up, O LORD, and go to your resting place,
> you and the ark of your might.

These verses suggest a mock expedition to seek and find the Ark, followed by its festal removal to Jerusalem, where it was lifted up and placed upon the site prepared by David. However, as older commentators (e.g. Poole 1962: 198) had already noticed, verse 10,

> For your servant David's sake
> do not turn away the face of your anointed one,

suggests that a successor of David is speaking. Moreover, the word 'there' in verse 17 is strange:

> There I will make a horn to sprout up for David…

This implies that the setting of the psalm is not in Jerusalem, but somewhere else (in Babylon during the time of the deportations?).

This section has not exhausted the royal psalms or the ceremonies that have been detected behind them. Approaching the psalms in this way has the merit of bringing the psalms to life as they are set in the great ceremonial occasions of the Jerusalem Temple. Yet a word of warning is needed. It is difficult to reconcile the suggestion that the Ark was regularly carried around in processions with the ritual of Leviticus 16, which specifies that the high priest could only enter the holy of holies (where the Ark was placed) once a year, and then only after elaborate rituals. Moreover, there is no hint in Leviticus 16 that the Ark could be removed from its place. It may be possible to overcome the difficulty by saying that in its final form Leviticus dates from, and reflects a time when, there was no king and thus no processions. It is not impossible that when Leviticus 16 reached its final form, there no longer was an Ark—it having been destroyed or carried off by the Babylonians. There is much that we do not know.

Form-Critical Study of the Psalms

The branch of psalm study known as form-critical is usually linked with the name of the German scholar Hermann Gunkel (1862–1932). It was a major aspect of psalms studies in the twentieth century; but its roots go back at least to the beginning of the nineteenth. Briefly, it involves grouping psalms together on the basis of content, and then trying to suggest the situation in the life of the individual or the community to which a particular psalm was appropriate.

A major group is known as individual laments, and a glance at Psalms 4–7 indicates that they have certain common features. Each begins with a prayer to God either to hear or to be gracious to the psalmist. Each implies that the psalmist is in some difficulty, chiefly from enemies; each ends on a positive note, as though the psalmist has been reassured of God's favour and can now face life once more in confidence.

Another major group is that of communal laments. Psalms 79 and 80 both imply that the people as a whole are in distress, and the speakers use the 'we' form of address to God, reminding him of how much they are suffering. Both of these two psalms end with a prayer for deliverance, not with a confident assertion that all is now right.

Parallel to individual and communal laments are individual and communal thanks-givings. Psalms 30 and 34 are examples of the former, Psalm 34 beginning with the words

> I will bless the LORD at all times;
> his praise shall continually be in my mouth.

In both cases, the psalmist celebrates how God brought deliverance in time of trouble. An example of a communal thanksgiving is Psalm 65. Another class consists of the 'wisdom' psalms, which reflect upon the problem of the suffering of the innocent and the prosperity of the wicked (e.g. Psalm 73). We have already men-tioned royal psalms in the preceding section.

The form-critical approach helps to bring the psalms to life, as texts bound up with the problems of individuals and the community; but again, the approach raises questions that are not easy to answer. Who are the individuals who composed or used these psalms? Were they ordinary worshippers? If the answer is yes, we must suppose that these psalms were composed during or after the time of Josiah; for it has been pointed out that Jerusalem was a royal sanctuary, and that ordinary Israel-ites made use of local sanctuaries when they needed them. Perhaps they were composed and used in regional sanctuaries, or the laments were composed by or for members of the king's entourage. We must be careful, in view of the limitations of our knowledge, not to read too much into the situations at which the psalmists hint. The psalms are vague, perhaps deliberately so, about their circumstances of compo-sition. This may be because they were meant to be used in all sorts of situations, in which case the search for greater precision would be self-defeating.

The Collection and Editing of the Psalms

We know very little about how the psalms were collected and edited; but what we can reasonably guess sheds some light which is quite instructive. The psalms are traditionally separated into five books: I, 1–41; II, 42–72; III, 73–89; IV, 90–106; and V, 107–50. There is some evidence that Book I, at the very least, was a separate collection, for beginning with Psalm 42 (the first Psalm of Book II), editors changed the divine name Yhwh to the more general word for God, *'elohim*. This can be seen if you compare Psalms 14 and 53, which are almost identical apart from the use of 'God' instead of Yhwh in Psalm 53. The fact that this process began at the beginning of Book II indicates that Psalm 42 was the first psalm of a collection separate from Psalms 1–41. It is also to be noted that whereas most of Psalms 1–41 are headed 'A Psalm of David', Psalms 42–49 are psalms of the 'Sons of Korah', and Psalm 50 is 'A Psalm of Asaph'.

We do not know the length of the collection beginning at Psalm 42. The changing of the name Yhwh to *'elohim* went as far as Psalm 83, that is into Book III but not quite to its end. Support for the traditional view that Psalms 42–72 were originally a separate collection can be found in the ending of Psalm 72, which takes the form of a doxology:

> Blessed be the LORD, the God of Israel.
> who alone does wondrous things.
> Blessed be his glorious name forever;
> may his glory fill the whole earth. Amen and Amen.

To this are added the words

The prayers of David son of Jesse are ended.

(It is worthwhile noting, however, that many psalms from 73 to 150 are also ascribed to David.)

Also supporting this division is the fact that Psalms 73–83 are psalms 'of Asaph', suggesting a new, or separate, collection. We may therefore guess that Psalms 1 (or perhaps 2—see later) to 41 and 42–72 and 73–83(?) were originally separate collections. The name Asaph is known to us from Chronicles (e.g. 1 Chronicles 25:2) as one of David's chief musicians; but how far this information is accurate we do not know.

For Books IV and V we have evidence from manuscripts from the Dead Sea Scrolls that even as late as the first century CE the order of the psalms was by no means fixed. The scroll known as 11QPs^a, and usually dated 30–50 CE has a most irregular order between Psalms 100 and 150, including ten pieces that do not appear in the final collection of the psalms in the Old Testament. The most spectacular deviations are as follows (see Wilson 1985: 124-25, for an outline): Psalms 106–108 and 110–17 are omitted. Examples of deviant order are the following sequences: 103, 109, 118, 104, 147, 105, 146, and 132, 119, 135; and 93, 141, 133, 144, 155, 142–43, 149–50. It is possible to argue, of course, that the evidence from Qumran is not representative, because the Qumran community was outside mainstream Judaism (if there was such a thing). But there is another approach, which looks for reasons for the order of psalms in 11QPs^a and uses these as a clue to the arrangement of the Psalter.

Wilson (1985: 124-31) points out that psalms 118, 104, 147, 105, and 146 in 11QPs^a all contain in their superscripts or postscripts either the word *hodu* ('praise') or *hallelujah* ('praise the LORD'). Furthermore, this block comes between psalms 101-103, 109 (ascribed to David), and 120-32, which are all 'Songs of Asents'. In other words, parts of 11QPs^a are grouped together in blocks, depending on the superscripts and postscripts, with 'hodu' and 'hallelujah' psalms marking a transition from one group to the next. Wilson detects similar phenomena in the Psalter as we know it. For example, Psalms 104–106, which end Book IV, are all 'hodu' or 'hallelujah' psalms, as are Psalms 146–50, which end Book V.

There are many things that remain unexplained, but the following points can be made about the collecting and editing of the Psalter in the light of the section on the psalms as a whole.

First, if there were royal psalms which were used in the way suggested above, they form no collection in the Psalter. This is evident from their numbers: 2, 24, 47, 110, 132, and possibly 93 and 96–99. This is not to say that it is wrong to try to identify royal psalms and to reconstruct the ceremonies at which they were used; but it is to say that the compilers of the Psalter were probably unaware that there was a group of psalms that had been thus used.

Second, the form-critical division of psalms into communal and individual laments, and so on, likewise represents an approach to the Psalter quite different from that of the collectors and editors. Again, it is not being suggested that the form-critical approach is wrong or useless.

Third, evidence from Qumran indicates that, by the second century BCE, the order of the psalms in Books I–III was more or less fixed, but that there was no fixed order, or even number, for Books IV–V. The principle of arrangement of Books I–III seems to have been that of presumed authorship. All but four of Psalms 2–41 are ascribed to David; Psalms 42–49 are ascribed to the sons of Korah; and then following the psalm of Asaph (50), there are seventeen more psalms of David (51–65 and 68–69). We have already pointed out that Book III begins with eleven psalms of Asaph (73–83), while of the remaining six in Book III, four are ascribed to the sons of Korah (84–85 and 87–88). In Books IV and V the situation is different. The only recognisable block of psalms according to their titles are the Songs of Ascents (120–34) and a group of David psalms (138–45).

Fourth, it is possible that at one stage the Psalter was completed by the addition of Psalm 1 at the beginning and Psalm 119 at what was, at that time, the end. Psalm 1 stresses the importance of delighting and mediating in the law (Torah) of God (Psalm 1:2), while Psalm 119 is an elaborate meditation upon the law in all its aspects (see Rogerson and McKay 1977: III, 90-91 for a plan of the psalm). This 'framing' of the Psalter with two psalms concerned with meditating upon God's law indicates an important shift in the understanding of the psalms. So viewed, they become not so much the words of worshippers addressed to God, but the word of God to worshippers.

Finally, although the Psalter may once have ended with Psalm 119, the fact that it now ends with a block of David psalms (138–45), followed by five 'hallelujah' psalms, indicates a further shift in intention on the part of the compiler(s). The Psalter can now be seen more or less as a whole in terms of the life of David (see Wilson 1985: 172-73 and 209-28). The prefacing of particular psalms with references to events in the life of David clearly suggests their intended use as texts to be read and meditated upon. The original cultic settings (if we are right about them) have receded so far into the background that not one single psalm title supports the cultic interpretation of psalms such as 2, 24, 47, 110, and 132. On the other hand, where there are psalm titles with cultic indications, they can surprise us. Psalm 30, for example, is described as 'A Song at the dedication of the Temple', although nothing in the content of the psalm suggests that this is so; and form-criticism would classify it as an individual thanksgiving for deliverance.

Wilson (1985: 209-28) suggests that each book of the psalms can be seen in terms of God's covenant with David. Book I introduces the covenant (Psalm 2) whereas Book II concludes (Psalm 72) with a prayer that its benefits be passed to David's son. Book III concludes (Psalm 89) with the extension of the covenant to David's descendants, while giving the impression that the covenant has failed. Book IV explores the reasons for this failure (the frailty of humankind [Psalm 90] and the disobedience of Israel [Psalms 105–106]), while Book V outlines the way back from exile: observance of the law (Psalm 119), hope of blessing for Zion (Psalms 120–34), and a shift back to David's confidence in God in Psalms 38–145.

Conclusion

The sacrificial and psalms traditions share the difficulty for the modern interpreter that they have taken a long time to reach their final form. In this chapter we have only been able to hint at these problems and at the fascinating questions that they raise. Taken together, however, the sacrificial and the psalm traditions are necessary complements. If each seems to be hardly aware of the other's existence, in spite of their presumed common setting in the Temple, this does not prevent us from reading each in the light of the other. The elaborate ceremonies for dealing with ritual impurity are offset by the sincere requests for forgiveness and salvation, while the joy in the psalms that God is the lord of the whole earth and of all the nations is seen in the light of the practical ceremonies which mark out those areas of life that properly belong to God and must be approached with reverence and awe.

References

Poole, M.
    1962   *A Commentary on the Holy Bible*, II (Edinburgh: Banner of Truth Trust [repr. of 1st edn, 1700]).
Rogerson, J.W., and J.W. McKay
    1977   *Psalms* (CBC; 3 vols.; Cambridge: Cambridge University Press).
Wilson, G.H.
    1985   *The Editing of the Hebrew Psalter* (SBLDS, 76; Chico, CA: Scholars Press).

Former Prophets
Joshua
Judges
1 Samuel
2 Samuel
1 Kings
2 Kings

Latter Prophets
Isaiah
Jeremiah
Ezekiel
Hosea
Joel
Amos
Obadiah
Jonah
Micah
Nahum
Habakkuk
Zephaniah
Haggai
Zechariah
Malachi

Chapter 12

PROPHETIC LITERATURE

The second division of the Hebrew Bible is called 'Prophets'. It comprises the 'Former Prophets', the books of Joshua–Kings (excluding Ruth), which describe, among other things, the activities of prophetic figures such as Samuel, Elijah, and Elisha; and 'Latter Prophets', consisting of four books: Isaiah, Jeremiah, Ezekiel, and the 'Book of the Twelve' (Hosea–Malachi). The Old Testament separates these two sub-groups: the Former Prophets, plus Ruth, are placed with other 'historical' books, and the Latter Prophets consist of thirteen books: the Twelve plus Daniel.

What is 'Prophecy'?

Most readers of the Bible will assume that they know what 'prophecy' is. But prophecy in ancient Israel and Judah, that is, the social and religious phenomenon of bringing messages from the deity, and prophecy as presented in the 'prophetic books' of the Bible, are not exactly the same thing. For example, often what we recognise as 'Prophecy' is carried out by a person who is not called a 'prophet'— Joshua, for example (see Joshua 7:10-15, especially verse 13) or Saul (1 Samuel 10:11; 19:24), or Balaam (Numbers 22–24), while prophets also do things that we would not normally regard as 'prophecy', such as performing miracles (as Elijah and Elisha often do). The Hebrew word generally used for 'prophet' is *nabi*'; but other terms are also used: 'holy man' (literally 'man-of-god') and *ro'eh* or *hozeh* ('seer'). (1 Samuel 9:9; even explains that 'the person now called a *nabi'* was once called a *ro'eh*'.) What we loosely call 'prophets' in ancient societies can in fact be divided into several specific roles. The common denominator of these roles is *intermediation* (see Wilson 1980). The Old Testament regards prophets as *legitimate* intermediaries, those truly called by Yhwh, while recognizing that there were also other 'prophets', dubbed 'false prophets'. It is only the 'true' prophets (as determined by the biblical editors) that are *really* 'prophets'.

But even in the Bible, 'prophecy' covers a range of different roles and activities. There are clear differences between an Elijah and a Hosea: on the one hand, a politically active charismatic 'holy man' who performs miracles, and belongs with a band of holy men, and on the other a poet who does little but talks, or writes oracles and acts only in symbolic gestures. Isaiah and Jeremiah combine political activity with speaking oracles, but of the majority of 'minor prophets' (Hosea to Malachi) we have only words. A further difference is that while some prophets are shown as operating within, the royal circle (Elijah, Elisha, Isaiah) or among temple officials (Jeremiah, Amos), many appear to speak from the fringes of society, denouncing its leaders. Some 'prophecy' does not even look like a 'message' (Nahum). And what about those instructions from Yhwh to perform a certain action (e.g. Jeremiah 18, Ezekiel 3)? Are these really 'prophecies', or just narrative devices used in explaining how such acts are 'prophetic' because inspired by a divine word?

The best way to begin is by looking generally at what we know of intermediation as an indispensable social and religious function.

Prophecy as a Social Institution

'Shaman', 'medium', 'witch', 'sorcerer', 'intermediary', and 'prophet' are all terms for different kinds of intermediating person or office. Intermediation between the society and its gods can occur through possession, in which the god takes over the intermediary, or through 'soul migration' or 'soul-loss' where the intermediary's soul or spirit temporarily leaves the body. Intermediaries can be formed through mental or social predisposition, by mystical experience or divine election. However, intermediation can also be effected by professional guilds, including diviners who read omens. They can be part of a cult, or stand outside it. But the roles are largely defined by the social structure and its requirements, and the role of society in creating and supporting intermediaries also varies widely. In some places we find prophets chosen by 'peer evaluation', in which a guild controls entrance into its profession, often through apprenticeship, or even by succession and inheritance—or by popular support, or royal appointment, or heredity. To put it simply, if we say that a prophet is 'someone called by a god to deliver messages' we have also to ask 'who determines this role: the god? the prophet? society?' It is clear that in the end a prophet unrecognised as such is useless; he (sometimes she) cannot deliver the message.

Prophets in the Ancient Near East

One of the richest archives of prophetic texts is the Mari library (see *ANET*: 623-25, 629-32), which contains descriptions of several quite specific and named prophetic types, but also mentions other, anonymous figures that give oracles. Texts from Assyria, Babylonia, and Syria also give us the names of classes of prophets, divinatory texts, and letters to and from intermediaries requiring or giving messages. Prophecy in Egypt, however, is represented largely in predictive texts, which belong, rather, to apocalyptic categories (see Chapter 14) and the range of 'prophetic' activities found elsewhere is absent.

Among the types of prophet at Mari (eighteenth century BCE) were *muḫḫu* ecstatics whose trances, probably induced, were often accompanied by violent behaviour and would produce oracles. *Muḫḫu* (plural *muḫḫum*) were found both at regional cult-centres and around the royal court. The Assyrian kings Esarhaddon and Asshurbanipal also employed such persons. Another type of prophet at Mari, known as *apilu*, delivered oracles, often in standard stereotyped language, including 'messenger' language (see below). However, these were apparently not influential with the monarch or in the royal cult. Yet another group, the *assinnu*, belonged to the cult of Ishtar. Their activities are unclear, but may have included female impersonation. In addition to all these, there were various individuals who uttered oracles, usually derived from dreams. But the most influential 'prophetic' representative was clearly the *baru*, an expert in divination and omens (see Chapter 14). Organised into guilds, they formed a major part of the religious and political establishment, and their practices were dictated by tradition and convention.

The classes of intermediary indicated at Mari apply also to Babylonia, and one important feature of their activity is that their messages are delivered in temples. The gods do not speak privately unless the recipient is in their house. Also, the final recipient of the message is nearly always the king, to whom the message has to be transmitted; and it is because this was so often done in a written form that we know as much as we do about 'prophecy' in the cities of Mesopotamia.

The other major archive is from a millennium later, from Nineveh (seventh century), where we find individual oracles of 'prophets' to the kings Esarhaddon and Asshurbanipal and several other references to prophetic types: alongside the *muḫḫu* appears the *raggimu* ('shouter') and the *sabru*, a 'revealer' of messages through dreams, as well as the female *selutu*.

Two important texts from Syria-Palestine also have a bearing on prophecy. The Zakir inscription (*ANET*: 655-56), probably from about 800 BCE, tells how Zakir, king of Hamath, prayed to Baal Shamen, who answered him through seers (*hzyn*) and '*ddyn*. However, we cannot tell by what methods intermediation was actually obtained here. The Deir 'Alla inscription from Transjordan, dating from about 700 BCE, contains a text ascribed to Balaam son of Beor who appears in the Bible in Numbers 22–24. He is called a 'seer (*hzh*) of the gods', and according to this text the gods visited him at night, The text is obviously of immense interest to biblical scholars because Balaam also appears in Numbers 22–24 (also alluded to elsewhere in the Old Testament); so far as our understanding of prophecy is concerned, it tells us, like the Zakir inscription, that the biblical word *hozeh* is also the name of a prophetic office in Syria–Palestine from the time of Israel's origins.

Prophets in Ancient Israel

This extremely sketchy review of ancient Near Eastern evidence confirms the variety of forms of divine–human mediation. But in the Old Testament not all mediation is regarded as prophecy: 'And when Saul enquired of Yhwh, Yhwh did not answer him, either by dreams, or by Urim [the drawing of a lot by the priest], or by prophets' (1 Samuel 28:6). Why are dreams and Urim excluded from prophecy? Dream-interpretation is assigned not to prophets but to wise men like Joseph and Daniel, while the manipulation of the lot—whether Urim and Thummim or ephod (Exodus 28:30; 1 Samuel 30:7)—is entrusted to priests. But even prophetic activity in the Old Testament, though excluding some kinds of intermediation, still includes several different techniques. Like the *muḫḫu* Elisha, in 2 Kings 3:15ff, goes into a trance, induced by music, upon which he is touched by 'hand of Yhwh', and utters an oracle. Saul's behaviour, described in 1 Samuel 10:10 as 'prophesying', when the 'spirit of God came strongly upon him', seems to have been an ecstatic but inarticulate experience. At least, if he uttered any valuable words, they were not thought fit to be recorded. Instances of violent behaviour associated with ecstasy, however, are attributed only to non-Israelite prophets, such as the prophets of Baal, who, in the Elijah story, 'cried aloud, and cut themselves after their custom with swords and lances, until the blood gushed out upon them' (1 Kings 18:28).

Prophecy is associated with a cult-centre (e.g. Gilgal, 2 Kings 2:1) as well as with the royal court. Prophetic guilds, the 'sons of the prophets' (e.g. 2 Kings 2:3ff.) are depicted, as in 1 Samuel 19:20ff., where three groups of men sent by Saul to capture David are seized with fits of prophesying. However, it is the 'messenger' language, as used by the *apilu*, that constitutes the most pronounced feature of Old Testament prophetic speech. In Genesis 32:3 Jacob sends messengers to Esau with the words 'Thus you shall say to my lord Esau: "Thus says your servant Jacob, 'I have sojourned...'"'. Compare Jeremiah 21:3: 'Then Jeremiah said to them "Thus you shall say to Zedekiah, 'Thus says Yhwh god of Israel: "Behold, I will turn back..."'"' in both cases we have a message within a message! Here, perhaps, a word of caution is needed. Messenger speech in the Old Testament may be associated with a theory of prophecy subsequently developed by the Deuteronomists, in which the 'prophet' conveyed the 'word of Yhwh'.

What of female prophets? Although it is usual to think of Israelite prophets as male, we must not forget Miriam, Deborah, or Huldah. Although the first two are called 'prophets', nothing is actually said of their prophetic activity (other than that both Miriam and Deborah sang songs: is this what female prophets were sometimes reduced to in the Old Testament?) Huldah, on the other hand, gives an oracle, exactly as many male prophets do (1 Kings 22:14ff.). Has the number of female prophets in ancient Israel and Judah been concealed in the Old Testament? We can suspect that this may be so, just as we might also suspect that other types of prophecy were concealed. For although divination is condemned, there is evidence that it might have been practised (see Chapter 14).

'Prophecy' in the Old Testament

'Prophecy' as a Largely Literary Product

Let us begin this topic by remembering the basic differences between the prophetic figures in the 'Former' and 'Latter' sections. Of course, the term 'Former Prophets' might simply reflect the later belief that prophets also wrote history (as Josephus claimed). If so, 'Former Prophets' is not supposed to imply that the subject matter is prophecy itself. But even so, there is a discrepancy between the prophets in the two sections. Only two of the Latter Prophets (Isaiah–Malachi) appear in Joshua–Kings: Isaiah in 2 Kings 18–20 and Jonah in 2 Kings 14:25. It seems as if the writers of these books did not regard the heroes of the Latter Prophets—or at least their words—as of great historical importance. Prophecy as a whole, is, of course, very important in these books, as a means whereby Yhwh indicates his wishes. But they tell us little about the figures among the Latter Prophets. Looking at it the other way: while the books of Isaiah, Jeremiah, and Ezekiel also tell us about lives and deeds of these prophets, among the other twelve we have only the rather exceptional case of Jonah and one small episode in Amos 7:10-14. Despite modern scholarship's emphasis on the time and place and character of the prophets, the Bible itself seems on the whole quite uninterested! In the book of the Twelve, at least, it is *prophecy* that matters, not *prophets*. In what follows, the peculiar biblical theological-literary category will be called 'Prophecy' to distinguish from the social function of intermediation ('prophecy').

To bolster this distinction we should mention an interesting analysis by Graeme Auld (Auld 1983 and 1996). Auld observes that Isaiah is named as 'prophet' (*nabi'*) only three times in his book, all in chapters 36–39, a narrative section that is paralleled in 2 Kings 18–20. Jeremiah is called 'prophet' twenty-one times, but in his own speeches he uses it only of those sent in the past and of contemporaries. Twice Ezekiel is indirectly referred to as a 'prophet' (2:5; 33:33); otherwise, as in Jeremiah, the title is also used of past figures or *other persons*. Hosea is not called a prophet, nor is Micah. Amos *denies* being one in 7:14; Zechariah is named merely as the son of a prophet. Only Habakkuk and Haggai are called prophets. To be fair, Jeremiah and Ezekiel are often said to 'prophesy', and Amos is forbidden to 'prophesy' by Amaziah the priest (before his denial of being a prophet). The verb 'prophesy' also occurs in Zechariah three times, but is nowhere applied to Zechariah himself.

But there is more to this: many of these 'prophets' actually *condemn* 'prophets'. Isaiah speaks of the 'prophet who teaches lies'; Micah (3:11) accuses prophets of prophesying for money: they 'cry "Peace" when they have something to eat, but declare war against anyone who puts nothing into their mouths'. Zephaniah (3:4) calls the prophets 'wanton, faithless men'. According to Jeremiah 14:14, Yhwh declares that 'The prophets are prophesying lies in my name; I did not send them, nor did I command them or speak to them. They are prophesying to you a lying vision, worthless divination.'

What all this means is that the title 'prophet' does not on the whole seem to have been used by the prophets of themselves: they saw people in the past as prophets and sometimes saw contemporaries as such—and disapprovingly! Yet in the Old Testament they now represent Prophecy. Although they are not mentioned on the whole in Joshua–Kings, they are offered as major representatives of the institution 'my servants the prophets' so common in these 'historical' books. Auld's conclusion means that Prophecy is a literary device, not to be confused with intermediation in the societies of Israel and Judah. This biblical device turns the many voices of intermediation into a single clear message running like a scarlet thread through the history of Israel and Judah: the voice of Prophecy is the voice of God.

It is often assumed that there was continuous tradition from the individual prophets themselves, through their disciples, who memorised and then copied out the sayings of their teacher. But this makes no sense. First, there is a lack of evidence that these prophets had disciples. One possible reference occurs in Isaiah 8:16, but 'disciples' is not necessarily the right translation—the meaning is not certain—and even if it were, a single reference in the whole Bible is hardly compelling (this passage is examined below). Jeremiah's assistant Baruch is not a disciple, but his scribe—although later tradition made him into a prophet as well. Second, the theory offers no good reason for the writing down of oracles in books in a society that is largely illiterate—unless the recipient is an individual or a group of individuals who can read. Third (and perhaps the most striking), most of the books of Prophecy contain no information (apart from an occasional heading which provides a date) about the prophet or his life or deeds, which is entirely contrary to what we expect of traditions passed on by disciples. At the very least followers wish to preserve something about their master to accompany the words. The table opposite illustrates the point.

In the same vein, we can see that the books of the 'Latter Prophets' are strictly speaking not the product of individual 'prophets' at all; prophets do not write books. The books come from editors. We can see the work of these editors in the superscriptions (which usually follow the same dating formula), the occasional narrative accounts, and the orderly arrangement that is visible here and there (for instance, oracles against Judah or foreign nations are often grouped in long sequences). In the case of Jeremiah we have two different editions of the book (both present among the Qumran scrolls). The contribution of the individual named prophet varies considerably; in the case of Isaiah, for instance, we have sections that contain references to later people and events (Isaiah 40–66); in the case of Jeremiah scholars range between regarding nearly all of it as his own to regarding very little of it as such.

Prophet	Date	Details
Hosea	'in the days of Uzziah, Jotham, Ahaz, and Hezekiah of Judah, and Jeroboam of Israel'	
b. Beeri		
Joel		
b. Pethuel		
Amos	'in the days of Uzziah king of Judah and Jeroboam of Israel, two years before the earthquake'	'among the herdsmen of Tekoa'
Obadiah		
Jonah	dates can be inferred from 2 Kings 14.25 but are not actually given in the book itself	a good deal, much, but probably to be understood as deliberate fiction
b. Amittai		
Micah of	'in the days of Jotham, Ahaz, and Hezekiah'	
Moreshet		
Nahum the		
Elkoshite		
Habakkuk		
Zephaniah	'in the days of Josiah b. Amon of Judah'	
b. Cushi etc.		
Haggai	'in the second year of Darius'	
Zechariah		
b. Berechiah	'in the second year of Darius'	
Malachi		

Making collections of prophecies, and inserting additional 'prophecies' or stories into them is the work of a learned book-maker. Why did they go to this effort to preserve words spoken—and fulfilled (or not) long ago? Before we turn to this question, we need to look at one major theological difficulty facing the compilers of the prophetic books: what makes (or made) a prophet a true prophet?

'True' and 'False' Prophecy

Inaccurate or unreliable prophecy is a universal problem. In Babylon, it was common for the respected *baru* to be consulted as a 'second opinion'. However, in the monotheistic religion of Judah, there was a serious theological dimension to the problem of prophetic disagreement. While elsewhere the many gods could give different messages, a single god could surely not do so. So what did the existence of wrong prophecy mean? Why did Yhwh allow it? A brief look at some Old Testament texts on this problem will show us a good deal about the *theological* dimension of prophecy, as it emerged in retrospect to the biblical editors.

Deuteronomy 18:20 considers the case of a prophet who has not been sent by Yhwh. But how will such a prophet be known? 'When a prophet speaks in the name of Yhwh, if the word does not come to pass or come true, that is a word which Yhwh has not spoken…' But people will know this only when it is too late—and no allowance is made for divine change of mind (as in the case of Jonah, who is therefore rather peeved, and not without reason). Conversely, a 'false' prophet might predict what would happen (Deuteronomy 13:1-3). So further help is given: if a prophet (or a dreamer) tells you to 'serve other gods', then Yhwh is testing you. But does Yhwh 'test' Israel by false prophets? If so, has he not therefore really given them a message? Such a case makes evaluation almost impossible: 'false' prophets may not have been 'sent by Yhwh' (as Jeremiah accuses them of doing: 14:15), or they might have been sent by Yhwh, but with misleading words! Let us look at this issue more closely.

In 1 Kings 22, despite the unanimous agreement of all the prophets to go to war, Jehoshaphat king of Judah insists on a final opinion from Micaiah. This prophet is unpopular with the king of Israel because 'he never prophesies good concerning me, but evil'. Micaiah first confirms the advice of the prophets; then, when challenged, he reverses his message. He explains that he had seen Yhwh instructing one of his spirits to trick the king of Israel by becoming a 'lying spirit in the mouth of all his prophets'. Micaiah is then put into prison, and the Deuteronomy 18 test of false vs. true prophets is applied; the kings go to war and the king of Israel is killed. Micaiah was therefore, according to the rules of Deuteronomy 18:20, a true prophet. But were the other prophets false? According to Micaiah they were only saying what Yhwh intended them to say. He *had* spoken to them! The 'true' prophet (in this case, anyway) was *not* instructed to say what he did—it was not a 'word of Yhwh'. In fact, by speaking the truth Micaiah betrayed Yhwh.

Another story deepens the confusion. 1 Kings 13 tells of a 'man of God' from Judah who completes a mission in Bethel and declines an invitation to stay because, he says, Yhwh has forbidden him to eat or drink in the northern kingdom, or to return the way he had come. However, an old prophet in Bethel invites the Judahite to his home, pretending that he has also received a divine word to do this. Persuaded that Yhwh's original instructions have now been superseded, the holy man goes with him. During the meal the host receives a *genuine* word from Yhwh condemning the 'man of God' for disobeying his original instructions, and sentencing him to death. On the way home he is killed. Upon hearing this, the other prophet penitently fetches the body and buries it, asking that when he dies he be buried in the same sepulchre. Perhaps this story is a warning to 'men of God' not to believe each other but to adhere to what they themselves have been told. But when a 'false' prophet can deliver a 'true' prophecy', and fatally deceive his own colleague, how can poor Israelites and Judeans know which prophet to believe?

The safest conclusion we can reach is that the 'true' prophets were those who in retrospect were deemed by the producers of the prophetic books to have been so. But it is also clear from the biblical texts that no satisfactory way was seen for assessing the truth or falsity of any *contemporary* prophet.

The Purpose of Old Testament Prophecy

We can start answering this question by reflecting that the editors of prophecies were working in Judah from the Persian period onwards, when there was no longer a king, and when local cults were being suppressed. The Judean community's religious life was now dominated by the Temple in Jerusalem, and Judah was politically an imperial province, yet functioning as a theocracy. Prophecy was an institution of the past, and although it ends with Haggai and Zechariah at the time of rebuilding of the Jerusalem Temple, most of it lies under the shadow of the disaster that befell the kingdoms of Israel and Judah. Why, in these post-monarchic times, would sayings of prophets from the past be assembled, amplified, arranged, and written down in scrolls? We moderns may be interested in the individuals and their times, but actually—unlike the three major figures—the Scroll of the Twelve tells us virtually nothing about the minor ones. What was it about these prophets that was so vital to later generations? With just a few exceptions, the books appear to offer explanations for the end of the monarchic era. Yhwh had finally destroyed (in prophetic code: 'would punish') the kingdom of Israel for its sins; Judah too had been punished but a remnant survived. Foreign nations would either come to worship Yhwh themselves or be destroyed for their hostility towards Israel and Judah. Collectively the books present a broadly hopeful message, though one accompanied by warnings: if the sins that led to Israel's destruction in the past were repeated, the promised future might not materialise.

The Latter Prophets are generally thought to have been formed, or completed, under the influence of Deuteronomistic thought (see Chapter 16). For the Deuteronomist writer, history demonstrates how the prophetic message is fulfilled. Prophecy explains why disaster struck (the Babylonian invasion), and uses Prophecy as vindication. But the prophets remain authoritative mouthpieces for times later than their own, for the possibility remained that history might repeat itself.

But as we have seen, Deuteronomy itself has a wary attitude towards prophecy. Its view is that the will of Yhwh is found in the revelation of his law to Moses, whom Deuteronomy represents as the prophet *par excellence*. Hence, prophets can be judged on whether what they say confirms what the law says. The problem of 'false prophecy' also shows how dangerous and unreliable *contemporary* prophecy can be. Therefore, Prophecy is confined to the past. This does not mean that prophetic words are not still generated: but they are attributed to the prophets of old: that procedure not only verifies the prophecy but also renders the true author of these prophecies (a scribe) less prone to persecution by those he is criticizing. Prophecy, on this understanding, has a real and serious contemporary function, served with the aid of figures safely in the past, whose words can be utilised (and expanded) so as to offer a *written* guide to the divine will.

A similar kind of transformation of Prophecy can be seen in Chronicles. Here Prophecy, a legitimate institution of the past, is converted into the more contemporary reality of the temple cult. The Chronicler describes certain levites as 'prophets', in conformity with his presentation of levites as Temple singers who should '...prophesy with lyres, with harps, and with cymbals' (1 Chronicles 25:1). Accordingly, in 1 Chronicles 25:2 the 'sons of Asaph' 'prophesied under the direction of the king'. In 2 Chronicles 20:14, the 'spirit of Yhwh' falls upon Jehaziel, who gives a short word of encouragement in the prophetic 'Fear not' oracle—a genre that seems to have originated in a prophetic oracle before battle! Here, as with the Deuteronomists, we see how the task of prophecy is absorbed into another institution: there the scribe, here the levite.

We see here an attempt to create an idealised notion of Prophecy into something of contemporary relevance. The move can be seen—though this would be a large oversimplification—as part of the longer process by which individual 'prophets' who had been critical of the 'establishment'—and of 'prophets'—became bastions of the new religious establishment in a society where official intermediation was conducted in the cult or by the 'scribe of the law'. But that is how ideology works. Successful rebels, protesters, or revolutionaries become the new 'establishment'. Prophecy came into being because the kind of intermediation these characters once practised was obsolete—at least in the eyes of the religious establishment.

Individual Prophets and Prophetic Books

We shall look very briefly at the individuals whose names adorn the books. Even in the case of Jeremiah, who is given the fullest description, little can be certainly known. But such individuals—with maybe one or two exceptions—did exist, and their words are contained (to a greater or lesser extent) in the books credited to them. If, as we have seen, they seem not to have liked the title 'prophet', what should we call them? Robert Carroll suggested 'poet' (Carroll 1983 and 1996). Indeed, in the case of Isaiah 40–55 ('Second Isaiah'), few scholars would offer a better title, and of course biblical Prophecy contains rather more poetry than prose. Now, poetry does not communicate in a literal vein; nor simply by sense. It communicates by sound, by word-association, word-play, rhythm; it plays on emotion, it evokes images, it is memorable. The turning of 'poets' into 'prophets' can therefore create a distortion where poetry is read as if it were prose: denunciations and descriptions become objective comment, dreams predictions, visions real psychological experiences.

How did the words become written in the first place? In Mesopotamia prophecies to the king were often written (by a scribe) as they were performed; such messages might have then been archived. But what about public performance? Before a largely non-literate audience what would be the point? Jeremiah 36 tells a story about how his prophecies were written down by Baruch; but the story is probably not historical (this chapter is discussed below). We should imagine some prophets as giving official oracles to the king. Isaiah is depicted as doing this, though the communication is represented (dramatised?) as oral. Amos perhaps delivered a written text at Bethel, and there is a letter in Jeremiah's name to deportees in Babylon (Jeremiah 29). There are also accounts (first and third person) of actions, such as Hosea's marriage or the antics of Ezekiel in eating a scroll (Ezekiel 3:1-3) or going about naked (Isaiah 20:2) or burying a loincloth by the Euphrates (Jeremiah 13: was this *really* done or was it an anecdote? Were there witnesses?). These different modes of communicating: poetry and prose, public and private, may accurately reflect a wide range of activities, but they represent artificial stagings of words by the editors of the books. How far the prophet is the *author* of a genuine anthology and how far the *leading character* in a reconstruction is often impossible to say and scholars are divided on the answer. This being the case, to offer any account of a prophet is a rather tenuous enterprise.

Prophetic Speech

The analysis of 'prophetic' speech has been used to try to recover the historical profile of prophets and their social context, since so little information is otherwise given. Genres such as the oracle of judgement, salvation oracle, 'lawsuit', woe-saying, proverb, account of a vision, prayer of intercession, and oracle against foreign nations have been identified, and some of these are paralleled in neighbouring cultures. But the use of these genres implies really very little, except that poets (and writers) borrow forms of speech from their society, using the form as part of the rhetoric. For us to use these forms to identify the author with a particular *role* is hardly justifiable. We can speak perhaps of 'role-playing', but only as far as adopting speech patterns that belong to a certain setting or function.

Isaiah

The book of Isaiah is the largest of the Latter Prophets. It also offers the best opportunity for explaining how the words of an individual grow into a complex literary
product over a long period.

Scholarship has long recognised in the book three different, related sets of writings, which it refers to as First, Second (or Deutero-), and Third (or Trito-) Isaiah.
The First, in chapters 1–39, is the Isaiah who is identified in the book. The Second,
in chapters 40–55, is anonymous (or pseudonymous) but is generally thought to be
a single person living under the Persians or immediately before. Finally, Third Isaiah,
chapters 55–66, is widely thought to be the work of many different poets. The
historical, as opposed to the literary relationship between the three Isaiahs is an
intriguing problem. The contributors to Third Isaiah are often thought to be disciples
of Second Isaiah or his work. But Second Isaiah has never been supposed to have
met First Isaiah, since the Second was alive 150 years or so later. So Isaiah gives us
a nice sample of the kinds of relationship between author and book which the Latter
Prophets as a whole gives us—a named and dated historical figure at one end; an
anonymous and only vaguely datable collection at the other.

The 'original' Isaiah—'Isaiah of Jerusalem' was born about 760 BCE and lived at
least until 701, when Sennacherib besieged Jerusalem. The major political events of
his life were the 'Syro-Ephraimite' war, in which Ahaz, opposed by Damascus and
the kingdom of Israel, called on Assyria to assist him; then later the unsuccessful
revolt by Hezekiah against Assyria, averted at great price. The story (told in almost
the same words in both 2 Kings 18–20 and Isaiah 36–39) relates a miraculous deliverance, but also mentions a pay-off. Isaiah seems to have spoken of the power of
Yhwh in history and the social ills of Judean society, which he portrayed as rebellion
against Yhwh's sovereignty. He viewed Judah as a remnant of the 'chosen people'
surviving after the end of the northern kingdom, confirming Yhwh's attachment to
his Temple and city of Zion (as he prefers to call Jerusalem). Later editors of First
Isaiah developed these themes further, enlarging his poems and adding new ones.

An example of enlargement is Isaiah's speech to Ahaz (7:3-24). The coalition of
Israel and Syria against Assyria is pressing Judah to participate, and Ahaz proposes
to respond by summoning the help of Assyria. Isaiah calls for trust in Yhwh and
predicts that Judah will be safe. Ahaz asks for a sign, which Isaiah offers: a young
woman will have a son, named Immanuel ('God with us'), and before this son
reaches a certain age (presumably only a few years) there will come 'such days as
have not come since the day that Ephraim departed from Judah' (i.e. since the kingdom was divided). The promise must have been in its original context a favourable
one, or the entire conversation makes no sense. But what seems a promise is then
turned into a threat by the addition of the sinister words 'the king of Assyria!'. The
'sign' is now a prediction that Assyria will afflict Judah. But immediately afterwards
(verses 21-22), the threat is turned into a promise of peace and prosperity. Finally, in
verses 23-25, that promise is reversed again: where there used to be a thousand
vines there will be briers and thorns; men will come with bows and arrows. The
'original' speech encouraged Ahaz to rely on Yhwh. As it happened he did not, and
the result was Assyrian control of Judah. This outcome is now reflected in the first
addition to the speech. But later Assyria was defeated, so that the Assyrian threat
given by Isaiah was now, later still, understood as having been meant to apply to the

fall of Samaria in 722/21 BCE—that is, that part had been fulfilled. However, Assyria itself was in turn overthrown (Nineveh fell in 612): so a better future could thus be read again from the *original* oracle: everyone would, like Immanuel (7:15) eat 'curds and honey'. But after that, the land of Judah was partly depopulated by the Babylonians! So again, the Prophecy was extended. We have in this extended speech something like an archaeological stratigraphy, in which its history can be read from the successive layers.

A different process by which the eighth-century prophet is made to speak to later days is illustrated in 39:5-7, where he warns King Hezekiah of the Babylonian deportations while Hezekiah is entertaining the king of Babylon. The inappropriateness and uselessness of such a prediction more than a century before it took place, is underlined by Hezekiah's understandably placid reaction: 'The word of Yhwh is good', he says, realizing that it would all happen long after he was dead! But we know that these words were written after the deportations had occurred, since they are copied from the Deuteronomistic History that records them (2 Kings 20:16-18).

The processes just described can make sense of many similarly obscure and contradictory passages in the Latter Prophets, and they demonstrate a concern with the continuing relevance of older prophetic speeches as predictions or criticisms of social practice. But in what sort of context has this taken place? Was there, as most scholars maintain, an 'Isaianic tradition', preserved by 'disciples'? The answer is probably no. The idea of a 'prophet' having 'disciples' who preserve his words is a product of modern imagination. The word translated 'disciples' in Isaiah 8:16-17 is better translated, 'those I have instructed', that is, the two witnesses to the tablet in 8:1-2, and the 'testimony' or 'deposition' to be 'bound up' is that tablet, not a prophecy.

Isaiah 1–39 displays some prominent themes, but hardly of such distinctiveness or coherence as to characterise a 'tradition'. As for the development of the Isaianic collection itself, some scholars propose a major edition in the time of Josiah while others argue that the bulk of chapters 13–39 is post-exilic. At the other extreme, Hayes and Irvine (1987) attribute most of the contents to Isaiah himself. Such disagreement about the extent of the original prophet's contribution is not unusual in the prophetic books.

Second Isaiah

Chapters 40–55 of Isaiah originated in a different time and place than Isaiah of Jerusalem, and contain a number of poems in which the Babylonian invasion of Judah is already in the past. Cyrus is mentioned twice as Yhwh's appointed liberator (indeed, as Yhwh's 'anointed', his 'messiah': 45:1), and as the restorer of Jerusalem and its Temple (44:28). The imminent downfall of Babylon is repeatedly and gleefully rehearsed, though whether before or after the event is debated. The returnees will be led back (or are being led back, or have been led back) across the desert in a repeat of their first entry in Canaan, but this time to a future radically different from the past. The best known and most studied poems concern a 'servant' (42:1-9; 49:1-6; 50:4-9; 52:13–53:12), described as a recipient of Yhwh's spirit—gentle, just, the victim of human reproach. The last song dwells on his abasement and humiliation, his suffering for others, his intercession for rebels, and his vindication. The identity of the 'servant' is much disputed. The poems were taken messianically by many Jews in the Second Temple period, as indeed they have been taken since by

Christians. The poet himself, or even other heroes of Israel's past, have also been proposed as candidates. The now traditional Jewish interpretation, like most biblical scholars, sees in the 'servant' the people of Israel collectively. But his identity could well be fluid, or multiple. Poetry, we should remember, thrives on ambiguity, metaphor, and multiple interpretation.

The poet regards Yhwh as the creator of the world, who also controls history. Yhwh is thus, as the only God, also the god of non-Judeans—though where exactly they fit into his plans is not made clear. Babylonian gods, the poet declares, are human artefacts of wood, metal, or stone. He writes about a new age, and offers a new god. But whether he speaks to stir up fellow-deportees in the hope and desire of returning or rather speaks later, in Judah, of the need for deportees and others who never left to embrace each other is still disputed. In either case, he welcomes Persian rule and it is even possible that his image of Yhwh is influenced by the Persian god Ahura Mazda, the author of light and darkness (see Isaiah 45:7). The poetry is of high quality and, like all good poetry, transcends its historical context.

Third Isaiah

In Isaiah 56–66 we are firmly in the world of the Judean community under the Persians, though the various poems come from different times: a rebuilt Temple is mentioned in 60:13, but still awaited in 63:18, while 66:1-2a seems to reject such a temple, whether rebuilt or not. There are signs of division within the community between those who represent themselves as loyal to Yhwh and others who, being called 'watchmen' and 'shepherds' in 59:9-15, may be community leaders. Similarities of style with Second Isaiah have been detected alongside sharp differences of subject matter. For example, 61:1-3 reads like a deliberate development of 42:1-4. But much of the content appears to be trying to come to terms with the fact that the eloquent promises given in Second Isaiah have not been fulfilled. One reason given (especially in chapter 59) is human injustice. Some scholars (e.g. Hanson 1975) find in this collection indications of a basic rift in ideology in late sixth-century BCE Judah between returnees from Babylonia and those who had remained. Many of the poems may be later still. It is always worthwhile remembering that one poet's view may be peculiar to that person. But the tone of protest is unmistakable.

The separate consideration of the three Isaiahs does not, of course, address the question of the shape, intention, and date of the book as a whole. Answering these questions is not easy. Clements (1985) has suggested that Second Isaiah makes direct allusions to First Isaiah, and that the two collections were combined through their common concern with the fate of Zion and the Davidic dynasty. Williamson (1994) has argued that Second Isaiah is responsible for editing First Isaiah, attaching his own work to it. Third Isaiah is thought by many to be a deliberate development of ideas in Second Isaiah, and it is possible that these two were combined even before being attached to First Isaiah. While the arrangement of the book into three parts is still largely maintained, its overall unity has come to be stressed in recent years. It is helpful that we can nevertheless discern major blocks of successive material in Isaiah. But the gradual and anonymous process of scribal copying and editing has fused them to some extent. In many of the other prophetic books, this process has obviously taken place, but in such a way that we cannot easily see the outlines of the original components.

Jeremiah

We are told more of the individual Jeremiah and his background than of any other of the Latter Prophets, both in narrative and in first-person speech. He is said (1:1-3) to have been a priest from Anathoth, Benjamin (but only 5 miles [8 km] from Jerusalem), and was active, according to 1:1-3, from 626 BCE until 586 (though many scholars now place the beginning of his activity after Josiah's death in 609). Most of the book is set against the background of the last kings of Judah (Jehoiakim and Zedekiah), but several speeches warn about an enemy from the north, and do not seem to refer to Babylon; these are placed earlier, in the reign of Josiah. The advice consistently given by Jeremiah is that because the impending fall of the city is, he says, a judgment from Yhwh, the Babylonians should not be resisted. Not surprisingly, Jeremiah met with popular and official displeasure.

Of how much of this profile can we be certain? Little information comes from material most plausibly ascribed to Jeremiah, and although many scholars feel confident in reconstructing quite precisely his life and the words that belong to each period in it, good reasons have also been given for viewing Jeremiah as a shadowy figure, and as substantially a creation of later groups who between them brought the present collection (or collections, for there are at least two ancient editions) into being. Of all the prophets, Jeremiah has attracted the most interest as an individual human being because of the so-called 'confessions' (11:18–12:6; 15:10-21; 17:14-18; 18:18-23; 20:7-13, 14-18) in which he complains to Yhwh about the pain of his calling. But many scholars doubt that these are words of Jeremiah rather than poems inserted in order to fill out the character: how can we know? At any rate, the book has been thoroughly worked over by an editor or group of editors who were strongly influenced by the language and theology of Deuteronomy. In the words generally agreed to be original to Jeremiah, by contrast, there is no acknowledgment at all of the reform that 2 Kings connects with the lawbook (clearly intended to point to Deuteronomy), even though, according to the view of most scholars, this is said to have been discovered in his own lifetime. On the other hand, there may be a good deal of useful historical material relating to the politics of Judah (and Benjamin, Jeremiah's own affiliation) in the late seventh century, enabling us to see some of the politics conducted by leading families—and carried on in Judah after the deportations (illustrated in Chapter 2, pp. 28-29).

Ezekiel

The problem of the book of Ezekiel, as B.S. Childs has pointed out (1979: 357), is the difficulty of reconciling it with the main features of Hebrew Prophecy as modern critical scholarship recognises it. According to the book, Ezekiel was taken to Babylon with the first group of captives in 597/96 and settled in Tel Abib. He was a priest, and we can calculate the beginning of his career to 593 (1:2). The major historical problem connected with the person of Ezekiel himself arises from the fact that many of the speeches are apparently addressed to the Judean community, rather than to the deportees. The book claims that he visited Jerusalem in visions (e.g. 8:1; 11:1); and it has sometimes been asserted that his deportation was a fiction and that he remained in Jerusalem. For we find here a great deal of allegory, vision, and symbolic acts. From his weird behaviour, mental illnesses such as schizophrenia or catalepsy have more than once been suggested. Much of the book reads very markedly as a first-person diary, and was once thought to be largely the work of Ezekiel. But the book is now widely regarded as a product of an Ezekelian 'school', following the work of the W. Zimmerli. If there is a character behind this book, he is complex: he is morbid, rather misogynist, even pornographic (see chapter 23), perhaps coprophiliac (see 4:15), and obsessed with the idea of Yhwh's total holiness and autonomy, since he restores 'Israel' not because they deserve it but in order to protect his own holy reputation. There is also, towards the end, an intensely futuristic focus: in chapters 38–39 a final war with Gog of Magog results in the destruction of the nations and restoration of Israel, and in chapters 40–48 visions of a new temple, a new Jerusalem, and a new Israel unfold. Were these the results of a fevered mind oppressed by having been deported, and imagining a new world when it was over? Or is Ezekiel a work of great literary fiction, disguised as the work of a 'prophet'. Or indeed, has one format been grafted onto another? Dispassionately viewed, Ezekiel, whether historical or literary, is not a particularly attractive character: but prophets are perhaps not supposed to be.

The Book of the Twelve

The twelve prophets from Hosea to Malachi were originally written on a single scroll, and indeed, probably viewed as a unity (Ben Sira, writing just after 200 BCE speaks simply of 'the bones of the twelve prophets': 49:10). There has been great interest recently in the structure of this single scroll, noting numerous catchwords and thematic links between adjacent books. In the Hebrew Bible the Twelve are given in more or less chronological order, though only some books have dating superscriptions (and in Qumranic and Greek manuscripts the order is also a little different). In Greek Bibles the scroll was divided into its twelve parts, and the prophets have been studied as individuals ever since, tending to represent less a *literary* collection than a succession of historical figures. The tension between this 'historical' approach and a literary approach—viewing it as a coherent corpus with interlocking themes—is not entirely resolved by regarding the Book of the Twelve as originating in individual books that were later collected together, because the editing seems to have continued after they were combined. Daniel, which appears before Hosea in English Bibles, is included in the Hebrew Bible elsewhere, among the Writings (see Chapter 17).

Hosea

The book of Hosea is dated by its superscription to the final decades of the kingdom of Israel. In chapter 1 Hosea is told by Yhwh to marry a whore; he does so, and she bears him three children, whose names proclaim Yhwh's rejection of Israel. Chapter 2 consists of a poem in which Yhwh reproaches Israel for her whorish behaviour in following other gods/lovers. In chapter 3 Hosea is told to take another woman. So far there is a certain coherence which may indicate the work of a single writer. After chapter 3 the structure falls apart, though there is a continuity of imagery and theme. The poetry attacks the transformation of the worship of Yhwh into a fertility religion, but it uses the language of fertility, characterizing Yhwh as Israel's true 'baal' (which means husband and lord and was a title of the major god of Palestine). The thrust of the poems is that after numerous betrayals by Israel, Yhwh is finally going to punish it, though (as with many marriages) there is an abiding sense of reluctance, and a hope for reconciliation and restoration occasionally surfaces.

Much of this book may have originated with Hosea, though we cannot be certain. The moments of hope and promise to Israel may be legitimate (there is some doubt) but references to Judah look very much later, added by Judahite writers to give reassurance that Judah would not necessarily go the way of Israel. Certainly, the book, like all the prophetic books, has been produced in Judah, as the superscription, which gives priority to Judean kings, shows. Perhaps, as many scholars think, the book's production was linked to the Deuteronomistic movement, whose language and themes it widely shares. If Hosea the man addressed the kingdom of Israel, the book of Hosea addressed Judah at a later period. Its theme of a husband's love for an erring wife has often been taken as theologically profound (even if inspired by the cult of Baal); but in the recent decades scholars have also become aware of its very patriarchal matrimonial politics.

Amos

A contemporary of Hosea, Amos is said (1:1) to have been 'among the *noqedim* from Tekoa', usually taken to be a village near Bethlehem, in Judah. A *noqed is* probably a sheep-rearer; the word occurs elsewhere only in 2 Kings 3:4, where it is applied to Mesha, king of Moab; yet a popular image of Amos is that of a simple shepherd. The text gives little evidence for this, apart from the writer's evident dislike of affluent city-dwellers. A single biographical passage (7:10-17) locates him at Bethel, where he is told to go to Judah and earn his living there. Amos denies being a prophet and claims that he was summoned by Yhwh 'behind the flock'. The book consists mainly of short sayings, but there are two long sections in 1:3–2:16 (denouncements of nations, culminating in Israel) and a series of visions in chapters 7–9 which must have been originally composed in this extended form. The unremitting thrust of this book is that social injustice in Israel will result in its utter annihilation through war. Assyria is nowhere mentioned as the agent, but there is no realistic alternative. Yet the book has been edited in Judah—as witness the superscription, the insertion of an atypically mild oracle against Judah in 2:4-5, and a promise of restoration for the 'falling booth of David' in 9:11-15. It also has some hymnic passages that seem obtrusive, but look as if they come from a single composition. There is plentiful evidence of careful editing, but the consistency of theme, rhetoric, and tone make this book one of the easiest in which to hear the voice of a passionate individual.

Micah

According to the superscription, Micah was a contemporary of Isaiah from Moresheth, in Judah. His words, however, are addressed to both kingdoms. The poems are arranged into two sets of threats (chapters 1–3 and 6:1–7:6) and two of promises (chapters 4–5 and 7:7-20). The threats are directed at social abuses—greedy landowners, deceitful prophets, corrupt judges, avaricious priests. These negative passages can fit quite easily into the historical context of Micah, but the promises often presuppose the Babylonian deportation, especially the final section, which has a marked liturgical character. The contents therefore seem to reflect a rather longer period of growth. A number of linguistic and editorial similarities link Micah with Isaiah, and it is possible that the books ascribed to these two figures were assembled by similar processes and within the same editorial circles (see Childs 1979: 434ff.).

Haggai

Haggai is mentioned in Ezra 5:1 and 6:14, along with Zechariah, as having 'prophe-sied to the Jews who were in Judah and Jerusalem in the name of the God of Israel who was over them', with the aim of building the Temple. The book contains four prose 'oracles' dated to the second year of Darius (521–520 BCE). The first two oracles indeed urge the building of the Temple: a third offers more encouragement in the work; and the fourth hails Zerubbabel's leadership in highly extravagant politi-cal terms. Haggai 1:12-15 records the consequences of the first oracle. But of the person or role of Haggai we know no more. The editors of this book seem to have tried to present him as a direct successor of pre-exilic and exilic prophets by using formulas such as 'the word of Yhwh came to'; but the profile of Haggai emerges as one quite different from an Amos or a Jeremiah. He is a champion of the Temple and supporter of the priesthood, a restorer of those institutions so often condemned in other prophetic books.

Zechariah

Associated in Ezra with his contemporary Haggai, Zechariah is mentioned also in Nehemiah 12:16, but only in a list of priests. It *is* common to separate chapters 9–14 from the rest as 'Deutero-Zechariah', since they are believed to be unconnected with Zechariah himself. This leaves us with eight chapters consisting of a series of visions, followed by a loose collection of sayings, apparently originally prompted by a discus-sion about fasting. The principal topic in chapters 1–8 is, as in Haggai, the building of the Temple, but the form and tone are quite different. The visions contain weird imagery, interpreted by an angel, and convey the expectation of great political upheaval. Other nations will be punished; Jerusalem will be preserved. Like Ezekiel, the contents of this book show very clear apocalyptic features (see chapter 14), with an increased interest in the notion of history as working out an elaborate pre-ordained plan of history conceived in heaven and carried out by heavenly agencies.

Anonymous Prophetic Books

Nahum, Joel, Habakkuk, Zephaniah, Obadiah, and Malachi are entirely unknown figures; possibly some are pseudonyms. Of the dates and circumstances of their composition, we can guess only from allusions to events like the fall of Nineveh in 612 (Nahum) or the advent of the Babylonians (Habakkuk). The book of Jonah, which describes the activities of a rebellious prophet, is best considered as a narra-tive (see Chapter 9). Malachi is especially significant for the question of the unity of the Book of the Twelve: some of the contents look as if they have been lifted from the preceding book, Zechariah, and the suspicion is hard to avoid that someone has created a prophet in order to make the total to twelve. The name 'Malachi' means 'my messenger' and may have been inspired by the mention of the 'messenger' in 3:1, probably meant to be Elijah. The Christian Old Testament ends with this announcement, before Mark's gospel describes the preaching of John the Baptist: a very happy (and for Christians, perhaps significant) juxtaposition.

On the whole, as this chapter has tried to show, Prophecy can more fruitfully be studied as a literary corpus containing the accumulated words of many generations, which have in their continual re-forming of poems, narratives, and oracles, overlaid whatever original 'prophetic' contribution may have existed. If this conclusion seems less straightforward and less satisfying than the biblical picture of a sequence of inspired individuals, it reminds us that the Old Testament is not the work of a few great individuals but of a host of mostly unknown and entirely forgotten Judeans who, as part of the creation of a new dialogue with the past and the future, were shaping the monotheistic religion of Judaism.

Further Reading

References in this chapter have been made to A.G. Auld, 'Prophets Through the Looking Glass': Between Writings and Moses', originally published in 1983 in *JSOT* 27: 3-23, and a following response by R.P. Carroll, 'Poets, Not Prophets: A Response to "Prophets Through the Looking Glass"' (pp. 25-31), both reprinted in Philip R. Davies (ed.), *The Prophets: A Sheffield Reader* (The Biblical Seminar, 42; Sheffield: Sheffield Academic Press, 1996): 22-42, 43-49; B.S. Childs, *Introduction to the Old Testament as Scripture* (Philadelphia: Fortress Press, 1979); P.D. Hanson, *The Dawn of Apocalyptic: The Historical and Sociological Roots of Jewish Apocalyptic Eschatology* (Philadelphia: Fortress Press, 1975); R.R. Wilson, *Prophecy and Society in Ancient Israel* (Philadelphia: Fortress Press, 1980); J.H. Hayes and S.A. Irvine, *Isaiah, the Eighth Century Prophet* (Nashville: Abingdon Press, 1987); H.G.M. Williamson, *The Book Called Isaiah: Deutero-Isaiah's Role in Composition and Redaction* (Oxford: Oxford University Press, 1994); W. Zimmerli, *Ezekiel: A Commentary on the Book of Ezekiel* (2 vols.; Philadelphia: Fortress Press, 1979) and R.E. Clements, 'Beyond Tradition-History: Deutero-Isaianic Development of First Isaiah's Themes', *JSOT* 31 (1985): 101-109.

There are several good collections of essays on prophecy. On anthropological approaches, see R.C. Culley and T.W. Overholt (eds.), *Anthropological Perspectives on Old Testament Prophecy* (Semeia, 21; Chico, CA: Scholars Press, 1982). On prophecy in the ancient Near East, see M. Nissinen (ed.), *Prophecy in its Ancient Near Eastern Context: Mesopotamian, Biblical and Arabian Perspectives* (Atlanta: SBL, 2000); on the issue of oral vs. written prophecy, see E. Ben Zvi and M.H. Floyd (eds.), *Writings and Speech in Israelite and Ancient Near Eastern Prophecy* (Atlanta: Scholars Press, 2000). *The Prophets: A Sheffield Reader* (see above) also covers a wide range of perspectives on biblical prophecy.

Dates: 800 BCE | 700 BCE | 600 BCE | 500 BCE | 400 BCE | 300 BCE

Biblical Dates of Prophets:
Elijah · Elisha
Amos · Hosea · Isaiah · Micah
Zephaniah · Jeremiah · Ezekiel
Zechariah · Haggai

Joel
Obadiah
Nahum
Habbakuk
and Malachi
are not dated
in the Old Testament

Period of Production of Prophetic Books:

Major:
'Former Prophets' (Joshua, Judges, Samuel, Kings)
Isaiah
Second Isaiah
Third Isaiah
Jeremiah
Ezekiel

Minor:
Amos
Hosea
Zephaniah
Haggai
Zechariah
Micah
Obadiah
Jonah
Nahum
Habakkuk
Joel
Malachi

Production of Collection of 'Minor Prophets'
Collection of 'Latter Prophets'
Collection of 'Prophets'

Historical Background:
End of Northern Kingdom 722 BCE
Deportations to Babylonia 596 and 586 BCE
Cyrus captures Babylon 530 BCE · Temple rebuilding 520 BCE
Nehemiah (and Ezra?) 445 BCE
Alexander overruns Persian Empire 33 BCE

Chapter 13

WISDOM LITERATURE

This chapter deals with a significant portion of Old Testament literature which—since it represents largely the ethos of the scribal classes to whom we owe the composition and final shaping of the Bible—takes us to the heart of the Old Testament itself. However, the category of Wisdom can also embrace popular lore, where traditional sayings, rules, and maxims about life constitute a great deal of social 'knowledge'. In what follows, we shall try to define Wisdom (it will be spelled with an uppercase letter when used in the technical sense), search for its adherents, explore its literary forms, and look at some wisdom books in the Old Testament and Apocrypha.

What is 'Wisdom'?

One is often led to think of the Old Testament as a testimony to a unique experience of God to a particular people, conveyed in their own historical traditions and inspired by the doctrine of a covenant; however, large parts of the Bible, namely the 'Wisdom literature', take a quite different approach. The major books of this category are Proverbs, Job, and Ecclesiastes, and, in the Apocrypha, Ben Sira and the Wisdom of Solomon. They share literary forms, such as the proverb, the parable, and the discourse, and also vocabulary: 'understanding', 'wisdom', 'counsel', 'justice', 'way'—much of it found in other forms of literature, but used here more frequently and in a more technical sense. Finally, the different literary forms are bound together by a similar understanding of the meaning of life, or at least a disposition to approach the problem in a certain way. The leading principle of these writings is 'wisdom', and even when this is not made explicit, a piece of Wisdom writing can usually be identified by the implicit acknowledgment of this principle.

However, as with many of the categories with which biblical scholars work, there are different ways of using the word 'wisdom' in this context. The primary sense is the literary one, for we can classify Wisdom literature on the basis of the criteria given above. But it is also common for biblical scholars to assume that behind a literary corpus lies a 'tradition' which implies a particular set of conventions or, we might say, a common interest pointing to a concrete social group as authors and transmitters. This gives us a second usage: the tradition of such writing, the social culture that sustains it. Thirdly, Wisdom has been understood as a set of ideas, an attitude; hence 'Wisdom thinking' or 'Wisdom theology'. In this sense it can be abstracted from its concrete social setting and analyzed as a system of thought.

As to the social setting of Wisdom within Israel, there are several views. The narrowest sees it as the product of a certain class, the 'wise', usually identified with scribes. A broader view sees Wisdom as the product of intellectuals in Israelite society generally. Nevertheless, some individual proverbs suggest a popular context, and it is well known that proverbs and fables are common forms of folk literature. However, popular culture is not literary and we have to assume that the scribes are responsible for the written collections. The Wisdom literature in the Old Testament is probably the product of deliberate collection and cultivation of Wisdom sayings by what we might call 'urban intellectuals'. It is their world-view that emerges most clearly from the Wisdom books. Any 'intellectuals' outside this circle (probably rather few, among the merchants, priests, and owners of large estates) might well share much of this world-view but they did not leave us their own views!

In any case there is a fairly coherent way of thinking in the Wisdom books, which suggests a consciously developed philosophy. And this philosophy makes best sense when put in a certain social context. In particular, it is an international phenomenon, and the authors of Wisdom seem to be sharing a world-view with their counterparts in other neighbouring cultures. Because of this international dimension we can know a good deal about the nature of Wisdom literature.

Types of Wisdom Literature

'Instructions'

Among the most striking parallels between Judean Wisdom writing and that in Egypt and Mesopotamia is the genre of 'Instructions'. These contain practical advice for successful living, and in Egypt (where they are especially common) they are largely written by or for pharaohs or their senior administrators. Hence the inference that this particular literary form derives from the court. It has long been recognised that Proverbs 22:17–24:22 (the 'Words of the Wise') borrows from the *Instruction of Amenemope*, dating from perhaps 1100 BCE, and the whole book of Proverbs is also ascribed to the court: indeed, to 'Solomon, son of David, king of Israel' (1:1; cf. 10:1), though 25:1 contains the heading, 'These are also the proverbs of Solomon which the men of Hezekiah king of Judah copied', which may take us a little nearer to the real locus of production: the royal scribes.

Why should this instruction belong to the royal court? The reason may be—in Egypt anyway—that the king was regarded as the upholder of cosmic order, being himself a divine or quasi-divine being. The Egyptians also venerated a goddess called Maat, who represented such order, which included the proper administration of justice. Justice in ancient Near Eastern societies, royalty, divinity, and Wisdom were interconnected. The biblical story of Solomon's acquisition of wisdom (1 Kings 3:5-15) is followed by wise judgment in a particular lawsuit (1 Kings 3:16ff.) and administrative organisation of his kingdom—bringing order to his realm. Social order was exercised through bureaucrats, whom Solomon is said to have appointed in large numbers (1 Kings 4:1ff.). Such bureaucrats would be the true authors of 'Instructions'. But as ever in political life, the credit rarely goes to the bureaucrat.

Instructions are frequently addressed (as in the early chapters of Proverbs) to 'my son', with the probable implication that the royal successor will inherit the divinely endowed wisdom of his father. If we can loosely say that Wisdom is about 'how the world really works' then that definition has, in the context of ancient royal ideology, a very clear and precise application, for the king rules as the regent of the gods.

Argument
Instructions are found in the Old Testament primarily in Proverbs, where the royal connection is most evident. But other literary genres take us into the arena of the 'wise men', the scribes. Job and Ecclesiastes (Qoheleth) do not offer definitive statements of a proverbial kind, but rather explore, through dialogue or extended monologue, the limits of human knowledge and challenge the confident belief in a divinely sustained order. There were similar kinds of writing in Mesopotamia and Egypt. A work often referred to as the 'Babylonian Job' (and sometimes as the 'Babylonian Qoheleth') consists of a dialogue between a sufferer and a friend from whom he unsuccessfully seeks comfort; another text, 'I will praise the Lord of Wisdom' (*ANET*: 434-37), is the monologue of a person of high rank; he describes his misfortunes and blames the 'lord of wisdom', Marduk, for these. He claims to have been righteous and records his deliverance, first through a dream and then in reality.

Narrative
A third genre of Wisdom literature, also connected with scribal and court circles, is the Wisdom tale. The foremost example of this is the story of Ahiqar, which seems to have been very well known throughout the ancient Near East. The earliest text we have of this tale is from the late fifth century BCE. It is quoted in the Apocryphal book of Tobit, and allusions have also been discerned in other biblical books, in both Old and New Testament. It is the tale of a wise courtier (an administrator, counsellor, a 'scribe') who, after misfortunes in life, is restored to an honoured place. The narrative is interspersed with Wisdom sentences. There are several other examples in the Bible and Apocrypha of stories whose heroes are also honourable men of the scribe/sage class and who, by various stratagems and despite setbacks, achieve the place they deserve. We may include among these the story of Tobit himself, Daniel 1–6, perhaps Esther, and the Joseph story (see Chapter 9). These stories, though in the guise of folk-tales, appear to be didactic in purpose, showing that virtue will, in the end, always achieve its due reward.

Manticism
In Mesopotamia, Wisdom was predominantly associated with quite a different form of practice and knowledge. The court and temples were administered by groups of practitioners of what we can call 'mantic Wisdom'. This worked on the principle that understanding earthly things meant understanding the secrets of the heavens, and that these could be known by the interpretation of 'signs' such as entrails, heavenly bodies, and unusual phenomena. It is therefore a combination of revelation and rationality: the signs and secrets are divine, but the code can be broken and then learnt and written down. This activity produced a vast amount of literature based on the observation of such 'signs', on the basis of which not only could the future be predicted but also, by means of appropriate forms of preventive action, its negative aspects avoided. In the next chapter we shall describe this form of Wisdom as the background to apocalyptic literature. In the Old Testament, mantics appear in Exodus 7:11-12, where Aaron surpasses them in skill. And, of course, Joseph (and Daniel) possesses mantic Wisdom in their ability to interpret dreams (and in Daniel's case, cryptic graffiti as well).

The 'Wise'

Wisdom and the Scribal Class

In a non-literate culture, writing (and reading) is highly valued. With the invention of writing bureaucracy became possible. The earliest texts were economic, but the value of writing for recording omens, sending letters, and creating permanent, visible, records of great royal deeds soon became evident; and scribes became indispensable to the running of court and temple. Scribes drew up contracts (Jeremiah 32:12) and took dictation (Jeremiah 36:26); there are royal administrators, the 'king's scribes' (2 Chronicles 24:11); and some scribes are attached to the army and the Temple, in which some had their own offices (Jeremiah 36:10). The many skills, of mastering not only languages and scripts, but also diplomatic and administrative conventions, required education. The scribes became the intellectuals of their age, their profession being the accumulation and ordering of knowledge, which they reduced to a tangible form. They sought to comprehend all forms of art and science, and the earliest literary works we have, such as the epic of Gilgamesh, are no mere myths but betray a sophisticated interest in human nature. In short, knowledge was their profession: not a technical knowledge of a particular trade, but knowledge of all the metaphysical and ethical issues of their day. Ben Sira illustrates this point wonderfully in 38:24–39:11, where he contrasts the humble artisans and labourers with the exalted calling of the scribe. The Hebrew term for 'scribe' is *sofer* (literally, 'writer'), but these also came to be known as *hakamim*, 'wise'.

Wisdom literature represents substantially the values of such a class. Trained in political and diplomatic skills, they advised the monarch on policy (as did Ahithophel, Absalom's 'counsellor': 2 Samuel 16:15–17:23), and were pragmatic, worldly, and committed to order in human affairs and the enjoyment of life's benefits to the privileged. The scribal schools of Mesopotamia and Egypt also instilled in the pupils something of the moral code of the scribe. These values were not so very different from those of reputable modern public servants: honesty, foresight, prudence, hard work, sobriety. Such schools at some point will have existed also in Israel and Judah. From these the scriptures as a whole emanate, but the Wisdom literature gives us a deeper insight into their particular values and concerns.

Folk Wisdom

The source of 'wisdom' among the vast majority of ancient Israelites and Judeans was within the extended family, and the village community. Here, ethical instruction was conducted, by parents and grandparents, while the moral code was defined and enforced by the social group, and justice administered by the elders (see Chapter 10). Research into folk elements within the Wisdom literature has strengthened and broadened this perspective. Fontaine (1982) detected in the diplomatic correspondence of the fourteenth-century Amarna letters sent to the Pharaoh references to the custom of using proverbs as a means of settling disputes among and between tribes. In comparative studies of folklore, the existence of 'folk wisdom' or 'traditional wisdom' is firmly established, and the growing scholarly attention to biblical folklore is showing particular interest in the Wisdom literature. Much of the ethics found in the prophets (and in the lawcodes) reflects traditional ethical beliefs and practices.

'Wisdom' therefore covers a large number of related environments, functions, and traditions. We are justified, nevertheless, in focusing attention on the formal preservation of Wisdom in literary forms only because it is through this medium that the biblical literature has come to us. Yet we should not entirely divorce the 'wisdom' of the 'urban intellectual' from that of the village and family: after all, many scribes had probably been brought up in villages, or may have owned rural estates.

The Book of Proverbs

Whether the proverb by itself implies a philosophy of life is doubtful, but proverbs often express the kernel of one. A proverb's authority does not rest on divine revelation, but is self-authenticating, drawing on experience and inviting the listener or reader to test its truth from his or her own practice. The proverb often carries some practical, even ethical element, being not simply a statement of fact, but a recommendation to behave in a certain way. The same is true of those closely related popular forms, the parable and the fable. Proverbs contains all these forms: it is not, despite its title, made up only of proverbs—though the Hebrew *mashal* has a wider connotation than the English 'proverb'; it can also mean 'likeness' (metaphor, simile).

The book of Proverbs is not merely a ragbag of wise sayings, either: it is a collection that includes other collections. It also contains extended addresses, such as the speeches of Ms Wisdom and Ms Folly in chapters 7–8. Among the proverb collections are the 'Proverbs of Solomon' (1:1; 10:1; and 25), the 'Sayings of the Wise' (22:17 and 24:23), the 'Words of Agur' (30:1) and the 'Words of Lemuel' (31:1).

Types of Proverb

The simple proverb, of which the second half of the book is mainly composed, comes in several different forms. It nearly always consists of two parts, but the types can be analyzed according to different criteria. For example, we can distinguish the following linguistic forms:

Statements of fact:

> 'It is bad, it is bad', says the buyer, but when he goes away, he boasts (20:14).

Statements in which the consequence is also pointed out, so that they are exhortations rather than observations:

> Fear the Lord and the king, and do not disobey either of them; for disaster from them will arise suddenly (24: 21-2).

Condemnations:

> The evil man has no future; the lamp of the wicked will be put out (24:20).

Antithetical comparisons:

> A wicked man earns deceptive wages, but one who sows righteousness gets a sure reward (11:18).

Commands:

> Leave the presence of a fool, for there you do not meet words of knowledge (14:7).

Antithethical commands:

> Do not reprove a scoffer, or he will hate you; reprove a wise man and he will love you (9:8).

Similes:

> As a door turns on its hinges, so does the lazy person in his bed (26:14).

Numerical sayings:

> Three things are too wonderful for me; four I do not understand... (30:18).

If such formal classifications shed little light on the content-matter of proverbs, at least they give an idea of the variety of approach and style used in communicating Wisdom. Moreover, the cumulative effect of a series of proverbs, even chosen at random, is not to be ignored. First, such a series produces reinforcement; the repetition of similar sorts of truth, especially if the external forms vary, tends, while it reduces the impact of any single proverb, to create a kind of awareness of the system of values being advocated. Second, the frequent contrast between types of behaviour or types of person: the 'wicked' and the 'righteous' or the 'foolish' and the 'wise' conveys the perception that there are no shades of grey in these matters. There is a right thing to do and a wrong thing; a person is either wise or foolish. That, perhaps, is the nature of a proverbial instruction. But it leaves plenty of grey area for other books (like Job and Ecclesiastes) to explore.

The everyday character of the proverbs listed above is rather removed from the more reflective Wisdom that occurs in the earlier chapters of the book (see below). But alongside sayings like 'Whoever digs a pit will fall into it, and a stone will come back upon whoever who starts it rolling' (26:27) are more cultivated ones, which have perhaps been composed as an exercise in literary skill; for example, 'Three things are too wonderful for me; four I do not understand; the way of an eagle in the sky, the way of a serpent on a rock, the way of a ship on the high seas, and the way of a man with a maiden' (30:18-19). This is not so much a proverb as a riddle. One of the better interpretations is that it refers to different patterns of movement: the eagle circles, the snake zig-zags, the ship rolls and pitches and the two young people... A third kind of proverb, rather less sophisticated, does not convey empirical wisdom but dictates what is or is not pleasing to God, or simply commands obedience to his will, without stating what that will is. Of these there are numerous examples, and although Wisdom certainly includes due piety towards heaven, a simple, rather crude appeal simply to do the divine will (without discerning what it is) strikes a false note. But, as will be explained later, divine law came to challenge the empirical spirit that undergirded Wisdom. We find, then, among the proverbs a very large range, and it is tempting to interpret this range in terms of a development from 'popular' to 'learned' to 'pious'—but such schemes are certainly too simplistic and probably wrong!

Wisdom Theology

If the origins of proverbs (and the contents of the book of Proverbs itself) are so diverse, how can we extrapolate from the contents anything like a 'Wisdom theology', or perhaps a Wisdom 'way of thinking'? In a rudimentary way we can: the proverb is a microcosm: one example illustrates the rule. But woe to whoever takes them as metaphysical truths! They are always *examples*. Just as 'many hands make light work' so do 'too many cooks spoil the broth'. Thinking beyond the individual case to general principles can be dangerous, but is the next step in Wisdom. The proverbs are not in the end assembled purely for amusement or learning, but as raw material for an argument about how the world works. Two important features of a 'theology' of Proverbs are the concept of order, particularly moral order; and retribution—which implies a kind of moral order, for getting what is deserved is what justice is about. Yet Proverbs does not discuss this in a philosophical way, but in the manner of an extended metaphor. Wisdom is a woman, a desirable woman, and she herself will explain her origin. She declares (8:22-36):

> Yhwh created me at the beginning of his work,
> > the first of his acts of old,
> Ages ago I was set up,
> > at the first, before the beginning of the earth.
> When he established the heavens,
> > I was there,
> When he drew a circle on the face of the deep,
> > when he made firm the skies above…
> then I was beside him, like a master workman
> and I was daily his delight.

Here the nature of Wisdom in the abstract is being discussed. What light does this throw on the collection of assorted sayings and exhortations in which it is embedded? It is saying that Wisdom was the criterion, or the blueprint, by which the earth was created. It is as old as the Creator himself. There are perhaps overtones here of a goddess, a consort, of the kind that Yhwh had once had, but which the official theology of Second Temple Judah banished. The scribes replaced her with something more chaste but no less dear. The world operates according to the principles of Wisdom which (like her Egyptian counterpart Maat) is feminine. Ms Wisdom's account of herself invites the natural and the human, the individual and the social elements in the proverbs. It reconciles the tension between the empirical basis of some of the proverbs and the religious claims that Wisdom comes from God. Since Wisdom was built into the world by God, observation of the world delivers to the wise the knowledge of God's will. The wise and the foolish get their deserts not because God intervenes in every case, but because the rules of the world ensure that this is what will happen.

The book of Proverbs also expresses conviction in retribution. That is to say, when a proverb states the consequence of an action, the consequence emerges as a natural outcome, a just result. Wisdom literature as a whole does not as a rule deal in miraculous events, but confines its observations and deductions to the operations of the laws of nature, and it is in accordance with these laws that human behaviour receives its due recompense. The lack of appeal to Israelite history or to covenant in Proverbs is understandable, since all people are equally subject to the laws of the natural world. The Wisdom of Proverbs is personal, universal, and also monotheistic; its only God is the creator of a world of physical and moral order. Or, at least, Proverbs tries to *impose* that order, believing that people should act as if it did exist.

We must not leave this topic without pointing out that there is an interesting social dimension to this ethic. Egyptian Wisdom includes belief in an afterlife, where retribution and justice can be exercised; but the Judean scribes did not (at least, not until the Hellenistic period). Hence people earned their deserts in the here and now. Wisdom brought honour, wealth, posterity in this life. If we turn this equation round, it can be expressed as follows: those who have honour, wealth, and posterity are wise and virtuous, and clearly know the mind of God. It is not surprising that the privileged scribal guild developed a theology that suited them well, especially when others, as we shall see, could very easily point out that in practice it did not work.

The Book of Job

Biblical scholarship often treats Job as if it were a retort to Proverbs. The books certainly represent different viewpoints although both belong in the Wisdom tradition. Job rebukes his companions: 'Truly you are men of knowledge, and wisdom will die with you!' (12:2-3)—for his own predicament is that of one who does not understand, to whom the natural order makes no sense. The reader, who knows the whole story (unlike Job), comprehends all. But, comprehending all, on whose side does the reader belong in the end? With Job or Yhwh? With or without the notion of a God who created order and remains just? The central challenge of the book is to decide whether, in the end, order is re-established; whether justice rules; and whether, if there is order in the universe, humans have the ability to discern or understand it.

The argument against the notion of a moral universe is nowhere more economically or cogently put than by the Satan (= the divinely appointed 'inquisitor' angel, not the Evil One he appears elsewhere) to Yhwh: 'Does Job serve God for nothing?' A philosopher might have devoted volumes to whether or not disinterested goodness is possible. If God is known to be just and thus to reward goodness, goodness can hardly be distinguished from self-interest. If God does *not* reward goodness, he is unjust and has no right to demand goodness from humans. There is, of course, no answer. If Wisdom is a way of thinking (and acting) that applies observation and reasoning, it will inevitably stumble upon the unanswerable question.

Apart from this large philosophical conundrum, Job also poses a structural problem: the actual story is contained in two and a half prose chapters, separated by nearly forty chapters of poetry, in which nothing happens but talk, and whose ending suggests there is no real answer to innocent suffering. For many scholars a solution can be found to this structure by supposing that the poem was originally separate from its framework. Considered by itself, the poem is open to a different interpretation: it ends, not with Job being given back his goods in double measure, but by receiving the divine response he demands. Job (in the poem) may then be either a righteous person, to whose legitimate challenge God (he is only called 'Yhwh' in the prose framework) responds with a personal reply, or a self-righteous prig whom only a divine rebuke can bring down to size. God's final speech (chapters 40–41) is indeed a rebuke, but not of Job's lack of innocence, but his *ignorance*. Job has been trying to understand things which he cannot. To illustrate what Job is up against, God invokes his creative power. This, as we have seen in Proverbs, is an argument especially dear to Wisdom literature, for the maker of the universe is the source of all ethics too. But here the order in creation is definitely *not* the argument—rather the opposite! God does not present himself as a grand designer of a magnificent, orderly system. Instead he speaks of himself as one who created monstrous animals like the crocodile and the hippopotamus (Leviathan and Behemoth). Let a person understand *these* creatures, mightier than human beings! For if one cannot understand even these, how can one understand God? Job has been challenging a God of order and of justice. God responds as one whose ways do not make sense—at least to humans. One cannot 'draw out' a crocodile, and one cannot 'draw out' God in debate, either. One can only fear these terrible beasts, and fear God, who conceived and made them.

So Job accepts, and the poem undermines any complacency that wisdom might induce, any security in the ultimate *reasonableness* of life, or of God. The poem affirms God as a free agent, answerable to no-one, nor to any principle such as justice. But in the opening narrative we are told that Job's suffering *does* have a rational basis, and God's behaviour *does* make sense. Job, of course, knows nothing of this, and God does not speak of them, even in the closing narrative. So the reader of the book knows more than Job does, and more than God admits to Job. For God has been challenged by the Satan to a test (1:8-12; 2:3-6), a wager, and he has accepted. Job's sufferings will determine whether righteousness really exists. In the story the test is a test not of Job but of God. And Job, not God, is the free agent.

How, then, does the ending of Job (chapter 42) strike the reader? After his power-ful speech rebuking Job, Yhwh turns his anger on Job's companions who had assumed that Job was guilty because of his afflictions, and endorses everything that Job has said, then restores Job's fortunes. This is a quite different divine response from that at the end of the poem. Job's insistence on his innocence, and on divine justice, was correct, and he is vindicated. The Satan's challenge has been rebuffed. But the ending poses many problems. By restoring the fortunes of Job twofold, the game is in danger of being given away; belief in God's justice and the prosperity of the righteous is reasserted. Job's companions, though rebuked, were basically right. Goodness is rewarded; God does not let the innocent suffer.

But the ending of the book is not as simple as it seems. Job now knows that his previous good fortune is a blessing which God gives and can withhold: it is not—if it ever was—to be taken for granted. Moreover, now that disinterested righteousness has been demonstrated, God can feel free to reward it *if he chooses*. So the nexus between virtue and prosperity in life is not automatic, and the view represented in Proverbs that the reward of wise behaviour is secure has been qualified. The prob-lem of the suffering of the righteous has not been solved, of course—but it was not solved in Proverbs, either, just ignored! The tensions between the search for order, which requires absolute divine justice, and the experience of disorder, and between the knowability and unknowability of God were at the heart of Wisdom from the very beginning.

Qoheleth

Qoheleth ('Ecclesiastes' represents the Greek translation) is the author's self-designa-tion. *Qahal* in Hebrew means 'congregation', and the usual English rendering is, therefore, 'preacher'. But both *qahal* and *ekklesia* can also mean 'assembly' and 'orator' might be a better translation. The contents of the book offer an even more direct challenge than that of Job to the competence of wisdom. The author, in ironic vein, uses traditional methods to undermine traditional teachings. He appeals to experience, but his own experience contradicts the traditional experience of Wis-dom. He appeals to the order of nature, but only to compare its permanence with the transience of human life. He recognises the difference between the righteous and the wicked, but finds that they meet the same fate. He looks for success in life, and finds that it is an empty thing. Ironical too is the author's assumption of the identity of Solomon (1:1; 1:12, 16), a figure who personifies everything that this book denies!

The book is not a random collection of statements, but presents a series of topics. It opens with a demonstration of the 'vanity' (better, 'emptiness' or 'futility') of human effort, which it characterises as 'toil' or 'labour' (1:12–2:26). Then it shows the futility of attempting to find what lies in the past or the future. Things happen in their appointed time, and although this can be observed, it cannot be understood or predicted (3:1-5). Therefore, justice is a vain pursuit (32:16-22), as is wealth (5:9-19). There follow observations on unpunished wickedness (8:10-15), on the fact that all humans share the same fate (9:1-10) and, finally, on the brevity of life (11:7–12:7), which is a continuing motif in the whole book. According to Qoheleth, there is a God, and there is a certain order that he has imposed. But humans cannot comprehend it and so cannot achieve any security, either material or spiritual. Reason and observation demonstrate no sense in human life.

Where Qoheleth stands apart from the wisdom of Proverbs is that he assumes an intensely personal perspective. Proverbs is essentially collective in its ethic, being an anthology of sayings from many sources and taking as its yardstick social values: respect, honour, wealth, posterity. It accords authority to society as a whole and to the tradition of wisdom sayings. Qoheleth does not. He observes on his own authority, and he is overwhelmed by the fact of death, presumably his own most of all. Does he, then, have any practical advice to offer? Despite the fact that he regards it as preferable not to have been born, he apparently does not advocate suicide, or even despair. He is more of a realist than a pessimist. Seven times he makes a specific recommendation: to be happy, enjoy life, eat and drink, have a cheerful heart (see Whybray 1982). But he does not suggest that this can be done by abandoning oneself to a life of dissipation. Joy is to be found in eating and drinking, to be sure, but as regular human activities, not in the sense of revelry. He enjoins pleasure in work also. The proper response to life, according to Qoheleth, is to accept it, and while one has the opportunity, make the most of it.

Qoheleth was undoubtedly a controversial book, and copiers or editors interlaced it with the sort of conventional and pious comments (e.g. 2:26; 7:18; 8:12-13) that also characterise a number of items in Proverbs (see above). The end of the book provides especial evidence of this. After Qoheleth has ended with his slogan, 'All is vanity', an appended note states that 'besides being wise, Qoheleth also taught the people knowledge… [He] sought to find pleasing words, and uprightly he wrote words of truth'—as if to anticipate criticism of the book? For then follows another comment: 'The sayings of the wise are like goads…my son, beware of anything beyond these'. Then, finally, 'All has been heard. Fear God and keep his commandments, for this is the whole duty of humanity.' For some readers, evidently, Qoheleth's words needed to have a health warning attached.

The pursuit of wisdom does not necessarily, then, lead to knowledge of God, and certainly not to a consensus. In Qoheleth we have seen the limits, at least within the Bible, of an independent and critical use of wisdom. But one other thing is important: the intellectual agenda of Wisdom does not recognise geographical, political, or social boundaries. Its principles apply to the one creator of the whole world and to all humans in the world. There is a tension here with the nationalistic traditions elsewhere in the Bible. Hence, most of Proverbs, Job, and Ecclesiastes might have been preserved in cuneiform or hieroglyphs and found in Mesopotamia or Egypt. (Job, after all, takes place in a foreign land.) But we have also noted occasional verses that orientate Wisdom towards Judah, specifically the name Yhwh and the command to keep his law. In the remaining wisdom books we shall find further evidence of the attempt to integrate wisdom with other Judean religious traditions and perspectives and thus to create a specifically Jewish Wisdom.

Wisdom Psalms

It has been suggested that Psalm 1 is intended as an Introduction to the Psalter, and if so its Wisdom character is significant for the way that the psalms were read privately, as distinct from being recited—to the extent that they ever were (see Chapter 11)—in the cult. The psalm compares the righteous and the wicked, likening the righteous to a tree planted by a stream, who prospers ('prosper' signifies the reward of Wisdom in Wisdom vocabulary). Other Wisdom words, such as 'way', 'counsel', and 'meditate', are also used: the psalm's language, tone, and structure are very like the 'Instruction' (see above). But it does not use the word 'wise', and it makes clear what the 'blessed man' should do: meditate on God's law day and night.

Within the Psalter are psalms that reflect the wisdom of Proverbs and others that identify wisdom with obedience to the law. Psalm 37, for instance, reads almost like a chapter from Proverbs: sinners will perish, the righteous will be rewarded. However, there are signs of an integration of these sentiments with other religious attitudes. There is increased emphasis on the promise that Yhwh himself will punish the wicked. He will look after the righteous and give them the 'desires of their heart'. The righteous person has the 'law of God in his heart' (verse 31). Rather than take refuge in the words of the wise, the psalmist urges refuge in God (verse 40).

In contrast, Psalm 39 is closer to Qoheleth and Job. Verses 4-6 dwell on the brevity of life, even its uncertainty: 'A human heaps up, and knows not who will gather' (verse 6). The psalmist also claims that he has committed no sin, but kept his mouth firmly closed, yet God has afflicted him. He asks God to 'look away from me, that I may know gladness' (verse 13).

The Wisdom of Psalm 119 is less obvious, but a careful reading will show that it derives much of its style from Wisdom literature. It is also saturated with the language of law: 'commandments', 'testimonies', 'precepts', 'ordinances'. In what we call the Second Temple period the scribes were involved in the political and religious reconstitution of Judah, which involved especially the installation of a distinctive Judean legal code and the anchoring of religious practice and governance in the now monopolistic Jerusalem temple. But as the influence and authority of the scribe waxed, so waned the independence of wisdom as a critical tradition, and its mantic aspects (see next chapter) developed into devices for interpreting the hidden meanings of sacred texts. In the emergence of 'Judaism' as a national religion (or even as a 'philosophy', as Greeks saw it) there was to be only a limited scope for 'wisdom' as a means of religious knowledge independent of law and sacred tradition, though any reader of the Talmud will recognise the ongoing power of wisdom traditions among the rabbis, the heirs of the 'scribes'.

Ben Sira

Yeshu ben Sira (or, in Greek Sirach) lived at the end of the third century BCE, and his book, included in the Apocrypha and also known as Ecclesiasticus, is a collection of his own sayings, presented in the well-known form of the Instruction. However, the book also includes some extended essays and hymns. The topics range widely, but Ben Sira's central theme is the 'fear of Yhwh'. What does this mean? 'Fear of Yhwh' is an attitude of reverence which will prompt the righteous person to do the divine will and to seek divine guidance in fulfilling it. But as to Ben Sira's understanding of the relationship between 'wisdom' and divine law ('torah'), understood as the revealed will of God to Israel, there remains some uncertainty. Some find him convinced that true wisdom is enshrined in the law of Moses; others claim that his allegiance was primarily to wisdom, and that he sought to explain the law as wisdom, rather than wisdom as the law. The most probable explanation is that Ben Sira regarded both wisdom and the law as leading to the 'fear of Yhwh', and as in principle in harmony. But if they came into conflict, he had no doubt as to the resolution:

> Better is the man who fears God without understanding than a man of prudence who transgresses the law (19:24).

> How great is one who has gained wisdom
> But there is none above him who fears the LORD (25:10).

> All wisdom is the fear of Yhwh
> And in all wisdom fulfilment of the law (19:20).

On the other hand, Ben Sira utters a great hymn to wisdom in chapter 24, and he advises the study of sages and obedience to elders. His allegiance to the priesthood is also manifest, for many of his greatest heroes are priests, and his description of the contemporary high priest is magnificent (50.6-8).

The way to understand Ben Sira is not as a great thinker, or even a very consistent one, but as a practical man. The overwhelming impression one gets from his words is of a great compromiser. On almost every question, he fudges. On the choice between wisdom and the law he wants (as we have just seen) to approve both. In chapter 13 he observes how wretched it is to be poor, and how much better to be rich, but 'poverty is evil only in the opinion of the ungodly' (v. 24), and elsewhere in many places he encourages giving to the poor, while advising prudence on giving credit (chapter 29). He advises a sick person to call the doctor but also to pray for healing (38:9-15). He says that sin came into the world through a woman (25:24), but praises a good wife (chapter 26). He does not seem to believe in an afterlife, but asserts that the wicked will get their punishment 'at the end' (e.g. 18:24).

It has been thought that Ben Sira can best be understood against a background of cultural conflict, when Hellenism was making an impact on religious belief within Judaism (see chapter 7). Possibly his work is an attempt to tread a middle ground between two ideologies. The extensive treatment of God's justice suggests that some Judeans were abandoning their religion because they did not accept the idea of this justice. On the other hand, there were those attracted by wisdom but preferring the Hellenistic kind. Ben Sira can be understood as trying to accommodate varying viewpoints and defining a form of Judaism that is worldly-wise but also rooted in law and priesthood and a sense of Judean identity. His book is also littered with references to the Scriptures (for a list see Crenshaw 1981: 150-51). The scribe, or wise man, is now a pillar of the religious establishment, an affirmer and an optimist, not a critic or questioner like Job or Qoheleth. Ben Sira has a conscience, but he is a snob. He is complacent and full of platitudes. But he does present a very important personal picture of a Judean scribe that enables us to see behind biblical Wisdom and its earlier, anonymous proponents.

The Wisdom of Solomon

This work, written probably in the first century CE in Alexandria, represents an attempt to adapt the wisdom tradition for a people living in one of the cultural centres of the Mediterranean world. The Solomonic ascription is a convention: the book employs the Greek language and a Greek literary style. A prominent theme is the election and protection of Israel by God, who has always exercised compassion on his chosen people, and there is a sustained attack on idolatry. Antagonism towards Egypt is evident in the reminiscence of the Exodus and deliverance by the sea, and there is more than a hint that this is what will come upon latter-day Egyptians. This book cannot be understood outside the context of bitter relations between (some?) Jews in Alexandria and the native Egyptians, and we know from other sources of such strife. But it seems that native Egyptian culture rather than that of the Hellenised population is the real target.

The concept of Wisdom itself is highly developed here. It becomes a projection of God, an advance on the personification in Proverbs. Whereas in Proverbs Wisdom claims to have attended God in the creation of the world, here Wisdom becomes the agent that guided Israel's early history, starting with Adam and culminating with Moses, as the author uses the Exodus story to develop his contrast between Israel and Egypt. Wisdom is also Solomon's bride; an emanation directly from God; the source of all knowledge, including all the sciences and arts learned in the Hellenistic schools. The connections between the Wisdom of Solomon and traditional Hebrew wisdom are more tenuous. The appeal to human experience is absent, and the universal dimension of human experience is obliterated by a concern to contrast God's treatment of Israel with his treatment of other nations (specifically Egypt). Concern with material well-being in this life, with death, and with individual suffering are absent. There is no place for doubt or questioning.

The book assimilates many ideas from its Hellenistic environment. In particular it believes in the immortality of the soul, which it describes as a mind imprisoned in a body. This permits the belief that long life is not necessarily a great reward and that retribution and recompense can take place after death (as in the native Egyptian religion).

We can explain the attitudes of Ben Sira and the Wisdom of Solomon, writings from the Hellenistic period, in terms of social and religious identity, so long as we realise that such an explanation is only partial and that individual authors do not necessarily represent their society in every respect. Qoheleth is probably much influenced by certain Greek notions, without any overt sign of concern about this. Ben Sira wrote in Palestine and in Hebrew, in a milieu that was open to other cultural influences and yet apparently had become increasingly wary of them. His attitude of compromise together with his dedication to the national institutions, addresses a society uncertain of how far to accommodate its beliefs to alien ways of thinking. The Wisdom of Solomon is more extreme case of a community seeking to define and assert its identity. It does this by reinterpreting its own traditions, but *in the presence and forms of its new environment* because this is where the community feels at home. Ironically, a group that has 'returned to Egypt' celebrates the deliverance from Egypt. But that deliverance is now transformed into the gift of Wisdom itself.

Wisdom, then, has travelled from the court, the extended family, and the individual protester, to the Jewish community in an alien environment. It has expressed scepticism and upheld religious dogma. Yet for all its variety, it remained an important aspect of the religious orientation of the Old Testament, and enabled the traditional tenets of the religion of Israel to be accommodated within the cosmopolitan culture into which Judeans found themselves increasingly drawn.

Further Reading

References in this chapter have been made to J. Crenshaw, *Old Testament Wisdom: An Introduction* (Atlanta: John Knox Press, 1981); R.N. Whybray, 'Qoheleth, Preacher of Joy', *JSOT* 23 (1982): 87-98. J.G. Gammie and L.G. Perdue (eds.), *The Sage in Israel and the Ancient Near East* (Winona Lake, IN: Eisenbrauns, 1990), contains very helpful essays, and J. Blenkinsopp, *Wisdom and Law in the Old Testament* (Oxford: Oxford University Press, 1995): 1-83, provides a very good account of most aspects of biblical Wisdom. Also recommended is R.N. Whybray, *The Intellectual Tradition in the Old Testament* (Berlin: W. de Gruyter). On Wisdom as formation of character, see W.P. Brown, *Character in Crisis: A Fresh Approach to the Wisdom Literature of the Old Testament* (Grand Rapids: Eerdmans, 1996).

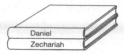

Chapter 14

APOCALYPTIC LITERATURE

The Meaning of 'Apocalyptic'

The word 'apocalyptic' is nowadays used to describe a scenario that heralds the end of the world, or of life, or civilization. This meaning lies some distance from the original. The Greek word *apokalypsis* means 'revelation' and is the title (because it is the first word) of the New Testament book of Revelation (which in fact calls itself 'prophecy'!). That book contains many descriptions of future events, particularly a time of great distress and persecution, followed by one of judgment and of bliss for the faithful. A number of books of this kind, describing the end of history, were written during the Greco-Roman period, not only by Jews and Christians, but also by Greeks, Romans, Egyptians, and Persians. These writings came to be known as 'apocalypses'.

A focus on the 'end-time' is a common feature of apocalypses, but in fact this ancient literary genre needs to be defined more widely. It conveys what are claimed to be direct revelations from heaven, given usually in a vision or by angelic dictation, or by a journey to heaven. They were often ascribed to a figure of antiquity, who would foretell what would happen in that person's future, but was in fact the past from the perspective of the real author and reader. A real prediction of the future, which was usually the main point, then formed the crux of this 'pseudo-prediction'. But the 'end-time' was not the only possible content of such 'revelations'. The origins of the world, the movements of the heavenly bodies, the meaning of history, the geography of heaven, the names of angels, or even the appearance of God himself, all counted among the secrets that could be learned only by revelations of this kind.

The characteristics of this literary genre of apocalypse have acquired a broader sense in biblical scholarship. 'Apocalyptic' or 'apocalypticism' is sometimes used to describe a way of thinking, even a kind of religion, which is other-worldly and focused on some imminent moment that will bring the existing world order to an end. 'Apocalyptic' may even be loosely used to mean 'eschatology', or 'eschatological', that is, concerned with the end or goal of history or the cosmos. It is even used of communities created or sustained by hope or belief that the order will soon change; and hence literary apocalypses have tended to be understood in some quarters as the product of millenarian sects. One can see how these meanings bring us to the contemporary usage of the term. But they are really not very helpful in the examination of ancient apocalypses, which were generally *not* produced by sects, often not concerned with the future, and, so far as their world-view is concerned, not very different from widespread beliefs in demons and angels, astrology, incantations, magic, and exorcism. Most citizens of the ancient Near Eastern and classical world believed in a realm of the gods from which mortals might access knowledge about this world. Apocalypses are a refined expression of an attitude that believes in the overwhelming reality of the transcendental world and its effects on everyday life. It is not surprising that this genre was especially popular in times of uncertainty or fear of the future, though some apocalypses seem to be a kind of proto-scientific attempt to get 'behind the scenes' of reality and show what makes things happen, and how.

In the Old Testament, apocalyptic literature (or simply 'apocalyptic', as the genre is often called) might not seem to occupy a prominent place. Only the book of Daniel falls into this category. But if we are interested in the world that the Bible reflects— and not just the physical world but the world of ideas as well—we must take account of a fairly large body of Jewish apocalyptic literature outside the scriptures, some of it older than parts of the Old Testament. In this chapter we shall try to describe the kind of religious and social background this kind of writing might reflect. Despite its poor representation in the Bible, apocalyptic literature is not a fringe activity, nor are its contents peripheral to an understanding of Judaism (or Christianity, for that matter).

It would be impossible even to begin to cover the range of apocalyptic writings now known to us that date from 300 BCE–100 CE; for this the reader can consult *Old Testament Pseudepigrapha* (Charlesworth 1983). Instead, we shall, in the last part of this chapter, focus attention on the books of Daniel and 1 Enoch, which contain the earliest and in many respects most important Palestinian Jewish apocalypses (Enoch himself is referred to in the New Testament, in Jude 14–15). The material in 1 Enoch dates from the third century BCE onwards and is often simply referred to as the Book of Enoch (though there are other 'books of Enoch' as well).

Apocalyptic Technique

In what way does an apocalypse differ from wisdom or prophecy or law, which also claim to derive from divine revelation? The differences lie, basically, in the words 'knowledge' and 'secrets'. Prophecy is a public announcement of a message that God wishes the recipient to hear. Wisdom instruction is knowledge derived from observation and experience by a sage and passed on in his name to his disciples or a wider audience. The apocalypse pretends to offer what cannot be normally known and what is not supposed to be known, or at least widely known. Unlike Prophecy and Wisdom, it is not directly an exhortation to behave in a certain way. It is rather essentially 'privileged information' which enables the recipient to know what is 'going on'. This knowledge is the key to salvation, and is often shared among restricted groups (what is the point of a secret that everyone knows?): hence its occasional association with sects. While the 'information' given in apocalypses may be intended to affect human behaviour (for instance, to join the privileged group with the 'knowledge'), it often serves to confirm that the present time, however bad, has been planned and that a better future lies ahead. For the technique of apocalyptic requires that the future is knowable and therefore, has been pre-determined.

Since this knowledge is presumed to be confidential, the apocalypse employs devices to explain how it has been acquired. The name of the recipient of the knowledge and (pretended) author of the book is given, along with details of the experience by which his (or her) knowledge was obtained. More often than not, the 'author' is a great figure of the past—Daniel, Enoch, Moses, even Adam—and hence many apocalypses are Pseudepigrapha, that is, given a fictitious authorship. The 'author' is often claimed to have written a book which the reader is to assume has remained a secret or been published just recently. In this respect, the book of Revelation, paradoxical as this may seem, is not like other apocalypses: whether it is pseudepigraphic remains unclear, but the name 'John' hardly points in that direction.

Apocalyptic literature is trying to grasp the sense that lies beneath the nonsense of the present world—or, more graphically, the sense, which lies *above* it! In that respect it is very closely linked to the ethos of Wisdom. In the Hebrew Bible, however, apocalyptic literature is—Daniel apart—found in the Prophets (see below). In the Old Testament, even Daniel is included with the prophets.

What sort of culture produces works that speculate on what happens behind the scenes? What sort of culture is concerned with the hidden, the mysterious, the unknown? Both Prophecy and Wisdom reveal the will and intention of the gods, but for the origins of apocalyptic writing we must go outside the orbit of biblical Prophecy and Wisdom and look at an aspect of religion that was prevalent throughout the ancient Near East, including ancient Israel: divination.

Divination

Babylonian Mantics
Manticism is a system of belief and practice about the discovery of heavenly secrets from earthly signs. The signs may be encoded in animal entrails, anomalous births, the movements of the heavenly bodies or dreams. These are collectively called 'omens', and each of these kinds of omen requires learning the decipherment appropriate to it. Omen lists are among the earliest cuneiform texts we have, and guilds of mantic specialists existed in Mesopotamia from the beginnings of monarchy.

Interpretation of omens presupposes a belief in the possibility of communication with supernatural forces that encode their secrets in *signs*. Interpreting such signs reveals the intentions of the gods and can help to avert what is projected for the future, be it for the nation or the individual. Two-way communication could sometimes be conducted through pouring oil on water or making smoke, and specific questions could also be asked about the favourability of certain tasks at certain times, or the outcome of a proposed action. The Babylonian omen lists typically have the form of a conditional sentence: 'if…then…', listing the consequences expected from certain phenomena. If the presupposition was not scientific, the procedures were, and observing the heavenly bodies led to astronomy as well as astrology. The key was an assumption that certain phenomena could be *interpreted* as signs of divine intentions.

The omen literature seems to have played a role in the development of other literary types, such as the so-called 'Akkadian prophecies' or 'Akkadian apocalypses'. These are essentially 'predictions' of past events, usually concluding with a genuine prediction. The statements about historical events past and present are markedly similar to the interpretation of an omen on an omen-list. These are not necessarily based on omens, but the point here is that the presuppositions of manticism and the language of the omen literature could be taken over into other literary forms. And all this was the product of a central cultic institution, the mantic priests/prophets or *baru*.

Divination in Israel

The extensive records of Babylonian manticism raise a question: did this sort of thing occur also in ancient Israel? Now, divination (which is what manticism deals in) was condemned in the Old Testament:

> There shall not be found among you…anyone who practises divination, a soothsayer, or an augur, or a sorcerer, or a charmer, or a medium, or a wizard, or a necromancer (Deuteronomy 18:10-11).

Jeremiah condemns prophets and diviners in the same breath:

> The prophets…are prophesying to you a lying vision, worthless divination (Jeremiah 14:14; cf. 27:9-10 and 29:8-9).

During their exile in Babylonia Judeans were of course exposed to a religious culture dominated by manticism. Isaiah 47:9-15 gives an eloquent condemnation of this practice:

> In spite of your many sorceries and the great power of your enchantments… Evil shall come upon you for which you cannot atone; disaster shall rain upon you which you will not be able to expiate; and ruin shall come on you suddenly, of which you know nothing. Stand fast in your enchantments and your many sorceries with which you have laboured from your youth; perhaps you may be able to succeed, perhaps you may inspire terror. You are wearied with your many counsels; let them stand forth and save you, those who divide the heavens, who gaze at the stars, who at the new moons predict what shall befall you…

The passion of this fervent Yahwist contrasts with the patient and faithful service of the 'wise man' Daniel, who learnt the wisdom of the Babylonians, surpassed them in his mastery of it, and rescued them from extermination (Daniel 2). He is superior because his god, the Most High, is the true source of all knowledge and can reveal secrets to whom he chooses. Nevertheless, deciphering writing on the wall is manticism, and writing pseudo-predictions of history (Daniel 11) a by-product. Daniel is a true mantic—a Jewish mantic. How has this come about?

Mantic Wisdom

In the Neo-Babylonian and Persian periods Babylonian mantic traditions were known as far west as Greece; eventually they reached Rome. By the time of the first Jewish apocalypses, in the late Persian or Hellenistic period, manticism formed part of a culture in which Judea was inevitably immersed. In Babylonia the mantic class, who increasingly focused on astrology, came to be called 'Chaldean' (as in Daniel); the mantic priestly class of the Persians were the Magi whose religion was Zoroastrianism and whose speciality was the interpreting of dreams. But the Magi gradually became identified with the Chaldean astrologers. Thus Matthew's 'wise men from the East' (*magoi*) are guided to Bethlehem by a star, and warned in a dream to return home without seeing Herod. Other Magian beliefs included Zurvan, a time-deity, and the notion of world-epochs. Ahura-Mazda, the creator, was their chief god, and they also believed in the pre-natal and post-mortem existence of the soul in the realm of light. Such beliefs profoundly influenced the development of Judaism.

In the period we are examining, however, manticism was no longer tied to a cult. We are talking less about priests and more about scribes using and developing its lore. As readers and writers of ancient texts, linguists, historians, and scientists, they were also concerned with the ultimate meaning of the world and of human history. The Deuteronomistic history (the Former Prophets) offers a theory: history depends on response to the demands of the covenant. But the idea that divine behaviour could depend on human activity was problematic, for in that way prediction was always conditional. Mantics were required to deliver something more reliable. Moreover, in an age of empires, when Judah had little autonomy in political matters, how could history be determined by such a small and insignificant province? Was history, then, dictated by the great empires? Again, no: it was the Most High God who decided these things. His promises to his chosen people were not being fulfilled; but were the chosen people to blame? Some Judean theologians thought yes: they were still being punished for their previous sins: others thought not. Either way, the Most High had his plans and what would happen would happen when he had decided.

In the last chapter it was noted that Ben Sira offered a portrait of a typical scribe at the end of the third century. In one famous passage he actually describes what a scribe was to do:

> ...he who applies himself to the fear of God,
> And to set his mind to the law of the Most High;
> Who searches out the wisdom of all the ancients,
> And occupies himself with the prophets of old,
> Who attends to what eminent men say,
> And investigates the deep meaning of parables
> Searches out the hidden meaning of proverbs
> And is acquainted with the obscurities of parables,
> He shall be filled with the spirit of understanding,
> He himself pour out wise sayings in double measure,
> He himself direct counsel and knowledge,
> And set his mind on their secrets;
> He himself declare wise instruction (Ben Sira [Sirach] 39:1-8).

Now, at first sight here is a definition of a seeker of Wisdom. But note the preoccupation with understanding secrets, which includes parables, proverbs, and prophetic sayings. And what is the 'wisdom of the ancients'? What does 'understanding' mean? We find here already the language of *interpreting*, deciphering. Ben Sira is already showing how the scribal ethos of Judah has become a *hermeneutical* one: it is interested in interpreting. Even though, as we saw in the last chapter, the law was imposing itself onto Wisdom, that law was itself subject to interpretation. In this way, the freedom of the wise could still operate, manipulate, and even control. In the sacred writings could be found out more of divine intentions than the surface meaning might convey. Ben Sira is quite at home with apocalyptic topics—myths, historical reviews, heavenly secrets, and profound old sayings. He was living at a time when apocalypses had already begun to be composed, and just before their heyday.

Jewish Apocalypses

We now turn to the earliest Jewish apocalypses, which modern readers of the Bible often find hard to understand. The language and even the point of apocalyptic writing can seem elusive. But, after the introduction, perhaps what follows will not seem so strange.

Enoch

1 Enoch, although not part of the Western Old Testament, is in the canon of some Christian churches (such as the Ethiopic) and in any case contains the earliest known Jewish apocalypses. Thanks to the discovery of literary fragments among the Dead Sea Scrolls, we can now confidently date the collection (except possibly for chapters 37–71) to the pre-Christian era, and the earliest parts to the third century BCE. These parts are the Astronomical Book (chapters 72–92), the Book of the Watchers (chapters 1–36), the Epistle of Enoch (chapters 91–105), and the Book of Dreams (chapters 83–90). They represent a body of traditions, rather than a single tradition, but these are related and suggest a more or less coherent pattern of ideas.

How did Enoch become a patron of apocalyptic literature? The biblical notice about him (Genesis 5:18-24) is brief: he was the son of Jared and father of Methuselah; he lived 365 years and then 'walked with God'. Then 'he was not, for God took him'. It is usual to consider this tantalising hint of something special as the origin of the Jewish Enoch tradition. But the Genesis notice probably stands not at the beginning but somewhere in the middle, or even towards the end, of Enoch's development as an apocalyptic sage. Enoch is probably derived from a figure in the Sumerian King List, a list of rulers of Sumer (the earliest civilization of Mesopotamia) before the Flood, and is preserved in several forms, including the third-century BCE historian Berossus (see *ANET*: 265). Here one of the kings, often appearing as the seventh, is called Enmeduranki or Enmeduranna. He is generally associated with the city of Sippar, which was the home of the cult of the sun god Shamash. Moreover, in other texts (see VanderKam 1984: 39ff.) this Enmeduranki was the first to be shown by the gods Adad and Shamash three techniques of divination: pouring oil on water, inspecting a liver, and the use of a cedar (rod), whose function is still unclear. These were to be transmitted from generation to generation, and became the property of the *baru*, the major group of diviners in Babylon.

So Enoch corresponds to Enmeduranki: he is also seventh in the list of names in which he appears; the number 365 preserves an affinity to the sun; walking with God (or perhaps, 'angels'?) suggests a special intimacy between him and heavenly world. The final connection links not with Enmeduranki, but with a fish-man (*apkallu*), with which each of the first seven kings associated and from whom they learnt all kinds of knowledge. Enmeduranki's *apkallu*, called Utu'abzu, is mentioned in another cuneiform text, where he is said to have ascended to heaven. The writer of Genesis 5:21-24 seems to be alluding briefly to a Judean version (as Noah is a Judean version of Utnapishtim or Ziusudra, the Mesopotamian Flood heroes) of a figure connected with the transmission of divine wisdom by divinatory means.

1 Enoch provides us with information about the Enoch that Genesis alludes to. In the Astronomical Book, Enoch reveals to his son Methuselah what the angel Uriel had shown him of the workings of the sun, moon, and stars. Most of this book is scientific, being a description of the movements of the heavenly bodies, ostensibly revealed in heaven, but obviously the result of generations of sky-watching. However, there is a brief section (chapters 80–81) which is especially important. Here Enoch also tells of the deeds of righteous and unrighteous persons, forecasting a disruption in the natural order. It is very likely that this passage is not original, but its presence shows us how a text of purely astronomical observations came to be used in the service of ethical exhortation and eschatological prediction—something closer to the usual interest of apocalyptic writers. According to Michael Stone, the origins of

apocalyptic writing lie in 'lists of things revealed' (see Stone 1976), including the names and functions of angels, and from there develops a focus on the origin and end of evil, on the final judgment, and on the identity of the righteous.

In the Book of the Watchers, these more ethical dimensions come to the fore. Here we find a story about the beginning and the end of the present order, particularly the origin of sin and its ultimate solution. These ethical concerns combine the 'listing of revealed things' with traditional concerns of Wisdom: right behaviour, harmony with the natural order, divine justice, the dualism of wisdom and folly, righteousness and wickedness. The Book of the Watchers opens (chapters 1–5) with a warning that moves from the observation of order in the natural world—in obeying the laws set for it by God—to the lack of order among humans. Those who adhere to these natural laws are righteous; those who do not are sinners. Note that righteousness, and wickedness are represented as functions of *knowledge* and *understanding*, rather than of simple obedience. In 1 Enoch (and apocalyptic generally) we find Wisdom categories rather than categories of law and covenant. Although the Enoch corpus does not contain very much direct or indirect interpretation of Scripture, chapters 1–5 seem to draw on the story of Balaam (Numbers 22–24)—though this tradition was not confined to Israel. Chapters 6–11 describe how sin first came into the world with the descent of heavenly beings called the Watchers. Here again is a fuller version of an episode that is only briefly related in the Old Testament.

The biblical episode is Genesis 6:1-6, where the 'children of God' have intercourse with women, producing a race of *Nephilim*, 'mighty men that were of old, men of renown'. 1 Enoch 6–11 describes how these heavenly beings (all named) teach the women about spells, root-cutting and plants, astrology, weapons of war, and cosmetics. The women give birth to giants, who turn to cannibalism and drinking blood. The earth cries out for help, and God orders the execution of the giants, the binding of the Watchers beneath the hills until the day of judgment, and thereafter in a fiery chasm. The leader according to one version, Azazel or Asa'el, is buried under a rock, until, after judgment, he is hurled into the fire.

Many scholars take the view that this story, in its various forms, is inspired by the Greek legend of Prometheus, the Titan who brought heavenly secrets to humans, and that it has also developed from the Genesis story. But that account makes little sense except as an allusion to some fuller version. More probably it is a version of an older myth about the origin of sin, which held sin to have originated in heaven and been brought to earth together with knowledge which enabled humanity to progress in arts and sciences. Isaiah 14:12 possibly echoes a story about a fallen rebellious angel whom it names as the morning star (= Lucifer, as he was named in later, Christian mythology). Even Psalm 82 may refer to a form of this myth, if we translate verse 7, 'Yet you shall die like Adam, and fall like one of the angels'.

Later in the Book of the Watchers Enoch enters the divine presence, and learns in more detail about the future. Here he is called a 'scribe of righteousness', who records the divine sentence on the Watchers. But he also intercedes for them with God. In the rest of this book, Enoch travels twice, to the west and around the world, including visits to Jerusalem, Eden, and Sheol, the abode of the dead—thus adding a knowledge of geography to his understanding of astronomy. In all this, we can see reflected the figure of the ideal scribe whose goal is universal knowledge, but gained not only by experience but also by revelation, and who hands it on to his 'children' (disciples). Yet elsewhere in 1 Enoch, he also becomes a heavenly figure, the patron 'angel' of the wise man, the 'recording angel', and a heavenly intercessor. Perhaps he is the scribal version of the 'messiah' (see Chapter 15). At any rate, the conversion of Enoch into a heavenly being is suggestive for the development of Christianity.

In the remaining two parts of 1 Enoch we find two substantial apocalypses (there is also a brief third one in 83:3-5) both dating from the first half of the second century BCE. The earlier of these, the Apocalypse of Weeks (93:1-10 and 91:11-17) divides Israelite history into ten periods ('weeks'), the time of the author being the seventh. This introduces us to another common feature of apocalypses: their division of history into periods—always culminating in the present time which stands on the eve of the End. This periodizing may be inspired by Persian ideas, and seems to have been a common practice among the scribal classes. The Apocalypse of Weeks makes a clear reference to the political and religious crisis beginning around 175 BCE (see Chapter 7), and takes the form of pseudo-prediction of past events followed by a genuine prediction of the (real) future. It foresees a restoration of order and righteousness, first in Israel, then in the world, and finally in the whole cosmos.

The other apocalypse in 1 Enoch is the 'Animal Apocalypse' (chapters 85–90), which is also an example of periodised history and prediction, and acquires its name from its depiction of individuals and nations in the guise of animals (animals being another favourite device of apocalypses). Unlike the Apocalypse of Weeks, this periodisation commences only with the exile, and it enumerates seventy shepherds who have ruled Israel—almost certainly inspired by Jeremiah 25 (especially verses 32ff.). This connection to a scriptural passage introduces us to yet another prominent feature of apocalyptic: the interpretation of scriptural books as if they, too, were encoded messages to be deciphered, especially in terms of what will happen in the future. The Animal Apocalypse is also detailed in its historical description (like Daniel 10–11), enabling us to discern the career of Judas Maccabee, whose successes inaugurate the eschatological section.

Neither of these apocalypses is concerned merely with periodizing history, however. Both are responding to problems raised by their own time that raise the question of the orderliness and purpose of history. In Jewish apocalypses accounts of history try to make sense of what is going on at the time of writing. Ben Sira had lamented the inequalities of his society; but he did not perceive in these inequalities any kind of crisis or any challenge to his belief in the orderliness and permanence of the world and his society. The apocalypses, by contrast, convey a radical account of the world order that assumes its imminent surrender to a new state of things.

From this overview we have been able to see how the world-view of the apocalypse develops from a more general concern with things unseen, with ancient secrets and their inspired revealers. But we can offer here only a sketch of apocalyptic; for it is the product of a very rich and varied culture. It is not an esoteric and intra-Jewish development but a cosmopolitan, variegated, many-sided, cross-cultural phenomenon. And while often connected with sects or religious groups, it is not always; and its authors (and readers) are privileged, literate, and influential persons.

Daniel

Like Enoch, the book of Daniel is a composite collection of stories and visions, not all of which have the form of an apocalypse, but which allow us to see how the apocalypse form emerges. The stories in the first part of the book (chapters 1–6) portray the adventures of a Judean youth initiated into Babylonian manticism. His gifts, which surpass those of the Babylonians, are those of interpreting dreams and (on one occasion) mysterious writing on a wall. However, as a Judean, he acquires his knowledge by direct revelation, not by divinatory technique. But the stories also tell of persecution and how the righteous are delivered through divine intervention. In these stories Daniel's profession is important, placing him in a prominent position that renders him vulnerable to the idolatrous or envious designs of kings and courtiers. Daniel is required under persecution to show exemplary behaviour, to teach in this case by his deeds rather than by his words. At the close of the book of Daniel, the authors reveal their own identity:

> Those among the people who are wise shall make many understand, though they shall fall by sword and flame, by captivity and plunder, for some days, but when they understand, they shall be helped a little. Some of those who are wise shall fall, to refine and to cleanse them, and to make them white, until the time of the end, for the time appointed is yet to be (Daniel 11:33-35).

> Those who are wise shall shine like the brightness of the firmament; and those who turn many to righteousness like the stars for ever and ever (Daniel 12:3).

The Hebrew word for 'wise' here is *maskil*, of which Daniel himself is one (1:4). Their task, according to this passage, is both to suffer and to reach righteousness, as did Daniel. An obvious model for this combination of roles is the 'servant' of Second Isaiah (chapter 53, especially verse 11). The profile of Daniel as an educated 'wise man', serving at court, a political administrator (2:48), an interpreter of the future for the king, is a profile of the scribe learned in mantic lore. The book of Daniel is indeed the product of 'Daniels'. It was created by appending a series of apocalyptic visions, which we can date to the mid-second century BCE, to an older cycle of stories reflecting life in the eastern diaspora. These stories are not apocalypses themselves: they belong to the genre of court-tale (see Chapter 9) but they lay a foundation for the second, apocalyptic part with its themes of knowing the future and suffering persecution.

Daniel 7–12 is an account of Daniel's visions in the first person, though from chapter 9 onwards the emphasis shifts from visions to Daniel's penitence and then to a detailed pseudo-prophecy (again with a genuine prediction attached) of the events of the writer's own time. In the first two visions (chapters 7 and 8) we find a form familiar from biblical prophetic literature, the 'symbolic vision', which constitutes the main technique for divine revelation in Jewish apocalypses.

In the simplest form of this literary device, as found in visions of Amos (7.1-9; 8:1-3; 9:1-4) or Jeremiah (1:11-19; 24), the objects seen in the vision belong to everyday life (e.g. a basket of fruit, an almond tree), and yield their meaning by metaphor or word-play. The accounts of the vision use a simple question-and-answer pattern: the prophet is asked what he sees, then the significance is given. In a second phase, represented in Zechariah 1–6, the vision develops into a more elaborate narrative, with more unusual objects seen, and an extended dialogue between the prophet and an interpreting angel in place of the deity. In Daniel, this type of vision is used to portray the succession of earthly empires as creatures. The origin of the description of the beasts remains disputed, but among the possibilities are zodiacal signs and catalogues of physical anomalies, such as are included in omen-lists as significant portents. The vision of judgment in Daniel 7 also borrows motifs from other scriptural writings. From Zechariah 1:18 it gets four horns, and perhaps from

Zechariah or from Ezekiel 40. The heavenly scene itself is reminiscent of those in Enoch, though no precise parallel can be cited. The theme of four world empires has long been thought to reflect a widespread notion (it is found in the Greek poet Hesiod, c. 700 BCE) but, like the phrase 'visions of his head as he lay upon his bed' (7:1, cp. 2:28), probably comes directly from Daniel 2.

Interpretation of scripture is indeed significant in Daniel. Daniel 9 shows the hero preparing for an inspired interpretation of a biblical passage in Jeremiah (25:11-12 or 29:10) that he cannot understand. He is given the meaning—seventy years means seventy weeks of years, that is, 490 years—and the events of those weeks are then enumerated in a manner similar to the 'Apocalypse of Weeks' in 1 Enoch. Another example of the use of biblical prophetic texts is the quotation from Isaiah 53:11 given earlier, while Daniel 11:17 quotes Isaiah 7:7. The use of Jeremiah is an excellent example of the mantic technique applied to biblical texts: the texts do not mean what they appear to say, but when properly deciphered contain a message about the here and now. This 'inspired' technique of interpretation is found in commentaries from Qumran and also in the Gospel of Matthew, especially the opening chapters.

The Danielic historical summaries—which become more detailed in each successive vision—are designed to account for a present crisis in terms of the meaning of history as a whole. The crisis is the destruction of the altar in Jerusalem (in 167 BCE), and first appears in Daniel 8:11. The daily offering used to take place twice a day, at sunrise and sunset, and the phrase 'evenings and the mornings' (8:26) recurs in later visions as a reminder of each missed offering. The visions of chapters 7–9 are reticent about exactly what will soon happen or when: they give assurance that it will come, for God has so ordained it. Only in chapter 12, at the end of the final vision, do we find a statement of what actually is predicted to happen, and even here it is not described in much detail. There will be trouble; the angel Michael will act; some will be raised from the dead to be punished or rewarded; the wise who set the example to the people will truly reach the pre-eminence which their exemplary behaviour in this present life merits.

Daniel's visions are provoked by a specific crisis. The nations challenged by the eastward expansion of Hellenism used the apocalypse to foretell the end of this domination. Examples of this evidence in Egypt are the 'Demotic Chronicle' and the 'Potter's Oracle' (Collins 1984: 94). A second burst of Jewish apocalyptic writing occurred when the Jerusalem Temple was destroyed (70 CE), and Christian apocalypses (starting with Revelation) react to the persecution of that new cult. The apocalypse is an ideal form for expressing hope in an imminent change to a desperate or unhappy situation, typically by a return to the past, to authoritative figures and texts that reassure present-day readers that they saw it all coming, and all will finally be well.

Other Apocalyptic Writing in the Old Testament

Two other passages in the Old Testament are often referred to as 'apocalypses' or 'apocalyptic'. The book of Ezekiel contains two major passages offering a detailed description of the future: chapters 38–39 give a description of a final great battle between Gog of Magog and Israel, while chapters 40–48 describe the future Temple and city of Jerusalem. Isaiah 26–29 has also long been regarded as a separate section added quite late to the book. It also describes in some details the scenario at the end of the world, as does Zechariah 9–14 (generally seen as a distinct composition from chapters 1–8); chapter 11 also uses the image of a shepherd to describe the good and the bad ruler, a device that may have inspired parts of 1 Enoch, though the metaphor of a shepherd for a ruler was widespread in the ancient Near East.

It is doubtful how far these writings can truly be called 'apocalypses'. If we include under the rubric of 'apocalyptic' any description, especially in supernatural terms, of the end of the world it becomes difficult to maintain a workable definition, since a great deal of biblical Prophecy obviously concerns itself with the future. What is essential to the apocalypse is the notion of secrets uncovered, knowledge gained through inspiration, or heavenly visit or inspired interpretation of signs. Apocalypses are not necessarily about the end of things; they are yet another genre in which writers express their view of a hidden reality that, if perceived, makes sense of an otherwise incomprehensible world.

Further Reading

References in this chapter have been made to J.H. Charlesworth (ed.), *Old Testament Pseude-pigrapha* (2 vols.; New York: Doubleday, 1983); M.E. Stone, 'Lists of Revealed Things in Apocalyptic Literature', in F.M. Cross, W.E. Lemke and P.D. Miller (eds.), *Magnalia Dei: The Mighty Acts of God* (Garden City, NY: Doubleday): 414-52; J.C. VanderKam, *Enoch and the Growth of an Apocalyptic Tradition* (Washington: Catholic Biblical Association of America, 1984); J.J. Collins, *The Apocalyptic Imagination: An Introduction to the Jewish Matrix of Christianity* (New York: Crossroad, 1984).

G. von Rad's definition of Apocalyptic as derived from Wisdom is highly important, and can be found in his *Old Testament Theology* (2 vols.; London: SCM Press, 1975): II, 301-15, though he did not distinguish 'mantic wisdom' from other forms.

Chapter 15

BEYOND THE OLD TESTAMENT

By the end of the second century BCE all the Old Testament books had been written. By 100 CE two religions, Christianity and rabbinic Judaism, were in the process of formation, each a product of these books and of the political events of the preceding two centuries. In this chapter we shall look at this transitional period (as it turned out to be), in particular at the religious developments that concerned what became in one religion 'Scripture' or 'Tenak' (Torah, Nebi'im, Ketubim) and in the other 'the Old Testament'. The period is a fascinating and controversial one, not only because of the complexity of the picture it offers, but also because of the often intense involvement with which Christians, in particular, deal with it. First, however, we ought to address some misconceptions about the period.

'Judaism'

For scholars of the nineteenth century and the early part of the twentieth, the word 'Judaism' (as distinguished from 'Modern Judaism') was used for the religion of post-exilic Judah/Judea, which was widely seen as a legalistic and hierocratic cult, bereft of the inspiration and ethical fervour of the prophets and represented by the 'scribes and Pharisees', who were rightly condemned in the New Testament for their hypocrisy. This Judaism could be more or less defined in terms of doctrines such as resurrection of the dead, messianism, sacrifice, law, covenant, and so on. It was seen as a foil to 'Christianity', understood to have inherited or 'fulfilled' some of these doctrines (such as messianism) and superseded others (such as Jewish law). Modern Judaism was regarded as a continuation of Pharisaism (and so was equally written off).

Ironically, Jewish scholarship of that time concurred in the description, though not the evaluation, regarding Judaism from the 'time of Ezra' (fifth century BCE) to modern times as essentially unchanged and indeed Pharisaic in a benign sense—that is, enshrining the legal and ethical values of these 'rabbis'. The judgment on both sides owed much to religious dogma. But even at the end of the nineteenth century, the influence of these traditional attitudes was weakening. Critical scholarship on Judaism came from Jewish scholars, especially in Germany (such as Leopold Zunz and Abraham Geiger), and from Christian scholars who attempted to study Judaism both critically and sympathetically (e.g. R. Travers Herford and G.F. Moore). The success of these scholars marked an important step forward. The reasons for this development are many. One factor was the emergence of critical historiography; another was the publication of Jewish and Christian apocalypses, which revealed quite different aspects of Judaism and a new dimension to the contrast (as then seen) between Judaism and Christianity. (There were also profound social and political reasons for the German *Wissenschaft des Judentums* movement.) Since the Second World War, more intense dialogue between Judaism and Christianity has prompted a more objective and sympathetic look at the historical relationship between the two religions, and new discoveries, especially the texts from Qumran, have altered the picture radically.

Early Judaism

The name 'early Judaism' applied to the religion of the Second Temple period is misleading in that it implies an exclusive continuity with rabbinic Judaism. By 'rabbinic Judaism' is meant the form of Judaism which, accepting first the loss of the Temple and its priests, and later (in 135 CE) expulsion from Jerusalem, devoted itself, under the leadership of rabbis, to the carrying out of the divine will as revealed in scripture. The rabbis recast the biblical Torah in terms of everyday laws governing personal and social life (halakhah) and moral lessons taught by scripture (haggadah). These laws and other teachings discussed and developed in the rabbinic academies in Palestine and then in Babylonia, were collected in the Talmud (sixth century CE). By then, rabbinic Judaism and Christian Judaism had diverged into two distinct religions. Both rightly claimed parentage in 'early Judaism', which therefore must be defined so as to embrace both. This is not a theological point but a historical one.

When, then did 'Judaism' begin? This is an unanswerable question because it depends on so many debatable criteria. For convenience, we shall take the view that the idea of 'Judaism' became embedded during the mid-second century BCE, which saw a protracted internal (and external) struggle for identity. Even then, it would take centuries for an orthodox 'Judaism' to emerge. Some would trace the beginnings of Judaism back to Abraham, to Moses, or to Ezra, but to call either Abraham or Moses 'Jewish' is historically problematic. (The problem is not unlike calling Jesus a Christian.) There is no doubt that early in the Second Temple period the religion of Judah evolved quite dramatically; but it continued to evolve. The question of 'origin' is unanswerable, but posing it is important because the effort of answering can help us understand better what we are dealing with.

The Idea of a 'Normative' Judaism

G.F. Moore, one of the twentieth century's greatest non-Jewish students of Judaism, although fully aware of different forms of Judaism, proposed Pharisaic Judaism as the 'norm', on the grounds that it did indeed become the norm in rabbinic Judaism. But, however Moore intended this to be understood, it is deceptive. In the period we are examining, there were many other subgroups and trends within Judaism (even among the Pharisees), and some of these movements were highly influential. Here are some instances of variety within Judaism of the Greco-Roman period.

'Apocalyptic' Versus 'Rabbinic' Judaism

During the last century many New Testament scholars worked with a distinction between 'mainstream' or 'official' Judaism and 'apocalyptic' Judaism—the latter represented by books not preserved in the Jewish canon, rejected by the rabbis, but preserved by Christians. The claim was often made that 'apocalyptic' Judaism was the forerunner or 'matrix' of Christianity, believing in the changing of the world order. But the notion of a kind of Judaism which was 'apocalyptic' is fanciful (see Chapter 14). Nevertheless, an important issue can be raised here. The literature of the period includes few if any elements of popular religion. It used to be customary to regard the religion of the sacred books and the authorities as defining a religion. But we now know that many Jews accepted astrology, magical spells, and mystical ascents to heaven as natural ingredients of their religion. We are also keenly aware of the political aspects of Jewish belief at this time. The suicidal revolt against Rome was provoked by corrupt administration (by Romans and locals), but fuelled by religious fervour. We have some inkling of this fervour from the Dead Sea Scrolls and other non-biblical Jewish writings, and hints in the Gospels but on the whole this aspect of Jewish religion is hidden in the sources. Much New Testament scholarship, however, is now keenly aware of the political context of Jesus' teaching, which is perhaps as significant to his career as anything in the Old Testament. The so-called 'apocalyptic world-view' of a history about to be overturned, as foretold by ancient writings, was the conviction of a number of Jews under Roman rule.

'Palestinian' Versus 'Hellenistic' Judaism
The distinction between 'Hellenistic' and 'Palestinian' Judaism is still attractive to many Jewish and Christian scholars. The former have often been tempted to regard 'Hellenistic Judaism' as degenerate; the latter to regard 'Palestinian' as Pharisaic. Alas, this convenient dichotomy is largely false. Palestine in this period was certainly 'Hellenised' to a considerable degree (see Chapter 7). The concept of a 'traditional' Judaism free of Hellenism, has had to go; but so has the notion that Greek ideas in Christianity must have been non-Jewish or alien to Judaism. It is more useful to draw a distinction between Diaspora Judaism(s) and Palestinian Judaism, since the social and political conditions inside and outside Palestine were different. In Palestine the unavoidable facts of life were the economic and political power of priesthood, of Temple, and Roman occupation. In the Diaspora (though it is, of course, simplistic to generalise) the emphasis was on identity and survival as social and religious groups, with the role of the Temple being largely symbolic. One kind of Judaism belonged to a majority, with a high degree of political relevance, the other to various minorities. Broadly speaking, the Old Testament is a product of Palestine, whereas the New Testament (despite the Palestinian setting of the Gospels) was written for a non-Palestinian audience (though only some of these were of course Jewish).

Three (or Four) Jewish 'Parties'
One favourite scheme for analysing early Judaism has been to start from the description of the Jewish 'parties' or 'sects' (Greek *hairesis*) given by Josephus at the end of the first century CE in Book 2 of his *Jewish War* (revised in Book 18 of his *Jewish Antiquities*). His parties are Essenes, Pharisees, Sadducees, and an additional 'fourth philosophy', which some scholars wrongly identify as Zealots (since the Zealots did not arise until the middle of the first century CE and probably did not constitute a single movement). The problems with following Josephus's account too closely are that it is addressed to non-Jewish readers and couched in terms of Greek philosophical schools. He wishes to project a suitable image of Judaism, and, for example, in his *Antiquities* he promotes the Pharisees as the representatives of the Jewish people, as they were perhaps bidding to become after the destruction of the Temple.

Josephus does not explain the origin of these parties, nor their interrelationship. Neither does he tell us about the majority of Jews who did not belong to any of these. We cannot therefore divide Palestinian Judaism at this time into such segments, though we ought to include these 'parties' in any description of the whole picture.

'Judaism' or 'Judaisms'?

Early Judaism was not, then, a uniform theological or doctrinal system. As we have seen, the world in which 'early Judaism' existed was culturally complex, and Jews absorbed a tremendous amount from their environment. One matter that is often overlooked is the extent to which Judaism, or at least some of its practices and ideas, attracted non-Jews, many of whom regarded it as a philosophy rather than a cult. (Many Jews also favoured this definition.) At the other extreme we find an ultra-legalistic sect described in the Dead Sea Scrolls organised like a Hellenistic religious association, holding a doctrine of dualism that is almost certainly Persian in origin and writing horoscopes. How can one classify such a sect? (Indeed, if there is no mainstream, how is a 'sect' defined?) It has become common in recent years to speak not of 'Judaism' at this time but of 'Judaisms', different systems of thought and practice from which just one (rabbinic) would emerge as the bearer of Jewish orthodoxy. From such a perspective, however, early Christianity would also qualify as a 'Judaism'. In the remainder of this chapter we shall try to describe some of the main institutions and ideological models of early Judaism(s), bearing in mind that what is said may not have applied without exception to all who called themselves 'Jewish' (for an excellent treatment of 'Jewishness' in this period, see Cohen 1999).

Outward Characteristics of Early Judaism

The measures taken against the Jews by Antiochus IV included the abolition of Temple sacrifice, the profanation of the Sabbath, worship of other gods, eating of 'unclean' food, suppression of the books of the Law, and a ban on circumcision. Assuming the reports to be correct, we have here a convenient list of matters that might be taken to constitute Jewish practice at that time. Practice is a good place to begin; religion is as much to do with behaviour as with belief. But these practices also relate to ideological components of early Judaism, such as law and holiness. The practices of circumcision, avoidance of idolatry, observance of the Sabbath, and dietary restrictions emerged as religious issues perhaps during the exile and shortly afterwards, with the challenge of defining a religious affiliation without any political entity. Later, with the encroachment of Hellenism, these outward practices again became tokens of identity. From the most conservative and xenophobic forms of Judaism to the most flexible and universalistic, these practices were accepted. They form the foundation of any description of early Judaism.

Circumcision

All Jewish males were, according to the Jewish law, to be circumcised eight days after birth. Circumcision was not exclusive to the Jews, and how it became adopted as a mark of Judaism is a rather intriguing question. But it came to be represented by Jews as the sign *par excellence* of membership of the Jewish people, as a mark of the covenant (see the story of its institution in Genesis 17). Some Jews were accused, during the time of Antiochus, of concealing their circumcision, presumably in order to perform (naked) in the gymnasium. According to Josephus, John Hyrcanus obliged the Idumeans to be circumcised (though probably they already were) in order to remain in their homeland, and Aristobulus, his successor, did the same to the Itureans. Judaism during this period was by no means exclusive, but circumcision, so far as we can tell, was always or nearly always required for membership.

Anti-Idolatry

The first two of the Ten Commandments forbid the placing of other gods before Yhwh and the making of images or pictures. These two provide the basis for the Jewish attitude towards other religions, and were combined in the common Jewish accusation that other gods were the 'work of human hands'. In the Greco-Roman period the importance of this principle lay in resisting the tendency, characteristic of Hellenism, to see every religion as a form of one universal religion and thus to pair deities—Thoth and Hermes, Baal and Zeus, Astarte and Aphrodite. Yhwh was identified by some non-Jews (and Jews?) with Jupiter or Dionysus.

There were two strategies for coping with the conflict between universalism and adherence to the national deity. The personal name was avoided in favour of titles like 'Most High', and he was presented as the god whom even other monotheists worshipped though without knowing him as Israel did. Another device was to consider other deities as heavenly beings inferior to the one supreme God worshipped by Jews. In Deuteronomy 32:8 God is said to have created the nations and their territories 'according to the number of the sons of God', with Jacob as his own charge. Other nations were thus under the patronage of subordinate deities, or, as we now like to say, 'angels'. In Daniel, the 'princes' (that is, patron angels) of Greece and Persia are mentioned, as is Michael, the 'prince' of Israel (Daniel 10:20-21; 12:1). It is worth noting (since many people assert the contrary), that Jewish literature of the Second Temple period does not attest a growing gulf between humanity and deity. On the contrary, it can suppose humans going to heaven without dying (Enoch, Moses, Elijah), or becoming heavenly beings after their death (Daniel 12:3) or even without dying (Enoch), and can accept that humans may have heavenly parentage. The basis of early Judaism, then, is not accurately defined as monotheism but as monarchical theism: the insistence that however many divine beings there were, there was only one supreme God.

Diet

Jewish dietary laws, as developed in rabbinic Judaism, are complex. The main biblical injunctions are not to drink blood and not to eat animals that are unclean (these are listed in Leviticus 11: the pig is the best known, but also excluded are the camel and the hare). The law forbidding 'boiling a kid in its mother's milk' (Exodus 23:19; 34:26; and Deuteronomy 14:21) came to be understood as a ban on mixing meat and dairy produce, but at what time we do not know. The ban on drinking blood, according to Genesis 9:4, was given to Noah and later regarded by the rabbis as forming part of the 'Noachic covenant', in principle binding on all humans. Meat slaughtered without removing the blood, or sacrificed to a god before being sold would not be acceptable to Jews. Dining with non-Jews was undoubtedly practised, but to those with a conscience presented a delicate situation.

Times and Seasons

The importance of time in early Judaism cannot be over-stressed. The Jewish calendar was (and still is) a major factor distinguishing Judaism from other religions. The Temple cult itself depended on both holy time and holy space. The Temple was in the correct place (the centre of the world, the meeting point of heaven and earth) and all sacrifices had to be performed there. But they also had to be performed at the right time. The account of creation in Genesis 1 states not only *what* God created but *when*. Or, to put it another way, God created time when he created the world. For this reason, sacred occasions were of great importance to Judaism, and differences over how to reckon time of considerable religious significance. We also find in writings from this period an interest in a world-calendar comprising pre-determined epochs, with the end of history foreseen.

Two different ways of reckoning the year were proposed in early Judaism. In one, the month is tied to the moon, and the year has to be adjusted by intercalating additional months periodically; in the other, the year is tied to the sun, and the months are thirty days regardless of the behaviour of the moon. An additional day is added quarterly. The lunar calendar had its new year in autumn; the solar calendar in spring. At some point during the Second Temple period the former system was officially observed and used to control the Temple worship, but some Jews believed that the other system was correct, and that therefore most of the Temple festivals were wrongly conducted, because at the wrong time. Their views are found 1 Enoch and Jubilees, and were adopted by the authors of the Dead Sea Scrolls. The calendar issue is far from a trivial one, as the Scrolls show. Doing the right thing at the wrong time was disobedience and nullified the act. Indeed, in 1 Enoch the calendar provides an important perspective on a much-debated question; the origin and nature of sin and evil. The fundamental problem is: if God made both sun and moon, why are they not in step? According to 1 Enoch, which adopts a solar calendar, the moon is out of phase. But if the heavens could go wrong, how can the earth be free from error also? The speculation that evil originated in heaven with a revolt of angelic beings (see Chapter 14) had a basis, for the writers of 1 Enoch, in such astronomical disorder.

For religious purposes, the day was considered to begin in the evening (for darkness obviously preceded light at the beginning of the world; see Genesis 1). There were two regular sacrifices in the Temple, evening and morning (the Tamid), and perhaps prayers were said at these times by pious Jews away from the Temple. However, in the solar calendar it is possible that the day began at sunrise.

The week is marked by the Sabbath. The biblical legislation concerning Sabbath observance is brief; however, before the first century CE, the Sabbath had become an important issue, and some Jews had detailed rules for its observance. The Temple had a special service for the Sabbath, and elsewhere it is probable that gatherings for prayer were taking place, possibly with a reading of scripture (see Luke 4:16ff.). A text from Qumran (the 'Songs of the Sabbath Sacrifice') provides a liturgy for the Sabbath, consisting mostly of descriptions of worship in heaven (where of course the Sabbath was also observed). In the second century BCE, the issue of whether to fight on the Sabbath seems to have been debated; and the book of Jubilees, later in that century, avoids having the patriarchs undertake any journey on the Sabbath.

The new moon, which had been a religious festival in earlier times, became relatively insignificant later, except that in the lunar calendar the beginning of a new month was not predetermined but announced when the new moon was seen. Naturally, the calculation of the months determined the dating of feasts, especially Passover, which occurred at the first full moon after the spring equinox. There were two calendrical years, the religious one (shared with the solar calendar) beginning in spring, the other in autumn, when it coincided with the Day of Atonement and the feast of Booths/Tabernacles. This was one of the three major annual festival complexes. In spring fell Passover (plus Unleavened Bread, which merged into it), in summer Weeks, or Pentecost, and in autumn Booths or Ingathering. According to both Deuteronomy and Leviticus, there was also a sabbatical year, during which fields were not to be sown and debts were to be remitted. It is difficult to see how such a system could really operate, and some scholars doubt that it was, but we have the evidence of a decree from Hillel (first century CE) that implies such a practice (by finding a way round it!). There was even a Sabbath of Sabbaths, a Jubilee year (see Chapter 1), either the forty-ninth or fiftieth. The book of Jubilees derives its name from the system of dating history by these units. Since the Sabbath symbolised both rest (Exodus 20) and deliverance (Deuteronomy 5), some texts from this period assert that history would be fulfilled in the final jubilee or sabbatical cycle of years. The Sabbath and its system thus offered a framework for the temporal dimension of early Judaism.

The Holy Place: Temple and Priesthood

Temple

Politically and economically, as well as religiously, the Jerusalem Temple was the focus of life in Judea. So far as we know, it was the only Jewish sanctuary in Judah, and all religious activity was conducted with reference to it. In addition to making various offerings, private sacrifices, tithes, and first-fruits, all males over twenty paid a Temple tax of half a shekel. Three times a year there were the pilgrim festivals of Passover, Weeks, and Booths, while Hanukkah celebrated the rededication of the Temple by Judas Maccabee. The Temple cult, at least in priestly theory, mediated between God and Israel in all important respects.

There is little evidence of resentment against the Temple, or rejection of its significance in Jewish writings of the period. But several texts are critical of its practices, and either condemn those priests running it, or anticipate a new Temple to be built in the future, or both. We may assume that these writings (e.g. Jubilees, the Temple Scroll from Qumran, and parts of Enoch) came from disaffected priests. Even the groups described in the Qumran texts, which seem to have boycotted the Temple, regarded this abstinence as an interim measure. After its destruction, the rabbis retained the Temple at the centre of their system and took the ideology associated with it into all areas of life.

The Temple was important to Palestinian Judaism in many other ways. It brought in wealth from visitors and overseas pilgrims, and it was a major consumer of produce. It was also a political symbol of Jewish independence. Even so, the Temple did not necessarily play a direct part in daily Jewish religion, and both rabbinic Judaism and Christianity developed without it. What it symbolised, however, could not be dispensed with. The synagogue—about which we know very little until the second century CE—eventually assumed a degree of Temple symbolism (the 'ark' housed the scrolls of law, for example, invoking the old 'ark of the covenant' in the pre-exilic Holy of Holies); while Christianity retained a doctrine of atonement by sacrifice and, unlike modern Judaism, has both priesthood and altars.

Priesthood

According to Leviticus (the priestly code of the Bible), Israel's destiny was to be holy, since God was holy. The priests were responsible for not only maintaining but also defining holiness: Aaron is 'to distinguish between the holy and the common, and between the clean and the unclean' (Leviticus 10:10). 'Holiness' was definable in cultic terms. Anything given to, or belonging to, God (such as sacrifices and priests) was to be 'holy'. What was not holy was 'common', and could be clean or unclean. Many things, from moral offences to accidental contact with unclean objects (such as corpses) could render one 'unclean'. Transition between these states is legislated for in Leviticus, and involves, generally speaking, washing for bodily impurities and sacrifice for 'sins'; sometimes both are needed (see Chapter 11).

The priesthood was hereditary and comprised two levels: levites (all members of the tribe of Levi) and, within this group, priests, who were descended from Aaron. Within the priesthood, moreover, were those who traced their descent from Zadok, and who, according to Ezekiel, should enjoy exclusive rights of sacrifice. At the head was the High Priest and a deputy, possibly the 'captain of the Temple'; these were permanently at the Temple. Otherwise, priests and levites were divided into twenty-four shifts, each serving for one week twice in the year. Within the shift each priest might expect to be on service one or two days. The priests' livelihood came from prescribed portions of the sacrifices, but also from first-fruits and tithes. With some over-simplification, it may be said that a priestly view of early Judaism would assert that the Temple and its cult guaranteed the holiness of the entire nation and earned God's favour. Without the Temple, no holiness, no forgiveness, no Israel, could be envisaged. Narrow though this view may sound, it was probably accepted, at least on the whole, by many laymen as well as by the priests.

Scripture, Law, and Scribes

Scriptures

As explained in Chapter 17, by the end of the second century BCE the Jews had a body of scriptures consisting of 'Law' and 'Prophets', with some other writings also. These provided a history of the Jewish people and defined who Jews were: chosen, promised, and given a law. Priests or scribes read these scriptures in other ways too: priests understood the Law to mean that Israel was commanded above all to be holy (see below). Scribes could read hidden meanings, finding either hints about the present time or moral truths. Writings from the period reveal a wealth of scriptural exegesis (or 'midrash'). The book of Jubilees, written in the second half of the second century BCE, combines many of these techniques. It is a retelling of the biblical story from Adam to Moses. It explains how even the patriarchs obeyed the Law and instituted the festivals and stresses the need for the separation of Jews from other nations. Other retellings of biblical stories are known, in the Dead Sea Scrolls and in the Pseudepigrapha. Examples of reading esoteric meanings into scriptural texts can be found in the biblical commentaries from Qumran, where the text is taken to speak of events in the recent past or near future.

The scriptures appear to have been read aloud in synagogues, and were probably accompanied by translations into Aramaic. These translations, or 'targums', may have been literal (like the targum of Job found at Qumran), or free, like the targums written later, which may nevertheless be of quite ancient origin. Additionally, the scriptures were probably studied privately by those who could read.

The Law

Since the beginnings of Second Temple Judah, the religion of the Judeans in Palestine had been centred almost as much on the law as on the Temple. Ezra was credited with having brought back the 'law of Moses' and had the people instructed in it. Thereafter, the task of developing and applying it was presumably set in hand. But, as we have seen, the Law, enshrined in the five books of Moses, deals mostly with cultic matters; on civil matters it is often vague. For instance, Deuteronomy 24:1-4 is the only piece of legislation on divorce: it requires a 'bill of divorce' in the case of 'some indecency', permits the woman to remarry, even to re-divorce, but forbids the first husband to remarry that woman. On the manner of marriage nothing is said; the custom is merely implied. Legal documents from the period show that Jewish practice on these matters was variable.

The law therefore needed to be more than was contained in the books of Moses. It was expanded in three ways: by exegesis, by tradition or custom, and by decree. Exegesis developed principles by which laws could be inferred from Scripture. Tradition and custom are self-explanatory, as is decree. Both were, where possible, rationalised by finding some justification in scripture. In the Mishnah the rabbis produced a legal corpus that combines biblical law, custom and practice, and rabbinic decisions and verdicts. A fourth possible means of lawmaking was by direct revelation. Such lawmaking was rejected by the priests and Sadducees (see below), but is found in the Dead Sea Scrolls, especially in the *Community Rule* (see columns 3-4).

Some groups sought to encourage adherence to their own understanding of divine law and formed themselves into associations for the purpose. The sects described in the Dead Sea Scrolls appear to have done just this, and we also know of religious associations called *haburoth*, which attempted to apply to their own lives the conditions of purity scripturally required only of priests. There were also differences of opinion about the interpretation of scriptural laws among the rabbis, going back at least as far as the famous schools of Hillel and Shammai, while in Matthew 19:8 Jesus is recorded as contradicting the biblical law on divorce (which he ascribes not to God but to Moses).

In the Hellenistic world, the notion of law was both politically and philosophically central. Cities were established with written constitutions. Those philosophers, then, who taught that the world was a single *polis* and that all were its citizens, taught that the world also had its constitution, its laws. Men who had written constitutions and laws for cities (e.g. Draco, Solon) were venerated. It was not difficult, therefore, for the Jewish law and its great lawgiver Moses to be understood and presented in this way. Within the Old Testament, wisdom had been understood as a kind of natural law; its equation with Torah was not merely an inner pietistic development, but was appropriate to Hellenistic ideas and perhaps partly inspired by them.

Scribes

What the Temple was to priests, literature (in this case, scripture) was to the scribes. As a class they belonged to no one religious group, though predominantly they seem to have been Pharisees, who were keenly interested in the development of legal theory. Scribes assumed responsibility for making Jewish law, and, as with so many developments in this period, we can see both internal and external factors at work. The first great scribe of the Old Testament is Ezra, who, according to tradition, brought a law book and had it read out and explained to the assembled people. The Greco-Roman period saw the preservation and study of national literatures and the growth of the scribal class everywhere. The introduction of schools for educating young Jews in their national literature was probably prompted by the need to counter the teaching of Greek culture. But the influence of scribes in Judaism was no doubt enhanced by the indifference of priests to instructing Jews in the law and the extent of widespread priestly participation in Hellenistic customs, seen by non-priests (but also by many other priests) as destructive of Judaism.

The Identity of 'Israel' in Early Judaism

What is the Hebrew term for 'Judaism'? There is none. The corresponding name is 'Israel'. In the Second Temple period Judah redefined itself as the one chosen people called Israel, and saw itself not as a state or a kingdom but a people, a society—one whose story was retrojected into the past and embraced the two now defunct kingdoms—and even earlier, back to a single family. But what was the essence of 'Israel'? Election? Covenant? Holiness? Wisdom? We can find all these responses in biblical and Early Jewish literature. As a result of the crises of the exile, then later the advent of Hellenism, the Maccabean wars and Roman rule, as well as the growing and diffuse Diaspora, the separateness of Israel and the need for a distinct, indeed a *visibly distinct* way of life was recognised. 'Separation' became a fundamental component for most definitions of Israel (or Judaism). How might different kinds of 'Jew' or 'Israelite' think of their identity? We can offer a partial answer in the following paragraphs.

Sadducees

The Sadducean party mentioned by Josephus (end of first century CE) and in the New Testament appears to have adhered most closely to the scriptural definition of Israel, in regarding temple and priesthood as central, and rejecting non-scriptural laws and the non-scriptural belief in resurrection. Josephus and the New Testament (Acts 23:8) also concur that they rejected a belief in angels—which appear in the Bible but in whose roles and names there is little interest. The Sadducees were composed of priests and aristocrats who were, also according to Josephus, wealthy and unpopular. We have no writings from them that we can identify, and thus they remain shadowy, described only vaguely by opponents. The preservation of the lucrative Temple and of a peaceful co-operation with Rome were presumably their aims. 'Holiness' for them meant the conduct of the cult: 'separation' meant not only separation of priests from non-priests, but also of rich Jews from poor Jews, of the privileged from the unprivileged. With the destruction of the temple and cult, the Sadducees apparently disappeared, at least as a party; they are remembered in the rabbinic writings on a few occasions as holding different opinions on some matters of law.

Pharisees

The Pharisees, who in Herod's time numbered, according to Josephus, more than six thousand families (not a large minority), were apparently both influential and concerned with promoting observance of the law, made possible by developing a code of obedience developed from scriptural law but incorporating other customs unwritten in scripture (Matthew 15:9 derides these as 'human commandments' but these were later embraced as 'oral law' in the Mishnah). Such 'laws' were presumably accumulated interpretations and rulings made by their scribes (see above) which defined the law in such a way as to make obedience possible. Their belief in resurrection underlines their personal commitment to piety; every Israelite was responsible for taking the 'yoke of the law' upon himself (and only to a very limited extent 'herself'). Such views might seem hardly sufficient in themselves to constitute a distinct party. But taking 'Pharisee' to mean 'separated', we might suspect that they carried their own observance of the law to the point of restricting contact with 'Israelites' who did not observe the Pharisaic definitions of law, and whom they referred to as 'am ha'aretz (literally 'people of the land' perhaps meaning 'rustic', 'uneducated'). Some formed themselves into societies (called *haburoth*, 'fellowships'), the chief communal activity of which was dining. This explains their emphasis on laws relating to the cleanliness of vessels and the necessity of tithing (untithed food was unclean). It is widely understood that the Pharisees aspired to the level of cleanliness required of a priest ministering in the Temple, and desired this status for all Jews. Such an ideology is fully worked out in the Mishnah.

What was the political attitude of the Pharisees? The party enjoyed political power in the first century BCE, and regained it after the destruction of the Temple in 70 CE. In between, they apparently eschewed politics. Being drawn from many different classes, including priests and scribes but probably also lower classes, they did not represent any single economic or social interest. There is evidence that on political matters, including 'messianic' beliefs, Pharisees held a variety of beliefs (see below).

Essenes

The Essenes, of whom Josephus gives a fuller description than he does of either Pharisees or Sadducees, are mentioned by other ancient writers but absent from the New Testament, a puzzle yet to be solved. They were, Josephus says, constituted in communities throughout Palestine—possibly with related communities in Egypt and Syria. The discoveries at Qumran prompted renewed interest in this group, since the contents of the some texts, and the remains of a settlement nearby correspond well to the details given about the Essenes by ancient authors.

The Qumran settlement was occupied somewhere around 100 BCE and was abandoned during the war with Rome, in 68 CE. But if Qumran was an Essene community—as we shall assume in what follows, though it is not undisputed and certainly needs qualifying— was it typical? Josephus notes that there were two 'orders' of Essenes, one of which did not marry (as mentioned in the Damascus Document). The Qumran documents contain, in addition to scriptural books and texts about sectarian communities, other writings which appear to point to an ideological movement from which the Qumran groups can plausibly have derived.

The authors of the Qumran scrolls believed that God had revealed to their founder the true law now lost to the rest of the nation Israel, and had made a covenant with the 'remnant' of Israel who survived capture by Nebuchadrezzar. During the period of divine anger which followed that capture, and which would one day end with the arrival of 'one who would teach righteousness', this true Israel, possessors of the true covenant and law, would live strictly according to the law revealed to them by God. They rejected both the (lunar) calendar and many of the laws followed elsewhere in Israel, and although they appear to have used the Jerusalem Temple, their participation may have been quite restricted. Their law was generally very strict with regard to holiness, and association with outsiders was severely regulated. (This description is drawn mainly from the *Damascus Document*).

The group depicted in the Qumran *Community Rule* offers a different profile. This group did not marry, had abandoned the Temple cult, and adopted the notion that they were participants in the worship of a presumed heavenly Temple. But in this text we also find a set of teachings that derive their authority not from the Mosaic law but from esoteric teaching about the 'god of knowledge', who has predestined the fate and character of all humans. The human race (and the angelic race too) is divided into parties of 'light' and 'darkness' who will battle until God intervenes to destroy darkness. In the related *War Scroll* is a description of a final battle in which the forces of light would defeat the forces of darkness (led by the Romans in thin disguise), and it would not be surprising to find that the writers and readers of this text participated in the war against Rome.

The authors of the *Damascus Document* and related texts had a fairly clear definition of what 'Israel' was. It was, of course, their own community, the true recipients of the covenant and the law. It is likely that they hoped one day to constitute a restored Israel, once the period of God's anger ended; until then, they were obliged to perfect obedience of the law—as they interpreted it. Where they came from remains unclear, and none of their ideas point to any specific moment in Jewish history.

Perhaps because of their different calendar or because they were banished from the Temple, this group lived in separate settlements. The group responsible for the *Community Rule*, perhaps an offshoot, had a more radical notion of Israel, if the dualistic teaching in this text does really reflect what they believed. For these dualistic and predestinarian views really cut across the notion of a chosen people, a law and a covenant, coupled as they are to a theology based on esoteric knowledge imparted by a teacher, and including a division of all humans into two camps (not 'Israel and 'nations'). Many of these ideas can in fact be rooted in aspects of biblical Wisdom theology, but they have travelled a long way further. If they do suggest the extent to which Jewish sectarian groups might depart from what we regard as 'mainstream' Jewish beliefs, they also fit quite well into the systems that we know challenged early Christianity, and are known as 'gnostic'. Here too, esoteric knowledge, not scripture, explains the reality of creation and constitutes the key to salvation from the coming judgment.

The 'Fourth Philosophy'

As we noted above, Josephus mentions, in addition to the three 'philosophies' of Judaism just described, a fourth, which was founded by Judas of Gamala and Zadok the Pharisee at the time of Quirinius's census (6 CE). This group, he said, called upon Jews to rebel against Roman 'slavery'. Some have identified this 'philosophy' with the Zealots, which is improbable—though many of the 'zealots' might have been adherents of this movement. Equally likely, there were a number of revolutionary movements that believed that Roman domination was intolerable and that Judaism could be practised only under the sovereignty of God. For these, Israel was as much a political as a religious concept. Let us not forget, though, that in the Bible Israel is described just as much in political as in religious terms, and the imaginary past that the Old Testament projects was taken in many circles as a blueprint for the future. The belief among some Jews that a messiah descended from David would soon liberate Israel testifies to the power of that history.

Other Jews

Still other Jews—among them Philo and the writer of the Wisdom of Solomon—expressed their religion in terms of Greek philosophies. Diaspora Judaism is simply too vast and varied to be considered here; we cannot be sure that holiness and strict obedience to the law were its common denominators, we do know that it incorporated many features of local culture.

And what of those Jews outside Josephus' parties, beyond our direct knowledge? We hear of messianic movements, baptizing movements, 'false prophets', 'Herodians', 'Boethusians', and other groupings. Then there are those populations who formally entered 'Israel' under the Hasmoneans, including from Galilee and Idumea. We have stories of itinerant miracle workers who healed and made rain, such as Honi the Circle-Drawer and Hanina ben Dosa, remembered in the Talmud. Or Jesus of Nazareth, for that matter. 'Judaism' embraced all these, and all of them, presumably, thought of themselves as members of 'Israel'.

Samaritans

Were Samaritans Jews or not? According to the famous New Testament parable (Luke 10:25-37) they were: the hero is a member of the most peripheral branch of the Jewish race. Until recently scholarly opinion had suggested that the rift between Judeans and Samaritans began in the time of Nehemiah, but most scholars think it developed gradually and somewhat later. After all, the Samaritans shared the same five books of Moses; the rift can hardly have occurred until after the Pentateuch was in more or less its present form. The causes of the rift were apparently not political, but concerned the location of the temple and the true priestly line. In the early Greek period, the Jewish inhabitants of the city of Samaria were displaced by Macedonians and moved to Shechem, where they built a temple on Mt Gerizim, one of two hills overlooking Shechem, where a Mosaic covenant ceremony had been recorded (Deuteronomy 27, especially verse 11). Serious antagonism between Samarian and Judean Jews probably dates from the establishment of this temple. Obviously, if by the time of Hyrcanus the two communities were not already completely divided, his destruction of their temple ensured this.

The Samaritans themselves would have claimed they were not Jews, but were Israelites, retaining the ancient religion of the ancient kingdom of Israel. This is true to a limited extent, and certainly it would be wrong to think of Samaritans as a Jewish splinter group. Rather, we have to see the Samaritans, in this period at least, as a sibling of early Judaism. The rabbis remained unsure whether Samaritans were Jews or not, and placed them in a special category.

Messianism

This unfortunate and inappropriate term is nevertheless commonly used to convey the widespread Jewish belief during this period that the course of history, which had recently turned against Jews in Palestine, would soon be brought to an end. 'Messianism' is worth discussing, even briefly, since it has two different but important aspects. One is the political, social, and economic frustration which existed in Palestine after the collapse of the Hasmonean monarchy and the arrival of the Romans. 'Messianic expectation' is largely not a religious doctrine but a political reflex. There is no evidence for it until the middle of the first century BCE. But allied to this reflex are opinions about the ideal political structure of Israel: should it be ruled by priests? Or kings? Or both? Or directly from heaven? Specific formulations of messianic beliefs were informed by such political opinions as much as religious inclination.

The other aspect of messianism is its religious or scriptural dimension. 'Messiah' by this time meant effectively the ruler of the people chosen by God, and had been applied in the Old Testament to kings or priests (and rarely to individual prophets). We have the hope of a king in the Psalms of Solomon (a collection of first century BCE/CE poetry, which called for a king like David to restore justice), making its author a critic of the high-priesthood; we also have the idea of two messiahs, one royal, one priestly, in the Dead Sea Scrolls and elsewhere—with priority given to the High Priest. We have the notion of direct heavenly rule, too. In one of the texts from Qumran is a description of a heavenly high-priestly messiah. There are also many texts that include no messiah whatsoever (1 Enoch). However important it has been in the past for Christians to imagine a Judaism waiting for a messiah, there was no 'messianic Judaism' and no 'messianic doctrine', but the notion of some kind of divinely appointed leader was common. Among Sadducees, of course, messianic ideas of any kind were rejected. And they reached diaspora Judaism only in the form of Christianity; for most of these the notion of a messiah was irrelevant (and politically unwise, anyway). This may be why Paul refers to Jesus as 'Christ', literally a translation of 'anointed' but in fact meaningless to most of his readers.

Further Reading

An indispensable resource is the thorough revision by G. Vermes and others of E. Schürer's *The History of the Jewish People in the Age of Jesus Christ* (3 vols.; Edinburgh: T. & T. Clark, 1973–87); E.P. Sanders, *Judaism: Practice and Belief* (London: SCM Press, 1992), argues for a 'common Judaism' in Palestine in the late Second Temple period; S.J.D. Cohen, *From the Maccabees to the Mishnah* (Philadelphia: Westminster Press, 1987), deals very well with the formation of 'Judaism'. On the Dead Sea Scrolls, the most recent comprehensive introduction is P.R. Davies, G.J. Brooke and P. Callaway, *The Complete World of the Dead Sea Scrolls* (London: Thames & Hudson, 2002). The most prolific and influential of writers on rabbinic Judaism, and on 'Judaisms' in the Greco-Roman period is Jacob Neusner; see, for example, *Judaism in the Matrix of Christianity* (Philadelphia: Fortress Press, 1986).

Part IV

THE FORMATION OF THE OLD TESTAMENT

Samaritan Pentateuch Scroll, Nablus, Palestine

Chapter 16

ORAL TRADITION AND COLLECTIONS
PRIOR TO THE DEPORTATIONS

When the first edition of *The Old Testament World* appeared it was still largely accepted that the most likely time for the beginning of the collecting and writing-down of the traditions that were to become the Old Testament was the reigns of David and Solomon. Their creation of a small empire, it was held, required a bureaucracy to administer it, most probably recruited from Egypt. The new archaeological picture of the history of Israel and Judah that has emerged in the meantime (see Chapter 4) has put large question marks against this view. As has been argued above (pp. 67-69), if David and Solomon controlled neighbouring territory, it was only by maintaining small garrisons in several border towns. There is no evidence that their kingdoms required or possessed the kind of extensive administrative apparatus that would also be conducive to the collecting and writing of national epics. On the other hand, there was probably sufficient of a Temple and palace administration to keep simple records of transactions and of the reigns of kings. These are possibly referred to in the books of Kings as the Chronicles of the Kings of Israel and Judah (see 1 Kings 14·19, 29).

A new emerging consensus is that it was not until the reign of Hezekiah, king of Judah (727–698), or later, that materials began to be collected and put together with a view to creating a national epic. There are two reasons for this. First, Hezekiah and his successors had the necessary administrative institutions to make this possible (see Jamieson-Drake 1991) and second, they had a strong motive. In 722/21 the northern kingdom, Israel, ceased to exist, and the population of Jerusalem was swollen by refugees from the north, probably including prophetic groups and others who brought with them written and oral traditions. From this point onwards, Judah sought to take over the mantle of Israel, and to put together a national epic that portrayed the northern kingdom, Israel, as a breakaway from a once united kingdom ruled from Jerusalem. As we have argued above (pp. 78-79) the likelihood is that Judah was a vassal kingdom of its immediate northern neighbour for many years, probably only gaining independence in the eighth century BCE.

An important qualification that needs to be made to this scenario, and one that Philip Davies intends to develop in future publications, is that after the destruction of the northern kingdom Judah retained parts, at least, of the territory of Benjamin. It is quite possible that some of the traditions that were incorporated into the national epic were preserved here, and did not need to be brought south from the former northern kingdom. Also, it should not be assumed that the Assyrian conquest of

Samaria in 722/21 ended all contact between people in the former northern king-dom and those in Jerusalem, and that no traditions could have been brought from the north, or have even been obtained from there, subsequent to 722/21.

Later in the chapter, the question will be asked about the form that the national epic of Judah had taken before the deportations of 597–582. For the moment the matter of oral tradition will be discussed. Interest in this subject dates particularly from the time when it was still believed that the national epic began to be written down in the time of David and Solomon, and that stories circulating in oral form might bridge the gap between their time (tenth century BCE) and events related in the Bible prior to the monarchy. Westermann (1964) pointed to the social setting and preoccupations of the patriarchal narratives: they are concerned with acquiring land (e.g. Genesis 12:7; 26:22) and ensuring that there are descendants (Genesis 16, 18, 24). There are quarrels between brothers (Genesis 25:27-34; 27:1-45), while the wives of the patriarchs find themselves in danger, so that the continuation of the family is put at risk (Genesis 12:10-19; 20:1-18; 26:1-11). These stories, it was argued, reflect the social conditions of migrant families, and are thus to be dated in the pre-settlement period, from which they had been preserved orally.

But how can, and should, the study of oral tradition be used in Old Testament interpretation? At the outset, it must be bluntly stated that oral tradition cannot help us to bridge gaps between the time of writing down of traditions and alleged earlier times or events which oral traditions portray. The view that we can do this rests upon a false assumption, the belief that society develops along a straight line from being pre-literate to being literate. If we take the example of the patriarchal stories we can explain this more fully. The fact that the patriarchal stories are concerned with prom-ises about land, with family rivalries, and with the need to protect the patriarch's wife, may show that they come from a particular social background; but it tells us nothing about the date of these stories. If it is argued that these stories must pre-date the monarchy, because in those times Israel's ancestors were migrants concerned with land and family matters, it can be replied that there must have been family groups during the period of the monarchy that had just the same concerns. The fact that a centralised monarchy introduced scribes and scribal schools into the court did not mean that oral storytelling immediately ceased among the people, so that anything that looks as though it was originally oral must pre-date the introduction of scribal schools. In fact, an oral and a literate culture must have existed side-by-side in Israel for many centuries.

'Oral' does not equal 'early' if a society is both oral and literate. The greatest probability is that the characters of the patriarchal story, Abraham and Jacob, were real ancestors of Judah and Israel respectively. Whether they pre-dated the monar-chy cannot be known, but even if they did, oral traditions told about them would change over the generations, as the storytellers adapted the tales to the needs or the situations of the hearers.

The same uncertainty exists with regard to the use of oral tradition to reconstruct tribal movements from the patriarchal stories. The classic instance is the interpreta-tion of the Jacob cycle. In the story, Jacob flees from his brother Esau and goes to Haran, where he marries his cousin's daughters, and later returns to his home in Canaan as a wealthy man. It has been widely held that the episode of Jacob fleeing and returning is a device to link together traditions about two different groups of people, one of which was settled in Canaan, the other of which came from Haran, in northeast Mesopotamia. But there is a possible alternative interpretation. The motif of the hero being forced to leave home and later returning as a rich and powerful person is a common one in folk literature (Propp 1968: 39, 55). We get a variation on it in the story of Joseph: the banished brother becomes powerful, and his family have to come to him and acknowledge his power. We cannot be certain, then, whether the Jacob cycle contains memories about social migrations, or whether it merely conforms to a typical folk-tale plot structure.

A Variety of Oral Traditions

The Book of Judges
The book of Judges contains no fewer than three stories that deal with the tragic hero; and these are the only instances of this theme in the whole of the Old Testament. The simplest is the story of Jephthah (Judges 11–12). He is an example of the brother who is rejected by his brothers (Judges 11:2) and who becomes more powerful than they (cp. Joseph). Jephthah is a tragic hero in that his vow to sacrifice the first person he meets if God grants his victory eventually forces him to sacrifice his only child, a daughter (Judges 11:34-40; cp. Gaster 1969: 430-31). He ends up victorious but without an heir. The story of Samson is more complex, but ends with him destroying his enemies and himself (Judges 16:30) after his weakness for women has led to his downfall. The story of Abimelech (Judges 9) transforms some themes found in the Jephthah and Samson stories; Abimelech eliminates his brothers instead of being rejected by them, and ends his life in defeat. His demise, too, is caused by a woman—one who throws a millstone onto his head from the top of a tower.

The three stories are not only about tragic heroes; they contain religious sentiments that are surprising when considered in the light of the Old Testament as a whole. Jephthah's vow to sacrifice a human being to God if he is granted victory is unparalleled in the Old Testament, and hardly represents its religion at its best. Samson, who is a Nazirite—that is, someone specially dedicated to God—hardly acts in a way that is creditable to God. He kills thirty men of Ashkelon in order to pay for a lost wager and seems to have a special liking for Philistine women. Abimelech also acts in an arbitrary and bloodthirsty manner. It is not unreasonable to conclude from these facts that the stories of Jephthah, Samson, and Abimelech were popular stories about local heroes, which, in the retelling, came to stress the tragic element, and which embodied popular superstition and crude morality.

The Books of Samuel
Even casual readers are likely to notice the great differences in style within the two books of Samuel. The first six chapters of 1 Samuel, apart from one short passage, are a coherent story, recounting the birth and dedication of Samuel; the wickedness of the priests, Eli's sons; the special message to Samuel from God, which with great artistry, is only vaguely hinted at (1 Samuel 3:18), and the sequel, in which Eli's sons are killed in battle, and the Ark is lost and then returned. 1 Samuel 2:27-36 is a later addition, which both supplies the word of judgment, which is deliberately only hinted at in 3:18, and spoils the artistry of the section. From 1 Samuel 7 to 24 the material becomes episodic, and sometimes chaotic. There is no clear picture, for example, of how and when Saul becomes king. At 10.1 he is privately anointed by Samuel; at 10:20-24 he is chosen by the casting of lots; and in 11:1-15 his kingship is 'renewed'

after he defeats Nahash the Ammonite king. From chapter 18 to 24 we have a poorly integrated series of episodes about David and Jonathan and about Saul's pursuit of David. It is very difficult to get the sense of a consecutive narrative. Then things begin to change from chapter 25, and from here until 2 Samuel 20, with only very occasional unevennesses, we get a highly artistic and connected narrative. But from 2 Samuel 21–24 we are back with episodes that do not form a connected whole.

The most likely explanation for the variations in style and coherence in the books of Samuel is that we have a mixture of original narratives, composed in a royal scribal school, and episodes that are written versions of oral stories. Because, during the reign of Saul and the beginning of that of David, there were no official chroniclers in Israel, it is not surprising that information about these periods could be obtained only from oral sources. Thus it is not surprising that there are differing accounts of how and when Saul became king, and that it is difficult, if not impossible, to trace the actual course of events once David appeared on the scene. Some points are clear from the episodes: David and Jonathan loved each other in spite of Saul's hostility to David, and Saul's daughter Michal was also faithful to David. Saul pursued David relentlessly once the latter had left the court. But these points are gleaned from originally unconnected stories rather than from a coherent narrative.

Genesis

Having considered Judges and Samuel, we can return to the stories about the patriarchs in Genesis. The Abraham cycle runs from Genesis 12 to 24:10. In its present form it is a combination of a priestly and a non-priestly version of the story, of which the former was probably not added after the return from the deportations. If, for the moment, we exclude the priestly material (Genesis 12:4b-5b; 16:15–17:27; 23:1; and 25:7-11), we are left with what is probably a mixture of oral-based traditions combined with literary compositions. The oral-based material probably consists of the Abraham–Lot cycle (13:2-5, 8-13; 18:1-15; and 19:1-38) and the story of Abraham purchasing a burial cave at Mamre (23:1-20). In the Abraham–Lot stories there are a number of folk motifs: the visit of unrecognised angelic guests (18:1-8), the promise of a child to a barren woman (18:9-15), the superior powers of angelic visitors (19:11), the dangers of looking back (19:17-26), and the incest of a man with his daughters (19:30-38). The account of the destruction of the Sodom area (19:24-5) is probably a folk explanation for the weird landscape in the Dead Sea basin.

If parts of Genesis 18–19 and 23 are correctly identified as oral-based traditions, it is possible to make suggestions about their origin. All have as their main setting the oaks of Mamre, near Hebron. They legitimate Abraham's settlement there, and they stress that Abraham's descendants came as a result of divine promise, whereas the neighbouring and related peoples of Ammon and Moab are descendants of a man who committed incest with his daughters. If these stories reflect the circumstances of the times when their spoken form was written down, this was most likely the seventh century, the time when Judah was creating what will later be described as the Israel of 'confession and belief' by presenting a picture of a united kingdom and small empire, over which David once reigned.

The Jacob cycle is much more extensive, stretching from Genesis 27 to 33. It shows every sign of being an expanded oral narrative on the theme of a hero leaving home because of danger, and returning a powerful man. It abounds with folk motifs: Jacob and Esau are twins and rival cultural heroes; the blessing intended for the elder is diverted by trickery; in Haran a false bride (Leah) is substituted for the intended one (Rachel); while the basis for Jacob's outwitting of Laban is the folk belief that what animals look at affects the colour of their offspring (30:5-43). The wrestling at the river Jabbok with a heavenly messenger that cannot endure the arrival of the dawn contains several well known motifs.

In its present form, however, the cycle celebrates the superiority of Jacob over the inhabitants of the northeast and over the people of Edom, personified by Esau. As part of the national epic fashioned by Judah, it helped to project a picture of the superiority of 'Israel' over surrounding peoples.

Exodus

With the account of the Exodus in Exodus 1–15, we are in a different situation. The stories of Abraham and Jacob were traditions preserved respectively in Judah and Israel, centring upon ancestors of those peoples; the story of the Exodus is the story of a corporate deliverance, and as such probably owes its existence to an annual celebration. In its present form it consists of priestly and non-priestly material; but it also has many folk motifs.

In Exodus 1:15-22 the pharaoh speaks to the two(!) midwives who deliver all the Hebrew babies. This extreme simplifying of matters is typical of oral narratives. When one considers what an exalted person the pharaoh was, and what an extensive bureaucracy he possessed, it is ludicrous to suppose that he talked personally to two midwives; but folk narrative necessarily simplifies these things. In Exodus 2, the birth of the hero in circumstances of danger is a well-instanced folk motif, while the flight of Moses to Midian and his subsequent return parallel the flight and return of Jacob.

In chapters 5–11 the narrative is shaped into a series of episodes in which Moses (accompanied by his brother Aaron) has interviews with the pharaoh. Each interview ends with pharaoh agreeing to let the Israelites go if the particular plague that is afflicting the people is ended. As soon as there is respite from the plague, however, the cycle begins again. The pharaoh goes back on his word, he is threatened with a new plague, and then temporarily relents when the plague comes. Behind this shaping is probably the art of the oral storyteller, holding the attention of the listeners, and building the story to a climax. Chapters 12–14 contain priestly regulations about the Passover and an evidently written literary account of the Exodus. Chapter 15 may be based upon an old hymn which celebrated the deliverance at the Red Sea.

There are no clues within Exodus 1–15 about the date of recording of the oral elements. If we could be sure that Exodus 15 was recorded at the same time as the other oral-based traditions, we would have an indication of the date. The hymn ends with the words

> You brought them in and planted them on the mountain of your own possession, the place, O LORD, that you made your abode, the sanctuary, O LORD, that your hands have established (Exodus 15:17).

This is clearly an attempt to link the Exodus deliverance with the establishment of Jerusalem as God's abode and is evidence of the appropriation by Jerusalem and Judah of traditions that must have originated in the north.

With the Exodus traditions, we come to the end of those parts of the Old Testament in which it may be possible to detect the presence of originally oral traditions.
This is not to say that material such as Numbers 12–24 or Joshua 2–12 are not
based upon oral tradition; it is just that we cannot be sure of this. Also, we must add
that Judges probably contains more oral-based material than we discussed above.
Further examples would be the traditions about the local heroes Ehud (Judges 3:15-
25), Deborah and Jael (Judges 4), and Gideon (Judges 6–8).

Written Forms of the Old Testament

So far, we have tried to identify material that seems to have existed as oral traditions. We now turn to the difficult, if not hazardous, task of describing in more detail
how the traditions that became the Old Testament began to be written down.
Fortunately, a most exhaustive examination of this process has been undertaken by
Kratz (2000), whose results we shall largely follow. Kratz makes it clear that the Israel
of the Old Testament is not the Israel (nor, we would add, the Judah) of history. The
Israel of the Old Testament is presented in the 'language of confession and belief'
(Kratz: 2000: 314), and that only as a result of a long and painful process in which
'Israel' came to understand itself to be the people of God. However, the traditions
that have become the 'language of confession and belief' contain remnants of material that functioned in many different settings in the period before the deportations of
597–582. These included smaller and larger family circles, locally administered
justice in villages, prophetic circles, situations of war and conflict, local communal
celebrations of an agricultural and/or religious nature, and the affairs of the royal
court and its scribes. These social situations embraced both the northern and the
southern kingdoms, and the religion that they followed contained many pagan
elements when viewed from the standpoint of the later orthodoxy of the Old Testament. Some of these have been indicated in the sections about oral traditions.

The crucial turning-point, as has been observed above, was the destruction of the
northern kingdom, Israel, in 722/21. As Kratz puts it (p. 320), the divine 'no' to Israel
pronounced by the prophets led to the demise of the northern kingdom but not to its
God. Yhwh survived in Judah, and Judah set out on the road to becoming the Israel
of the 'language of confession and belief'. It did this by projecting back into its pre-
history the view that Israel and Judah had once been united, not just as one nation,
but as one family.

In the course of the seventh century BCE, three literary works were composed that
described the origins of Israel (the Israel of 'confession and belief') and which clarified Judah's relation to this Israel. The works were, first, a story of the beginnings of
the kingship and of David's empire in 1 Samuel 1 to 1 Kings 2 (only, of course, certain parts of these chapters). Secondly, there was an account of the origins of the
world and stories of the patriarchs in Genesis 2–35, and, thirdly, the story of the
Exodus in Exodus 2 to Joshua 12. In the first work, great pains were taken to show
that David had not usurped the kingdom of Saul, but that he was Saul's legitimate
heir by virtue of delivering the people from the Philistines. This was an apology for
Judah (David) taking over the role of Israel (Saul). Again, the story of the Patriarchs
put the ancestor of Judah (Abraham) before that of Israel (Jacob), by making Jacob
Abraham's grandson. Only in the story of the Exodus was a northern viewpoint still
discernible. The nucleus of Exodus 2 to Joshua 12 were the Israelite (or possibly

Benjaminite, so also Kratz) traditions retained in Exodus 14, Joshua 6 and 8 and the song of Miriam in Exodus 15:20-21.

The catastrophe of 587 and its aftermath would, of course, have a significant and transforming effect on the growth of the traditions towards the Israel of 'confession and belief', but a step in this direction was taken by the incorporation into the Exodus material of the *mishpatim*, the laws in the Book of the Covenant. According to Kratz (2000: 322) the redaction prefaced these laws with the law of the altar in Exodus 20:24-26, and concluded them with the cultic calendar of Exodus 23:14-17. This put the laws in a new context, a context which was further emphasised by putting the laws in the form of a direct address by Yhwh in the second person singular. In this way the idea was expressed of the solidarity of a people bound by allegiance to Yhwh by observance of social and cultic ordinances.

This chapter has dealt with the beginnings of the traditions found in the Pentateuch and the Former Prophets (Joshua to 2 Kings). What of the remainder of the Old Testament? Of some parts we can definitely say that they were composed after the deportations, and therefore did not exist before 587 BCE. These would include Chronicles, Ezra, Nehemiah, Esther, Isaiah 40–66, Jeremiah, Ezekiel, Daniel, Joel, Jonah, Haggai, Zechariah, and Malachi. About the remainder we are uncertain. It is quite likely that parts of the book of Proverbs existed, as indicated by Proverbs 25:1:

> These are other proverbs of Solomon that the officials of King Hezekiah of Judah copied.

Whether or not these proverbs were really spoken by Solomon, it is likely that proverbs believed to be by him were copied in the royal scribal school of Hezekiah's time (late eighth century BCE).

Some of the oracles attributed to Isaiah, Hosea, Amos, Micah, Nahum, and Zephaniah were probably written down and were preserved among prophetic groups. There were probably collections of laws and of psalms, while details of priestly rituals, if not written down, were passed from generation to generation. Whether any of these materials at this stage were regarded as scripture is most unlikely. For the collecting together of books that began to be regarded as authoritative for Israel's faith, certain conditions were necessary. A beginning had been made from the latter part of the eighth century onwards. It would be the destruction of Jerusalem and its aftermath that would provide the circumstances in which the idea of an authoritative collection of sacred books would become an actuality.

References

Gaster, T.H.
    1969   *Myth, Legend and Custom in the Old Testament* (London: Gerald Duckworth).
Gunkel, H.
    1988   *The Folktale in the Old Testament* (Historic Texts and Interpreters in Biblical Scholarship; Sheffield: Almond Press).
Kratz, R.G.
    2000   *Die Komposition der erzählender Bücher des Alten Testaments* (Göttingen: Vandenhoeck & Ruprecht).
Propp, V.
    1968   *The Morphology of the Folktale* (Austin, TX, and London: University of Texas Press).
Westermann, C.
    1964   *Genesis* (Biblischer Kommentar, Altes Testament; Neukirchen–Vluyn: Neukirchener Verlag).

Chapter 17

THE FORMATION
OF THE SCRIPTURAL CANON

In this concluding chapter we shall consider the processes by which the scrolls that made up the Jewish biblical canon were created, edited and assembled, and the canon finally closed. We shall also see how and why the Old Testament and Hebrew Bible differ and how the text of the biblical books was also fixed. But before looking at the process in detail, let us reflect on what a 'canon' is and how canons arise. To understand Jewish/Judean canonizing entails understanding canonizing generally as human social activity. For the scriptural canon is not a unique phenomenon; it can be illuminated by parallels from the ancient Near Eastern and the classical worlds.

When the first edition of *The Old Testament World* was published, a division between 'pre-exilic' and 'post-exilic' processes still seemed a useful one. However, two more recent developments obliged us to think before we retained that division. First, whether the 'exile' really marks a decisive watershed is rather dubious. Yet a very significant sequence of events did occur between 722 and the mid-fifth century. The incorporation of the territory of Benjamin into Judah, the destruction of the Judahite state (following that of Israel by over a century), the transfer of political power (and religious influence) away from Jerusalem, the restoration of Jerusalem as major (then only) sanctuary of a new universal monotheistic religion, and the creation of a new community going by the name 'Israel' as the chosen people and ministers of its deity Yhwh, constitute the matrix of the biblical literature. The 'exile', both as a deportation and later resettlement in Judah, and as an identity marker and ongoing literary and theological theme is an encapsulation of those traumatic processes.

Second, the process of forming the biblical literature does not separate neatly into first oral then literary then canonised. The three aspects all overlap: writing never replaced speaking, and canonizing occurred from the moment that literature began to be produced. No simple distinction, then, can be made in the mode of activity by which the contents of the Old Testament were put together. Yet there is some value in looking at the process from different perspectives. The previous chapter focussed on the oral narratives that lie behind some of the literature and the manner in which written forms adopted and reinterpreted them. In this chapter, the focus will be on the literary activity within the scribal communities who were responsible for creating the literary texts, copying and editing them—and canonizing them.

What are Canons?

The obvious starting point is the term 'canon' itself, though the history of the *term* must not be confused with the history of the *phenomenon*. The term itself is Greek, and denoted a physical ruler (such as a carpenter would use for measuring) and an abstract standard (as we might nowadays say 'yardstick'). It referred to the rules by which poetry or music could be composed, or geometrical shapes measured. The notion of a perfect work of art as representing the ideal, to be studied and copied, is fundamental to the Greek concept of canon. For such a work is itself a 'canon' because it both enshrines and demonstrates the 'rules' or the 'art' in question (the eternal, as against the ephemeral). Individual works or collections of works could be created in the Greek and Hellenistic world *specifically as canons*, and such works could cover a range of topics, whether art, medicine, technology, or philosophy.

Canons are not usually exclusive or closed, either. Such an act fossilises a literary repertoire and has a specific reason—often when a culture sees itself as in decay, when the best lies in the past and must not be diluted by more recent additions. It is a function of a culture that sees itself as committed to preserving a heritage rather than adding to it. Classic works do not inspire new ones: they are now venerated for their own sake.

But canons are older than the Greeks. Millennia before the Greeks learned to write, other civilizations had produced highly complex bureaucratic systems in which the art of writing was indispensable. This requirement in turn necessitated a society of scribes, and over time this society defined and replicated itself through a body of literature that served as a kind of genetic blueprint of its social and political functions, its own values and world-view, and its theoretical and practical philosophy. By means of the scribes' own educational system and the constant copying and refining of this corpus, the Mesopotamian and Egyptian civilizations produced literary texts that acquired a classical status and would be copied and recopied.

The Canonizing Process

Closing a canon is a single authoritative decision (often confused with 'canonizing' itself). Canons grow, on the other hand, slowly and by natural processes, for they are an inevitable by-product of any consciously literary culture. The production of an ancient literary corpus involved many stages: not only composition, copying, editing, but also classifying, collecting, and archiving, since the growth of a corpus depends on its physical preservation. A work becomes canonised by being preserved until its status as a classic is ensured; and only later by being classified in a collection of some kind. There is a parallel with the evolutionary theory of natural selection; the best, the fittest pieces of writing are reproduced, others die. Some works can of course be more firmly 'canonical' than others. In Greek literature Homer first, Herodotus and Thucydides next, and so on. In the Hebrew Bible there are three divisions, one at least of which was at one time a canon in itself (Torah). The Torah enjoys a higher degree of authority than the rest of the canon, and sometimes the entire Jewish scriptures are called 'Torah'. In the Christian scriptures, the New Testament is a similar sense more 'canonical' than the Old. And until a canon is 'closed' there will remain works on the fringes of being canonised. Perennial candidates, they leave room for dispute about their quality.

But this is how the Old Testament/Hebrew Biblical canon was formed: its contents were those writings that the literate class wished to preserve, or needed to preserve—for various reasons. In the following review all stages of the process will be reviewed, from the composition of a work to the ultimate freezing of its canonised text. But whatever the *sorts* of processes and histories that the various scrolls—and sets of scrolls—have undergone, the precise reconstruction is nearly always disputed.

The 'Primary History'

The Structure of the Pentateuch

The process by which the Pentateuch was formed is especially opaque and therefore disputed. Towards the end of the nineteenth century the influential (Graf–Wellhausen) theory was developed that it had been put together from four major literary 'sources', which, understood in their correct sequence, also provided a framework for a critical history of Israel's religion. These sources are traditionally identified as follows: J (the 'Yahwist', so named because it uses the divine name Yhwh), who wrote in the ninth century BCE; E (who uses *'elohim*, 'God'), dated a little later; D (mostly the book of Deuteronomy), in the seventh century; and P (the Priestly writer), who dates from the exile. This analysis was known as the New Documentary Hypothesis. However, these sources were not simply laid side-by-side: each one was overlaid by a later one or combined with another source by an editor. While D was relatively independent, it is also recognisable in the occasional editorial insertion outside Deuteronomy. Working within this framework of understanding, however, scholars early in the twentieth century also become accustomed to tracing a pre-history of some of the contents, going back to shorter and often oral compositions. A climax was reached in the work of Gerhard von Rad and Martin Noth in Germany in the 1930s and 1940s, each of whom produced an account of the history of the composition the Pentateuch (in von Rad's case, the Hexateuch, for he included Joshua in the Documentary Hypothesis) from its very beginnings to its final form. Noth argued that five originally independent themes—'promise to the patriarchs', 'guidance out of Egypt', 'guidance into the arable land', 'guidance in the wilderness', and 'revelation at Sinai'—had been combined into a continuous history even before J and E wrote early in the monarchic period, while he saw P as a final editor, rather than merely another source-document. A variation on this view was offered by Cross, who suggested an 'early Israelite epic'. Von Rad, on the contrary, saw the Hexateuch as growing up around a kernel which contained nearly all the main components—promise to patriarchs, exodus, and land occupation—and which was filled out with stories until the outline of the Pentateuchal story was achieved. Only the Sinai story, in his view, was originally independent. For von Rad, the Yahwist was the author of the earliest draft of the Hexateuch. Working in the reign of Solomon, J wrote down the emerging national tradition of Israel's beginnings and history up to the occupation of the land after the Exodus, and prefaced it with an account of the origins of the world and humanity (Genesis 1–11).

Neither of these (whose work dominated German and Anglo-American scholarship for decades) cast doubt on the existence of the four component documents. The only major alternative to this view was in Scandinavia, where many scholars preferred to think of two circles of tradition (corresponding to D and P) that committed their stories to writing at a relatively late stage, when they were also combined.

In the last fifty years, Pentateuchal criticism has taken new directions. Many of the above conclusions are now being abandoned. Of the original sources, the only one that is not debatable is the book of Deuteronomy, though its traditional dating in the reign of Josiah can be questioned. Of the three other sources, E has long been doubted as an independent source. The Priestly writer has still tended to be seen as the final or near-final creator of the Pentateuch in its present form, an editor rather than author. But a group of especially Jewish and Israeli scholars argue for P's antiquity. The Yahwist has been dated by some later than Deuteronomy, perhaps in the exilic period or later. Other scholars doubt the existence of any of the documents and prefer to see the Pentateuch as the work of a single author (so Whybray 1987). Unlike Noth's scheme of 'themes' combining at an early stage to form a written 'Pentateuchal tradition', Rendtorff proposed that these 'themes' developed independently and were combined only at a relatively late stage to form the connected Pentateuchal narrative.

Can We Unravel the Pentateuch?

The problem is, essentially, that Genesis–Numbers can be sliced up in two ways, 'vertically' or 'horizontally'. One can see passages spread across the Pentateuch that share linguistic and ideological features, providing a basis for a *horizontal* stratification of more or less continuous sources, such as the Documentary Hypothesis provided. But one can also see blocks of materials dealing with their own theme or episode strung together sequentially in a later editing process to create a continuous history. In either case, some kind of editing ('authorship'?) is involved in achieving the final complete story. This could be ascribed to one of the 'sources' (J or P), or to others. In fact, Noth's masterful analysis perceived both perspectives: he assumed that the various episodes came together at an early stage to form the continuous narrative that both J and E reproduced. In view of what we now know about the history of Israel and Judah, however, the Pentateuchal story as a whole seems very unlikely to have been compiled before the monarchic period at the earliest, and probably not before the Persian period.

The 'Deuteronomistic History'

Another complicating factor is the relationship between the Former Prophets (the 'Deuteronomistic History') and the Pentateuch. Many early adherents of the Documentary Hypothesis were inclined to think that the Pentateuchal sources originally told of the conquest of the land—a 'Hexateuch' rather than 'Pentateuch'. Noth, on the other hand, argued for an original 'Tetrateuch' with a 'Deuteronomistic History' (see Chapter 16) comprising Joshua–Kings and with Deuteronomy as a preface. Only when this work was placed after the equivalent of Genesis–Numbers was Deuteronomy detached and integrated into what became the 'Pentateuch'. The assumption that we are dealing with two large extended narratives that were linked together at some point is generally favoured at the present—with some interpreters preferring to think of the complete sequence as a 'Primary History'.

Future Progress

The present state of uncertainty about the composition of the 'Primary History' should be welcome to the scholar, for whom problems are what scholarship is about! But the general reader, or even the student may feel dismayed at our lack of certainty. The way forward will perhaps emerge not from further detailed source-criticism but from archaeology and from a study of scribal methods. The Documentary Hypothesis was developed in relative isolation from any knowledge about the real history of Israel and Judah, and even in the mid-twentieth century our information was still a good deal less than it is now. But recent decades have seen a decisive verdict on the historicity of the stories from Genesis to Joshua, possibly even to the end of 2 Samuel. The earlier notion of an extensive early version of 'national' history now seems unrealistic (and even the notion of a twelve-tribe 'nation' of Israel may be a relatively late one). And while the Documentary Hypothesis was intended to provide a framework for the development of Israelite and Judean religion, archaeology is now providing some clarification; most of the distinctive religious ideas of the Bible (monotheism, ban on images, centralised worship) are late monarchic at the earliest and probably even later. In one superficial way this later dating explains why the contents of Genesis–Deuteronomy are apparently unhistorical; but more importantly, it has focussed attention on what the 'Primary History' of Israel is really about and why it was created. Why does this story tell of a written law, of a covenant, of a people originating from first Mesopotamia and then Egypt, of the massacre of Canaanites (but then, in Judges, their absorption!). Why does it end in Babylonia, with the figure of the deported king?

A study of scribal practices, and of the function and self-understanding of that class, is also important. Biblical scholarship is still inclined to speak of 'traditions', of 'circles', of 'editors', and of 'redactors'. The answer to 'who wrote the Bible?' is not to give a name, or a cipher like 'J', but to realise that 'wrote' is the wrong word and that we are dealing with processes that took place in real contexts by real social groups having very precise agendas. These people not only initially wrote down, but also continually added, altered, combined, annotated—and in all this, were creating a canon of writings. The Qumran scrolls have been enormously helpful in our understanding of scribal schools and libraries, since they contain multiple editions or versions of basically the same 'document' preserved side-by-side in the same cave. They also show us the creative rewriting of existing biblical texts was undertaken. If we can appreciate the social, political, and economic location of the scribal class, their responsibilities, values, social world, and professional craft, we will understand a great deal about why the Old Testament came to be as it is.

One further point needs to be made. The freezing of canonised books in a stable form means we only see the end product; any history of that literature is theoretical (which is not to dismiss it). The recent interest in the 'final form' of biblical books rather than their literary history, and in literary rather than literary-historical scholarly reading, even where this approach is essential non- or even anti-historical, has shown how valuable is such a holistic approach in identifying the architecture of large compositions. Simply, we can often miss the wood for looking at the trees. Literary critics have also shown how rhetoric and ideology can never be ignored: all texts are 'persuasive' ('propaganda' is perhaps too strong a term on the whole, but it is not always inappropriate). The starting-point of Pentateuchal criticism (and of Joshua–Kings) ought to be the architecture of its final form. Even if that architecture is not the result of any individual's deliberate decision, it exposes the principles on which the overall conception grew.

In the case of the Pentateuch that task is actually not so difficult. Its narrative shows first how human nature, then different nations, came into being, then how a small family of nations, then 'Israel' alone, emerged. 'Israel' sprang from an ancestor (Jacob), and acquired a constitution (at Sinai) then a land—all the things that define a nation. But that nation is chosen by the creator deity, which makes it very special. Hence, inserted into this narrative are idealised descriptions of this 'ideal' nation itself, found in Leviticus, Numbers, and Deuteronomy. These utopian 'Israels' are all located in the 'wilderness' period, and they are all different. For Leviticus, Israel is a holy nation, with Yhwh at the centre, his priests surrounding his place and ministering to him, and, beyond the confines of Israel, chaos, sin, and death. The contours of this world are contours of holiness: packed closely in the centre, more widely spaced at the outside. For Numbers, Israel is a Sparta, marching in military formation, governed by strict discipline, with any rebellion severely punished, and fighting behind the Ark upon which Yhwh leads his warriors from their 'camp'. For Deuteronomy, Israel is governed by an exclusive contract with Yhwh that regulates their occupation of the land.

This overview shows that 'Law' is not what the Pentateuch is about. Nor is it 'history'. It is a definition of 'Israel' that bridges the gap between the reality of a small Judah, subject to a larger empire, and a people once (and still) chosen by the one and only God for a better destiny. In Deuteronomy that bridge becomes an address to each individual to preserve the covenant, and here we can even see the beginning of the religion of Judaism emerging.

As for Joshua–Kings: the overall shape is of a land gained and lost by military conquest, through failure to follow the words of God. 'Israel' failed also to find the true leadership. After Joshua's death his efforts collapsed: the Judges could not impose permanent security and themselves were increasingly flawed. Neither Saul, David, nor Solomon were perfect (their faults are clearly expressed), and as a whole the kings of Israel and of Judah led their people to destruction. The story is not a glorious one, but its lesson was to be learnt: true leadership and obedience to the covenant alone would restore divine favour. This is not a 'theological interpretation' of real history: it is a dramatic statement of what 'Israel' is and should be.

The 'Prophetic' Collections

'Former Prophets'

We have just looked at the books of Joshua–Kings under the rubric of 'Primary History' (following the canonical structure of the Old Testament): but in the Hebrew Bible, these books (minus Ruth) are called 'Former Prophets' and their implied relationship with 'Latter Prophets' ought to be considered too. In the case of the Pentateuch, it was suggested that 'Torah'/Law was a misleading term. The same seems to be true of 'Former Prophets', for although they include stories of prophets, they contain little Prophecy.

Yet there is a connection between some of the books of 'Former' and 'Latter' Prophets. Jeremiah and Isaiah both include passages paralleled in 2 Kings, and Jeremiah is strongly influenced in places by the language of Deuteronomy. Moreover, several books of the Minor Prophets have headings that draw on the chronological system of 2 Kings. More broadly, the Former Prophets shows a great interest in the role of prophets in history, while the Latter Prophets together and individually are deeply concerned with the processes of history and sometimes with the culmination of history, since they couple their social comment with the historical outcome:

there is a nexus between human deeds and historical outcomes; history is not pre-determined, and Israel and Judah can make their own. So it is very plausible that the Former and Latter Prophets were conceived to have a close connection in their process of compilation and canonisation. Blenkinsopp has suggested that Prophecy was developed as a corpus, and canonised, as a deliberate counterpart (or even counterweight) to Torah. Deuteronomy is again very important in this process, since both conceptually and canonically it effectively makes Prophecy subject to Law, and presents Moses the lawgiver as the ultimate prophet. Thus we might well see, in the later stages of the collection of writings, a creative process of bringing together Prophets and Law just as Wisdom and Law also came to be associated. Does the canonical sequence of the Hebrew Bible better reflect these processes than the apparently more logical order of law, history, poetry, and prophecy in the Old Testament? Not necessarily; but we may, after all, have to reckon with later stages of a canonizing process among Jews who read Greek also.

Latter Prophets

We have looked in some detail (Chapter 12) at the composition of Isaiah, as an example of how the prophetic books were assembled. Here we shall briefly look at the remaining books as 'collections' that over a period of time assumed a settled shape (in the case of Jeremiah, two shapes).

Isaiah

The division of Isaiah into three discrete collections (chapters 1–39; 40–55; 56–66) is still commonly accepted, and shows us one way in which prophetic books might grow—by juxtaposition. But it has recently been argued that the three parts are more closely connected than this, and that as we now have the book, the first part has also been shaped by the second, while the third part may also have shaped both the second and the third! This, however, is not unexpected, for in the later stages of copying of scrolls, cross-references, harmonisations, and general integrative devices are to be expected: a collection has become a 'book' and in the process of turning it into such a good deal of editing will be expected. Despite the ingenuity of modern literary critics, it is in the end unlikely that we can accurately reconstruct this process in any detail. We can just accumulate plenty of evidence that it did.

Jeremiah

Scholarship on the book offers little consensus as to how the book was assembled. There is, though, widely accepted classification of the materials into four kinds: (a) poetry attributed to Jeremiah himself, found in chapters 1–25; (b) historical tales about him (sometimes attributed to Baruch) in chapters 26–45; (c) prose speeches attributed to Jeremiah but not authentic, in chapters 1–45; and (d) a 'book of consolation' in chapters 30–31. The remaining chapters, 46–52, are usually considered secondary (though secondary to what remains an open question). But there is little consensus on how these relate to each other or to Jeremiah. Among the material in (a) are the so-called 'confessions' (11:18–12:6; 15:10-21; 17:14-18; 18:18-23; 20:7-18, possibly more). Are these Jeremiah's own experiences, his words, or are they psalms, or, at least, used by later editors of the book to create the prophetic character? The prose speeches, the most coherent body of material in the book, are thoroughly Deuteronomistic in style and ideology. Did Jeremiah himself write them? Nowhere in the other material in Jeremiah is there any hint of a pro-Deuteronomy stance from the prophet. Indeed, there are certainly internal contradictions. Material in (a), which is most likely to contain original sayings of Jeremiah, opposes prophets in general, thinks little of the Temple, and calls for submission, rather than repentance. The speeches assigned to (c) are dominated by criticism of cultic impurity, and by calls to repentance. The book also offers hope and consolation, and presents Jeremiah to us as a prophet who speaks to those exiled, perhaps also those who have returned. A good example is 24:4-10:

> Like these good figs I will regard as good the exiles from Judah, whom I have sent away from this place to the land of the Chaldeans...like the bad figs...so will I treat Zedekiah the king of Judah his princes, *the remnant of Jerusalem who remain in this land* and those who dwell in the land of Egypt...

Here Jeremiah's own political situation is reinterpreted into the 'restoration' community, where the *golah* (Hebrew 'exile', those priding themselves on having been in exile and preserving their religion intact) is turning upon those who remained in the land, using Jeremiah, the 'true' prophet whose words were fulfilled as a pretext.

If to many readers Jeremiah seems the most immediately accessible of all the prophets, scholarship therefore deems otherwise. The book has grown around the words and the figure of one who interpreted the Babylonian invasion as divine punishment and was persecuted by the leaders of the community. Around that core have developed sermons that create of this figure a Deuteronomistic prophet par excellence, who can provide a lesson for exiles. While scholarly attempts continue to be made (Holladay 1986 and 1988) to write Jeremiah's biography from the contents of his book, analysis of the way the contents have been put together suggests a long process of expansion. McKane sees the growth of the book as a *literary* and organic one, not one tied to external events or historical 'occasions'. Carroll (1986), who likewise finds little overall coherence, believes that the context of any passage can be gained only by investigating the theological interests that inspire it, and finds many different circles in the exilic and Persian periods to have been responsible. The important thing to bear in mind is that copying and editing and expanding a book are not operations that *precede* 'canonizing' but are part of the very process by which classic collections of texts are preserved.

Ezekiel

The book of Ezekiel presents a different profile from both Isaiah and Jeremiah, suggesting further processes of editing, copying, and canonizing. It also has a tighter structure than either Jeremiah or Isaiah: chapters 1–24 contain speeches of denunciation, chapters 25–32 deal with foreign nations, and 34–48 with salvation. The whole book is written in the first person, and there are frequent datings (based on the reign of Jehoiachin), which assign the contents between the years 593 and 571 BCE; these, together with the formula 'the word of Yhwh came to me: "son of man..."' (or some element of this) divides the book into exactly fifty units. The initial impression of an orderly autobiographical sequence disintegrates under scrutiny, however: there are signs of revision (e.g. 1:15-21 actually amends the description that surrounds it), and some individual groups of units can be discerned (e.g. chapters 29–32). These units are more extended, more impersonal and abstract, and more developed in their imagery and argument than the shorter pieces of Isaiah or

Jeremiah. The conscious literary creation of 'prophecy' also takes place in the re-use
of older texts (such as Isaiah 5, Psalm 46, and Jeremiah 4–6) in chapters 38–39; the
'call' of Isaiah and Jeremiah—as well as Exodus 24—is evoked in Ezekiel's own
'call' (1:1–3:15). This process is now referred to as 'inner-biblical exegesis', and it
even happens *within* the book (compare chapters 16 and 23). Much more than
Isaiah or Jeremiah, Ezekiel bears the marks of a coherent literary shaping. Was it
shaped by Ezekiel? The autobiographical style, weird imagery use of angelic guides
(chapters 40–48), re-use of Scripture, appropriation of mythical motifs, speculation
about the end of history, and many other features point towards the kind of scribal
activity that produced apocalypses (see Chapter 14).

The signs are that the book is the product of several authors, who share a common outlook and even a common literary style. It is certainly a much more coherent,
complex, highly artistic, and, above all, literary product than Isaiah or Jeremiah and
results from a different kind of literary history.

The Minor Prophets

The Minor Prophets were originally a single scroll. Of the origin and composition of
most of the individual books we know, in fact, very little. The arrangement is
apparently chronological, according to the superscriptions (and in the case of Jonah
his dating in 2 Kings 14:25). Other signs of inter-connection are repeated phrases
such as 'the word of Yhwh which came to' and 'which he saw'; and the collection
ends with three sections called 'saying' in Zechariah and Malachi (Zechariah 9:1;
12:1; Malachi 1:1).

What principle or process controls the assembly of this multiple book? First, the
number twelve is suspiciously indicative of a complete, whole unit. Just as the
individual 'judges' in the book of Judges have little to do with each other but are
brought under a scheme of consecutive all-Israel 'judges', so Prophecy is here presented as an ongoing phenomenon to every generation, one that stretches to include
Israel as well as Judah. Secondly, all of these books point in some way towards the
eschaton (Greek 'last things'), the definitive act of God at some time in the future
which will resolve all the tensions of history and fulfil the purpose of creation and the
election of Israel. This is a theme we ought to consider for all the Latter Prophets.

Prophecy and Eschatology

The final chapters or passages of all the prophetic books give, in different ways, a
picture of how things will be. Much of Isaiah 40–66 dwells on this theme, while the
last chapter, for example, speaks of gathering the exiles of Israel to the 'holy mountain' of Jerusalem, 'all flesh' worshipping Yhwh, a new creation of heaven and earth,
and the destruction of all those who rebelled against Yhwh. Jeremiah 46–51 contains oracles against foreign nations, promising their punishment or destruction,
though in most cases a short statement at the end of each oracle promises their
restoration (Egypt: 46:26; Moab: 48:47; Ammon: 49:6; Elam: 49:39). Ezekiel also
ends with oracles against foreign nations, but these in turn are followed by a description of the final battle with Gog and then with a picture of the New Jerusalem.

Among the Minor Prophets, we also find signs of an eschatological message.
Hosea, Amos, Micah, Malachi, though not books of promise about Israel's future,
nonetheless all end with such passages. Joel, Obadiah, Nahum, Habakkuk, Zephaniah, Haggai, and Zechariah are all based predominantly on eschatological themes.

Jonah in this perspective can also be seen to be a book about the future, raising the possibility of repentance and salvation for Israel's enemies. It can be no accident that nearly all of the prophetic books end on a note of promise for the future of Israel or of woe to its enemies. It is here, then, that we probably locate the function of the Latter Prophets as a *collection*. According to such texts as Ben Sira 48.17ff., Acts 3:24, and 1 Peter 1:10-12, Old Testament prophecy was seen cumulatively as a message of salvation for Israel. Of course, many of these books were perhaps originally created out of other themes and for other purposes. The ideology of the various books also differs widely—for example, in their attitude towards non-Israelites, the cult, the law, and other criterion by which we might discriminate between different theological viewpoints.

Prophecy as Texts to Study

A final point of interest is the last verse of Hosea, which begins, 'Whoever is wise, let him understand these words; whoever is discerning, let him know them'. Why does this book in particular end with such a comment? Is it the allegory of the opening chapters, about the wayward wife, which attracts attention? Or the sexual language which invites decoding? Whatever the answer, it shows us that one way in which the prophets were understood to function was as literature for the 'wise' to study—confirmed by what Ben Sira says in 39:31 about the scribe being 'concerned with prophecies'. We have seen in Chapter 13 that Wisdom began to accommodate itself to the Law; but it also became attracted to prophecy as a resource full of hidden predictions. Daniel 9 has a 'wise man' being shown a hidden meaning in Jeremiah, and the biblical commentaries from the Dead Sea Scrolls show us 'secret messages' decoded from Isaiah, Habakkuk, Nahum, and even Psalms. Hence we can see how the scribe united his Wisdom with Torah and with Prophecy, just as the canon presents itself.

Writings

The Writings comprise Psalms, Proverbs, Job, Ruth, Song of Songs, Lamentations, Ecclesiastes (Qoheleth), Esther, Daniel, Ezra, Nehemiah, and Chronicles. Many of these books can be classified as Wisdom, but not all. The very name 'writings' perhaps betrays the lack of any unifying category. The references to the scriptures in the Dead Sea Scrolls and New Testament imply that Law and Prophets comprised the two major categories, with psalms and possibly some other writings occasionally mentioned. However, it also seems that Prophets was also taken to include everything not in Torah. The formation of the third division, Writings, may be due to the desire of the rabbis to create a single category from those writings that did not fit the other two.

Psalms

As we have noted earlier in this book, Psalms contains five books (chapters 1–41, 42–72, 73–89, 90–106, and 107–50), each of the first four ending with a short doxology. Psalm 1 is generally seen as an introduction to the entire Psalter, and there is evidence that in many mediaeval Hebrew Bibles it was unnumbered (see Wilson 1985: 204-205). This psalm places the psalms as a whole within the orbit of obedience to the Law. But it also seems to presuppose not public performance of the psalms, but private meditation on them. Wilson has suggested that the five books of

Psalms exhibit a clear shape: Book I (starting with Psalm 2) concentrates on the relationship between King David and God; Book II on David's royal descendants; Book III on the Davidic covenant, but ending on a note of despair (Psalm 89: 'How long, O Lord?'). The fourth book, where Wilson sees a good deal of editorial activity having taken place, offers assurance that Yhwh, who is Israel's king, will be its refuge, thus answering the cry of Psalm 89. The final book, where the overall theme is least explicit, nevertheless emphasises obedience to Yhwh's law and reminiscence of his great acts for Israel in the past. The Psalter ends emphatically with hymns of praise.

The ascription of the Psalms to David may have come about gradually as part of the canonizing process. We can see the traces in the headings of some as 'Psalms of David' and in superscriptions that relate some psalms to events in his life. In the Dead Sea Scrolls and in the early Greek translation (the Septuagint), there are more such connections than in the Hebrew Bible, showing the process taking place.

'Solomonic' Works

Proverbs, the Song of Songs, and Ecclesiastes are attributed to Solomon. But, unlike the psalms, both Ecclesiastes and the Song are intrinsically connected with Solomon rather than having a mere ascription. His reputation as the representative of wisdom explains two of these books, but why the Song? Is it because of his reputation as a 'lover of many foreign women' (1 Kings 11:1)? The allegorical interpretation representing Solomon and wisdom at first, but later Israel and God (and, in Christian interpretation, Christ and the Church), is probably a justification for its canonical status, not a reason.

The Canon

Why is the Jewish canon a collection of sacred and authoritative writings, 'oracles of God'? There were canons in Mesopotamia and Egypt and also in Greece. But these did not become religious scriptures. One answer is that the culture of Judah became a religious one: Judaism (though elsewhere in the Diaspora Judaism was also presented more as a 'philosophy', which is more akin to the Greek conception of what we now call a religion). We can see how this canon was already viewed as a religious resource from within the scriptures themselves (e.g. Psalm 1) and from Ben Sira. But when and why was this canon closed?

The move can only have taken place when there existed an authority that could declare the canon of Jewish literature to be 'closed', and second, only when there was some political or social reason for this to happen. Perhaps the scribes themselves felt that a 'golden age' had passed. A common view is that only after 70 CE was Judaism so formally constituted that an official canon could exist and that the canon was agreed at a rabbinic council in Yavneh/Jamnia. But discussion at Yavneh was, the story goes, apparently confined to the Song of Songs, Ecclesiastes, and Esther. 'Scriptures' were already in existence, and in Judea, by the first century CE, their extent was not much disputed, either. Luke 24:44 speaks of 'the Law of Moses, the Prophets, and the Psalms'; Josephus *(Against Apion* 1:8), at the end of the first century CE (the same time as the reported 'council of Yavneh'), mentions twenty-two books 'justly believed to be divine'. 4 Ezra, a Jewish apocalypse, also from the end of the first century CE, enumerates twenty-four (14:18ff.). A century earlier, however, different Jewish groups had other scriptural books besides these. The Qumran caves contained fragments of probably every biblical book (except Nehemiah and Esther, possibly also Ezra), but also other books, which may have been regarded as of equal authority, such as Jubilees (which is part of the scriptures of the Ethiopian Church). Outside Palestine, Jewish Scriptures in Greek contained additional books, namely those now included in the Apocrypha of the Christian Old Testament.

We may therefore need to look a little earlier for a definitive constitution of a fixed and closed canon. The early Hasmoneans came to power amid an internal battle over what 'Judaism' was, and, as Josephus reports, they found themselves confronting different groups once they had gained political power. These groups were lobbying for influence over the management of a Jewish kingdom: how would it be governed according to Mosaic law? Who should run the temple and how? What religious duties should the population fulfil? There was also a specific challenge (to which the Hasmoneans personally succumbed in large measure) to allow Hellenistic cultural features to be absorbed, and among the main features of this culture was education. The educated classes of Judea (and many of the lower classes) could speak Greek, and with the language came the literature. The dominance of Greek culture could only be resisted if Jewish literature, a Jewish canon of writings, were also taught. We cannot be sure that this was the context in which an existing body of writing was made into a formal corpus of Judaism, but the chronological data fit and the political and social imperatives also exist. Beyond Judea, the canon remained more fluid, but gradually (and helped by the adoption of the scriptures in Greek by Christians), the 'Hebrew Bible', endorsed by the rabbis, prevailed.

Text and Versions

It is wrong to think that once a book—or, in this context, 'scroll'—has come into existence, its form remains fixed. The composition of the biblical scrolls came to an end only with the concern to *preserve* the form already in existence. The process of copying ('publishing' in the ancient world meant copying) inevitably led to variations in the content, and over time a good deal of corruption found its way into copies. We know that Greek scholars in Alexandria, aware of this problem, took measures to rectify the text of their 'canon' (Homer especially). The Jewish authorities did the same, but rather than, as their Alexandrian colleagues, engage in textual research to determine the original form, they rather lazily opted for a single manuscript of each writing and made that the official text. The evidence of how many forms of the text existed prior to that stage is clear from the Dead Sea Scrolls, where no two copies of any scriptural scroll are identical. The 'authorised' Hebrew text is called the Masoretic text, after the Masoretes or 'Traditionists' who in the following centuries embellished it with vowel marks, marginal notes, official 'corrections' (such as 'blessing' rather than 'cursing' God), division into liturgical units, and marks to indicate how to sing it. Our earliest Masoretic Bibles date from the ninth century CE (much later than our earliest Christian Bibles, which date from the fourth century CE and include the Old Testament in Greek). The Greek translation sometimes differs from the Masoretic text (MT), and represents a Jewish, not a Christian version.

A story of how a Greek translation of the Torah was produced is told in the 'Letter of Aristeas'. Seventy-two Jewish elders were commissioned by Ptolemy Philadelphus (285–247 BCE) to work on a translation for his library. Hence the product of their work is called the Septuagint ('Seventy', commonly abbreviated to LXX). In truth, the translation was not a single process, and does not always follow the Masoretic text.

Later Greek translations, however, were undertaken on the basis of the new official Hebrew version. In the case of Jeremiah, the most notorious example, we have, in effect, a different edition of the book.

We must also not forget the scriptures of the Samaritans. This group separated from the Judeans but shared the Torah as scripture—we know it as the Samaritan Pentateuch. This version has about six thousand differences from the MT, about a third of which agree with the LXX.

The biblical manuscripts discovered at Qumran dating from the third century BCE–first century CE (about a quarter of all the manuscripts in the caves) contain texts both like and unlike the MT. There are some texts agreeing substantially with the Samaritan Pentateuch, which suggests that this text is not necessarily Samaritan in origin or exclusive to them. No single authoritative text had been established by this time—or at least among those who wrote and kept the Scrolls. The history of these different forms of the Hebrew text is currently in dispute. One dominant theory, that of Cross, is that there were three major text types prevalent in Egypt, Babylonia, and Palestine. But, according to Emanuel Tov, the LXX, Samaritan Pentateuch, and MT are three from a number of ancient texts that varied from and agreed with each other in a multitude of ways. In short, the text of books of the Jewish scriptural canon was rather fluid; and no-one seems to have bothered until the canon was closed and the matter of a single authoritative edition became an issue.

Students of the Old Testament or Hebrew Bible therefore need to realise this: the official Jewish text, the MT, goes back about two thousand years but is not the original or the best text. But we cannot really reconstruct the 'original' text anyway, since all scrolls underwent generations of copying. The scrolls do not come, as they are now, from a single copyist, let alone a single author: they are collective products. Whatever issues of inspiration or authenticity may arise, these facts cannot be disputed. But in antiquity there were Jews, like those who wrote and copied the Dead Sea Scrolls, who were aware of the differences in the text but still regarded them as authoritative.

Nevertheless, the impression must not be given that all these ancient versions differ very widely; many of the deviations are slight. In places, however, they are significant. The corruptions in a text generally involve *expansions* (e.g. to remove ambiguity, enhance clarity, or eliminate accidental writing of words or phrases twice); *conflations*, where a scribe adds extra words from another text or passage; *omissions*, where a scribe's eye jumps accidentally from one group of letters or words to another group a little later, missing the text in between; or *misreadings*, where a letter is incorrectly written (scribes did not always read carefully what they were copying). (For examples of these, and a readable guide to text criticism generally, see McCarter 1986.) However, not all alterations are accidental, and sometimes a scribe deliberately updates or improves the text he is copying. By comparing versions one can often suggest which is more primitive. We can learn about what scribes did, and how they liked to make the text (just a little) say what they wanted it to say (like many interpreters today).

At the time the canon was closed, most Jews did not speak Hebrew, but Greek or Aramaic. How did they learn the contents? Most modern Christians know their Bibles only from their parents or from church—and they do not know much of it as a rule. The same was probably true for most Jews in antiquity (in contrast to a few learned Jews who may have known it all by heart). In the synagogue the readings were translated into Aramaic, and this tradition was kept up in written Aramaic translations called targums. These translations range in date between about the first century BCE (there are two or three among the Dead Sea Scrolls) and the Middle Ages, and vary a lot: some are very literal, others more like paraphrases.

From about the first century CE comes a translation of the Jewish scriptures into Syriac, an Aramaic dialect of northern and northeastern Syria. This translation was later revised by the Syrian Christian Church and has been influenced by the LXX. Two Latin versions are also known: the Old Latin is a general term for early Latin translations, while the Vulgate is the work of St Jerome (fourth–fifth century), translated from the Hebrew. Jerome resorted to the Hebrew rather than the LXX that the Church regarded as its sacred text, and met with opposition, raising as he did the question of whether it was the Jewish or the 'Christian' Old Testament text which was truly inspired. It is fortunate that Jerome and his antagonist (on this issue), St Augustine, were unaware of, and thus undistracted by, other Hebrew and Greek translations of the text which had existed only a few centuries earlier! But ever since Western Bibles have had two forms the 'shorter' Hebrew canon (adopted by most Protestants) and the 'larger' Christian one, derived from the Greek. However, both forms retain the Greek, not the Hebrew order!

Those books found in the earliest Greek Christian Bibles but not in the Hebrew scriptures are now commonly called 'apocryphal'. Modern Bibles include these books, either gathered together at the end of the Old Testament, or in their original position (which makes more sense, especially with texts that are additions to other books, like the 'Additions to Daniel'). These variations, of course, extend only to the Bibles of the Latin-derived Western Church: what 'Old Testament' means to other non-Western (e.g. Ethiopic) Churches is another story altogether. Perhaps it is a fitting way to end an Introduction to the Old Testament by pointing out that there is, really, no single 'Old Testament'.

Further Reading

References in this chapter have been made to J. Blenkinsopp, *Prophecy and Canon: A Contribution to the Study of Jewish Origins* (Notre Dame: University of Notre Dame Press, 1977); W. McKane, *Jeremiah 1–25* (Edinburgh: T. & T. Clark, 1986); R.P. Carroll, *Jeremiah: A Commentary* (London: SCM Press, 1986); W.L. Holladay, *Jeremiah: A Commentary on the Book of Jeremiah* (2 vols.; Philadelphia: Fortress Press, 1986, 1989); G.H. Wilson, *The Editing of the Hebrew Psalter* (Chico, CA: Scholars Press, 1985); F.M. Cross, *Canaanite Myth and Hebrew Epic: Essays on the History of the Religion of Israel* (Cambridge, MA: Harvard University Press, 1973); F.M. Cross and S. Talmon, *Qumran and the History of the Biblical Texts* (Cambridge, MA: Harvard University Press); P. Kyle McCarter, *Textual Criticism: Reconstructing the Text of the Hebrew Bible* (Philadelphia: Fortress Press, 1986); E. Tov, *Textual Criticism of the Hebrew Bible* (Minneapolis: Fortress Press, 2nd edn, 2001).

The account of canonisation given here is more fully explained in P.R. Davies, *Scribes and Schools: The Canonization of the Hebrew Scriptures* (Louisville, KY: Westminster/John Knox Press, 1998), and the formation of the canon (among other topics) is also discussed in J.W. Rogerson, *An Introduction to the Bible* (London: Penguin Books, 1999).

INDEX